This book belongs to

MARTHA STEWART'S
COOKING SCHOOL

MARTHA STEWART'S COOKING SCHOOL

Lessons and Recipes for the Home Cook

BY MARTHA STEWART

WITH SARAH CAREY

PHOTOGRAPHS BY MARCUS NILSSON

PORTRAITS BY DITTE ISAGER

CLARKSON POTTER/PUBLISHERS

NEW YORK

All rights reserved.
Published in the United States by Clarkson Potter/Publishers,
an imprint of the Crown Publishing Group,
a division of Random House, Inc., New York.
www.crownpublishing.com
www.clarksonpotter.com

www.marthastewart.com

Clarkson N. Potter is a trademark and Potter and colophon are
registered trademarks of Random House, Inc.

Library of Congress Cataloging-in-Publication Data is available
upon request.

ISBN 978-0-307-39644-0

Printed in Hong Kong

Design Director: William van Roden
Design Assistant: Yasemin Emory

10 9 8 7 6

First Edition

To home cooks everywhere, may
you always continue to learn

CONTENTS

Introduction

I was in third grade when I knew that I would grow up to be a teacher. I was so interested in the challenges that my wonderful petite "career" teacher, Miss Weyer, dealt with regularly, as well as the solutions she devised to get our attention, focus our attention, and keep our attention every hour of every day of the entire school year.

All this without shouting, without rapping her desk with a ruler, and with only a tiny bit of discipline. Her secret? Her method?

By constantly inspiring us with fascinating facts and procedures, by informing us about how things happened and why, and by entertaining us with the greatest stories and articles about a vast number of subjects and current events. We were always involved with art and science and history projects and were consistently spoken to as if we were intelligent adults with a thirst for knowledge and a quest for the best. And most important, our teacher infused everything with just the right amount of humor and the correct amount of seriousness. She was, after my parents, the greatest role model for me on the most difficult course of study: how to be a great teacher, an inspiring instructor, a successful purveyor of factual and creative knowledge.

Much of what I learned that year in Yantacaw School I still know, and I attribute that to how I was taught those facts and figures. I thought of this while I prepared to write this book and compile its vast table of contents. Food editor Sarah Carey and I had extensive meetings to determine just what information we would attempt to convey. I am very proud to report that this volume is very, very close to the original outline. Of course we have had to edit out some of the recipes—we have always been overzealous in providing an enthusiastic quantity of inspired information—but we have not eliminated any of the valuable techniques, tips, or bits of knowledge that we have deemed invaluable for the home cook.

This book has been designed and written as a course of study, very much like a college course in chemistry, which requires the student to master the basics before performing more advanced experiments. The lessons here begin just as they would in a true cooking school, with instruction about the essential tools and equipment, and perhaps the most basic lesson of all: how to hold and use a chef's knife. You'll also learn about fundamental ingredients, such as onions, garlic, and herbs and spices, and how they are used to build flavors. Then the book is organized in seven chapters, each offering indispensable lessons, such as the proper way to make a rich brown stock; poach eggs; braise meats, fish, and poultry; prepare fresh pasta; simmer and puree vegetables; and cream butter to produce a fine-crumbed cake. The lessons are followed by recipes — a tutorial in stock-making, for instance, is followed by a soup recipe that calls for the stock. This practical approach works throughout the book, which means that you build your recipe repertoire along with your skills.

You'll also find useful information on what to cook in addition to how to cook it. You'll discover which cuts of meat are right for which cooking methods; how to decipher the often confusing language of food labels; how to select nearly any vegetable; and how to cook rice and less familiar whole grains, so you can incorporate more healthful ingredients into your diet.

What's more, all of this information is offered in a thoroughly modern fashion. So while you'll find fundamental French techniques in these pages, there are tips, techniques, and ingredients that acknowledge the way we cook today. There may be shortcuts, but there is no skimping. For example, you will learn how to thicken a soup with a velouté, one of the French "mother sauces," as well as how to make a very quick (and healthful) Japanese miso soup. Similarly, you get fresh takes on sauces — in the form of salsas, chutneys, and relishes — that represent our expanding food worldview and are a departure from the heavier, cream-laden sauces of classic cookery.

As you work your way through the "curriculum" here, I am quite sure you will find that you have both the skills and the confidence to improvise and experiment in the kitchen. And if that is the case, then I will feel that I have done Miss Weyer proud.

Martha Stewart

Basics

A Cook's Golden Rules

The best cooks develop routines that make them more efficient in the kitchen. Incorporate these tips into your routine (and keep them in mind as you work your way through the techniques in this book) and you'll soon be cooking with confidence. After all, cooking should be fun and enjoyable. Keep these rules in mind and you will never be overwhelmed but, rather, eager to learn more and more.

Getting Started

☐ Read a recipe all the way through before you begin cooking; knowing what needs to happen and when will help you avoid any mistakes as you prepare each step.

☐ Establish good habits: keep work surfaces and tools pristine and at the ready; wash and put things away as you work.

☐ Don't try to rush things, especially when you are first starting out. Give yourself plenty of time to work and avoid taking shortcuts.

☐ Keep your culinary ambitions in check: don't try to make too many dishes at once that require a lot of hands-on time at the stove; learn to make one thing really well and then build from there.

☐ Keep notes while you are cooking. Don't be discouraged if something doesn't turn out exactly as you expected it to. With practice you can learn to cook anything successfully, and taking notes is the best way to remember what happened the first time you attempted a recipe.

☐ Develop a system for organizing recipes that works for you, whether putting them on a computer, flagging them in cookbooks, or keeping copies of favorites in a binder.

☐ Learn to trust your instincts, so you can cook according to visual cues, smell, and taste, rather than always following a specific time or instruction in the recipe. Also, use tools (such as thermometers) as suggested for accuracy, especially when learning.

☐ Master basic techniques first and then feel free to improvise, creating your own variations on recipes.

☐ Plan your kitchen spaces efficiently. Make sure you have ample room to chop and prep, and that there is proper storage for everything.

☐ Balance the components of your meals. Pair rich dishes with lighter ones, vibrantly colored vegetables with deep brown meats.

☐ If you are entertaining, don't attempt a new recipe at the same time. Go easy on yourself, and make something you've prepared before (even if that means giving something new a test run first).

Stocking the Kitchen

☐ Don't buy more kitchenware than you need. Instead, invest in the best-quality products you can afford; good-quality pots and pans and knives will serve you well for a lifetime.

☐ Use tools that are multipurpose rather than cluttering your kitchen with specialty gadgets. Use a fine-mesh sieve, for example, for sifting flour, rather than a specialty sifter.

☐ Ingredients are your most important tool. Buy wisely and with an eye toward quality, not quantity.

☐ Cook seasonally, and shop with an open mind. Don't go to the market determined to buy just the thing (and only the thing) that you plan to make. See what's fresh (and often, on special) and adjust your cooking plans accordingly.

☐ Seek out excellent vendors in your area. A farmers' market will have the best seasonal produce; a good butcher or cheese shop will offer service and selection you may not find in your supermarket.

☐ Keep a well-stocked pantry and freezer, but don't buy more than you need. Don't purchase a variety pack of spices, for example, if you are not yet in the habit of cooking elaborate meals.

☐ Replace spices and other pantry items each year, as they lose their flavors over time.

As You're Cooking

☐ Get in the habit of doing what the French call *mise en place*, or preparing your ingredients (chopping, peeling, measuring, etc.), before beginning a recipe.

☐ Use your time efficiently. Make whole dishes or components in advance whenever possible.

☐ Keep coarse (such as kosher) salt and freshly ground pepper in little dishes by your cooktop so you can season as you go.

☐ Season well, and appropriately as you go— don't overseason (or, equally important, underseason), especially with salt and pepper.

☐ Keep a bowl near your workspace for produce scraps to go into a compost bin.

☐ If you are entertaining, decide in advance what serving dishes you will use. You might even set everything out the night before, with labels indicating which recipe should be served in which vessel.

WOK

ROASTING PAN AND RACK

SAUTÉ PANS

STRAIGHT-SIDED
SKILLET

NONSTICK
SKILLET

CAST-IRON
GRILL PAN

SAUCEPAN

SAUCEPAN

LARGE STOCKPOT

CAST-IRON
SKILLET

DUTCH OVEN

Equipment

The right cookware is essential to successful cooking, but that doesn't mean buying many items, just the most useful (and versatile) ones.

Pots and Pans

CAST-IRON GRILL PAN

A grill pan is a practical indoor alternative to a gas or charcoal grill, although you won't get the same charred flavor. The ridges allow fat to drip off meat and also produce grill marks. Look for cast-iron or enameled cast-iron pans. A long rectangular model that fits over two burners is convenient; these pans often have a flat side that doubles as a griddle for pancakes, and a ridged side for grilled meats and pressed sandwiches. The larger size will accommodate large or multiple pieces of meat for searing; a smaller handled pan is another good option. Clean a cast-iron grill pan as you would a cast-iron skillet (see below).

CAST-IRON SKILLET

An iron pan retains heat and distributes it evenly, making it well suited for searing, sautéing, and even baking. Look for a heavy pan that's at least an eighth of an inch thick. A new pan will look gray and raw, but will turn black once seasoned. Properly cared for, a cast-iron pan will last a lifetime. Season the pan before using it to prevent rusting and create a virtually nonstick surface: rub it evenly inside and out with vegetable oil, and put the skillet in a 300°F oven for an hour. Never put cast iron in the dishwasher. To clean cast iron, sprinkle with coarse salt, rub with paper towels, then wipe clean. Or, to clean more thoroughly, rinse with hot water and rub with a scrubber, avoiding anything but mild detergent; dry completely with a kitchen towel and rub with a small amount of vegetable oil before storing. Avoid cooking wine or anything acidic, such as tomato sauce, in a cast-iron pan—it can cause the patina to be worn off.

DUTCH OVEN

This versatile pot is indispensible for braising meats and vegetables, as well as for making stews. Look for a heavy 5- to 6-quart Dutch oven made of enameled cast iron, anodized aluminum, or stainless steel around a copper or aluminum base. The thick sides and bottom retain and evenly distribute heat, and the tight-fitting lid traps in moisture and flavor. With the lid off, it can be used to brown meat or vegetables on the stovetop. The pot can also go into the oven (make sure you choose a model with ovenproof handles and knob).

LARGE STOCKPOT

An 8- to 10-quart pot is perfect for making soups and stocks and for cooking pasta.

NONSTICK SKILLET

A nonstick skillet can make certain tasks, such as scrambling eggs or making omelets, even easier. An 8- or 10-inch one is ideal.

ROASTING PAN AND RACK

Use a generous-sized pan made of heavy-gauge stainless steel with sturdy handles to roast meats, poultry, fish, and vegetables. A pan with 3-inch-high sides is best for turkeys and other large roasts; for everything else, choose a pan with 2- to 2½-inch sides, to prevent foods from steaming. A roasting rack will elevate the food, allowing air to circulate underneath. It also lets drippings collect underneath, perfect for making pan gravy.

SAUCEPANS

A traditional saucepan has tall, straight sides that prevent rapid moisture loss, which is exactly what you need when steaming, blanching, or making sauce or soup. The walls should be as thick as the bottom, for even heat distribution. Do not use a cast-iron or regular (nonanodized) aluminum pot for sauces; their reactive surfaces can discolor and alter the taste of butter and acidic ingredients such as tomato. Instead, opt for stainless-steel pans with aluminum or copper cores. Use a 4-quart lidded pan for cooking small amounts of pasta, and a 2½-quart lidded pan for reheating soups and sauces.

SAUTÉ PANS

Used to sauté and pan-fry meats and vegetables, these pans have sloped sides that allow you to flip foods easily as you cook. Choose sturdy stainless-steel models with aluminum or copper cores; stainless steel is durable and nonreactive, while aluminum and copper are excellent heat conductors. A 10- or 12-inch is practical for most recipes.

STRAIGHT-SIDED SKILLET

This pan's straight sides and lid make it a good option for pan-frying or braising smaller cuts of meat. An extra handle makes it easy to transfer the pan to and from the oven.

WOK

Invest in a wok if you plan to do a lot of stir-frying. Its rounded shape evenly spreads heat, cooking food rapidly. Traditional woks are completely round; some newer models have flat bottoms, allowing them to sit level on the stovetop.

Baking Equipment

ANGEL FOOD CAKE PAN

The straight-sided pan's construction allows it to distribute heat from the inside out and the outside in, evenly baking the batter and keeping it from collapsing. In some pans, the central tube is higher than the sides; other pans have legs. Both of these designs allow you to invert the delicate cake to cool without compressing it.

CERAMIC BAKING DISH

A rectangular dish is indispensable for gratins, baked pastas, cobblers, and crisps. Porcelain is durable and attractive enough to go from oven to table.

COOKIE SHEET

These sheets have a small rim on one or two of the sides for easy gripping; flat edges on the other sides make it easy to slide off cookies without disturbing their forms. The open sides allow air to circulate in the oven, so cookies brown evenly. Choose sheets made from light-colored metals, such as heavy-duty aluminum, which will not curl or warp. Light-metal sheets are best, but if you must use dark-metal sheets, such as nonstick, be aware that these tend to brown baked goods faster; you may need to lower the oven temperature (by 25°F) and reduce the baking time slightly.

FLUTED TART PAN

Tarts owe much of their elegant appearance to the pans in which they're baked. Traditional pans have short, fluted sides and removable bottoms (for easy unmolding). A 9-inch round pan is typical, but you can find tart pans in a variety of shapes and sizes.

GLASS PIE PLATE

Heat disperses well in a tempered-glass pie plate, allowing for more even browning. The clear glass also lets you see the color of the bottom crust. A 9-inch pan works for most recipes.

LOAF PAN

Two sizes are considered standard for loaf pans: 8½ by 4½ inches and 9 by 5 inches. Choose metal or glass pans; they work equally well. Lining a pan with a piece of parchment paper with a 2-inch overhang on two sides will let you quickly and cleanly lift out baked goods.

MUFFIN TINS

A typical muffin pan has 6 or 12 cups, each with a ½-cup capacity. Pans with smaller cups, which generally hold 2 tablespoons of batter, are handy for making mini-muffins. You can bake any muffin or cupcake batter in mini-muffin pans, but be mindful that the baking time will need to be greatly reduced.

NONSTICK BAKING MAT

A heat-resistant silicone mat, such as a Silpat, can be used instead of parchment paper to line baking sheets; it's washable and reusable. Wipe after each use with a damp sponge or, for more thorough cleaning, run it under warm water. Never scrub the mat with an abrasive sponge, which damages the surface. After it's dry, store the mat flat or rolled up. Don't fold it or store objects on top of it. If you bake frequently, you might want to invest in a few mats.

RIMMED BAKING SHEET

These sided sheets (essentially very shallow baking pans) are used to make jelly rolls, bar cookies, and more. You should also position one under a fruit pie as it bakes to catch the juices, preventing them from dripping onto the oven floor. Buy sheets made from shiny, heavy-duty aluminum.

ROUND CAKE PAN

The most frequently used cake pans are 9 inches in diameter and 2 inches deep, with straight sides. You should have two, for making layer cakes. Avoid nonstick cake pans, as they can cause the crust to darken too much or too quickly; opt for light-colored aluminum instead.

WIRE RACK

Raised wire racks allow air to flow around cooling baked goods. Look for a rack with stainless-steel mesh and feet on the bottom. Avoid plastic racks, and skip those with bars that go in only one direction (small items won't sit level on them).

ROUND CAKE PAN

CERAMIC
BAKING DISH

NONSTICK
BAKING MAT

made in France A 08

RIMMED
BAKING SHEET

GLASS PIE PLATE

FLUTED TART PAN

ANGEL FOOD
CAKE PAN

MUFFIN TINS

COOKIE SHEET

WIRE RACK

LOAF PAN

BOX GRATER

SLOTTED
SPATULA

POTATO
MASHER

FOOD MILL

MIXING BOWL

ADJUSTABLE-BLADE
SLICER

KITCHEN TIMER

PEPPER MILL

LONG-HANDLED
METAL SPOON

CUTTING BOARD

MEAT
THERMOMETER

POTATO RICER

VEGETABLE PEELER

TONGS

SPIDER

SLOTTED
SPOON

COLANDER

LADLE

CITRUS REAMER

Tools

ADJUSTABLE-BLADE SLICER
This tool quickly slices fruit and vegetables into thin, even pieces. Japanese slicers, like the one pictured here, are made of plastic and are a less expensive alternative to the traditional stainless-steel French mandoline. (See page 15 for how to use a mandoline.)

BOX GRATER
Use an all-purpose four-sided box grater to grate hard cheeses (coarse or fine) and to shred vegetables. After using the grater, let it soak in warm water to loosen stuck-on bits of food. Then scrub it with a stiff brush, rather than a sponge, which can rip on the teeth.

CITRUS REAMER
Pick out seeds from halved citrus fruits with the tip of this wooden tool; twist the ridged body to express juice.

COLANDER
A stainless-steel footed colander with abundant holes is invaluable for draining pasta and vegetables. Stainless steel doesn't react with acidic foods; the holes and feet ensure that water flows out easily. Avoid plastic colanders.

CUTTING BOARD
Whether you prefer wood or plastic cutting boards, you should have one for raw meat and fish and another for produce; this will prevent bacteria from raw meat from contaminating other foods. It's also a good idea to use a separate board for garlic and onions so their strong flavors, which tend to linger, don't transfer to other foods. Do not put wooden boards in the dishwasher or soak them, as that will cause them to crack, split, and develop mold. Instead, clean them with hot water and mild dishwashing liquid; dry completely. Periodically you should rub them with coarse salt and the cut side of a lemon half to remove stains and odors. Plastic cutting boards are dishwasher-safe.

FOOD MILL
Use a food mill to puree fruits and vegetables for soups and sauces, without having to further strain. Many come with three interchangeable disks, with holes in graduated sizes, so you can puree to a desired consistency.

KITCHEN TIMER
Even if your oven comes with a built-in timer, it's a good idea to have a stand-alone timer as well. Some digital models allow you to time several jobs at once.

LADLE
Although most frequently used to serve soups and stews, or to ladle sauce onto bowls of pasta, a stainless-steel ladle is also useful for tempering eggs to be added to cream sauces and custards.

LONG-HANDLED METAL SPOON
Use this utensil to skim impurities from a simmering stock or stew.

MEAT THERMOMETER
Testing the internal temperature of meat lets you know when it's done cooking. An instant-read or rapid-response thermometer is inserted near the end of the cooking time (it is never left in the meat as it cooks). It has a thin, 4- to 5-inch-long stem that is inserted into the roast, and a dial that indicates the temperature. Insert the thermometer deep into the thickest part of the meat, without touching a bone, which can result in an incorrect reading.

MIXING BOWL
Keep a set of graduated mixing bowls on hand for myriad kitchen tasks. Stainless-steel bowls, which are heatproof, are useful for recipes that require setting a bowl over simmering water; tempered-glass models are another durable option. Avoid plastic bowls, which retain flavors and traces of grease.

PEPPER MILL
Use a pepper mill to grind whole peppercorns. Freshly ground pepper has a more pronounced taste than its preground counterpart. Many models can be adjusted to make fine or coarse grinds. The fine setting is for general use, such as seasoning soups and sauces; use the coarse setting when seasoning meat before cooking and for garnishing salads.

POTATO MASHER
This tool coarsely crushes potatoes or other vegetables, making it a better option for mashes and other rustic purees than a food mill.

POTATO RICER
A potato ricer, which produces tiny, even strands of boiled potato, gives mashed boiled vegetables a smooth, uniform texture. It's also essential for making the lightest, fluffiest gnocchi.

SLOTTED SPATULA
Use this versatile kitchen helper to lift or flip foods as they cook. In addition to a basic all-purpose spatula, such as the slotted one shown, you may want a couple of specialty spatulas, such as a fish spatula, which has a flexible blade, or a wedge-shaped cake server.

SLOTTED SPOON
Use a slotted spoon to remove vegetables from hot water, or to extract delicate foods, such as fish or eggs, from poaching liquid. Spoons with large holes or long slots offer good drainage. Make sure to choose one made of heatproof material, such as stainless steel. It should have a long handle that is comfortable to hold.

SPIDER
The wide, shallow bowl-shaped mesh of this wire skimmer is great for removing vegetables and short pastas from boiling water or deep-fried foods from hot oil. The long handle, available in metal or wood, keeps your hands away from the heat. Wire skimmers are sold in kitchen-supply stores and some supermarkets, and come in a wide range of sizes; 5-inch is useful for most tasks.

TONGS
Use tongs for turning meat when browning or roasting, or lifting pasta out of boiling water. Look for heavy-duty, professional-grade tongs; a long-lasting spring allows for easier storage.

VEGETABLE PEELER
Choose a model with a steel blade. Use it for peeling vegetables and fruit, shaving hard cheeses, and making chocolate curls.

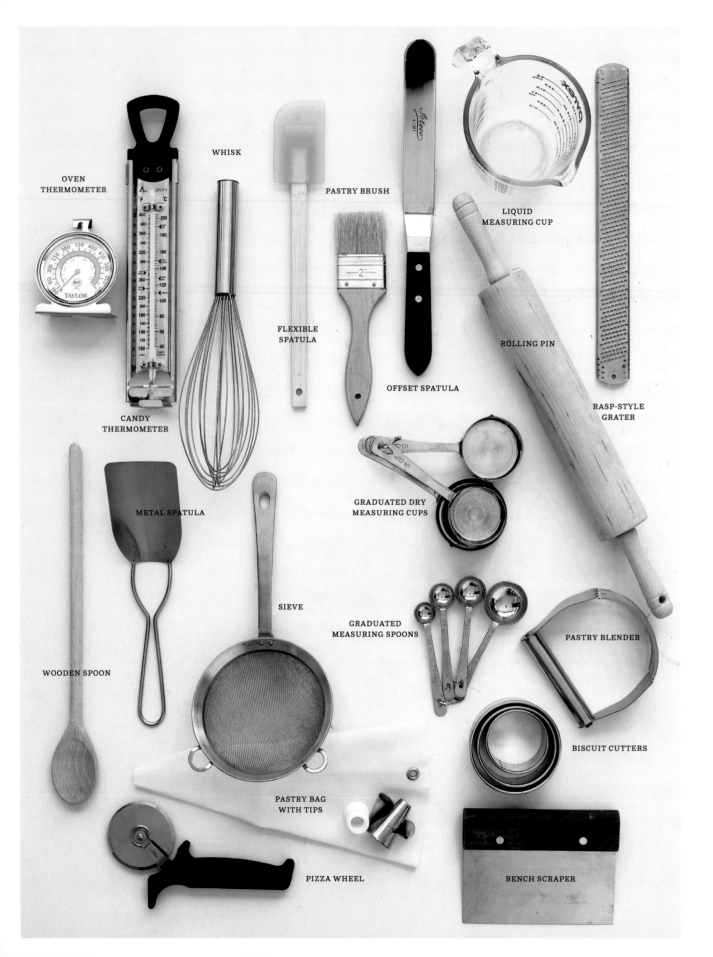

OVEN
THERMOMETER

WHISK

PASTRY BRUSH

LIQUID
MEASURING CUP

FLEXIBLE
SPATULA

OFFSET SPATULA

ROLLING PIN

RASP-STYLE
GRATER

CANDY
THERMOMETER

METAL SPATULA

GRADUATED DRY
MEASURING CUPS

SIEVE

GRADUATED
MEASURING SPOONS

PASTRY BLENDER

WOODEN SPOON

BISCUIT CUTTERS

PASTRY BAG
WITH TIPS

PIZZA WHEEL

BENCH SCRAPER

Tools *continued*

BENCH SCRAPER

A metal bench scraper is helpful for loosening dough from a work surface and for dividing dough into neat, even portions. The flat surface can also help transfer chopped ingredients from a cutting board to a bowl or pan.

BISCUIT CUTTERS

A clean cut helps biscuits rise higher, so metal cutters are the best choice (plastic cutters are not sharp enough). Buying a boxed set provides a variety of diameters to work with.

CANDY THERMOMETER

A candy thermometer is useful for making Italian meringue or caramel. One that's long enough to reach into a deep pot, and is attached to a flat metal backing, is easier to handle and to read.

FLEXIBLE SPATULA

Flexible spatulas are heat-proof up to 800°F, won't pick up or impart flavors from foods, and are safe to use on nonstick pots and pans. They are great for scrambling eggs and for folding cake batters or transferring them from bowl to baking pan.

GRADUATED MEASURING CUPS

Measure dry and semisolid ingredients (such as sour cream and peanut butter) in graduated dry measuring cups, preferably long-lasting metal. Make sure they sit flat.

GRADUATED MEASURING SPOONS

A set of spoons is convenient for using and storing; look for those with deep bowls, which won't spill as easily.

LIQUID MEASURING CUP

For measuring liquids, choose a clear, heat-resistant glass cup with a spout for pouring and clearly marked lines for accuracy. Remember to measure at eye level.

METAL SPATULA

A wide metal spatula with a thin edge is excellent for sliding under just-baked cookies, cream puffs, and other delicate baked goods.

OFFSET SPATULA

The thin metal blade and angled design of an offset spatula make it invaluable for frosting cakes, smoothing batter in a pan, and lifting cookies from baking sheets. Steer clear of plastic ones; they are thick and not as heat-resistant. Depending on the task, you might prefer a large spatula or a small spatula, so it's a good idea to have both.

OVEN THERMOMETER

An inaccurate oven temperature can ruin a baking project or roast, so an oven thermometer is essential. Keep it in the oven to make sure your thermostat is accurate; if not, adjust the temperature accordingly. It's a good idea to replace your thermometer annually, or sooner if you drop it on the oven floor a few times.

PASTRY BAG WITH TIPS

Pastry bags are essential for decorating cakes, but they can also be used for other kitchen tasks, such as piping pâte à choux into rounds. A pastry bag has three components: the bag, a tip, and a coupler, which connects the tip to the bag, making it easy to switch tips as you work. Before filling a pastry bag, drop the base of the coupler (the larger piece) into the bag. Fit the pastry tip over the base, and secure with the coupler ring. To change tips, remove the ring.

PASTRY BLENDER

This tool with sturdy, rounded blades or wires is indispensable when making biscuits, pie dough, streusel, or anything that requires you to cut butter into dry ingredients.

PASTRY BRUSH

The best pastry brushes have natural, tightly woven bristles that are securely attached to the handle. Use them to apply egg wash to pies, brush excess flour from rounds of dough or countertops, and sweep crumbs from cakes before icing. They are also used to coat baking pans with softened butter. Reserve one brush for dry tasks and one for wet ones; label each and store separately.

PIZZA WHEEL

This tool, most frequently used for slicing pizza and other flatbreads, can also stand in for a pastry wheel to make lattice strips for pies.

RASP-STYLE GRATER

This stainless-steel grater has tiny, razor-sharp teeth that remove brightly colored citrus zest. It can also be used to finely grate chocolate, hard cheeses, or whole nutmeg.

ROLLING PIN

Look for a 12-inch-long wooden pin with tightly sealed joints between the handle and barrel to protect the inside from flour, and stainless-steel ball bearings inside, which make the pin glide easily. This classic American rolling pin, with handles, is called a baker's pin.

SIEVE

A mesh sieve can be used to sift ingredients such as flour, or to strain purees and sauces. Look for sturdy mesh that won't stretch or bend, and choose sieves in several sizes and levels of coarseness.

WHISK

Metal whisks are used to combine dry ingredients, make vinaigrettes, and beat eggs. Look for one with fine spokes that wiggle when you shake the handle. The best whisks are stainless steel and weighted for strength and comfort. Use a balloon whisk for whipping whites and cream; straighter, stiffer ones for other tasks.

WOODEN SPOON

A wooden spoon is the most essential tool for mixing almost everything in the kitchen, including all manner of sauces and soups. Buy good-quality, smooth hardwood spoons with no jagged edges. Designate some for sweet foods, others for savory. Because wood is absorbent, soaking wooden spoons or putting them in the dishwasher will saturate them, making them more likely to mildew. Instead, clean them by hand with hot, soapy water, and dry immediately with a dish towel.

ESSENTIAL KNIVES

SPECIALTY KNIVES

Knives

The Essentials

These utensils should help you accomplish most kitchen cutting jobs. As you take on more culinary challenges, consider adding one or all of the specialty knives that follow.

1. SANTOKU

The Japanese santoku is similar to a traditional chef's knife (and in most cases can be used in its place), but with a shorter, broader, thinner blade. The evenly spaced indentations along the blade, called a granton edge, create air pockets as the knife cuts through food, reducing friction and keeping particles from sticking to the blade. Use a santoku as you would a chef's knife, for chopping, dicing, and mincing.

2. CHEF'S

This multipurpose knife is the most essential of all. It is long, broad, and weighty, with leverage and heft that make it the best choice for mincing, chopping, and slicing vegetables, fruits, and herbs. The most common sizes for a chef's knife are 8 and 10 inches; choose the length that is most comfortable for you.

3. PARING

With its short blade, a paring knife is good for small jobs requiring precision, such as trimming, coring, and peeling.

4. SERRATED

The scalloped teeth on a serrated knife can cut through bread and other soft foods, such as tomatoes and cake, without sliding off or crushing them. It's also used to chop chocolate and nuts.

5. KITCHEN SHEARS

Use high-quality stainless-steel shears for tasks such as cutting lobster or chicken, and snipping herbs; they're also good for cutting twine and parchment.

Specialty Knives

6. CLEAVER

A cleaver, hefty enough to cut through bones, is used to chop meat.

7. UTILITY KNIFE

A smaller, lighter version of a chef's knife, a utility knife is handy for a variety of cutting jobs, such as filleting fish or slicing meat.

8. BONING KNIFE

The narrow, slightly curved blade of a 5- or 6-inch boning knife can wiggle between meat and bone, making it ideal for trimming off fat, tendons, or cartilage. The narrow, rounded tip is designed to work around bones.

9. SLICING KNIFE

The long blade of this knife is excellent for slicing meat, fish (especially smoked salmon), and produce thinly and precisely.

fig. 0.1 SHARPENING ON A WHETSTONE

fig. 0.2 HONING WITH A STEEL

Sharpening on a Whetstone

Following the manufacturer's instructions, treat a sharpening stone with food-grade mineral oil or water. Place stone, coarse side up, on a damp towel. Hold blade at a 20-degree angle to stone, starting at the tip and working your way back to the base. Firmly and evenly draw blade back over stone *fig. 0.1*. Repeat, turning the blade each time to sharpen both sides and maintaining an even pressure angle as you work. After ten to twenty swipes on each side, turn the stone fine side up; repeat process. Wipe blade clean before using.

Honing with a Steel

To hone a knife, hold the blade at a 20-degree angle to the steel, with the base of the blade near the steel's handle *fig. 0.2*. Draw its length down the steel; when you finish, the tip of the knife should be at the end of the steel. Repeat ten times. Repeat on other side of blade. Wipe blade clean. Since a steel is magnetized to attract particles, store the steel separately from knives.

Holding a Chef's Knife

Hold the handle near the blade *fig. 0.3*, grasping the blade between your thumb and forefinger (called choking). With the other hand, secure the food to be cut, curling your fingers under so they're safely out of the way. Begin to cut with fluid motions, moving the curled hand back with each chop to expose a portion of the food to be cut.

fig. 0.3 HOLDING A CHEF'S KNIFE

Chopping Vegetables

The key to making uniform pieces is to first trim away all the rounded parts for an even-sided shape. Then, following the three steps below, you can make the basic cuts. When a recipe calls for something to be finely chopped, cut into small dice; brunoise is used only for garnishing refined dishes, such as consommé. 1 With a sharp, heavy chef's knife, cut off the rounded edges of the vegetable—in this instance, a turnip—to make a block with flat sides. Slice the turnip lengthwise at even intervals. 2 Stack the slices and cut lengthwise again into strips. 3 To dice, gather the strips and cut them crosswise into cubes.

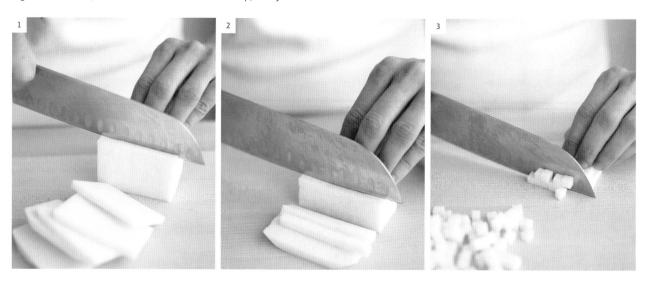

Basic Cuts

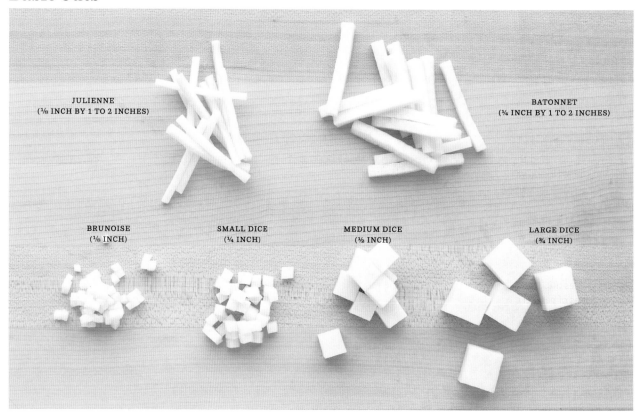

JULIENNE
(⅛ INCH BY 1 TO 2 INCHES)

BATONNET
(¼ INCH BY 1 TO 2 INCHES)

BRUNOISE
(⅛ INCH)

SMALL DICE
(¼ INCH)

MEDIUM DICE
(½ INCH)

LARGE DICE
(¾ INCH)

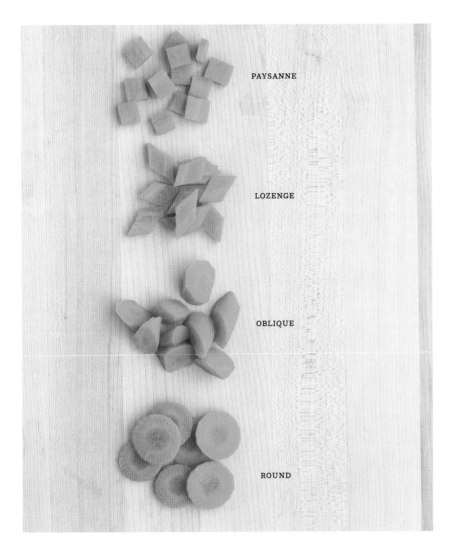

PAYSANNE

LOZENGE

OBLIQUE

ROUND

Using a Mandoline

If desired, trim vegetables' rounded edges into flat surfaces (see step 1, opposite) to make slicing easier. Adjust the blade to desired width. Hold the mandoline at an angle with the end on cutting board. Keeping your hand flat on top, slide the vegetable away from you to slice; slide it back up and repeat.

Specialty Cuts

Once you've mastered the basic cubes and matchsticks, you can begin to experiment with different shapes to add variety to your presentation. Whichever shape you choose, make sure all your pieces are the same size and thickness, so that they'll cook evenly.

PAYSANNE
Square off vegetables—in this case, carrots—and slice them into sticks, as you would for julienne or batons; the wider the cut, the more rustic your pieces will look. Gather the sticks together and thinly slice crosswise in even intervals to create squares.

LOZENGE
Cut vegetables into thin slices, about ⅛ inch wide, then stack the slices and cut into strips. Make a series of parallel cuts on the bias (diagonally) to achieve a diamond shape.

OBLIQUE
This method is usually used for carrots and other cylindrical vegetables. Slice off the stem at a diagonal. Keeping your knife in the same position, roll the vegetable a quarter turn; slice it again on the same diagonal. Work your way down the vegetable, rotating it with each cut.

ROUND
Slice a round vegetable into coins of even width. As a variation, cut on a bias to make elongated disks. Or cut the vegetable in half lengthwise first, then slice into half-moons.

SPEARMINT

BASIL

CHERVIL

CHIVES

CILANTRO

OPAL BASIL

THAI BASIL

CURLY PARSLEY

PEPPERMINT

DILL

FLAT-LEAF
PARSLEY

TARRAGON

Herbs

Here are some of the more common and versatile herbs used in cooking, classified according to their texture and flavor. The ones pictured opposite are tender and more delicate; they are generally added at the end of cooking or as a garnish. Those on page 19 are more sturdy (some are described as woody) and robust, and can withstand longer cooking.

Tender Herbs

BASIL

Used in Mediterranean dishes, basil has a slightly peppery flavor and a licoricelike fragrance. It is a member of the mint family and very easy to grow. Its delicate leaves are often torn by hand and used raw or added at the end of the cooking process. The leaves should be uniformly green, crisp, and free of black or slimy spots; the stems should be tender, not woody. Deep purple-leaved opal basil adds color and flavor to summer salads; or use it to make basil-infused white-wine vinegar. Thai basil has sharp-pointed leaves and tastes of mint, cinnamon, and licorice. It is widely used in Asian cooking, particularly Thai and Vietnamese cuisines. Also known as holy basil, Thai basil makes a nice addition to salads, fish, and curried dishes.

CHERVIL

Similar to parsley but far more delicate, chervil also has hints of anise. It's delicious with eggs or fish. Along with tarragon, parsley, and chives, chervil makes up the traditional French herb blend known as *fines herbes*.

CHIVES

The long, slender chive is the smallest member of the allium family, which includes onions and garlic (see page 29 for more on alliums); its flavor is also the most delicate. Snipped chives are a common garnish, especially for pureed soups, but they also add bright flavor to dips, salads, and Asian dumplings. Look for bright green leaves, with no signs of drooping or dehydration.

CILANTRO

A key ingredient in Asian and Latin American cooking, this herb has a pronounced flavor that stands up to spicy foods. Add finely chopped leaves to salsas, salads, and stews; toss whole sprigs or stems into a pot of simmering black beans.

DILL

Commonly known as the pickling herb, dill has a green taste that works well in salads, soups, and sauces, as well as savory baked goods. It pairs especially well with fish, and is traditionally used to flavor salmon for gravlax.

MINT

Peppermint has a pronounced flavor that adds zing to desserts and frozen drinks. With its mild scent and vibrant, refreshing taste, spearmint is used to flavor meats, vegetables, teas, and cocktails. For both varieties, look for leaves that are bright green with no signs of bruising or wilting.

PARSLEY

Curly parsley has a bright, grassy flavor. Use it in salads and sauces. Also known as Italian parsley, flat-leaf parsley has a more vibrant taste than curly parsley. It stands up well to heat in stews and sauces; it's also the key ingredient in the Mediterranean salad known as tabbouleh.

TARRAGON

This versatile herb is a member of the sunflower family. Essential to French cooking, it has a mild, aniselike taste. Heat intensifies the taste of tarragon, so use it sparingly. It is often used in egg, cheese, or tomato dishes; it pairs well with chicken, fish, and many vegetables, including beets and tomatoes.

SAVORY

ROSEMARY

THYME

LEMON THYME

CURRY LEAF

MARJORAM

OREGANO

SAGE

LEMONGRASS

BAY LEAF

Robust Herbs

BAY LEAF
The bay leaf comes from the laurel tree and is an essential ingredient in French, Mediterranean, and Indian cuisines. The leaves are usually sold dried, which mellows their flavor, eliminating some of their natural bitterness. Use bay leaves to infuse stocks, soups, and sauces; always remove the leaves before serving the finished dish.

CURRY LEAF
An important aromatic ingredient in South Indian cuisine, curry leaves can be bought fresh or dried. You can find curry leaves at Indian and other Asian specialty markets. Despite its name, commercial curry powder often doesn't include any curry leaf.

LEMONGRASS
This herb is widely used in Southeast Asian cuisines. The delightful, almost floral flavor is more highly concentrated in the lower, fleshy parts of the plant's stalks; discard the long, flat blades and remove any dry or tough outer layers from the stalks. Use the stalks whole or cut into slices. For a more pronounced taste, bruise the stalks with the back of a knife to help release the flavor.

MARJORAM
This relative of the mint family tastes like a sweeter, gentler, more aromatic oregano. Crush the herb in your hand before using to release its flavor. Add at the end of cooking to fish, poultry, eggs, tomato dishes, sauces, soups, stews, pastas, and vegetables. It enhances the flavor of meat dishes and is especially delicious with lamb.

OREGANO
Another member of the mint family, oregano is highly aromatic and has a pungent flavor. Try it in tomato-based dishes such as pasta sauces, or to season grilled or roasted seafood, poultry, and lamb.

ROSEMARY
This multitalented herb has the look and smell of pine needles, and a strong, slight camphor taste. It is often paired with garlic, and gives a pungent Mediterranean flavor to grilled fish, roasts, and vegetables.

SAGE
Sage's velvety gray-green leaves have a somewhat bitter flavor. Thought to aid in digestion, sage is often paired with richer meats; it's also commonly used with sausage, poultry, white beans, and stuffing. Add sage early in a recipe, if possible: longer cooking helps mellow its strong taste.

SAVORY
This herb from the mint family has a mildly sharp, sweet-and-salty taste that's best released by crushing it in a mortar and pestle. It adds piquant flavor to meat, poultry, fish, eggs, soups, and stews.

THYME
A common ingredient in French and Mediterranean cuisine, this member of the mint family has more than 100 varieties. It's among the most versatile herbs. Thyme adds depth to poultry, fish, vegetables, stuffings, soups, and sauces. As its name implies, lemon thyme has a citrus scent and flavor and a milder taste than regular thyme, making it just right for seasoning fish and seafood.

PARSLEY

THYME

ROSEMARY

fig. 0.4 **STRIPPING A LEAFY HERB**

fig. 0.5 **STRIPPING A ROBUST HERB**

Working with Herbs

Many basic techniques, such as making stock or soup, call for adding an herb sprig or two to the pot along with the liquid and any other aromatics. Each sprig is a single, small stem, like the parsley, thyme, and rosemary shown above. Other recipes call for just the leaves (either to use whole or chopped). If only a handful of leaves are needed, pull them from each stem *fig. 0.4*. When more are called for, use a knife to shave the leaves from the stems (and keep these stems for flavoring stocks and soups, since some of the leaves will remain intact). For woody herbs, such as thyme, rosemary, and oregano, grasp the tip of a stem with two fingers; run the thumb and index finger of your other hand along the stem, from tip to bottom, against the direction of the leaves *fig. 0.5*.

COARSELY CHOPPED

FINELY CHOPPED

fig. 0.6 **CHOPPING HERBS**

Chopping Herbs

Whether for use in cooking or as a garnish, fresh herbs are often chopped. This allows them to more readily release their flavor. Start by removing the leaves from the stems as described (opposite); then place the leaves in a pile on your cutting board. To chop herbs, press the tip of a chef's knife against the cutting board to stabilize it, then rock the blade up and down repeatedly without lifting or moving the tip *fig. 0.6*; as you work, guide the herbs under the knife with your free hand and, again keeping the tip of the knife in the same position, rotate the knife from side to side over the herbs until all are evenly chopped, either coarsely or finely as shown above. Basil, sage, and other herbs with bigger leaves are often cut into chiffonade; to do this, stack several leaves, then roll them tightly lengthwise; slice thinly crosswise with a very sharp knife *fig. 0.7*. The pieces will unroll into fine green ribbons.

fig. 0.7 **MAKING A CHIFFONADE**

fig. 0.8 IN A PLASTIC BAG

fig. 0.9 ON THE COUNTERTOP

Making a Bouquet Garni

A bouquet garni is a bundle of aromatic herbs that infuses soups and broths with flavor. Tying the herbs together with kitchen twine makes it easy to remove them before serving. A classic bouquet garni consists of parsley, thyme, and bay leaves; sometimes celery or leeks are included as well.

Storing Herbs

You can store fresh herbs in the refrigerator in a resealable plastic bag between layers of barely damp paper towels *fig. 0.8*; they should keep for a few days and up to a week. Herbs can also be stored in a bowl or glass of water at room temperature, as you would a bouquet of flowers *fig. 0.9*. Keep the herbs in a cool spot out of direct sunlight, and change the water daily; they'll last for several days. Their constant presence on the countertop can also be a reminder to use the herbs instead of letting them linger, out of sight, in the refrigerator drawer.

fig. 0.10 BLANCHING TENDER HERBS TO
MAKE HERB OIL

Making a Sachet d'Epice

Like a bouquet garni, a sachet d'epice adds flavor to soups and stocks. *Epice* is French for "spice," and this cheesecloth-wrapped bundle usually includes peppercorns, other spices, and sometimes garlic, along with the herbs.

Making Herb Oils

Herb oils can be used in cooking and garnishing. To infuse oil with tender herbs, combine ½ cup extra-virgin olive oil and ½ cup vegetable oil (olive oil alone would overpower the flavor of the herbs). Blanch one bunch of fresh leafy herbs, about 5 seconds *fig. 0.10*. Immediately transfer to an ice bath. Drain and squeeze out excess liquid, than process herbs in blender with half of the oil until smooth. Add remaining oil and process until herbs are very fine, about 1 minute. Refrigerate in an airtight container 8 hours or overnight. Return to room temperature, then strain oil through two layers of cheesecloth set in a sieve; discard solids. Store in an airtight container, refrigerated, up to one month. For herbs such as thyme or rosemary, combine with oil in a saucepan over medium heat for about 5 minutes. Transfer to an airtight container and steep at least 1 hour and up to overnight *fig. 0.11*. Strain oil through cheesecloth before using or storing in an airtight container in the refrigerator up to one month.

fig. 0.11 STEEPING ROBUST HERBS IN OIL

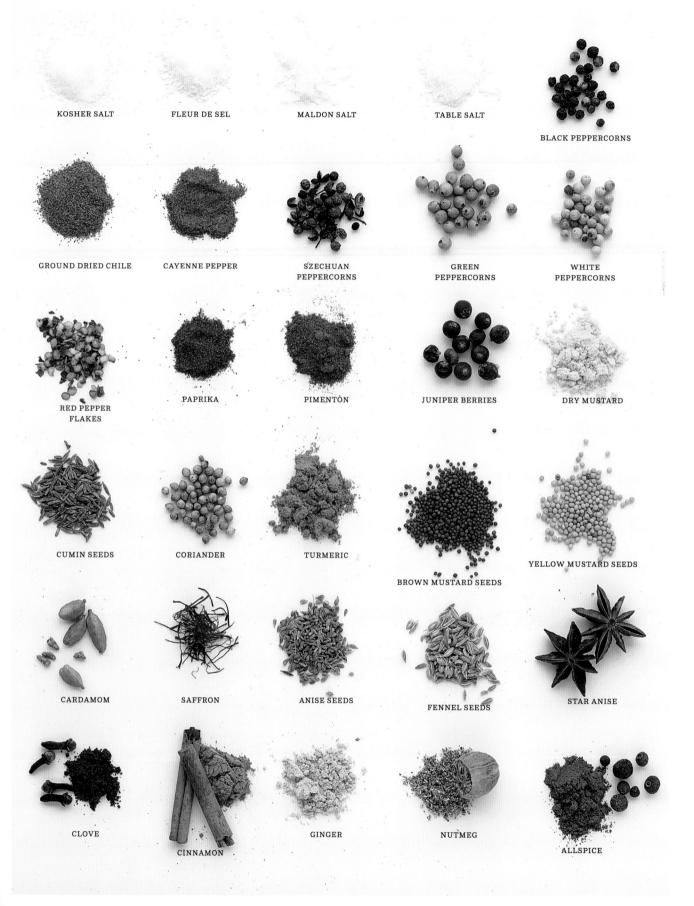

KOSHER SALT

FLEUR DE SEL

MALDON SALT

TABLE SALT

BLACK PEPPERCORNS

GROUND DRIED CHILE

CAYENNE PEPPER

SZECHUAN
PEPPERCORNS

GREEN
PEPPERCORNS

WHITE
PEPPERCORNS

RED PEPPER
FLAKES

PAPRIKA

PIMENTÒN

JUNIPER BERRIES

DRY MUSTARD

CUMIN SEEDS

CORIANDER

TURMERIC

BROWN MUSTARD SEEDS

YELLOW MUSTARD SEEDS

CARDAMOM

SAFFRON

ANISE SEEDS

FENNEL SEEDS

STAR ANISE

CLOVE

CINNAMON

GINGER

NUTMEG

ALLSPICE

Seasonings

Here is a list of spices to keep on hand, including peppercorns and, although not a spice, four common types of salt. Each one has distinct benefits in the kitchen: some offer pronounced flavor, others serve as delicate finishers, still others enliven sweet, as well as savory, dishes. For optimum freshness, buy whole spices whenever possible and grind or grate as needed. Store all spices and seasonings in airtight containers, away from heat, moisture, and direct sunlight. Replace every year or two, as the flavors' potency will diminish over time.

KOSHER SALT
This coarse-grained variety is an excellent multipurpose salt and can be used at the table and in most recipes, except for tender doughs and other finely textured desserts. The taste is clean and bright, as it contains no iodine; some brands are also additive-free.

FLEUR DE SEL
Harvested by hand in the Brittany region of France, this delicate, crystalline variety is considered one of the finest finishing salts. Its name translates as "flower of salt," and the flavor—pure, almost sweet, with faint floral notes—can enhance desserts, such as caramels, as well as savory dishes.

MALDON SALT
These pyramid-shaped white flakes pack an intense, salty flavor, so a small amount may be sufficient. Produced in Essex, England, the crystals are wholly natural and contain no artificial additives. It is generally used as a finishing salt, not an ingredient in recipes.

TABLE SALT
Finely granulated table salt dissolves faster than coarser varieties, which is why it is often recommended for baking. It contains additives that prevent the small grains from clumping and may also be fortified with iodine, a nutrient supplement that can impart a metallic, bitter flavor and can react with certain foods. If you have to use it in place of coarse salt, cut the amount approximately in half.

BLACK PEPPERCORNS
Black peppercorns are the dried, dark berries from the pepper plant, picked unripe and allowed to dry. Whole ones are often used in sachets d'epice (see page 23) to flavor stocks and poaching liquids; cracked with a rolling pin or heavy pan, they can encrust steaks and roasts before cooking. The coarser the grind, the more kick the pepper delivers.

GROUND DRIED CHILE
A pure chile powder contains only one type of pepper, such as Anaheim (pictured), ancho, or habanero, and the level of spice varies according to the particular chile. This is not to be confused with chili powder, a blend of dried red chiles, cumin, oregano, and garlic, often used in Southwestern and Mexican dishes, most notably chili con carne.

CAYENNE PEPPER
Also called ground red pepper by some manufacturers, this pungent seasoning, originally from South America, is made from the dried flesh of a variety of red chiles. It is generally used more for flavoring than for heat, and often appears in gumbos and chilis.

SZECHUAN PEPPERCORNS
Despite the name, Szechuan peppercorns are not part of the pepper family. Instead, the rust-colored dried berries come from the prickly ash tree and have a fragrant, woody aroma with citrus overtones. They are also known to create a mild numbing sensation on the tongue. Used in Chinese, Japanese, Tibetan, and Nepalese cuisines, they are best toasted over low heat before using to release their flavor.

GREEN PEPPERCORNS
Black, white, and green peppercorns are all harvested from the pepper plant, yet the green ones are harvested the earliest, when they are still soft and underripe. More perishable than the other two varieties, they are often packed in brine, though they are also available dried or freeze-dried. Slightly fruity with a mild, peppery flavor, green peppercorns work well in marinades, mustards, cream-based sauces, and meat dishes.

WHITE PEPPERCORNS
In contrast to black ones, white peppercorns are ripened berries with the outer husk removed. Beige in color and very aromatic, they are often used in light-colored sauces, soups, and other dishes. White pepper should not be used as a substitution for black pepper.

RED PEPPER FLAKES
Also known as crushed red pepper, this coarse seasoning comprises not only the flesh of dried chiles but also the seeds, which provide the most heat. The level of spiciness can vary greatly depending on the chiles used and their age. Red pepper flakes add spice to sautéed and stewed vegetables, as well as many sauces.

PAPRIKA
Available only as a powder, this crimson-hued seasoning combines several types of dried red peppers. Hungary produces the most well-known paprika, which can vary from mild to bold in flavor, and from reddish-orange to brick red in color. It is commonly used in goulashes and other Eastern European dishes, as well as a colorful garnish on foods such as deviled eggs.

PIMENTÒN
Also known as Spanish paprika, this blend of dried (and often smoked) red peppers is incorporated into many Spanish foods, including paella. There are three varieties: dulce (sweet), agridulce (medium), and picante (hot). Use of the word "pimentòn" is regulated, so look for "Denomination de Origen," or "D.O.," on the label.

JUNIPER BERRIES

This small bluish-black fruit is actually the cone, not the berry, of the evergreen juniper shrub. They are usually available dried but can sometimes be found fresh in season. With a piney, clean aroma, the spice complements rich meats, especially pork and game, as well as stuffings, sauerkraut, marinades, and brines. Juniper berries are also used to flavor gin.

DRY MUSTARD

Also called mustard powder, this spice is simply finely ground mustard seed. Pungent in flavor and bright yellow in color, dry mustard adds flavor to barbecue sauces, salad dressings, and meat dishes, as well as its namesake condiment.

CUMIN SEEDS

Essential in Latin American and Indian cuisines, cumin plays an important role in two seasoning blends, chili powder and curry powder. Dry-roasting the seeds before grinding helps bring out the flavor. Ground cumin can be a flavorful addition to spice rubs, marinades, and dressings.

CORIANDER

These dried seeds of the cilantro plant have a sweeter flavor than the fresh leaves. Coriander seeds are often incorporated into Asian, Indian, and Middle Eastern dishes.

TURMERIC

This ginger-related root, native to South Asia, is sold dried and powdered. Peppery and bitter, turmeric appears in many Indian and Middle Eastern dishes, providing the mustard-yellow hue often associated with curries.

MUSTARD SEEDS

Members of the cabbage family, these seeds come in two varieties: brown and yellow (sometimes called white). The yellow ones are staples in American-style mustards and are used to flavor pickles and sausages. Brown seeds are smaller, spicier, and more pungent, and are traditionally part of North African and Asian cuisines.

CARDAMOM

The seeds come in white, green, and black, and are popular in Scandinavia, India, and parts of Africa. Uncracked pods ensure the freshness of the aromatic seeds inside. With a sweet, somewhat spicy flavor, they are often used in baked goods and curries, and are available as pods or seeds, or ground into a powder.

SAFFRON

These red-orange threads, known for turning food a vivid shade of yellow, are dried crocus-flower stigmas. Each blossom has only three stigmas, and it takes 225,000—all hand-collected—to make a pound; as a result, it is the most expensive spice available. It is a prized addition in many Near Eastern and Mediterranean dishes, including tagines, bouillabaisse, risotto Milanese, and paella Valenciana.

ANISE SEEDS

Small and oblong, anise seeds are the dried ripe fruit of an herb found in Mediterranean regions, as well as in South Asia. Similar to fennel seeds, they have a distinct licorice taste and aroma and are used to flavor savory and sweet foods, as well as liqueurs, such as Pernod.

FENNEL SEEDS

Small, oval, and pale greenish-brown, fennel seeds come from a plant related to the fennel bulb. With an aroma and flavor akin to licorice, they are used in various Indian and Mediterranean dishes, and add characteristic flavor to Italian sweet sausage.

STAR ANISE

As the name suggests, this brittle fruit pod is star-shaped, with eight points on average and a seed contained within each. Collected from a Chinese evergreen in the magnolia family, the spice has a strong licorice aroma and is widely used in China, as well as in Thailand, Vietnam, and other parts of Southeast Asia, lending flavor to braises, stews, and soups, among other uses. It is also a key ingredient in Chinese five-spice powder.

CLOVE

Named after the French word for nail (*clou*), these dried and unopened myrtle-flower buds have a distinctive spiked shape. They can be used to stud and flavor a roast or to make an onion pique, as in Pot-au-Feu (see page 235). Ground cloves are also used in gingerbread, as well as in other spiced desserts, cookies, and cakes.

CINNAMON

This reddish-brown spice is the dried bark of a tropical evergreen tree, hand-rolled into "quills," or sticks, or ground into a powder. True cinnamon, a pale brown, is Sri Lankan and comes from a tree of the same name, but the widely distributed variety comes from the Indonesian cassia. Ground cinnamon is used in many desserts, as well as in savory dishes in the Middle East and South Asia.

GINGER

This tropical and subtropical plant is cultivated for its fibrous, knobby rootstock. Available fresh (in root form), dried, ground, pickled, or candied, it has a sweet, spicy flavor and is traditionally used in Indian and other Asian cuisines. Ground ginger appears in many baked goods.

NUTMEG

These large, egg-shaped seeds grow on tropical evergreens found in the West Indies. Dark brown in color and pungent in flavor, nutmeg is used in savory and sweet foods and is particularly good used sparingly in egg dishes, including quiche and custards. Use freshly grated nutmeg when possible for best results.

ALLSPICE

This dried pea-sized berry comes from the evergreen pimiento tree, native to the West Indies and South America. The dark russet-brown spice is available whole or ground, and yields a scent that is reminiscent of clove, cinnamon, and nutmeg.

Toasting and Grinding Spices

For extra intensity, toast whole spices just before grinding; this releases their flavorful oils. Preheat a dry skillet over medium heat. Spread spices in an even layer. Shake or swirl the pan constantly to keep spices from burning; you'll know they're ready when you smell their rich, heady aroma. Transfer immediately to a bowl or plate to cool.

Grind whole spices in an electric coffee grinder *fig. 0.12*. Run a few bits of soft white bread or a handful of uncooked white rice through the grinder when you're done to pick up any left-behind spice particles and oil. To avoid cross-contamination with your coffee beans, buy a separate grinder and designate it for spices only.

You can also follow the traditional method of grinding: Place the spices in the bowl of a mortar and use a pestle to pound and grind them in a circular motion until they reach the desired texture *fig. 0.13*. If necessary, sift through a coarse sieve to remove any large particles.

fig. 0.12 ELECTRIC SPICE GRINDER

fig. 0.13 MORTAR AND PESTLE

CHIVES

LEEKS

SCALLIONS

RED ONIONS

SHALLOTS

GARLIC

GLOBE ONIONS

PEARL ONIONS

CIPOLLINI

Onions

The most common of aromatics, onions are essential ingredients for many savory dishes and preparations. Onions and their kin—shallots, leeks, scallions, chives, and garlic—are collectively known as alliums. They add depth and character to everything from stocks and sauces to hearty braised dishes and roasts. They also serve as important components in flavor builders such as mirepoix and soffritto.

Peeling and Slicing Onions

1 Using a paring knife, cut off the stem end of the bulb. Catch the skin between your thumb and the flat side of the knife blade, and pull off the peel. 2 Using a chef's knife, cut the onion lengthwise in half, through stem and root ends. 3 Make a *V*-shaped notch around the root end to remove it. 4 Place halves flat side down on cutting board. Trim the stem end, then thinly slice onion lengthwise.

Alliums

GLOBE ONIONS are available in three colors—red, yellow, and white—and a range of sizes, from petite "boilers" to jumbo, or Spanish, onions. Yellow onions, the most common type, have a robust flavor that's perfect for caramelizing. Red onions' sweetness and bright hue make them ideal for finely chopping and using as a garnish. White onions are frequently used in soups and stews, and are also a staple of Mexican cuisine.

CIPOLLINI, which are Italian in origin, are slightly sweet onions, perfect for braising or roasting.

PEARL ONIONS are usually white but are also available in red or yellow. They are often used in stews and pot pies.

SHALLOTS, available year-round, have purple-tinged white flesh and copper-colored skin. Classically used in French cuisine, they are more mild-tasting than onions. Minced shallots make an excellent addition to vinaigrettes (and can also be substituted for onions in a variety of recipes).

LEEKS are used in place of onions in many soups (including vichyssoise), stews, and sautés whenever a milder, more delicate flavor is desired. They are also wonderful on their own—steamed, sautéed, grilled, or poached and marinated.

SCALLIONS, also called green onions, have a light, slightly sweet taste. They are available year-round, but are at their peak in spring and summer. As a general rule, the most slender bulbs are the sweetest. Scallions are often used in Chinese and other Asian cuisines.

CHIVES, although sometimes classified as herbs, are actually alliums. They add bite to soups, baked potatoes, egg dishes, and compound butters.

GARLIC can be sweet or fiery, subtle or sharp. Each bulb, or head, of garlic contains a cluster of cloves that are connected at the root but separated by papery skins. Garlic can be used raw in salads and vinaigrettes or cooked in sauces, stews, and soups. Garlic that's crushed, chopped, or minced gives dishes a stronger flavor than whole or sliced cloves; the taste mellows upon cooking.

Chopping Onions

Begin by peeling and slicing the onion in half lengthwise through the root and stem ends as described on page 29; place halves flat side down on cutting board. Follow the steps below to chop the onion, varying the intervals to achieve the desired cut (opposite). **1** Slice lengthwise at even intervals, almost but not quite to the root end. **2** Holding the root end, slice horizontally toward root end at even intervals. **3** Then make even, perpendicular cuts. The pieces will fall away as you chop.

Sautéing and Caramelizing Onions

1 In a skillet or saucepan, heat a thin coat of oil or butter over medium-high heat. When oil is shimmering, add thinly sliced onions. **2** To sauté, cook, stirring occasionally, until onions are softened, translucent, and just starting to turn golden around the edges, 5 to 10 minutes. **3** To caramelize onions, reduce heat to medium-low and continue to cook, stirring more frequently to keep the onions from sticking to the pan, until onions are very soft and brown, 30 to 40 minutes more. To further play up the vegetable's natural sweetness, try adding 1 teaspoon of sugar to the pan once the onions are soft and translucent. If onions begin to stick or appear to darken too quickly, add a tablespoon of water to pan.

Onion Cuts

MINCED   FINELY CHOPPED   DICED   SLICED

Peeling Pearl Onions

Prepare an ice-water bath. Bring a pot of water to a boil. 1 Add onions and blanch for 30 seconds. Transfer to ice bath until cool enough to handle, then remove. 2 With a paring knife, cut off the root end and squeeze the onion from the skin. It should pop right out.

Chopping Leeks

1 Leeks are commonly chopped into half-moon shapes before cooking. First, trim and discard root ends and dark green tops from leek, leaving just the creamy white bulbs and pale-green parts, which are more tender. 2 Use a chef's knife to halve leek lengthwise. 3 Place halves flat side down on a cutting board and thinly slice crosswise. Wash according to instructions below before using.

Washing Leeks

Leeks are notoriously difficult to clean, as dirt, sand, and grit can collect between their many layers. There are two ways to wash them effectively. If you've sliced them into rounds or half moons, place the pieces in a bowl of cold water, swishing to loosen grit *fig. 0.14*. Repeat several times with fresh water, until you no longer see grit at the bottom of the bowl. Lift leeks from water and drain on paper towels. If your recipe calls for long leeks instead of thin, crosswise slices, first trim and discard the tough, dark greens. Halve leeks lengthwise and cut off root ends, leaving as much of the bulb intact as possible. Rinse each half under running water *fig. 0.15*, carefully separating layers to loosen dirt.

fig. 0.14 WASHING LEEK HALF MOONS   *fig. 0.15* WASHING SPLIT LEEKS

Peeling and Slicing Garlic

When the goal is to cut garlic into neat slices or slivers, peel by this method: 1 With a paring knife, slice off the root end of a whole, unpeeled garlic clove. 2 Grip the peel between your thumb and the flat part of the knife blade, and pull off the skin.

3 To slice, hold a peeled clove in place with your fingertips (curve fingers inward). Carefully slice very thinly with a sharp chef's knife, moving your fingers back as you cut.

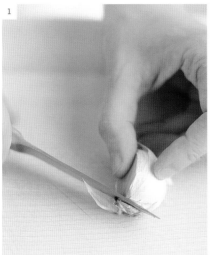

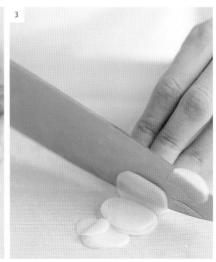

Crushing and Mincing Garlic

An easy way to remove the skin is to crush the clove, good for when the garlic will be minced or turned into a paste. Place the flat side of the knife over the clove. 1 Put the heel of your palm on the knife blade and press down firmly to smash the clove. Pop out the crushed clove. 2 To chop or mince garlic, run the blade of a sharp knife back and forth over peeled cloves until garlic reaches the desired consistency (small pieces

for chopped, very small for minced). Because raw garlic is sticky, you may have to wipe the blade while you work. 3 To make a paste, sprinkle crushed cloves generously with coarse salt. With the flat side of a large chef's knife blade, mash everything together until a paste forms. The salt works as an abrasive, making it easier to form a paste.

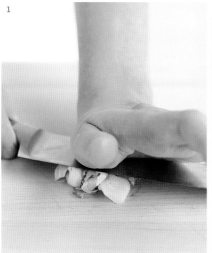

Citrus

Zesting Citrus

There are several ways to remove the zest from the fruit, and the one you use will depend on how the zest will be used in a particular dish. Here are three common methods: A rasp-style grater is the best tool for finely zesting citrus *fig. 0.16*; it removes only the brightly colored peel, leaving the bitter white pith behind.

For bright garnishes, use a vegetable peeler to remove citrus rinds, creating wide ribbons of zest *fig. 0.17*. For thinner, more delicate strips, slice the shaved peel lengthwise into fine julienne.

For tiny strips of zest, use a zester, pressing lightly to avoid removing the bitter white pith *fig. 0.18*.

fig. 0.16 **USING A RASP-STYLE GRATER**

fig. 0.17 **USING A VEGETABLE PEELER**

fig. 0.18 **USING A ZESTER**

Suprêming Citrus

1 Cutting citrus fruits into neat segments is called suprêming (from the French *suprême,* meaning "fillet"). First, slice off both ends of the fruit with a knife, exposing the flesh. Stand the fruit on one end and, working from top to bottom, cut away the rind and pith with long strokes, following the fruit's curve. 2 Holding the fruit over a bowl (to catch the juices, which are often used with the segments), cut between the membranes to release each segment into the bowl. 3 Squeeze the remaining juice from the membrane into the bowl.

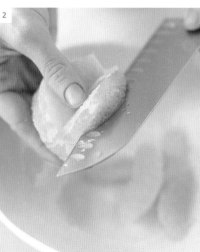

Using a Hand-Press Juicer

A hand-press juicer quickly and easily extracts juice from lemons and limes. Place one half of the fruit in the cup, with the cut side facing the holes. Hold the juicer over a measuring cup and squeeze firmly. The pulp and seeds stay in the press, so there's no need to strain the juice.

Juicing Citrus

Room-temperature fruits will release their juices more easily than cold ones. To get the most juice from a citrus fruit, roll it firmly between your palm and a work surface before slicing in half crosswise. The pressure crushes the fruit's inner membranes, causing them to release more liquid. A reamer is an old-fashioned tool that works with lemons, limes, oranges, and grapefruits. Set a fine-mesh sieve over a liquid measuring cup or a bowl. Working over the bowl, insert the ridged cone of the reamer in the center of a citrus fruit half, and twist to release the juice. The sieve will catch the seeds and pulp.

1

Stocks & Soups

STOCKS AND SOUPS

IT HAS BEEN SAID that the measure of a good cook is how well he or she makes soup. Not a complicated, multicourse meal or a delicate soufflé, but a simple soup. The dish's humble nature is exactly what makes it so telling—there is no hiding behind elaborate presentation. Success lies in using the best ingredients and combining them well, seasoning them correctly, and cooking them just enough to bring out their elemental flavors.

STOCKS

Making soup, of course, whether a crystal-clear consommé or thick, chunky minestrone, usually begins with stock. Perhaps you've never made your own stock. Maybe you can't imagine why you should, when the grocery store has such a variety, including organic, low-sodium versions in cans and even convenient, resealable boxes. You need only taste a homemade version to know the answer. No mass-produced broth can rival the freshness and authentic flavor of a good, home-simmered stock, nor will it come close in versatility. Aside from serving as a base for soup, your own stock, which will be rich with gelatin, can be reduced to its essence and enriched with butter or cream for a delectable sauce. It can stand in for plain water to infuse rice or other grains with flavor. It can take braised meat to a more complex level. It can do another, very important thing: Stock, and the process of making it, informs your palate and teaches you fundamental cooking principles that you will turn to again and again as you become more confident in the kitchen.

In this chapter you will learn how to make the essential and familiar chicken and beef stocks, as well as variations on them. Expand your repertoire with fish fumet, vegetable stock, and the Japanese soup base called dashi.

Making stock isn't difficult, but there are some useful rules of thumb to keep in mind:

■ A good stock starts with good ingredients. Your goal when making stock is to transfer all the flavor from those ingredients to the cooking liquid; every flavor, therefore, should be as pure and appealing as possible. Good ingredients, however, don't have to be expensive. In fact, inexpensive, tough cuts of meat and their bones (such as chicken necks, backs, and wings; oxtails; and veal knucklebones) are some of the best choices for stock, as they are loaded with connective tissue that will break down and enrich the liquid with gelatin. Vegetables that have had time to mature and develop deep flavor are likewise better choices than young, more delicate-tasting specimens, but avoid using any that are past their prime, which often taste bitter.

■ If you plan ahead, you can ask your butcher or fishmonger to start setting aside bones for you a few days before your cooking session. Additionally, you should always save backs and necks from chickens you butcher yourself; you can freeze them up to 3 months. Leftover cooked ingredients (the carcass from a roast chicken, for instance) can be used with moderate success, but the stock won't be as flavorful as one made with raw bones, nor will it have the same clarity.

■ Cut your ingredients to size, according to how long the liquid will be cooking. A beef stock might simmer all day long, so the bones and vegetables that flavor it can be roughly chopped into big chunks; a delicate vegetable or fish stock, on the other hand, will cook quickly—in less than an hour, in some cases—so everything should be chopped more finely, so the flavors can be more quickly and easily drawn out.

■ Use a good, heavy soup pot—it should be taller than it is wide so the steam doesn't escape too quickly, but it's more important that the pot be large enough to hold all the ingredients with about three inches of room on top. Make sure ingredients are submerged at all times, adding more liquid as necessary.

■ To prevent the stock from becoming cloudy, skim it frequently as it cooks, especially during the first hour. Use a ladle or wide, flat spoon to remove the impurities and fat that rise to the surface.

■ Keep your eye on the heat. The water should be brought just to a boil, then reduced to a bare simmer; more bubbling than that and the impurities that are drawn out of the ingredients will be incorporated back into the liquid, the fat emulsifying with the stock instead of floating, for an unpleasant, murky result.

■ Remember that it is possible to cook a stock too long. You want to simmer those ingredients until they are virtually flavorless—meaning all that goodness has made its way into the liquid—but no longer. Too much cooking can lead to bitterness.

SEASONING STOCK

Use reserve when seasoning your stock. Keep flavorings simple, as with a bouquet garni of parsley, thyme, and other mild herbs. Add salt and any assertive seasonings later, while making the soup, sauce, or other recipe in which the stock will be used. A stock in which the raw ingredients are merely cooked in water is called white stock, the type called for in many soups and milder, lighter-bodied preparations. If you want a more intensely flavored stock, roast the bones and vegetables in the oven before simmering, a process that produces a deeper colored and flavored result called brown stock, ideal for rich sauces and braises.

Another way to enhance a stock is to reduce it by straining and defatting the liquid, and boiling it down to concentrate the flavors. If you're planning to reduce a stock, however, for use in a sauce or another preparation, it's especially important not to overdo it with spices and salt—those flavors will also intensify, perhaps unpleasantly so, as the liquid level drops.

STORING STOCK

To protect the investment of time and effort that you put into your stock, make sure you store it right. A finished stock should be carefully strained: use a sieve or colander lined with cheesecloth, or even a coffee filter. Cool the liquid quickly by placing it in an ice-water bath, or divide it into several small, shallow containers, and then refrigerate it (allowing a large quantity of stock to cool on its own could present a safety hazard because it will take much longer to cool, thus exposing it to bacteria for a longer period of time). After being chilled overnight, a layer of fat will form on the surface of the stock, which can be easily removed. All stocks can be frozen in different amounts, so you can thaw only what you need. Freezing

stock in 1-cup measures is a safe choice, allowing you the option of thawing one (say, for a sauce) or many (such as for risotto). Be sure to label the containers with the date the stock was made so you know when to use it by (most keep for several months).

Once you have taken the time to prepare a few batches of stock, whether chicken, meat, vegetable, or fish, you'll find that you've made your day-to-day cooking considerably easier and more successful. Having stock at the ready in the refrigerator or freezer means a soup, stew, or pan sauce is only a few steps away.

SOUPS

Once you've stocked up on stock, it's time to make soups. Many of the techniques here are templates, easy to vary depending on what you like and what you find in the market. Showcase the pure flavor and pretty colors of fresh vegetables in silky cream soups or lighter purees. Learn how to make classic chicken soup, which is the foundation for such variations as matzo ball soup and a lovely springtime soup with watercress and peas. You'll also find recipes for Mexican tortilla soup, French onion soup, minestrone, and consommé, each with a singular flavor and valuable lessons for the cook. Finish the chapter—and your soups—with homemade garnishes, a delicious detail to make a bowl of homemade soup even more enticing.

GLOSSARY OF TERMS

Though the terms that describe stocks are sometimes used interchangeably, the distinctions are useful to understand as you start to cook. A *stock* (with the exception of vegetable stock) is made of water simmered with bones. The meat on them provides flavor while the bones, and the gelatinous connective tissue between them, slowly break down and add body to the liquid. A *broth*, on the other hand, is usually made with just meat (or bone-in meat, such as a whole chicken) and/or vegetables; it is typically lighter bodied and served on its own. The word *bouillon* is sometimes used interchangeably with *broth*, but often refers to a concentrated, dried, salt-laden grocery-store product that can be reconstituted for a poor-quality brothlike substitute (in a pinch, a can or carton of low-sodium broth is a much better choice). *Fond* is the French word for stock, and it literally means "foundation." *Fumet*, French for "aroma," usually refers to a concentrated fish stock.

ASSORTED STOCKS

LESSON 1.1
How to Make White Stock

The first lesson in stock making is also the simplest: everything (bones and aromatics) is covered in a pot with water and gently simmered, yielding a stock with a pure, clean flavor. This technique can be applied to making stock with chicken, meat, fish, or only vegetables. Of these, no stock is more versatile and flexible than white chicken stock, which is flavorful but not overpowering, lending itself to a vast array of uses: white sauces, such as velouté; any number of soups (it is the default choice for many); and many stews and braises, among other dishes where there are layers of flavor (think risotto). White beef stock is equally classic, and a better option in dishes such as Wine-Braised Short Ribs (page 188).

For this stock, there are several ways to alter the outcome, depending on how it will be used. The longer the stock simmers, the stronger it will taste. Simmer for 1½ hours for vegetable soups or other delicate dishes (including white sauces), longer for more robust sauces and soups. To give the stock a more pronounced chicken flavor, add 1½ pounds chicken thighs along with the other parts (take them out of the pot as soon as they are done if you plan to reserve the meat for another purpose, returning bones to pot after removing meat).

BASIC CHICKEN STOCK Makes about 2½ quarts

For flavor base

> 5 POUNDS ASSORTED CHICKEN PARTS *(backs, necks, and wings)*

For aromatics

> 2 MEDIUM CARROTS, *peeled and chopped into 1- to 2-inch lengths*
>
> 2 CELERY STALKS, *chopped into 1- to 2-inch lengths*
>
> 2 MEDIUM ONIONS, *peeled and cut into eighths*
>
> 1 DRIED BAY LEAF
>
> 1 TEASPOON WHOLE BLACK PEPPERCORNS

Bring water with chicken to a boil Place chicken parts in a stockpot just large enough to hold them with about 3 inches of room above (an 8-quart pot should do) and add enough water to cover by 1 inch (about 3 quarts) [1]. Bring to a boil over medium-high heat, using a ladle to skim impurities and fat that rise to the top [2].

Add aromatics and simmer Add vegetables, bay leaf, and peppercorns and reduce heat to a bare simmer (bubbles should just gently break the surface) [3]. Cook, skimming frequently, for 1½ to 2½ hours (depending on taste preference).

Strain Pass the stock through a cheesecloth-lined sieve into a large heatproof measuring cup or another bowl or pot [4]; do not press on solids. Discard solids.

Remove fat Skim off fat if using immediately, or let cool completely (in an ice-water bath, if desired) before transferring to airtight containers. Refrigerate at least 8 hours to allow the fat to accumulate at the top; lift off and discard fat [5]

ABOUT MIREPOIX

Mirepoix is a combination of aromatic vegetables that gives a subtle background flavor to dishes such as soups, stews, and braises. To make mirepoix: Rinse, trim, and peel vegetables—typically two parts onion to one part carrot and one part celery—then chop them into uniform pieces. The shorter the cooking time of your recipe, the smaller the pieces should be, so that they effectively infuse the food with flavor.

You can add the mirepoix uncooked to stocks and broths for a light dose of flavor. To add richness to heartier stews and braises, "sweat" the vegetables first, cooking them with a little oil or butter over low heat until they start to release their juices into the pan.

Mirepoix, a French term, is only one of many possible variations. The Italian soffritto, like mirepoix, calls for onions, celery, and carrots, and sometimes pancetta and garlic. Mushrooms, parsnips, leeks, peppers, tomatoes, and garlic are all considered aromatic vegetables, and can be used in endless combinations.

before using or storing stock. The stock can be refrigerated up to 3 days or frozen up to 3 months; thaw completely in the refrigerator before using.

WHITE BEEF STOCK

Follow the above recipe, using 4 pounds of beef bones, such as knuckle or shin, and 2 pounds oxtail or short ribs (or just use 7 pounds total beef bones) in place of chicken parts, and about 6 quarts of water. Also, add 4 crushed garlic cloves, 6 sprigs parsley, and 4 sprigs thyme to the aromatics, and use 2 bay leaves and 2 teaspoons peppercorns. Simmer for 8 hours, then proceed with recipe to strain, skim off fat, and store. Makes about 3½ quarts.

Basic Chicken Stock, Step by Step

SOUPS AND STOCKS | **43**
How to Make Chicken Soup

LESSON 1.2
How to Make Chicken Soup

If soup-making is an indication of a cook's talents, chicken soup is the truest test, since the soup should ideally offer warmth and nourishment as well as flavor. It is, after all, the ultimate comfort food. Once you've committed this basic soup technique to memory, the possibilities for variations—and other meals—are limitless. Making the soup is essentially a form of poaching chicken in an aromatic broth. The chicken should always be just covered with liquid—in this case, water—which should remain at a gentle simmer. Skimming the surface is critical to the soup's success, since the impurities from the chicken would cause the broth to become cloudy. Straining out the aromatics will also help produce a cleaner broth; the vegetables will have become very soft and lost much of their individual flavors by this time, so it is necessary to replenish them with "garnish" vegetables, added at the end. The variations below provide flavorful alternatives to the basic soup recipe—one with matzo balls and the other with springtime vegetables, including green beans, peas, and watercress.

CHICKEN SOUP Serves 6 to 8

For chicken and broth

1 WHOLE CHICKEN *(3 to 4 pounds), cut into 8 parts (page 110)*

1 MEDIUM CARROT, *peeled and cut into 1-inch pieces*

1 MEDIUM PARSNIP, *peeled and cut into 1-inch pieces*

2 CELERY STALKS, *cut into 1-inch pieces*

1 MEDIUM ONION, *peeled and cut into 1-inch pieces*

3 SPRIGS PARSLEY

2 SPRIGS THYME

1 DRIED BAY LEAF

¼ TEASPOON WHOLE BLACK PEPPERCORNS

1 TEASPOON COARSE SALT

7 TO 8 CUPS WATER

For garnish vegetables

2 MEDIUM CARROTS, *peeled and cut into ½-inch pieces (1 cup)*

2 CELERY STALKS, *cut into ½-inch pieces (½ cup)*

1 MEDIUM PARSNIP, *peeled and cut into ½-inch pieces (¾ cup)*

COARSE SALT AND FRESHLY GROUND PEPPER

Make broth and cook chicken Place chicken in a large stockpot (it should be just large enough to hold chicken with 3 inches of room on top). Add vegetables, herbs, peppercorns, salt, and enough water or stock to just cover chicken. Bring to a boil, skimming foam from surface as necessary [1], then reduce heat and simmer until chicken is just cooked through (the juices should run clear when

MATZO BALL SOUP

CHICKEN SOUP

CHICKEN SOUP WITH
SPRING VEGETABLES

pierced and an instant-read thermometer inserted into thickest part should register 160°F for breasts and 165°F for legs and thighs), 7 to 10 minutes for breasts and 10 to 15 minutes for legs and thighs. Use tongs to remove each part as soon as it is finished cooking. (The meat will be added back to the soup later, so it is important not to overcook.) When cool enough to handle, pull off and discard the skin, then separate the meat from the bones and tear into bite-size pieces [2] (or dice for a more elegant presentation). You should have about 3 cups chicken (reserve 2 cups for soup and the rest for another use).

Fortify broth Cover chicken and refrigerate until needed. Return the bones to the pot [3] and simmer broth for another hour.

Strain broth and add garnish vegetables Strain broth through a fine sieve [4], discarding solids. You should have about 6 cups of broth (add more water if necessary). Skim off fat, then add broth to clean pot. Add carrots, celery, and parsnip [5], and return to a boil, then reduce heat and simmer until the

Chicken Soup, Step by Step

vegetables are tender, 5 to 8 minutes. Add reserved 2 cups chicken [6] and cook just to heat through. Season to taste with salt and pepper and serve immediately. The chicken and broth can be made up to 3 days ahead. Refrigerate separately in covered containers, then proceed to finish the soup. If making ahead (or if you desire a lighter broth), refrigerate the broth at least overnight to allow the fat to accumulate at the top, then lift off with a spoon before proceeding.

CHICKEN SOUP WITH SPRING VEGETABLES

Follow the recipe above to cook the chicken and make the broth. Replace garnish vegetables (celery, carrot, and parsnip) with 3 ounces green beans, trimmed and cut into ½-inch pieces (¾ cup), and 3 ounces shelled (or frozen) peas (½ cup). Simmer soup until beans and peas are crisp-tender and bright green, about 5 minutes, then add 1 cup watercress (tough stems removed) and simmer just to wilt slightly, about 30 seconds. Season with salt and pepper and serve immediately. Serves 6 to 8.

MATZO BALL SOUP

Make broth and cook chicken as directed above, reserving meat for another use. Strain broth and pour ¼ cup into a medium bowl (reserve the rest for serving); whisk in 2 large egg yolks (reserve whites), 2 tablespoons melted chicken fat (also called schmaltz; available from a butcher), ¾ teaspoon coarse salt, and a generous pinch of freshly ground pepper (or more as desired). Stir in ½ cup matzo meal and 2 tablespoons chopped flat-leaf parsley. Beat reserved egg whites on medium-high speed until stiff peaks form, then stir into matzo mixture until smooth [1]. Cover and refrigerate mixture until slightly thickened, about 30 minutes.

Bring 4 cups water and 2 cups reserved chicken broth to a boil in a large pot; add 1 tablespoon coarse salt. Using 2 tablespoons at a time, roll matzo mixture into balls, then drop into pot with a spoon [2]. Reduce heat, cover, and gently simmer until matzo balls are cooked through [3], about 15 minutes (do not overcook; they should be only slightly firm). Transfer 2 matzo balls to each of four serving bowls. Meanwhile, bring remaining 4 cups broth to a boil in a medium saucepan. Add 1 carrot, peeled and sliced into coins, and reduce heat to a simmer; cook until the carrot is tender, about 5 minutes. Ladle broth and carrot into bowls and garnish with coarsely chopped fresh dill or parsley, if desired. Serves 6 to 8.

Making Matzo Balls

TORTILLA SOUP Serves 8

Unlike other chicken soups that begin with water, this Mexican version starts with chicken stock; the resulting broth is richer and more complex than for basic chicken soup (page 43), since stock will impart flavor to (and be fortified by) the chicken. To make the soup, a whole chicken is simmered in chicken stock, which is then strained and combined with a fiery puree of dried chiles, charred tomatoes, and sautéed onion and garlic. Before being pureed, the chiles are toasted in a dry skillet to enhance their smokiness, then soaked in water to soften, a process that is widely used in Mexican cooking as a building block for many types of dishes (this is comparable to the way spices are toasted in Indian cooking as a flavor-building component for masalas and curry pastes).

What distinguishes tortilla soup is the way it is served, since the garnishes are essential to the overall flavor; plus, they are incorporated at the table—not in the kitchen—so that each guest has a hand in creating and customizing the

Ingredients

Commonly used in moles, pasilla chiles are 6 to 8 inches long, with blackish brown skin and a mild flavor. Look for them in Mexican or Latino markets and the specialty foods sections of supermarkets. Other dried chiles, such as ancho or mirasol, are good alternatives.

Cotija cheese is a semi-hard Mexican cheese made from cow's milk. It is available in two varieties: the moist type is similar to feta and is perfect for crumbling over soups, salads, and tacos; firmer ones resemble Parmesan cheese in taste and texture and are more easily grated.

Tortilla Soup Tips

The soup components can be prepared a day ahead: Cook and shred the chicken, then refrigerate in a covered container. Proceed with the recipe to make the chile puree, heating with the strained stock for 15 minutes. Let cool, then refrigerate in an airtight container. When you are ready to proceed, heat the stock, then add the chicken and cook just until it is heated through. Stir in lime juice at the end.

Except for the tortillas, which can be fried 1 to 2 days ahead and kept at room temperature, the garnishes should be prepared as close to serving as possible. Once the stock is simmering, slice the onion and cabbage, cut the limes, grate the cheese, and dice the avocado (toss with a bit of lime juice to prevent it from turning brown).

---

final dish. The garnishes suggested below are traditional and offer a nice balance of taste and texture, but sliced jalapeños (seeded for less heat) or radishes, diced fresh tomatoes, or other types of cheese (such as queso fresco or queso blanco) are also authentic, as is a dollop of *crema* (Mexican sour cream) or sour cream.

For chicken and stock

1 LARGE WHOLE CHICKEN *(about 4½ pounds), cut into 10 pieces (page 110), or use 4½ pounds chicken parts*

8 CUPS BASIC CHICKEN STOCK *(page 41)*

¼ TEASPOON WHOLE BLACK PEPPERCORNS

1 DRIED BAY LEAF

2 TABLESPOONS COARSE SALT

For chile puree

2 DRIED PASILLA CHILES

½ CUP WATER

2 TEASPOONS SUNFLOWER OR OTHER NEUTRAL-TASTING OIL, *plus more for tomatoes*

3 TOMATOES *(about 1¼ pounds), halved*

1 LARGE ONION, *halved lengthwise and thinly sliced*

3 GARLIC CLOVES, *finely chopped*

For finishing soup

2 TABLESPOONS FRESH LIME JUICE

For garnishes

FRIED TORTILLA STRIPS *(page 75)*

¼ WHITE OR GREEN CABBAGE, *halved lengthwise, cored, and thinly sliced (1 cup)*

½ RED ONION, *finely diced (½ cup)*

½ CUP FINELY GRATED COTIJA CHEESE *(1 to 2 ounces)*

¾ CUP CILANTRO LEAVES

1 RIPE, FIRM AVOCADO, *peeled, pitted, and diced*

LIME WEDGES

Cook chicken and fortify stock Place the chicken, stock, peppercorns, bay leaf, and the salt in a large stockpot. Bring just to a boil, skimming foam from the surface, then reduce heat and simmer until chicken is just cooked through, 9 to 12 minutes for breast pieces and 12 to 18 minutes for legs and thighs. (Always check the thickest part to determine whether the chicken is cooked; the juices should run clear and an instant-read thermometer should register 160°F for breasts, 165°F for thighs.) Remove chicken from stock. Once it is cool enough to handle, slip off skin and pull meat from bones, then shred meat into bite-size pieces. Strain stock through a sieve into a clean saucepan.

Meanwhile, prepare chiles Toast the chiles in a dry medium skillet over high heat until fragrant and charred, about 1 minute on each side [1]. Let cool a bit, then split chiles lengthwise and scrape out seeds [2]; discard seeds. Put chiles in a bowl and cover with warm water to soften, about 20 minutes (do not drain). If necessary, weight chiles with another bowl to keep them submerged.

Make puree Heat broiler with rack about 5 inches below heat source. Lightly oil tomatoes and broil until charred in spots [3], about 5 minutes. Let cool briefly, then coarsely chop. Using the same skillet as above, heat oil over medium-high heat and sauté onion and garlic until translucent, about 3 minutes, stirring to prevent sticking. Add the tomatoes and cook 2 minutes more [4]. Stir in chiles and soaking liquid [5]. Allow mixture to cool slightly before pureeing in a blender until smooth. Strain mixture through a sieve [6], pressing with a flexible spatula to extract as much liquid as possible (discard solids).

Finish soup Add puree to fortified stock and simmer over medium heat for 15 minutes, to allow the flavors to blend. Add shredded chicken and cook just to heat through, then stir in lime juice.

Serve Ladle soup into serving bowls and serve garnishes in individual bowls alongside.

Making Chile Puree

LESSON 1.3
How to Make Brown Stock

Brown stock gets its color—and its flavor—from the initial step of roasting bones and vegetables, often with a bit of tomato paste added to promote browning and impart a caramelized flavor, as well as a touch of acidity. After the contents of the pan are transferred to a stockpot, the pan is deglazed (either with water or red wine) to incorporate all the flavorful browned bits, which then, too, get added to the pot. In classical French cooking, brown stock is made with veal bones to produce a delicate-bodied soup. In the recipe that follows, beef is added for deeper flavor, but you can replace the beef with more veal bones (or veal stew meat) for the traditional version. Brown stock can also be made with chicken (see variation); this would be ideal for using in more robust dishes, such as braised meats. Heed the general rules for making all stocks, including simmering very gently, skimming frequently, and keeping enough liquid in the pot so that everything is submerged at all times. Brown stock is also the basis for other classic preparations, including demi glace and glace de viande (see page 52).

BASIC BROWN STOCK Makes 3½ quarts

For flavor base

4 POUNDS VEAL BONES, *such as knuckles and shin*

2 POUNDS SHORT RIBS OR OXTAIL *(optional; add 3 more pounds of veal bones if not using)*

3 TABLESPOONS SUNFLOWER OR OTHER NEUTRAL-TASTING OIL

2 TABLESPOONS TOMATO PASTE

2 ONIONS, *unpeeled and quartered*

2 CELERY STALKS, *each cut into thirds*

2 CARROTS, *peeled and cut into 2-inch pieces*

4 GARLIC CLOVES

For deglazing pan

1 CUP WATER OR RED WINE

For aromatics

6 SPRIGS FLAT-LEAF PARSLEY

4 SPRIGS THYME

2 DRIED BAY LEAVES

2 TEASPOONS WHOLE BLACK PEPPERCORNS

Roast bones and vegetables Heat oven to 400°F. Arrange bones and beef in a single layer in a large heavy roasting pan [1]. Drizzle with the oil and turn to coat. Roast, turning once and stirring often for even browning, until beginning to brown, about 45 minutes. Remove from oven, add tomato paste, and stir to combine. Cook over medium heat for about 30 seconds (to let it brown a little, which cooks out some of the acidity and intensifies the sweetness), then add vegetables [2], stirring well. Return to oven and roast until vegetables are browned and tender and bones are deeply browned, about 40 minutes [3].

Deglaze pan Transfer bones and vegetables to a large stockpot, then spoon off fat from roasting pan and discard. Set the pan over two burners. Add the water or wine and bring to a boil, scraping up any brown bits from bottom with a wooden spoon *fig. 1.1*, boil until liquid is reduced by half, about 3 minutes. Pour everything into the stockpot.

Make stock Add enough water (about 6 quarts) to stockpot to cover bones and vegetables by 2 inches. Bring to just under a boil, then reduce heat to a bare simmer (bubbles should just gently break at the surface). Add herbs and peppercorns and very gently simmer, uncovered, over low heat for 8 hours, adding more water as necessary to keep everything submerged.

Strain stock Carefully pour stock through a fine sieve (do not press on solids) into a large heatproof bowl or another stockpot and discard solids. Stock will be dark brown. Skim off fat if using immediately, or let cool completely (in an ice-water bath, if desired) before transferring to airtight containers. Refrigerate at least 8 hours to allow the fat to accumulate at the top; lift off and discard fat before using or storing. Brown stock and its variations can be refrigerated for up to 3 days or frozen for up to 3 months; thaw completely in the refrigerator before using.

fig. 1.1 DEGLAZING PAN

> ## Roasting Ingredients for Basic Brown Stock

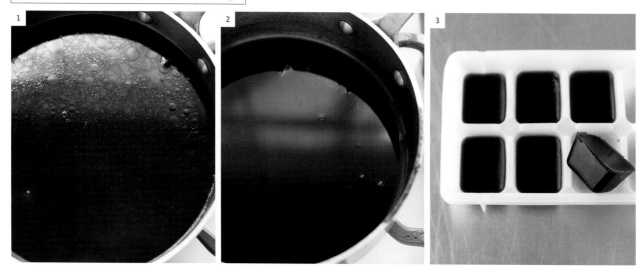

BROWN STOCK, AFTER CHILLING

BROWN CHICKEN STOCK

Follow the above recipe to roast the flavor base and deglaze the pan using 5 pounds chicken parts (backs, necks, and wings) in place of veal and beef; omit garlic and use only 1 tablespoon tomato paste. Then make stock, adding enough water to cover everything by about 1 inch (about 3 quarts). Bring to a boil, then reduce heat to a gentle simmer. Add 1 dried bay leaf and 1 teaspoon peppercorns and cook 1½ to 2½ hours, skimming surface frequently. Strain, chill, and store as directed above. Makes 2½ quarts.

GLACE DE VIANDE Makes ¾ cups

This dark, thick, flavorful reduction adds an inimitable richness to meat stews and braises (one or two cubes is sufficient for boosting the flavor). In classic French cooking, demi glace is made by combining brown veal stock with sauce espagnol (a veal stock thickened with roux), which is then reduced by half. Because demi glace is rather laborious to make (and a bit heavy for modern palates), so many chefs use this straight reduction of stock (without the espagnol) instead. (Julia Child called it a "semi-demi glace.") This simplified method results in a lighter-bodied sauce, or glaze. To make glace de poulet, substitute veal stock with brown chicken stock.

MAKE BASIC BROWN STOCK AS DIRECTED above [1]. After chilling and removing the fat, transfer 1 quart stock to a small pot. Bring to a boil, then reduce the heat to medium-high. Cook, skimming frequently, until the liquid is reduced to about 1½ cups, 30 to 35 minutes. It should be dark and viscous [2]. Let cool 10 minutes, then pour into an ice-cube tray or 8-inch square pan and let cool completely. Cover tightly with plastic wrap and refrigerate overnight. Pop the cubes from the tray [3] or cut with a sharp knife into 1- and 2-inch squares;

> ### Glace de Viande, Step by Step

place cubes in a large resealable storage bag. Glace de viande can be frozen up to 3 months (there is no need to thaw before using).

FRENCH ONION SOUP Serves 8

One of the best reasons to make your own basic brown stock is that it means French onion soup from scratch is within easy reach. (You can also make the soup with white beef stock, page 42.) Like many other bistro classics, French onion soup has humble origins as a staple of thrifty households, where a pot of stock—itself born of frugality—was the foundation for many family meals. Even those with limited resources could make *soupe a l'oignon* since it calls for little else: pounds of inexpensive and readily available onions, a crusty baguette (providing a way to use up day-old bread), and a chunk of sharp Gruyère cheese, grated to turn a little into a lot. Because there are so few components, each one is enhanced in some way to contribute to the final dish. The homemade stock provides both color and robust taste, as well as ensuring a silky consistency. Caramelizing the onions gives them a wonderful sweetness (and more dark brown color). Toasted bread adds a textural note, while gratinéed cheese introduces another pleasing component. Similar to the burnt-sugar shell atop crème brûlée, the molten, golden crown invites tucking into with a spoon. This recipe can be halved, but since the soup freezes well, it is worth making the full amount.

fig. 1.2 SPRINKLING FLOUR OVER CARAMELIZED ONIONS

For caramelizing onions

    5 TABLESPOONS UNSALTED BUTTER
2½ POUNDS ONIONS, *peeled, halved lengthwise, and cut into ¼-inch-thick slices*
    1 TEASPOON SUGAR

For soup

    1 TABLESPOON ALL-PURPOSE FLOUR
    7 CUPS BASIC BROWN STOCK *(page 50) or white beef stock (page 42)*
    3 TABLESPOONS COGNAC
½ CUP DRY WHITE WINE
    COARSE SALT AND FRESHLY GROUND PEPPER

For croutons

½ BAGUETTE, *cut into 16 rounds (¾ inch thick)*
    3 TABLESPOONS UNSALTED BUTTER, *melted*
    6 OUNCES GRUYÈRE CHEESE, *grated on the large holes of a box grater (4 cups)*

Caramelize onions Melt the butter in a medium Dutch oven or stockpot over medium-high heat. Add onions and sprinkle with sugar. (The pot will be quite full but the onions will cook down significantly.) Cook, stirring only occasionally to prevent sticking, until onions are translucent, about 15 minutes. Reduce heat to medium and continue cooking, stirring frequently, until onions have turned deep brown, 30 to 45 minutes more. (If the onions are sticking to the bottom of the pot, or browning unevenly, stir in a tablespoon of water. Adjust heat if onions are cooking too quickly or too slowly.)

54

fig. 1.3 TOPPING SOUP BEFORE BROILING

FRENCH ONION SOUP

Make soup Sprinkle flour over onions and stir to combine *fig. 1.2*, then stir in wine and Cognac. Bring to a simmer over medium heat. Cook 2 minutes, then stir in stock. Partially cover the pot and cook until flavors have melded, 20 to 25 minutes. Season with salt and pepper.

Meanwhile, toast croutons Heat broiler. Spread bread slices on a baking sheet and broil, turning once, until lightly toasted, 2 to 4 minutes (watch carefully so they don't burn). Brush both sides with the melted butter.

Broil and serve Divide soup among eight flameproof crocks or bowls. Float two croutons in each crock and sprinkle with ¼ cup cheese *fig. 1.3*. Broil until cheese is melted and browned in spots. Serve immediately.

LESSON 1.4
How to Make Fish Fumet

Fumet is a white stock made from fish bones and aromatic vegetables, which are first "sweated" (cooked until soft but not taking on any color), then simmered in water. That initial step is a crucial building block, eliciting a touch of sweetness from the leek and developing the flavors for the next step, though it will produce a stock with less clarity than when the aromatics are simply brought to a boil with the rest. (To achieve that result, follow recipe for Basic Chicken Stock on page 41, bringing the fish bones and heads to a boil, then adding vegetables, bay leaf, and peppercorns and simmering 30 minutes before straining.) With its concentrated flavor, fumet is ideal for making fish soups and stews, or for steaming shellfish, such as the Clams in Herbed Broth on page 219.

Like other stocks, fumet can be altered for different effects. Increase the ratio of bones to water and you will have a stock with more pronounced fish flavor. For a Mediterranean-style stock, chopped garlic and fennel (and its fronds) can be sweated with the other aromatics, then crushed tomatoes, crumbled saffron, and a few parsley stems added and simmered in the pot along with everything else.

FISH FUMET Makes about 2 quarts

- 2 TABLESPOONS SUNFLOWER OR OTHER NEUTRAL-TASTING OIL
- 2 POUNDS FISH BONES AND HEADS
- 1 CELERY STALK, *cut into 1-inch pieces*
- 1 LEEK, *white and pale green parts only, cut into 1-inch half-moons and washed well (page 32)*
- 1 CUP DRY WHITE WINE
- 1 DRIED BAY LEAF
- 5 WHOLE BLACK PEPPERCORNS

Ingredients

Ask your fishmonger to save the bones and heads from the fish in advance; firm-fleshed white fish, such as snapper, bass, and halibut, work best. Avoid oily fish (such as mackerel and tuna).

Sweat the bones and vegetables Heat the oil in a medium stockpot over medium heat until hot but not smoking. Add fish parts, celery, and leek. Cover and cook, stirring once or twice, until vegetables are soft and translucent and flesh on the bones has turned opaque but not brown, about 3 minutes.

Make stock Add wine and reduce by half, 3 to 5 minutes, then add enough water to cover by ½ inch (about 2 quarts) along with the bay leaf and peppercorns. Bring to just under a boil over medium-high heat, skimming foam with a ladle as it rises to the surface, then reduce heat and gently simmer (bubbles should just gently break the surface) for 35 minutes, skimming frequently.

Strain stock Pass mixture through a fine sieve into a heatproof bowl or another pot (do not press on solids), discarding solids. Skim off fat. If not using immediately, let cool completely (in an ice-water bath, if desired) before transferring to airtight containers. Fish fumet can be refrigerated in airtight containers for up to 2 days or frozen for up to 3 months; thaw completely in the refrigerator before using.

MAKING FISH FUMET

How to Make Vegetable Stock

For true vegetarian soups, stews, and other dishes (such as risotto), vegetable stock is a flavorful alternative to water and meat-based stocks. Some recipes call for the vegetables in the mirepoix to be added to the simmering liquid without first cooking; others call for them to be sweated first, without browning. In this recipe, the vegetables are lightly browned to give the stock intense flavor. The resulting richness and complexity are particularly important when there is no base of flavor provided by chicken, beef, or fish.

You can vary the flavor by increasing the amount of garlic, replacing the carrots with parsnips, or changing some of the fresh herbs for others. Or add any of the following: dried mushrooms, such as porcini or shiitake (no more than two or three, since they can be overpowering), a few corncobs, some chopped tomato (seeded, if desired), or thinly sliced leeks. If the stock will be used to make Italian dishes, add a rind of Parmigiano-Reggiano cheese once the water has been added. If making a vegetarian dish with other vegetables, use the scraps to flavor the stock, such as beet greens for beet risotto. But be careful to avoid adding anything that is less than fresh or that has too strong a flavor, such as most cruciferous vegetables (including broccoli, cauliflower, and cabbage).

VEGETABLE STOCK Makes about 2 quarts

3 TABLESPOONS OLIVE OIL

1 LARGE ONION, *peeled, half coarsely chopped, the other half kept whole*

2 LARGE CELERY STALKS, *cut into ½-inch pieces*

2 MEDIUM CARROTS, *peeled and cut into ½-inch pieces*

2 GARLIC CLOVES, *thinly sliced*

8 SPRIGS FLAT-LEAF PARSLEY

8 SPRIGS BASIL

4 SPRIGS THYME

1 DRIED BAY LEAF

¼ TEASPOON WHOLE BLACK PEPPERCORNS

COARSE SALT AND FRESHLY GROUND PEPPER

Brown vegetables Heat the oil in a medium stockpot over medium until hot but not smoking. Add chopped onion and cook, stirring often, until beginning to brown, 10 to 15 minutes. Add celery, carrots, and garlic; cook, stirring occasionally, until vegetables are tender and lightly browned *fig. 1.4*, about 10 minutes.

Make stock Pour in enough water to cover vegetables by 1 inch (8 to 10 cups) and add the herbs, peppercorns, and remaining onion half. Season with salt and pepper and bring to a boil. Reduce heat to a gentle simmer and cook (uncovered) 1 hour.

fig. 1.4 BROWNING VEGETABLES

Strain stock Pour stock through a fine sieve into a large bowl or another pot, pressing on vegetables to extract as much flavorful liquid as possible. Discard solids. If not using immediately, cool in an ice-water bath before transferring to airtight containers. Vegetable stock can be refrigerated for up to 2 days or frozen for up to 3 months; thaw completely before using

MINESTRONE Serves 6 to 8

Vegetable stock is an essential ingredient in many vegetarian soups, but it also provides incomparable flavor to many well-loved vegetable (but not necessarily meat-free) soups such as this one. Minestrone has become so familiar in the American kitchen that it might be easy to forget its Italian origins. But the name—*minestre* is the word for soup, while the suffix *(-one)* indicates bigness—hints at its universal appeal as a simple pantry-based soup that is also hearty and substantial. The foundation of flavor, called a soffritto, is a common element in soup-making: a trio of celery, carrots, and onion is sautéed first, then stock and more vegetables are added and slowly simmered to coax out their flavors. Beans are what distinguish minestrone from other vegetable soups; the type varies by region, as does the addition (if any) of pasta or rice (this version has neither). The beans are also what give the soup such heft, making it a good option for a meatless one-pot dish (if you leave out the prosciutto) that can stand as the centerpiece of any casual dinner.

The beans need to soak overnight in the refrigerator, so plan accordingly. Then they need to boil for at least a half hour, so use that time to prepare the rest of the ingredients for the soffritto and soup.

For beans
- ¾ CUP DRIED CANNELLINI BEANS *(5 ounces)*
- 8 CUPS WATER, *plus more for soaking*
- ½ LARGE ONION
- 1 DRIED BAY LEAF
- 2 OUNCES PROSCIUTTO ENDS *(optional)*

For soffritto
- ⅓ CUP EXTRA-VIRGIN OLIVE OIL
- 1 LARGE CELERY STALK, *minced*
- 1 MEDIUM CARROT, *peeled and minced*
- 1 LARGE ONION, *peeled and minced (1 cup)*

For soup
- 1 MEDIUM LEEK, *white and pale-green parts only, quartered lengthwise, sliced ¼ inch thick, and washed well (page 32)*
- 3 GARLIC CLOVES, *minced*
- 2 LARGE CELERY STALKS, *sliced ¼ inch thick*
- 2 CARROTS, *peeled and sliced on the diagonal ¼ inch thick*
- 1 LARGE RED POTATO, *cut into ½-inch pieces*
- 1 MEDIUM ZUCCHINI, *quartered lengthwise and sliced ¼ inch thick*
- 4 OUNCES GREEN BEANS, *trimmed and cut on the diagonal into 1-inch pieces (about 1 cup)*
- 1 CAN (14½ OUNCES) WHOLE PEELED PLUM TOMATOES, *crushed and juice reserved*

Ingredients

The soup is traditionally flavored with scraps of cheese and ham, which every frugal Italian home cook keeps in the larder. This recipe calls for end pieces of prosciutto (the bit left when the rest has been sliced), available from many butchers, and the rind from a wedge of Parmigiano-Reggiano cheese. It's a good idea to save these rinds so you can add them to this and other vegetable soups; wrap them in plastic and freeze in resealable plastic bags.

Tuscan kale is also called *cavalo nero* and dino kale; look for it at greenmarkets, Italian groceries, and some supermarkets, or substitute regular kale.

1 BUNCH TUSCAN KALE *(about 5 ounces)*, *tough stems removed, leaves cut crosswise into ½-inch strips*

¼ HEAD SAVOY CABBAGE, *cored and very thinly sliced (about 2 cups)*

4 CUPS VEGETABLE STOCK *(page 56)*

1 RIND (ABOUT 3 INCHES) PARMIGIANO-REGGIANO CHEESE, *plus freshly grated cheese for serving (optional)*

4 OUNCES PROSCIUTTO ENDS *(optional)*

1 DRIED BAY LEAF

¼ TEASPOON RED PEPPER FLAKES

   COARSE SALT AND FRESHLY GROUND BLACK PEPPER

   BASIL PESTO, *for serving (page 379; optional)*

fig. 1.5 SEASONING BEANS WITH AROMATICS

fig. 1.6 COOKING SOFFRITTO

Soak and cook beans Place beans in a large bowl and cover with cold water by 2 inches. Refrigerate 8 to 12 hours, then drain. Combine beans and 8 cups water in a large saucepan. Add onion, bay leaf, and prosciutto ends, if using *fig. 1.5*. Bring to a boil, then reduce heat and simmer until beans are just tender (but not at all mushy, as they should hold their shape in the soup), 30 to 45 minutes. Drain, reserving beans and 4 cups liquid; strain liquid. Discard onion, bay leaf, and prosciutto, and cover beans.

Meanwhile, cook soffritto Heat the oil in a large stockpot over medium-low heat until shimmering. Add celery, carrot, and onions, and cook *fig. 1.6*, stirring often to prevent them from scorching on the bottom, until deep golden brown, 20 to 25 minutes.

Cook vegetables Add leek and garlic to soffritto and cook, stirring often, until soft, about 4 minutes. Raise heat to medium-high, then add sliced celery and carrots along with the potato, zucchini, and green beans. Cook, stirring often, until vegetables are golden, about 5 minutes.

Make soup Stir in reserved bean liquid, the tomatoes and juice, kale, cabbage, stock, cheese rind, prosciutto ends (if using), bay leaf, and red pepper flakes; season with salt and black pepper. Bring to a boil, then reduce heat to a simmer. Cover and cook 1 hour.

Add beans Stir in beans and continue cooking until all vegetables are very tender, 20 to 30 minutes more.

Serve Ladle into bowls, incorporating beans and vegetables in each, and top with pesto and grated cheese, if desired. The soup can be refrigerated in an airtight container up to 3 days; thin with water, if necessary, before reheating over gentle heat.

MINESTRONE

LESSON 1.6
How to Make Dashi

Ingredients

Kombu (also called kelp) is a type of sun-dried seaweed that has been processed into sheets. It should not be rinsed with water before using or it will lose some of its flavor; instead, lightly wipe it with a dry cloth. Unopened packages will keep indefinitely; after opening, store kombu in a resealable plastic bag in a cool, dry place and use within six months.

Bonito flakes are made by boiling, smoking, sun-drying, and then flaking fresh bonito, a type of small tuna. Store in an airtight container in a cool, dry spot for as long as a year (check the label for a freshness date).

This quick and easy stock has many uses in Japanese cooking, including dipping sauces (such as the one on page 336), noodle dishes, and, most commonly, as the base for miso soup. It calls for just two ingredients—kombu and bonito flakes—and water.

DASHI Makes 6 cups

3 STRIPS (EACH ABOUT 6 INCHES) KOMBU, *wiped with a dry cloth*
6 CUPS COLD WATER
2 CUPS BONITO FLAKES *(do not pack)*

COMBINE KOMBU AND WATER [1] in a medium saucepan and bring to just under a boil, then remove from heat. Use tongs to remove and discard the kombu [2]. Sprinkle the bonito flakes [3] into the pan and let steep until they sink to the bottom, about 3 minutes. Strain broth through a fine sieve before using. Dashi can be kept in an airtight container in the refrigerator up to 4 days.

Dashi, Step by Step

MISO SOUP Serves 4

The simplicity of miso soup belies its significance to Japanese cuisine, where it is a common course for breakfast, lunch, or dinner. It is ubiquitous on Japanese restaurant menus here in the United States, but miso soup is so uncomplicated to prepare that any home cook can make it. Variations are numerous, from the type of miso to the addition of vegetables, such as mushrooms or spinach, or other ingredients, such as tofu.

Miso, or fermented soybean paste, is a staple of Japanese cooking. Depending on the amount of salt and *koji* (the mold used in the fermentation process) used, miso varies in color, flavor, and texture. Lighter versions, such as the white miso called for here, have a mild flavor and lower salt content; they are best reserved for delicate soups and sauces. The pronounced flavor of darker varieties (which include reddish-brown and dark-brown pastes) is better for more robust dishes. Shinshu miso, an all-purpose paste with a golden color and salty but mellow taste, would be a fine substitute for the white miso in this recipe.

fig. 1.7 COMBINING MISO WITH DASHI

Wakame is another type of seaweed widely used in Japanese cookery, most often in soups and simmered dishes. It is available fresh or dried; to rehydrate dried wakame, soak in warm water for 20 minutes and drain before using.

TO MAKE MISO SOUP, pour ½ cup dashi into a small bowl and set aside. Bring 3½ cups dashi to a simmer in a medium saucepan over moderate heat. Add 6 ounces silken tofu, cut into ½-inch cubes, and simmer 2 minutes, just to heat through. Stir ¼ cup white miso into the reserved dashi with a flexible spatula until smooth *fig. 1.7*. Pour this mixture into the pan and cook just until soup is hot (do not boil or miso will lose much of its flavor). Serve immediately. If desired, garnish with rehydrated wakame and thinly sliced scallions.

LESSON 1.7
How to Make Cream Soups

Classic cream soups were traditionally based on béchamel sauce, essentially milk thickened by roux—a paste made by whisking flour into melted butter and cooking until combined. Today you are just as likely to be served a cream soup that is based on velouté, another of the so-called "mother sauces." Velouté is made by thickening stock—chicken, beef, or fish fumet—with roux. The distinction seems insignificant; after all, the only difference is using stock instead of milk. But the outcome is noticeable, especially if the two are compared side by side. (Notice the color of the two broccoli soups in the photo opposite—the one on the top is made with milk; the more vibrant one to the right is made with stock.) Béchamel-based soups have a more pronounced vegetable flavor, since milk is milder-tasting than stock, while velouté-based soups will be richer and more complex (just how much will depend on which type of stock is used). Although velouté soups were classically finished with a liaison (page 207) made by whisking an egg yolk with cream, the more modern practice is to skip that step and instead enrich with a bit of cream at the end, since the sauce base imparts a sufficiently velvety texture.

BROCCOLI CREAM SOUP Serves 4 to 6

Broccoli is used here to demonstrate the basic method for making a velouté-based soup; cauliflower can be easily substituted for the broccoli, resulting in a soup that is creamy in color and texture. Or use asparagus: Cut off the tips and blanch to use as a garnish, then trim the tough ends of the stalks before cutting into 1-inch pieces. Proceed with the recipe as written, cooking the stalks for 5 to 8 minutes. For any of these, simply replace the stock with an equal amount of whole milk to make a béchamel-based soup.

For aromatic and roux

    5 TABLESPOONS UNSALTED BUTTER
    1 MEDIUM ONION, *peeled and cut into small dice (about 1 cup)*
    ¼ CUP PLUS 1 TABLESPOON ALL-PURPOSE FLOUR

BROCCOLI CREAM
SOUP (WITH MILK)

SPINACH CREAM
SOUP

BROCCOLI CREAM
SOUP (WITH STOCK)

ASPARAGUS
CREAM SOUP

MUSHROOM CREAM SOUP

CAULIFLOWER
CREAM SOUP

For velouté sauce base

4 CUPS BASIC CHICKEN STOCK *(page 41)*

For base vegetable

1 HEAD BROCCOLI *(1¾ pounds), trimmed and cut into florets,
stems peeled and cut into ½-inch-thick coins*

COARSE SALT AND FRESHLY GROUND PEPPER

For finishing

½ CUP HEAVY CREAM *(optional)*

Sweat aromatic and make roux Melt the butter in a medium saucepan
over medium heat. Add onion and sauté until translucent [1], about 5 minutes.
Add flour and cook, stirring constantly, for 1 minute (the flour should not take
on any color) [2].

Make velouté base Pour in stock, whisking to incorporate fully, and bring to a boil. Reduce to a simmer and cook for 10 minutes, whisking fairly often, to cook out raw flour taste and thicken the liquid (it should reach the consistency of heavy cream) [3].

Add base vegetable Add broccoli stems and season with salt and pepper. Return to a boil, stirring to combine, then add florets and return to a boil [4]. Reduce heat and gently simmer until tender enough to mash with the back of a spoon, 10 to 20 minutes.

Puree soup Working in batches (do not fill more than halfway), pour contents of pot into a blender and puree until smooth. (Alternatively, puree soup in a food mill, using either fine or coarse disk, a food processor, or with an immersion blender.) Pass soup through a fine sieve into a clean pot [5], pressing on solids with a flexible spatula to extract as much liquid as possible [6].

Cream Soups, Step by Step

Finish soup Set pot over low heat and whisk in cream, if using. (Thin with more stock or water, if necessary.) Season with salt and pepper and serve immediately. Cream soups are best made just before serving, especially when using green vegetables, as the soup can lose some of its vibrant color. You can make the velouté (or béchamel) base the day before; let cool completely, then refrigerate in an airtight container.

MUSHROOM CREAM SOUP

Mushrooms need to be cooked briefly to remove some of their liquid—and concentrate their flavor—before being simmered in the stock. For added flavor, sherry is used to deglaze the pan. Serves 4 to 6.

SWEAT ONION AS DESCRIBED ON PAGE 63, ADDING 1¾ pounds cremini mushrooms, stemmed and quartered (about 6½ cups) after the onion is translucent; cook mushrooms until they soften and release liquid, about 5 minutes, stirring periodically. Then whisk in the flour and cook for 1 minute, stirring vigorously with a wooden spoon and scraping the bottom of the pot so the brown bits don't burn. Deglaze the pan with 2 tablespoons dry sherry, cooking and scraping the brown bits from the bottom until the liquid has evaporated. Pour in stock (or milk), whisking until smooth, and proceed with recipe, simmering mushrooms until tender, about 15 minutes. Strain and finish as above (adding cream, if desired). Makes about 5½ cups.

SPINACH CREAM SOUP

Spinach and other greens (such as watercress or sorrel) should be blanched and then squeezed to remove excess liquid; blanching helps to set their color and squeezing afterwards keeps the soup from being watered down. After that, the spinach does not require extra cooking, making this version the quickest of the cream soups. Serves 4 to 6.

SWEAT THE ONION AND MAKE the roux as described on page 63, then make the velouté sauce base. Meanwhile, blanch spinach: Wash well and trim tough ends from 2 pounds spinach while bringing a large pot of water to a boil. Prepare an ice-water bath. Salt the boiling water generously and submerge all of the spinach. Blanch 30 seconds, just until wilted and bright green, then remove spinach with a spider or slotted spoon and immediately plunge into the ice-water bath to stop the cooking, stirring to cool more quickly. Squeeze the spinach with your hands to remove excess liquid. Puree spinach with the velouté base. Strain and finish soup as directed above (adding cream, if desired).

TOMATO SOUP

PUREED MIXED VEGETABLE SOUP

WINTER SQUASH
AND PEAR SOUP

PEA AND SPINACH SOUP

VICHYSSOISE

CARROT AND GINGER SOUP

POTATO AND CAULIFLOWER SOUP

LESSON 1.8
How to Make Pureed Vegetable Soups

Pureeing is another way to produce creamy vegetable soups, without much (if any) added cream or other thickeners. Consequently, the soups have a pure, unadulterated vegetable taste. The texture can be as fine or coarse as you desire, and will depend on the equipment you choose. A blender—called a liquidizer in England because that's what it is capable of doing—produces the smoothest, creamiest consistency, followed by a food processor. If you prefer a less refined texture, use a food mill; even when fitted with the fine disk, the soup will remain slightly coarse.

These soups generally contain three components—aromatics, base vegetables (the primary flavor), and liquid—plus salt and pepper for seasoning.

This recipe for a mixed vegetable soup demonstrates the basic formula, which can be adapted to make the variations that follow by replacing base vegetables. Stock (especially chicken) will produce a soup with the richest flavor, but you can use water instead, which will allow the flavor of the base vegetables to remain unobscured. Experiment to determine which one you prefer. Some variations are enriched with cream and/or buttermilk, but that is usually an optional step (with the exception of vichyssoise, which is meant to be rich and luscious).

PUREED MIXED VEGETABLE SOUP Serves 6

The onion can be substituted with one leek or two large shallots (this is true for the variations, too) and the spinach with other leafy greens, such as chard, kale, watercress, or sorrel. For a soup with brighter color, the leafy greens are added in the last five minutes of cooking, just so they are given a chance to wilt.

For aromatics

   2 TABLESPOONS UNSALTED BUTTER

   1 ONION, *peeled and coarsely chopped (1 cup)*

   1 TO 2 GARLIC CLOVES, *peeled (optional)*

For base vegetables

   12 OUNCES RUSSET POTATO *(1 large or 2 small), peeled and cut into 1-inch chunks*

   6 OUNCES BROCCOLI *(½ head), trimmed, florets separated and stems cut into pieces*

   6 OUNCES CARROTS *(2 medium), peeled and coarsely chopped*

   COARSE SALT AND FRESHLY GROUND PEPPER

   8 OUNCES FRESH SPINACH *(1 bunch), washed well and stems removed*

For soup

   3 TO 4 CUPS BASIC CHICKEN STOCK *(page 41), vegetable stock (page 56), or water*

For finishing

   ½ CUP HEAVY CREAM OR BUTTERMILK *(optional)*

Sweat aromatics Melt butter in a medium stockpot over medium heat. Cook onion and garlic (if using), stirring constantly, until softened and translucent [1], about 3 minutes.

Add base vegetables and stock Add potato, broccoli, and carrots along with enough stock (or water) to just cover. Season with salt and pepper and bring to a boil, then reduce heat and simmer 10 minutes. Add spinach and continue cooking until vegetables can easily be mashed with the back of a wooden spoon [2], about 5 minutes more.

Puree Reserve 1 cup liquid for thinning soup. Puree the rest of the contents in a blender, food processor, or food mill [3], working in batches as necessary (do not fill blender or processor more than halfway, and cover the lid with a kitchen towel while machine is running).

Finish soup Return puree to clean pot, and set over low heat; whisk in cream (or buttermilk), if using, and add enough reserved liquid to thin soup to desired consistency. Season with salt and pepper. Serve immediately, or let cool completely, then refrigerate in a covered container. Reheat over moderate heat, just to warm through, thinning with more liquid as necessary.

Pureed Mixed Vegetable Soup, Step by Step

POTATO AND CAULIFLOWER SOUP

FOLLOW THE BASIC RECIPE, adding ½ teaspoon ground cumin and ½ teaspoon ground coriander when sweating the aromatics and using 1 pound cauliflower (1 head), trimmed and cut into 1-inch pieces and the same amount of potato for the base vegetables. Proceed with the recipe to simmer and puree. Serves 6.

CREAMY TOMATO SOUP

Tomatoes contain a lot of water, so the soup calls for less stock than other pureed soups. Adding cream will lend body, but the soup is refreshing without it. Herbed Croutons (page 75) make a perfect garnish. Serves 4.

TO MAKE THE SOUP, FOLLOW basic recipe to sweat the aromatics, then add 1 can (28 ounces) whole peeled tomatoes or 2 pounds fresh tomatoes, blanched and peeled (page 381), as the base vegetable, and 1½ cups stock or water. Proceed with recipe, simmering tomatoes 10 minutes (they should be soft and beginning to fall apart). Puree and finish with heavy cream, if desired.

CARROT AND GINGER SOUP

Water is particularly good in this variation, creating a soup with a pure, clear taste. Adding fresh ginger to the aromatics is an example of a secondary flavoring component that pairs well with the base vegetable—in this case, carrot. Don't omit the garlic, since it adds another flavor component (and goes well with ginger). Garnish each cup of soup with a sprig of crisp watercress. Serves 4.

FOLLOW THE BASIC RECIPE, sweating 1 piece (1 inch) fresh ginger, peeled and thinly sliced, along with the onion and 1 small clove garlic. Then add 1½ pounds carrots (8 medium), peeled and cut into ½-inch-thick rounds, as the base vegetable, and 4 cups water. Proceed with recipe to simmer and puree. Do not finish with cream or buttermilk.

VICHYSSOISE

Perhaps the best known cold pureed soup, vichyssoise is a simple puree of potato and leeks that is traditionally enriched with cream; adding a bit of buttermilk along with the cream gives this version a pleasant tangy flavor. Here, leeks serve as both an aromatic, replacing the onion, as well as one of the base vegetables. Garlic is typically not used. The amount of stock or water called for is also reduced, since both cream and buttermilk are added. If making the soup for company, buy an extra leek to prepare the Leek Frisée (page 75) for the garnish. Serves 6.

FOLLOW THE BASIC RECIPE, sweating 3 medium leeks, white and pale-green parts only cut into ½-inch-thick half-moons (2¼ cups) and washed well (page 32), for aromatics, then adding 1½ pounds russet potatoes (2 large), peeled and cut into 1-inch chunks (4 cups), for the base vegetable, and 3½ cups stock or water. Proceed with recipe, simmering for about 15 minutes, then remove from heat. Puree, then add ¾ cup each heavy cream and buttermilk. Thin with water or stock to reach desired consistency. Cool soup completely before refrigerating in an airtight container, up to 3 days; thin with stock or water as necessary before serving.

WINTER SQUASH AND PEAR SOUP

To intensify the flavor of the squash, you can roast it before simmering in the soup: Halve squash lengthwise and scoop out seeds, then season squash halves with salt and pepper; place cut sides down on a lightly oiled baking sheet and roast in a 400°F oven until tender when pierced with a knife, about 30 minutes. Scoop the squash from the skins and discard skins, then proceed with the recipe, simmering in stock for 8 to 10 minutes, to let flavors meld. Serves 4 to 6.

FOLLOW THE BASIC RECIPE, omitting garlic and sweating 1 Bosc pear, peeled, cored, and quartered, along with the onion. Then add stock or water and use 1¼ pounds winter squash (butternut, acorn, or kabocha), peeled, seeded, and cut into 1-inch chunks, for the base vegetable, and proceed with recipe to simmer until tender and puree. Finish with ½ cup buttermilk, if desired.

PEA AND SPINACH SOUP

This soup is best made with farm-fresh peas, but you can substitute a ten-ounce package of frozen peas in a pinch. Since spinach and peas cook in such a short amount of time, do not add them to the pot until the stock has reached a boil. This soup is finished with lemon juice rather than cream or buttermilk. For an elegant presentation, garnish the soup with Frico (page 75). Serves 4.

FOLLOW THE BASIC RECIPE to sweat the aromatics, then add 3½ cups stock or water and bring to a boil. For the base vegetables, add 2 pounds fresh green peas, shelled (2 cups), and return to a boil, then reduce to a simmer and cook until bright green and tender, 2 to 3 minutes. Then stir in 1 pound (2 bunches) fresh flat-leaf spinach (in batches if necessary, stirring until each is wilted) and cook until wilted, 2 to 3 minutes. Puree and finish, thinning with water as desired, then season with 2 teaspoons fresh lemon juice along with salt and pepper.

> LESSON 1.9
> # *How to Make Consommé*

Consommer means "to accomplish" or "to finish" in French, and consommé is indeed a "finished" stock. (In a culinary context, one could say that to make a consommé is to bring out in full all of the flavors.) What gives consommé its purity and clarity is a bit of culinary magic: Egg whites (combined with mirepoix and ground meat) coagulate in the soup and rise to the top (forming a "raft"), drawing up any impurities that would otherwise cloud the stock. This mixture also infuses the broth with deeper flavor, as does an *onion brûlé* (or charred onion), which imparts deeper color to the broth. After an hour or two of simmering, the raft is also discarded, leaving behind a clear, intense broth.

Consommé can be served either hot or cold, usually garnished in some way or another (there are literally hundreds employed in formal French cuisine); one of the more common embellishments is vegetables cut into julienne or brunoise (page 14), such as the blanched carrot and leek shown here.

Consommé Tips

- The clarification mixture should be kept as cold as possible until needed (always add tomato, or other acidic ingredient, just before using, since it will cause the egg whites to coagulate too soon).

- Monitor the temperature of the consommé as it cooks to make sure it is at a gentle simmer.

BEEF CONSOMMÉ

BEEF CONSOMMÉ Serves 4 to 6

For clarification (raft)

½ YELLOW ONION, *peeled and coarsely chopped, plus ¼ onion (root intact)*

1 SMALL CARROT, *peeled and coarsely chopped*

1 CELERY STALK, *coarsely chopped*

5 LARGE EGG WHITES

1¼ POUNDS GROUND BEEF (93% LEAN)

For consommé

2 QUARTS WHITE BEEF STOCK *(page 42)*

1 SMALL TOMATO, *coarsely chopped*

COARSE SALT

Prepare clarification mixture Pulse chopped onion, carrot, and celery in a food processor or mini-chopper until finely chopped. Whisk egg whites [1] until frothy, then add ground beef and chopped vegetables and mix well with your hands. Cover and chill in the refrigerator for at least 1 hour (or overnight).

Make onion brûlé Sear the remaining onion wedge in a small cast-iron skillet over medium-high heat on both cut sides until blackened [2], then coarsely chop.

Clarify stock Pour stock into a stockpot. Remove the clarification mixture from the refrigerator and add the browned onion and the tomato, then add this mixture to the pot. Set over medium-high heat and whisk briskly until thoroughly incorporated with the stock [3]. Use a wooden spoon to stir at a slower speed until the solids rise to the top, then stop stirring. Continue cooking until frothy bubbles start to form around the sides of the raft. Reduce heat to medium-low and use a spoon or a ladle to make a hole in the raft [4] so the consommé can bubble freely, and you can see the color and clarity of the broth. At this point the broth should be clear; further simmering is to develop more flavor.

Remove raft and strain consommé Cook for 1½ to 2 hours, or until the raft starts to sink a bit [5]. Ladle the consommé from the pot through the hole in the raft (or you can crack it at this point, since it has solidified) into a cheesecloth-lined sieve set over a heatproof container. Discard the raft. Then strain broth again, this time through a coffee filter. Remove fat by sweeping a paper towel across top of consommé several times [6]. Reheat if necessary. Season with salt and garnish as desired. If not serving immediately, allow consommé to cool and then refrigerate overnight in an airtight container. Before using, remove and discard solidified fat that has accumulated at the top and reheat consommé over gentle heat, just until hot.

CHICKEN CONSOMMÉ

Follow the directions above for beef consommé, substituting ground chicken and chicken stock for the ground beef and beef stock.

Consommé, Step by Step

FRICO

BASIL OIL AND
MOZZARELLA CROSTINI

LEEK FRISÉE

FRIED TORTILLA
STRIPS

HERBED CRÈME FRAÎCHE

FRIED SHALLOTS

PROSCIUTTO CRISPS

CROSTINI

HERBED
CROUTONS

FRIED HERBS

LARDONS

> EXTRA CREDIT
> ## *Soup Garnishes*

If you'd like to add an extra touch to your soup just before serving, here are a number of simple garnishes you might try. Herbed crème fraîche for flavor and tang, crisp prosciutto for a salty note, croutons for crunch — all are ingredients that can complement a soup without over-powering it. Of course, if you don't have a suitable garnish on hand, you can simply ladle your carefully prepared soup into bowls and feel confident in serving it unaccompanied. A good soup, after all, will speak for itself.

FRICO

Heat oven to 400°F. Grate **Parmigiano-Reggiano cheese** on the medium holes of a box grater. Using 1½ tablespoons of grated cheese for each frico bowl, sprinkle into rough 4-inch rounds on a nonstick baking mat set on a rimmed baking sheet. Bake 3 minutes, then use a small offset spatula to gently transfer to a small bowl (or mini muffin tin) and let rest for 25 seconds to allow the shape to set. Frico can be carefully stacked and stored in an airtight container at room temperature for 2 to 3 hours.

BASIL OIL AND MOZZARELLA CROSTINI

Make crostini (see right), leaving slices whole. Remove from broiler and immediately brush with a bit of **basil oil** (page 23). Top with a thin slice of fresh **mozzarella cheese** and broil until cheese is melted and bubbly (but not browned), about 1 minute. Use immediately.

FRIED TORTILLA STRIPS

Cut 6-inch **corn tortillas** into ¼-inch strips. In a large straight-sided skillet or pot, heat 2½ inches **sunflower or other neutral-tasting oil** over medium-high heat until 350°F on a deep-fry thermometer. Fry the strips in batches until golden brown and crisp, about 2 minutes, then use a spider or slotted spoon to transfer the strips to paper towels to drain. Season with **salt** while still hot. Store in an airtight container at room temperature up to 2 days.

LEEK FRISÉE

Cut **leek** (white and pale-green parts only) into fine julienne and wash well (page 32). Heat 2½ inches of **sunflower or other neutral-tasting oil** in a small pot over medium-high heat until 300°F on a deep-fry thermometer. Working in batches, fry until golden and crisp, 1 to 3 minutes. Use a spider or slotted spoon to transfer to paper towels to drain. Store in an airtight container up to 2 days.

HERBED CRÈME FRAÎCHE

Pulse ½ cup **crème fraîche**, 2 tablespoons chopped **fresh herbs**, and ¼ teaspoon each **coarse salt and freshly ground pepper** in a food processor until thoroughly combined. Refrigerate, covered, up to 2 days.

CROSTINI

Heat broiler. Slice an **Italian rustic bread** (such as pan pugliese) on the diagonal ½ inch thick, then cut slices in half. Place bread on a rimmed baking sheet. Brush with extra-virgin olive oil and season with salt, if desired, and broil until lightly browned around the edges. Store in an airtight container at room temperature up to 3 days.

FRIED SHALLOTS

Slice **shallots** into very thin rings. Heat 2½ inches of **sunflower or other neutral-tasting oil** in a small pot to 300°F. Working in batches if necessary, fry shallots over medium-high heat until golden and crisp, 1 to 3 minutes. Use a spider or slotted spoon to transfer to paper towels to drain. Refrigerate in an airtight container up to 2 days.

PROSCIUTTO CRISPS

Heat oven to 400°F. Lay thinly sliced **prosciutto** in a single layer on a baking sheet. Bake until crisp, 13 to 15 minutes. Drain on paper towels. Store in an airtight container, between layered sheets of parchment, up to 2 days.

FRIED HERBS

Heat 2½ inches of **sunflower or other neutral-tasting oil** in a small pot over medium-high heat to 275° to 300°F. Working with a few leaves at a time, drop herbs, such as basil, sage, or parsley, into oil and fry until translucent but not taking on any color, 20 to 30 seconds. Remove carefully with a spider or slotted spoon; drain on paper towels. Use immediately.

LARDONS

Cut **slab bacon** into ¼-inch pieces. Fry in a skillet over medium heat until fat has rendered and bacon is crisp, about 8 minutes. Drain on paper towels.

HERBED CROUTONS

Heat oven to 350°F. Trim crusts and cut six slices of **white sandwich bread** into ¼-inch cubes. Toss bread with 1 tablespoon melted **unsalted butter** on a rimmed baking sheet. Toast in oven, tossing once, until pale golden, 9 to 10 minutes. Toss with a tablespoon of chopped **herbs**, such as parsley, basil, or marjoram, before using. Store in an airtight container at room temperature up to 3 days.

2 Eggs

EGGS

THE EGG IS A food that lets us perform magic in the kitchen. We've all seen it: Someone pillages the shelves of a nearly empty fridge and comes out with a few staples—eggs, cheese, some leftover vegetables—then turns them into a scrumptious meal. What we don't always remember about that particular trick is that the eggs themselves do most of the work. They are perhaps the world's most versatile protein, taking imaginative variations

in flavoring and cooking method in stride. They form the basis of so many perfect dishes, from hearty, spicy huevos rancheros to tender, gently coddled eggs that are mild enough to please even the most finicky toddler. Once you understand the techniques for cooking eggs, you'll find them to be a delightful—and easy—canvas for your culinary creations.

There are just a handful of primary cooking methods for egg dishes—and many variations. On the pages that follow, you'll find the basics, starting with—what else?—hard-cooking (though this preparation is often called hard-boiling, an egg should never be boiled). Other egg cookery techniques follow: soft-cooking, scrambling, baking, coddling, poaching, and frying. In addition to the fundamental techniques, there are recipes to help you elevate the everyday egg, such as Scrambled Eggs with Caviar in Eggshell Cups, as well as how-tos for easily adaptable preparations such as omelets and frittatas.

Whatever the technique, the keys to success lie in temperature and proper timing. Eggs should be cooked on low to moderate heat until the whites set and the yolks reach the desired firmness; if a higher heat is called for, as with omelets, it should be brief. Overheating or cooking too long can lead to disappointing results, including rubbery, tough egg whites and scrambled eggs sitting in a watery puddle (since too much heat can cause the protein in an egg to separate from the liquid).

If eggs are among the simplest and most versatile of ingredients, the equipment needed to prepare them should be equally straightforward—in spite of all the gadgets you'll find on those kitchen-supply store shelves. Items such as poachers and divided omelet pans can be nice to have, but keep in mind that in almost every case you can do without them, or substitute something

you're likely to have in the kitchen, without sacrificing quality. Don't overthink eggs—just take a gentle hand and let them work their magic.

BASIC EGG-SENSE

The egg, of course, is much more than a quick breakfast staple. It's an indispensable cooking ingredient that makes many of your favorite recipes possible. Crack an egg or two into seasoned ground beef to bind a batch of meatballs; brush a beaten one on pastry for a golden brown crust; blend a few yolks into a sauce to emulsify and thicken it; then whip the remaining whites into airy peaks and bake an ethereal meringue. All of these tasks are possible because of the egg's simple, but remarkable, composition. It consists of two primary parts: the white, also called the albumen, and the yolk. The yolk contains all of an egg's fat and much of its flavor. It's that fat that gives hollandaise sauce such luscious body. The white, on the other hand, contains more than two-thirds of the egg's liquid and more than half of its protein. When beaten, egg whites whip up to many times their volume. Any fat will inhibit that foaming, stiffening process. Therefore, knowing how to separate an egg, to isolate just the part you need for your recipe, is a must (see "Separating an Egg," page 95).

When you crack a very fresh egg, the yolk will be plump and firm and the white will be thick. Open an egg from the same carton a couple of weeks later, and you'll find both parts to be more slack and watery. Assuming the eggs have been well refrigerated in their carton (a package that not only protects against breakage but also helps block the porous eggs from absorbing odors and losing moisture in the refrigerator), this difference won't affect the egg's flavor or the nutritive value. It can, however, impact your cooking. If you're frying or poaching, a fresh, firm egg will hold its shape most beautifully; on the other hand, if you're hard-cooking an egg, a slightly older one is actually a better choice than one straight from the henhouse. Because the membrane inside the shell loosens with time, you'll find that older egg much easier to peel. For scrambled eggs, omelets, or most other recipes, fresh or older eggs will do. Take care, though, not to lose track of the "pack date" noted on the carton. Eggs will keep for four or five weeks past that day; beyond that, quality deteriorates. A very old egg will not have as much volume because it will have a large air pocket inside.

ARE EGGS HEALTH FOOD?

Eggs have long been maligned as a dangerous indulgence, thanks mostly to a convincing scare about dietary cholesterol. But owing to recent studies, the tide has started to turn. Here's the lowdown:

The cholesterol question: An average large egg contains 213 mg cholesterol. That's fairly high as foods go, but studies have failed to find a link between moderate egg consumption (about an egg a day) and cardiovascular disease. The latest research shows that saturated fat consumption, genetics, and other factors play a much larger role in blood cholesterol levels than dietary cholesterol intake. And today you can find eggs that are low in cholesterol (see below).

Calories and fat: If you're watching caloric intake, an egg is a relative bargain, with about 75 calories in an average large one. It serves up about 5 grams of fat, only 1.5 of those saturated.

Vitamins and minerals: An egg yolk is a rich source of vitamins B_2 (riboflavin) and B_{12}; it also contains a small amount of vitamin K and is one of the few food sources of vitamin D, which strengthens bones. Additionally, it has the minerals selenium (which protects against cancer-causing free radicals) and choline (which helps brain function).

Protein: An average egg white contains about 6 grams of high-quality, complete protein, which means it can be easily processed and efficiently used by your body.

A NOTE ABOUT RAW EGGS

As a precaution, raw eggs should always be avoided by pregnant women, babies and young children, the elderly, or anyone whose health is at all compromised. If you are concerned, substitute liquid pasteurized eggs. Liquid eggs are widely available at supermarkets, next to whole eggs.

READING THE LABELS

Why do egg carton labels seem more complicated than they used to be? Here's what you need to know:

Size Eggs are classified in sizes peewee to jumbo, but large is the standard size used in recipes, particularly in baking.

Grading The USDA grades eggs as AA, A, or B, as determined by appearance, texture, and flavor. Grade B eggs are rarely found in supermarkets, but are used by commercial bakeries and the like.

Color Contrary to popular wisdom, brown eggs are not inherently healthier, fresher, or more natural than white eggs. An egg's color is determined by the color and breed of the hen that laid it. Sometimes brown eggs are more costly than white eggs, in part because brown-egg-laying chickens are more likely to be found on smaller farms, while large commercial producers prefer white-egg layers; also, brown-egg-laying hens eat more, so they cost slightly more to maintain.

Organic Eggs with this label come from hens fed certified organic feed, which means it was grown without pesticides or commercial fertilizers. No antibiotic use is allowed, either. The "organic" designation is regulated by the USDA.

Free-range/cage-free Hens that are free-range have regular access to the outdoors, while cage-free eggs come from hens that aren't confined to cages, whether or not they actually make it out to fresh air.

Low-cholesterol These eggs contain at least 25 percent less cholesterol than standard eggs, thanks to the hens' special diet.

Omega-3 eggs Omega-3 fatty acids reduce the risk of heart disease and stroke. Some producers feed their hens a diet rich in foods such as flaxseed and fish oil, which yields yolks with omega-3 levels three to five times higher than standard eggs.

SOFT-COOKED EGGS

LESSON 2.1

LESSON 2.1
How to Boil

Hard-cooked eggs should never actually be boiled for any length of time, or they will turn rubbery and dry. Instead, follow the directions below for gently cooking eggs—the whites will be tender and yolks still slightly soft in the center. These eggs would be perfect for sprinkling with salt and pepper and eating whole, halving and scooping out the yolks to make deviled eggs, or cutting into wedges for salads. They are also the starting point for making the classic mayonnaise-based egg salads. Soft-cooked eggs are classically served in their shell in a cocottier (small egg cup), with a tiny silver spoon and toast points (triangles) or soldiers (baton shapes) for dipping into the still-soft yolks. The eggs are also delicious scooped out of the shells and served on slices of toasted buttered rustic bread.

TO HARD-COOK EGGS, place them in a deep saucepan and cover with cold water by 1 inch. Bring to a boil over high heat, then immediately remove from heat, cover, and let stand 13 minutes. Use a slotted spoon to transfer eggs to an ice-water bath to stop the cooking. Serve warm, or leave in the bath to cool completely, about 10 minutes. Unpeeled eggs can be refrigerated up to 1 week.

TO SOFT-COOK EGGS, bring a deep saucepan filled halfway with water to a rolling boil. With a slotted spoon, gently lower eggs into water. Cover pan and remove from heat. Let stand 4 to 6 minutes (depending on how soft you like the yolks). To serve egg in the shell, quickly crack the wider end with a knife and remove the top. To serve out of the shell, hold egg over a small bowl, tap around center with a knife, and gently pull shell apart, then scoop out egg with a spoon into the bowl.

PEELING HARD-COOKED EGGS
To peel a hard-cooked egg, place it on your work surface and roll it under your palm to crack the shell (rather than cracking against the edge of a bowl, which might cause the peel to mar the egg white). Cold eggs are easier to peel. Holding the egg under cold running water as you peel it can also help.

LESSON 2.2
How to Poach

Because they are cooked in water, with no oil or other fat added, poached eggs are a healthful alternative to eggs cooked by many other methods. But their true appeal is in their texture, the ideal being a still-runny yolk surrounded by a just-set white. Their no-fat cooking method also suggests that the eggs might benefit from being served with a rich, flavorful hollandaise sauce (see page 96), as in eggs benedict. But they are also delicious on a slice of toast, which soaks up the yolk.

A bit of practice is required to prevent the egg white from dispersing into the water, causing the edges to become frayed. Some cooks prefer to add a drop of white vinegar to the water to help the white coagulate; others swirl the water vigorously to create a whirlpool (technically a vortex, which traps the egg inside) just before sliding in the egg. Generally, though, you should not have a problem if you heed these suggestions: Use very fresh eggs; keep the water at a bare simmer (it should hardly move); gently slide the broken egg into the water; and spoon the edges of the whites over the egg as soon as it is in the pan.

TO POACH 4 LARGE EGGS, fill a large deep saucepan with 2 inches of water and bring to a boil. Reduce the heat to medium. When the water is barely simmering, break one egg into a small heatproof bowl. Placing lip of bowl in the water, gently tip the bowl to slide egg carefully into pan [1]. Use a small spoon to "fold" the edges of the white over the egg, for a neater edge. Repeat with remaining eggs. Cook until whites are just set but yolks are still soft (they should still move around inside), 2 to 3 minutes. Lift out eggs with a slotted spoon or small mesh sieve [2] and briefly rest on paper towels to allow eggs to drain. Trim the edges of the whites with a knife for a prettier presentation [3].

Poached Eggs, Step by Step

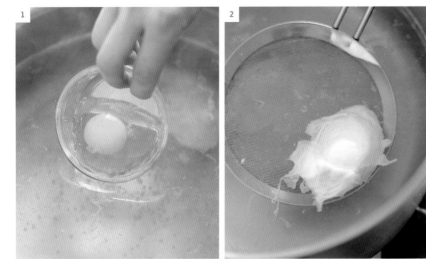

STEAMED ARTICHOKES WITH SMOKED SALMON, POACHED EGGS, AND HOLLANDAISE Serves 4

This elegant dish is perfect for brunch. The artichokes resemble flower petals, with the eggs, hollandaise, and thin slices of smoked salmon their centers. See page 296 for how-to photos of trimming artichokes.

- 4 MEDIUM OR LARGE ARTICHOKES
  COARSE SALT AND FRESHLY GROUND PEPPER
- 4 LARGE EGGS
  HOLLANDAISE SAUCE *(page 96)*
- 4 THIN SLICES SMOKED SALMON *(2 ounces total), plus more for serving (optional)*

Prepare artichokes Cut off stems of artichokes flush with bottoms and discard. Using kitchen shears, trim outer three layers of leaves to 2 inches. Fill a large stockpot with 2 inches of water and set a steamer basket over the water. Stand artichokes upright in basket, cover pot, and bring to a boil over high heat.

Steam until bottoms of artichokes are tender when pierced with the tip of a paring knife, 30 to 40 minutes. Remove artichokes from pot. When cool enough to handle, remove and discard inner leaves, leaving trimmed outer leaves to create a flowerlike shape. Using a teaspoon, remove fuzzy choke and any purple leaves and discard. If necessary, gently spread apart artichoke leaves with your fingers (to make room inside for the egg). Season with salt and pepper and cover to keep warm.

Poach eggs Follow instructions on page 82 to poach the eggs and briefly drain, trimming the edges as desired.

Serve Using a tablespoon, place one egg inside each artichoke (be careful not to pierce yolk). Spoon about 1 tablespoon Hollandaise Sauce over each egg, then drape with a slice of salmon. Serve immediately with more Hollandaise Sauce and salmon (if desired) on the side.

Poached Eggs Tip

Poached eggs will hold up well for up to 24 hours. To make ahead, immediately place them in an ice-water bath to stop the cooking, then transfer them to a bowl of cool water (it should just reach the tops of the eggs). If storing for longer than an hour, place bowl in the refrigerator (covered). Reheat by briefly placing eggs in a pan of barely simmering water, just until warmed through.

LESSON 2.3
How to Fry

Unlike when poached, eggs that are fried are intended to brown ever so slightly, with a hint of a crust around the edges that contrasts wonderfully with the soft, runny yolk. That's the hallmark of eggs prepared "sunny side up." When a fresh egg is cracked into a skillet, the thickest part of the egg white clings around the yolk. To ensure that the white sets throughout, you need to break the thick albumen sac, and distribute the whites evenly. Fried eggs are often served on toast or as a component of a heartier breakfast dish such as Huevos Rancheros (opposite).

TO FRY AN EGG, begin by heating an 8-inch skillet over medium heat; add 2 teaspoons unsalted butter (or bacon drippings). When butter begins to sizzle, crack an egg into pan. Cook until white is beginning to set, then use the edge of a spatula to break the albumen sac [1]. Continue cooking until white is light golden underneath, 2 to 3 minutes, spooning butter over the yolk to cook it slightly [2]. For "over easy," flip egg with a spatula and cook for 30 seconds [3]. Season with coarse salt and freshly ground pepper, if desired. Serve immediately.

Fried Eggs, Step by Step

HUEVOS RANCHEROS Serves 4

This dish was originally named for the tomato and chile sauce it was served with; now it is often topped with any chile-spiked salsa, such as the tomatillo version on page 179. Start by heating the salsa in a skillet with a tablespoon of sunflower or other neutral-tasting oil.

Toast tortillas Working with one at a time, use tongs to hold an 6-inch corn tortilla directly over the flame of a gas burner until it just starts to blacken, then flip and heat other side until it begins to puff. Keep warm in a clean kitchen towel while repeating with 3 more tortillas.

Assemble Place a toasted tortilla on each plate and spoon warmed salsa on top (about ¼ cup on each). Fry 4 eggs (see opposite), then slide one onto each tortilla. Season with salt and pepper, if desired. Serve at once, with sour cream, if desired.

fig. 2.1 SCRAMBLING EGGS

Equipment

Although a nonstick pan might seem the obvious choice for scrambled eggs and omelets, it's not essential, as long as your pan is well-seasoned. The butter and the near-constant motion of moving the eggs should keep them from sticking.

LESSON 2.4
How to Scramble

The secret to light, fluffy scrambled eggs is to cook them over moderate heat and to move them fairly constantly; this will ensure that the eggs do not take on any color. Also, cook the eggs just until they form plump, soft curds with no more runny parts in the pan (the curds should appear slightly wet, not dry) and immediately remove them from pan, as they will continue cooking.

TO SCRAMBLE EGGS, use a fork to beat together 4 large eggs and 2 tablespoons heavy cream (or milk); season with salt and pepper. Melt 2 tablespoons unsalted butter in a medium skillet over medium heat. Add egg mixture. Using a heatproof flexible spatula, gently pull the eggs to the center of the pan and let the liquid parts run out under the perimeter. Cook, continually moving eggs with the spatula, just until eggs are set *fig. 2.1*, 1½ to 3 minutes. Serve hot.

SCRAMBLED EGGS WITH CAVIAR IN EGGSHELL CUPS Serves 4

8 LARGE EGGS

4 TABLESPOONS (½ STICK) UNSALTED BUTTER

CRÈME FRAÎCHE OR SOUR CREAM (optional)

SEVRUGA OR OSETRA CAVIAR

Prepare eggshell cups Bring a large pot of water to a boil. Hold a large egg in one hand, tapered end up. Place an egg topper (a special tool for neatly snipping off the tip of the shell) over the top and squeeze, using a scissor motion. Discard top of egg. Pour egg into a medium bowl. Repeat with remaining eggs. Boil shells for 5 minutes. Using a slotted spoon, transfer to a wire rack. Let dry, cut sides down.

Prepare eggs Scramble eggs as above, using the butter and a large skillet. Transfer eggs to a pastry bag fitted with a ½-inch plain round tip (wrap bag with a kitchen towel if necessary, as eggs will be very hot). Pipe eggs into shells. Transfer shells to egg cups. Serve with a dollop of crème fraîche or sour cream, if desired. Top with caviar.

LESSON 2.5
How to Make an Omelet

Because it involves some practice to perfect, making an omelet has become one of the tests of a cook's true talents. The end result leaves little room for error, as any rips, tears, or other flaws are impossible to mask (other than by topping with a sauce or garnish). Just follow the tips at right, and don't give up after an unsuccessful attempt. (Remember, even imperfect omelets taste delicious.) Done often enough, omelet-making should soon become second nature.

HERB-FILLED OMELET Serves 1

This three-egg omelet is strewn with fresh herbs for the simplest of fillings. See the variations on page 89 for other ideas. If you'd like an omelet with a bit more heft, add another egg.

3 LARGE EGGS

COARSE SALT AND FRESHLY GROUND PEPPER

1 TABLESPOON CLARIFIED BUTTER (page 88)

1 TABLESPOON FINELY CHOPPED MIXED FRESH HERBS, such as tarragon, basil, chervil, chives, and flat-leaf parsley

Prepare skillet and eggs Heat an 8-inch skillet over medium-high heat. (It's ready when your palm feels warm when held just above the skillet.) When the pan is hot, heat the clarified butter until hot but not smoking. While the butter is heating, whisk the eggs in a medium bowl and season with salt and pepper.

Omelet Tips

> Whisk the eggs together very well to incorporate lots of air; this is how you get a light, fluffy omelet. But don't whisk too early or the eggs will deflate while you wait for the pan to heat up.

> Use clarified butter (page 88); since the milk solids have been removed, it will not burn as quickly as regular butter or cause the eggs to brown or stick to the pan.

> Get the skillet nice and hot, but don't let the butter smoke before adding the eggs.

> Work quickly after pouring the eggs in the pan; constant motion is key, whether jerking the pan or running a spatula across it to allow the eggs to cook more evenly (similar to scrambling).

> Cook just until there are no more runny parts. Omelet will continue to cook when off the heat.

HERB-FILLED OMELET

CLARIFYING BUTTER

Because clarified butter has no milk solids, it can withstand higher cooking temperatures without burning. Melt 1 cup (2 sticks) unsalted butter in a small saucepan over low heat until foamy and milk solids have fallen to bottom of pan, about 15 minutes. Remove from heat and let cool. Carefully skim foam from top and discard. Slowly pour melted butter through a cheesecloth-lined sieve into a bowl or storage container, leaving the solids behind. Use immediately, or store covered in refrigerator up to one month. Makes ⅔ cup.

Cook omelet Working quickly, pour the whisked eggs into the hot skillet. Reduce heat to medium. Simultaneously stir the eggs with a heatproof flexible spatula [1] and shake the skillet vigorously back and forth over heat for about a minute. You want to keep the eggs moving, incorporating some of the runny parts with the more-cooked parts until there are some curds swimming in the eggs. Continue cooking, using a spatula to pull cooked eggs from the edge and allow uncooked parts to run underneath [2], until the eggs are just set, with no more runny parts (this should take 15 to 30 seconds). Sprinkle herbs evenly over eggs [3], then run the spatula around all sides of omelet to loosen it from the pan. Use spatula to lift opposite edge of omelet and gently fold over one third [4]. Then, holding pan over plate, simultaneously slide and roll omelet onto plate so that it lands with the seam side down [5]. (Alternatively, flip over one half to form a half-moon shape.) Serve immediately.

Variations Replace the herbs with about ¼ cup of any of the following (or a combination), adding them to the pan when the eggs are just set:

- Grated cheese, such as Gruyère, cheddar, or fontina
- Crumbled soft cheese, such as goat cheese or feta
- Wilted greens (page 297)
- Slow-roasted tomatoes (page 316)
- Caramelized onions (page 30) or shallots
- Chopped blanched asparagus
- Diced or thinly sliced ham
- Sautéed mushrooms (page 419)

Herb-filled Omelet, Step by Step

fig. 2.2 CODDLING EGGS

Equipment

Egg coddlers are available at some kitchen-supply stores. Ramekins or custard cups covered tightly with foil can be used instead.

LESSON 2.6
How to Coddle

Coddling, which in cooking terms means to heat food in water that is just below the boiling point, is a gentle steaming method that yields a tender egg. The traditional way to prepare and serve these eggs is in coddlers — special cups with tight lids that trap in steam when the cups are placed in a pan of simmering water. Buttering the coddlers and adding a bit of heavy cream impart richness. For a garnish, sprinkle with chopped fresh herbs, such as *fines herbes* (a mix of chives, chervil, parsley, and tarragon), finely diced red onion, or crumbled bacon. Soldiers (toasted bread cut into batons) are the traditional — and sole — accompaniment.

TO CODDLE 4 EGGS, fill a large saucepan with enough water to come just below the rim of the coddlers. Bring to a boil over medium-high heat. Meanwhile, brush the insides of coddlers generously with softened butter. Into each pour 1 teaspoon heavy cream and then break in an egg (the cream will surround the egg and keep it moist) *fig. 2.2.* Season with coarse salt and freshly ground pepper and clamp or screw lids on tightly.

Use tongs to carefully lower coddlers into boiling water and immediately reduce the heat to medium. Simmer for 4 minutes, then turn off heat. Cover pan, and let stand until the whites are just set, 4 to 7 minutes. Lift coddlers from water, remove lids, and serve immediately with toast soldiers.

LESSON 2.7
How to Bake

Often referred to as "shirred," baked eggs are known in France as *oeufs en cocotte* (*cocotte* being both an endearing name for a hen and the name for the individual serving dishes the eggs are cooked in). To prevent the whites from drying out in the oven, they are usually drizzled first with a bit of cream or other liquid. Similar to coddled eggs, baked eggs have a tender white and a soft, runny yolk, perfect for dipping with toast soldiers or toast points. For a simplified version of the recipe below, follow the directions to bake the eggs, drizzling each egg with a tablespoon of heavy cream (and omitting the shallot and mushroom mixture).

BAKED EGGS WITH MORELS Serves 4

In this recipe, the eggs are paired with a heady sauté of shallots and morels — wild mushrooms prized in French cuisine for their distinctive taste and rarity (they grow largely in areas recently stricken with forest fires). They are in season during the spring months; substitute other wild mushrooms, such as oysters or chanterelles, if morels are unavailable.

1 TABLESPOON UNSALTED BUTTER, *plus more, softened, for dishes*

1 SMALL SHALLOT, *finely chopped*

1 CUP FRESH MORELS, *washed (page 341) and halved lengthwise (quartered if large)*
COARSE SALT AND FRESHLY GROUND PEPPER

fig. 2.3 COMBINING EGGS WITH MORELS

BAKED EGG AND
CODDLED EGG

1 CUP HEAVY CREAM

4 LARGE EGGS

1 TABLESPOON FINELY CHOPPED FRESH CHIVES, *plus more for garnish*

Heat oven and prepare mushrooms Heat oven to 375°F. Melt butter in a medium skillet over medium-low heat until foamy. Cook shallot, stirring constantly, until softened, about 2 minutes, then add morels and season with a pinch of salt. Cook, stirring occasionally, until morels have softened, about 5 minutes. Add heavy cream and bring just to a simmer, then immediately remove from heat and let the mixture cool for 5 minutes.

Bake eggs Butter four 6-inch shallow baking dishes (such as gratin dishes) and set on a rimmed baking sheet. Crack one egg into each dish, keeping yolk intact; season with salt and pepper. Spoon the morel mixture into the dishes *fig. 2.3*, dividing evenly, and sprinkle with chives. Bake until egg whites are just set (they should be firm to the touch), 9 to 12 minutes. Serve immediately.

LESSON 2.8
How to Make a Frittata

Although an Italian frittata is similar to an omelet in that it combines seasoned eggs and a flavorful filling, the result is more rustic, and the technique more forgiving. A frittata starts out on the stove — the filling is cooked first and the eggs poured over. When the eggs are just about set, they are given a last-minute browning under the broiler. Because of the broiler's intense heat, the frittata will also puff up slightly, like a soufflé, contributing to its light, fluffy texture. Unlike for an omelet, there's no flipping involved, and the eggs benefit from being browned just a bit, for color and texture. Moreover, there's no need to serve a frittata right away; it is equally delicious hot, warm, or at room temperature.

SQUASH AND GOAT CHEESE FRITTATA Serves 6

The squash filling in the recipe can be replaced with virtually any precooked vegetables you like. You can also omit the goat cheese and sprinkle on more grated Parmigiano-Reggiano or Asiago, or use Gruyère cheese instead.

For filling

- 1 TABLESPOON UNSALTED BUTTER
- 1 MEDIUM YELLOW ONION, *thinly sliced*
- ½ POUND MIXED SMALL ZUCCHINI AND YELLOW SQUASH, *halved lengthwise and sliced crosswise ¼ inch thick (1 ½ cups)*

For eggs

- 12 LARGE EGGS
- ¼ CUP HEAVY CREAM
- 4 BASIL LEAVES, *sliced into chiffonade (page 21)*
- 2 TABLESPOONS FINELY CHOPPED FRESH CHIVES
  COARSE SALT AND FRESHLY GROUND PEPPER

For topping

- 3 OUNCES FRESH GOAT CHEESE
- 2 OUNCES PARMIGIANO-REGGIANO OR ASIAGO CHEESE, *finely grated (½ cup)*

Sauté filling Heat butter in a 10-inch nonstick straight-sided skillet over medium heat. Cook onion until soft and translucent, stirring occasionally, 3 to 4 minutes. Add zucchini and squash and sauté until it begins to turn golden brown, about 4 minutes [1].

Prepare egg mixture Heat broiler. Use a whisk to lightly beat eggs in a large bowl, then whisk in cream, basil, and chives and season with ½ teaspoon salt and ⅛ teaspoon pepper.

Frittata Tips

> For the fluffiest frittata, whisk together the egg mixture while making the filling (not further in advance), and allow the broiler to heat sufficiently before putting the pan in the oven (so the intense heat will cause the eggs to puff like a soufflé).

> Do not stir eggs vigorously while cooking on the stove but, rather, draw the heatproof spatula across the bottom of the pan in deliberate strokes to form large curds, pushing them toward the center and allowing the runny parts to flow underneath. It is much like a slower, more controlled version of scrambled eggs.

> Avoid overcooking; the top should still be very moist and not quite set when it goes under the broiler.

Cook frittata Pour egg mixture into skillet. Cook, using a heatproof flexible spatula to stir and push egg from edges to center of pan so runny parts run underneath [2], until eggs are almost set (they should still be wet on top but otherwise set throughout), 2 to 3 minutes.

Broil frittata Drop dollops of goat cheese on top of frittata, distributing evenly and pressing down into eggs a bit with the spatula. Sprinkle evenly with Parmigiano-Reggiano cheese [3]. Broil until frittata is set on top and has puffed slightly, and cheese is melted and golden, 1 to 1½ minutes.

Serve Gently run the spatula around the edges and underneath the frittata and carefully slide out of pan onto a plate. Slice into six wedges and serve hot, warm, or at room temperature.

Frittata, Step by Step

Mayonnaise and Hollandaise Sauce

These two egg-based sauces are examples of emulsions, among the most ethereal of the sauces in the classic canon. Emulsions are mixtures of two substances, such as oil and vinegar, that would not usually combine; made properly, they are perfectly smooth and delectably rich yet surprisingly light. Although other ingredients, such as butter and mustard, can act as emulsifiers, the egg yolk is the most effective. It is also a stabilizer, holding the emulsion over time.

MAYONNAISE Makes 1 cup

Making your own mayonnaise is a great way to observe the process of emulsification—and the result is far superior to the store-bought variety. The key to preparing any emulsion is to add the oil very slowly while whisking constantly and vigorously. In this case, you end up with a creamy concoction in which tiny droplets of oil are suspended in the lemon juice.

> 1 LARGE EGG YOLK
>
> 1 TEASPOON DIJON MUSTARD
>
> 2 TEASPOONS FRESH LEMON JUICE
>
> ¼ TEASPOON COARSE SALT, OR TO TASTE
>
> 1 CUP SUNFLOWER, SAFFLOWER, OR GRAPESEED OIL

PLACE EGG YOLK, MUSTARD, 1 teaspoon lemon juice, and salt [1] in a mixing bowl and whisk together until mixture is smooth and thoroughly combined. To add the oil, start with one drop at a time and whisk constantly until the mixture begins to thicken [2]; add remaining teaspoon lemon juice, then pour the oil in a very slow, steady stream and continue whisking until all the oil is incorporated and the sauce is thick and emulsified [3]. Use immediately, or refrigerate in an airtight container for up to 1 week.

SEPARATING AN EGG
Crack the side of a cold egg on a flat surface—not on the rim of a bowl, which could shatter the shell—then use thumbs to pull it apart. Pour the yolk back and forth between the eggshell cups, letting the white run out into a bowl beneath. Then drop the yolk into a separate bowl. Transfer the white to a third bowl before repeating; if any yolk breaks and lands in the first bowl, you won't have to discard all the whites.

Mayonnaise Tip

> To fix a broken emulsion (it will appear curdled), put 1 teaspoon of water (cold if it's a warm emulsion, warm if it's cold) in a bowl. Whisk sauce into water until it's smooth and creamy again.

Mayonnaise, Step by Step

1

2

3

HOLLANDAISE SAUCE Makes about 1½ cups

This rich yet airy, velvety sauce is made by enriching an acidic liquid with egg yolks and then thickening with butter. Here, we used a wine reduction, but you can skip that step and simply whisk eggs with 1 teaspoon lemon juice and ¼ cup boiling water. As one of the French "mother sauces," its preparation is a basic culinary technique that can be varied to create other sauces in the same family (often referred to as "warm emulsions"). By changing the acidic liquid to blood orange juice and zest, you get sauce Maltaise, typically served over steamed asparagus; tangerine juice and zest flavor Mikado sauce. Perhaps the best-known variation is Béarnaise, a traditional accompaniment for steak. To make it, prepare the hollandaise as directed, adding tarragon (the defining flavor of Béarnaise) to the reduction mixture. As it is designed to demonstrate, the method is the key to making the sauce, not the specific ingredients used to give it flavor.

When making hollandaise or any of its variations, using gentle heat is critical to achieving the right consistency. The best—and classic—way to do this is to "cook" it in a bain marie, or hot-water bath, instead of directly over a burner.

- ¼ CUP DRY WHITE WINE
- 1 TABLESPOON WHITE WINE VINEGAR
- 1 TABLESPOON MINCED SHALLOT (½ medium)
- ½ TEASPOON CRACKED BLACK PEPPERCORNS
- 3 TABLESPOONS BOILING WATER
- 3 LARGE EGG YOLKS
- ¾ CUP (1½ STICKS) UNSALTED BUTTER, room temperature, cut into tablespoons
- 1 TEASPOON FRESH LEMON JUICE
- ½ TEASPOON COARSE SALT
- PINCH OF CAYENNE PEPPER

Make reduction Combine wine, vinegar, shallot, and peppercorns in a small skillet [1] over medium-high heat; cook until reduced to 1 tablespoon [2], 3 to 4 minutes. Add the boiling water and strain through a fine sieve into a heatproof nonreactive (stainless-steel or glass) bowl [3].

Prepare bain marie (hot-water bath) Fill a medium saucepan with 2 inches of water and bring to a boil, then reduce heat so water is barely simmering.

Heat egg yolks Add egg yolks to strained reduction [4] and whisk, off the heat, until they become pale [5]. Place bowl over the bain-marie. Whisking constantly, cook until the mixture is thick enough to hold a trail from the whisk and begins to hold its shape when drizzled from the whisk [6]. Remove from heat. Wipe off any mixture that may have cooked onto the side of the pot with a damp paper towel to prevent any lumps from forming.

Incorporate butter Whisking constantly, add butter 1 tablespoon at a time [7], whisking until each addition is incorporated completely before adding the next. When all the butter has been added, season with lemon juice, salt, and cayenne [8]. The sauce should be thick but still able to drizzle from a spoon (and it should form a pool, not a mound) [9]. If it is too thick, thin it with a little water.

Hollandaise Tips

- Do not overheat the egg yolks; "temper" them instead by mixing with a bit of boiling water before placing in the hot-water bath to keep them from scorching.
- Simmer over very low heat. If the egg mixture is heated too quickly, it turns grainy; if cooked too long over too high a temperature, it will scramble.
- Add butter gradually to allow the mixture to emulsify. Adding too quickly will cause the emulsion to "break" or separate, preventing the liquid and butter from combining.
- Adjust the finished sauce with water to thin, and add lemon juice, salt, and cayenne pepper to flavor.
- If not serving immediately, cover with plastic wrap, pressing it directly on the surface of the sauce to prevent a skin from forming, and set over a pot of water that has been brought to a simmer and then removed from heat, or in a warm spot on the stove for up to 1 hour. Alternatively, store in a clean thermos warmed with hot but not boiling water, holding it for 2 or 3 hours at most.

Ingredients

Although traditionally made with melted clarified butter (page 88), softened butter emulsifies more readily with the egg yolks and produces a lighter texture.

> ## Hollandaise Sauce, Step by Step

3

Meat, Fish & Poultry

MEAT, FISH & POULTRY

WHEN IT COMES TO COOKING meat, fish, and poultry, many new cooks are easily overwhelmed with questions and concerns. What is the right cut for a particular dish? How do you know what a good cut should look like? And, perhaps most vexing of all, how can you tell when meat is done (but not overcooked)? These questions arise in part from the fact that meat, fish, and poultry dishes are usually the centerpiece of dinner. After all, if

you've spent a lot of money, energy, and effort on a standing rib roast or a side of salmon, the last thing you want to do is dry it out completely or season it incorrectly.

At the same time, you don't want to undercook certain meats — for obvious reasons, including safety. But preparing a meal should not be an intimidating venture. The key is to rely on your senses, and to build on your experience. The more you cook, the more you'll know to look for visual cues, taste for just the right level of seasoning, gauge the aromas wafting from the oven, and touch a piece of meat or fish to determine exactly its degree of doneness. Eventually, you'll be able to stray from strictly following recipes, and perhaps even create your own distinctive dishes. The recipes in this chapter are designed as a means to that end, each one offering a lesson of sorts that will give you valuable experience and the confidence to keep experimenting.

This chapter is organized by techniques, rather than divided into types of food, because once you understand the basics of each method you'll find you can cook a variety of meats using the same principles. The techniques used to roast a turkey, for example, so that it comes out with crisp, golden skin and moist meat are essentially the same — with a few variations — as for roasting a pork loin, a rib roast, or even a whole fish. In the following pages you'll find lessons on roasting, grilling, braising, stewing, steaming, poaching, simmering, sautéing, stir-frying, and frying. You'll also find information on the method of salting and preserving known as confit; how to grind and bind your own meats to make the best-tasting hamburgers and pâtés; and recipes for pre- and post-grilling flavor enhancers, such as marinades, salsas, and chutneys.

While the lessons in this chapter lay the foundation for culinary success, no amount of proper technique can

improve the quality of your ingredients. Before you attempt to create the recipes themselves, read through the sections that follow on purchasing meat, fish, and poultry. The goal here is to demystify the experience of shopping for these foods, so that you start out with the very best components.

Beef, Pork, Lamb, and Veal: Making the Cut

If you've ever found yourself confused in the meat aisle of your local market, wondering which cuts are tender enough for quick-cooking methods, such as grilling or broiling, or which are better suited for braising or other long, slow methods, you're not alone. Trying to decode the names of various cuts (and knowing how to prepare them) can baffle even experienced cooks. Understanding what makes meat tender versus tough will clear up a lot of the confusion.

At its most basic level, meat is made up of a collection of muscle fibers, fat, and connective tissues. As an animal grows and exercises, its muscle fibers and connective tissues get stronger, which also makes the meat tougher. This is why meat from older animals tends to be more stringy, and why, for the most part, animals that are bred for consumption are slaughtered at a relatively young age.

Take a look at a diagram of a cow, pig, or lamb (see pages 102–103). Think about how these animals move, and it becomes easier to comprehend the tender-versus-tough equation. The most tender cuts generally come from the middle of the animal — the back and rib sections — where there are suspension muscles that don't do much work. Here you'll find the loin and ribs in beef, pork, and lamb. These cuts tend to be leaner and are generally best suited for quick, dry-heat cooking methods such as grilling, broiling, sautéing, and sometimes roasting. Most steaks, for example, come from the loin or rib sections. Because they make up a small proportion of the entire animal, these tender cuts are also the most prized and expensive. As you move toward the shoulders and rump, and lower down to the chest and legs, you reach the harder-worked muscle groups that give the animal mobility and support its weight. The higher proportion of connective tissue in these areas makes the meat tougher. To break down the connective tissue in these cuts you need to cook them at a lower temperature, most likely using a wet cooking method such as braising, stewing, or simmering. The low, moist heat will melt the collagen — part of the connective tissue — into gelatin, which helps keep the meat from drying out.

PRIMAL CUTS

Meat is labeled by its primal cuts — also called the wholesale cuts (see pages 102–103 for diagram). For beef, these are the chuck, rib, short loin, sirloin, round, shank, brisket, plate, and flank. Pork, lamb, and veal have only five primal cuts. (Bear in mind that these are standard cuts in the United States; other countries define the cuts differently.) The primal cuts are further divided into retail cuts (see below). Cuts from the middle of the animal (short loin, sirloin, and rib in beef; loin in pork; and rack and loin in lamb and veal) are more tender than other cuts, and are therefore better suited for dry-heat cooking methods. Cuts from the extremities (from the chuck and round in beef, shoulder and ham in pork, and shoulder and leg in veal) are often best when cooked with wet heat. There are, of course, exceptions — leg of lamb, for example, is excellent roasted or butterflied and grilled. But, in general, each of the primal cuts is particularly well suited for specific cooking techniques.

RETAIL CUTS

These retail cuts are specific roasts or steaks that come from the larger primal cuts, such as the porterhouse and T-bone steaks from the beef loin, or the Boston butt roast from pork shoulder. Names for different cuts can vary from store to store, and region to region, which can make looking for an exact one specified in a recipe confusing. As an example, strip steak, from the loin, is alternately called a New York strip, New York sirloin, Kansas City strip, shell steak, and loin steak. This is why knowing your primal cuts is important — if a particular

retail cut you're looking for is not available, you can look for another cut from the same area of the animal. In the charts listing the best cuts for specific cooking techniques within each section, you'll find a few alternate names to help clear up confusion.

HOW TO BUY THE BEST MEAT

Befriend your butcher A surefire way to guarantee that you get the best quality meat is to get to know a local butcher, whether in a specialty shop or behind the meat counter in your grocery store. A good butcher can guide you to the best cuts for sale on any given day and should also be able to suggest the best ways to cook them. But having access to a good butcher is not always possible; in fact, these days many people shop in large supermarkets and warehouse stores, where the meat is often fabricated and packaged before it arrives at the store. In this case, you have to rely on your own knowledge about what to look for when you buy a piece of meat.

Check the grade The U.S. Department of Agriculture (USDA) grades meat for quality, which should give you a preliminary indicator of what to look for. The grades indicate how much fat is marbled throughout the meat. The more marbling there is, the more tender and flavorful the meat will be.

Beef is graded Prime, Choice, or Select. The grade is indicated by a purple shield stamped onto the outside layer of fat on the meat. This mark is not always on retail cuts (because it has been cut away); in that case, the package label should include the grade. Prime cuts, which have the most marbling, often go directly to restaurants and high-end butchers. Choice cuts have slightly less marbling than prime, but are still considered high quality. Select cuts have less marbling and often require a marinade to tenderize them if cooked with dry heat, otherwise these cuts are cooked with moist heat to maximize flavor and tenderness.

Veal and lamb are also graded as Prime or Choice; lower grades are usually ground and used in sausages and other processed meats. Pork is regulated for wholesomeness by the USDA, but not graded for quality, because today's pork is bred to be leaner than it was in the past.

Know what to look for Beyond the USDA's grading system, simply looking at a piece of meat can tell you a lot about its quality. Red meat, particularly beef, should be evenly marbled with fat, which gives it good flavor. As the meat cooks, the fat will melt and essentially baste the meat from the inside, keeping it moist. The fat should be a creamy white color; yellowish fat indicates that the meat comes from an older animal and won't be as tender.

Red meat is naturally a dark purple color, but when it is exposed to air it oxidizes, turning bright red. Some vacuum-packed meat will retain the purple color, but otherwise meat should be red. This is why the outer layer of a steak is often bright red, but the interior is a darker purple color. Never purchase meat that has a brownish tint — this is a good indicator that the meat has been sitting on the shelf too long. When shopping for pork, look for meat

Beef Cuts

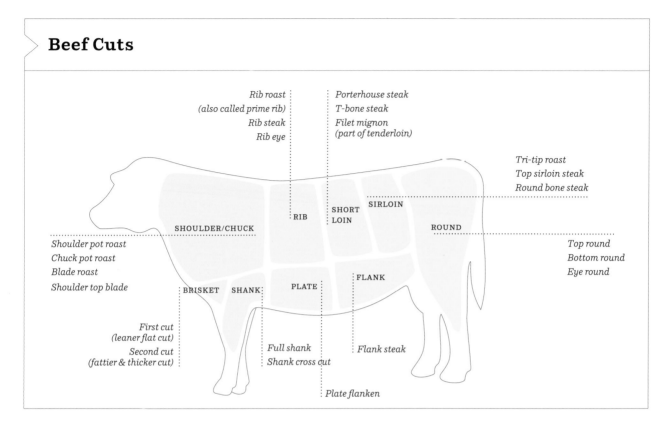

Rib roast
(also called prime rib)
Rib steak
Rib eye

Porterhouse steak
T-bone steak
Filet mignon
(part of tenderloin)

Tri-tip roast
Top sirloin steak
Round bone steak

RIB
SHORT LOIN
SIRLOIN
ROUND
SHOULDER/CHUCK

Shoulder pot roast
Chuck pot roast
Blade roast
Shoulder top blade

Top round
Bottom round
Eye round

BRISKET
SHANK
PLATE
FLANK

First cut
(leaner flat cut)
Second cut
(fattier & thicker cut)

Full shank
Shank cross cut

Flank steak

Plate flanken

Pork Cuts

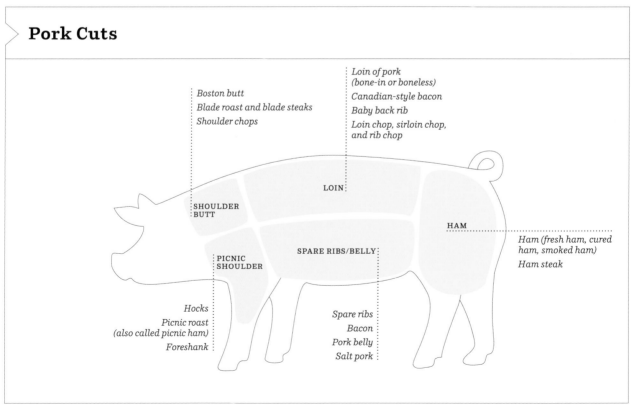

Boston butt
Blade roast and blade steaks
Shoulder chops

Loin of pork
(bone-in or boneless)
Canadian-style bacon
Baby back rib
Loin chop, sirloin chop,
and rib chop

LOIN
SHOULDER BUTT
HAM

Ham (fresh ham, cured
ham, smoked ham)
Ham steak

PICNIC SHOULDER
SPARE RIBS/BELLY

Hocks
Picnic roast
(also called picnic ham)
Foreshank

Spare ribs
Bacon
Pork belly
Salt pork

Lamb Cuts

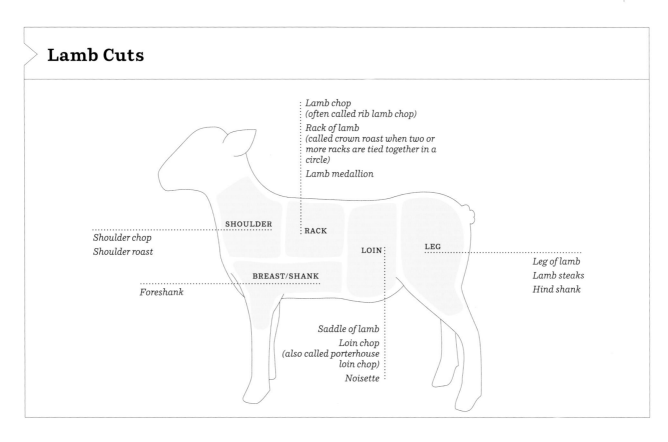

Lamb chop
(often called rib lamb chop)

Rack of lamb
(called crown roast when two or more racks are tied together in a circle)

Lamb medallion

SHOULDER

RACK

Shoulder chop
Shoulder roast

LOIN

LEG

BREAST/SHANK

Leg of lamb
Lamb steaks
Hind shank

Foreshank

Saddle of lamb
Loin chop
(also called porterhouse loin chop)
Noisette

Veal Cuts

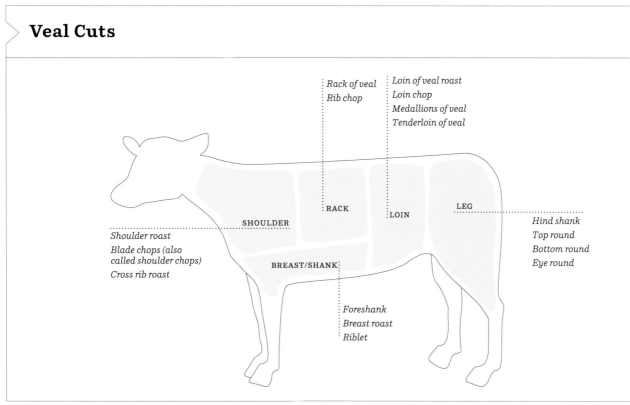

Rack of veal
Rib chop

Loin of veal roast
Loin chop
Medallions of veal
Tenderloin of veal

RACK

LOIN

LEG

SHOULDER

Shoulder roast
Blade chops (also called shoulder chops)
Cross rib roast

BREAST/SHANK

Hind shank
Top round
Bottom round
Eye round

Foreshank
Breast roast
Riblet

with a pinkish color that is streaked with creamy fat. The meat should also have a fine grain, rather than a coarse texture. Packaged meat should not have a lot of blood that has pooled at the bottom of the container, which is a sign that it has been sitting for a while. Always check the label for a date, and avoid any meat with a strong aroma.

DRY AGING MEAT

You may be familiar with the image of a whole side of beef or pork hanging in a butcher's meat locker. This is more than just a practical way of storing the meat until it's ready to be butchered—hanging meat for a brief period of time actually improves its flavor. The technique, called dry aging, is done in a humidity- and temperature-regulated room. As the meat hangs, natural enzymes break down the fibers, and in turn tenderize the meat. A layer of fat left on the outside of the meat protects it from bacterial contamination. Meat is aged for a range of time periods, depending on the type. Beef can be aged for as long as one month (though twenty-one days is most common). Veal, lamb, and pork (which are more tender to begin with) are hung for no more than a few days.

Dry aging has actually become something of a lost art, mainly practiced by specialty butchers—which is why it's hard to find meats labeled "dry aged" at grocery stores. Instead, most retail meat is "wet aged," meaning the cuts are vacuum-packed and stored until they are ready to be fabricated into retail cuts. Meat that is aged this way will tenderize to a certain extent, but won't gain the noticeable improvement in flavor that dry-aged meats have.

Poultry: Making the Cut

The cuts of poultry are much more straightforward than those of beef, pork, lamb, and veal. Chicken, turkey, duck, goose, and a variety of smaller birds, such as quail and game hens, are all categorized as poultry. The harder-worked muscles in poultry are the legs and thighs, which—for larger birds—makes these cuts appropriate for stewing and braising. Because the breast meat is leaner, it cooks best when prepared by a quick technique, such as grilling, broiling, and poaching. The fat content in poultry can range widely. Chicken and turkey are leaner meats, and can dry out easily if overcooked. Duck and goose have much more fat, and usually require more time at a lower cooking temperature to render the fat and baste the meat. Birds such as quail are too small to be cut into pieces and are cooked whole, most commonly by pan roasting or grilling.

GRADING POULTRY

Just as with meats, poultry is graded for quality by the USDA, with an A, B, or C rating system. Grade A indicates that the product has no discolorations or bruising and that bones are not broken. The bird should look plump with a well-distributed, even layer of fat in the skin. There should also be no tears in the skin or discoloration or bruising of the flesh, which can sometimes show up as a purple or yellow color. Also, there shouldn't be any blood that has pooled at the bottom of the package. You won't usually see lower grades of poultry (B and C) in stores, as these are used to make ground chicken or sausages.

SIZES OF POULTRY

The age of a chicken, turkey, duck, or other poultry will determine how tender it is. The younger the animal, the more tender the meat. The age of a bird can be determined by its size—the smaller it is, the more tender it will be. For example, chickens that are labeled "broiler" or "fryer" are usually raised for forty-five days and weigh up to 5½ pounds; those labeled "roasting chickens" are bred for a few more days (usually forty-nine), weigh up to 6 or 7 pounds, and are perfect for roasting. Sometimes you'll find older chickens in the store that are either labeled stewing, baking, or roasting chickens—not to be confused with young roasters. These are egg-laying hens raised to about fifteen months, and will usually have "hen" listed on the label. The age of these birds makes their meat tougher, but also more flavorful. They are good for simmering, braising, and stewing—all moist cooking methods that will better break down the connective tissue. If you're unsure whether a chicken labeled for roasting is a young one or an older hen, ask your butcher, if possible.

Fish and Shellfish

Fish are among the last wild creatures on Earth that we eat in abundance. Visit any commercial fishing dock, from Seattle, Washington, to Gloucester, Massachusetts, and from the Great Lakes to the Gulf of Mexico, and you'll find fishermen unloading their catch, soon to be rushed to grocery stores and fresh fish markets across the country. Of course, a variety of fish are also farmed in the United States and abroad. There are advantages and disadvantages to both wild and farmed fish; see page 107 for more on both.

TEXTURE AND FLAVOR

Fish are very tender creatures. Life suspended in water makes the tough tendons and cartilage that connect muscle to bone in land animals superfluous in fish. The parts of fish that are tough are grouped around their fins and tails — pieces that humans generally don't eat. There are thousands of types of fish in the seas and fresh waters of the world, and an equally wide range in consistencies of their flesh. At one end of the spectrum are the firmest-textured fish, such as tuna, bluefish, and swordfish, which are sometimes described as "meaty." In fact, these fish are often cut into steaks and cooked just as you would a beef steak — on the grill, under the broiler, or pan-seared on the stovetop. At the other end of the spectrum are the most delicate fish and shellfish, such as flounder and scallops, that virtually melt in your mouth. These fish are often cooked by gentle methods — by steaming or shallow poaching, although they also take well to sautéeing. Other fish fall somewhere between the benchmarks of the dense tuna and delicate flounder. Salmon, for example, is a firmer fish that cooks just as well on the grill as it does when roasted in the oven.

How strong- or mild-tasting a fish is will also determine what flavors you'll want to pair with it. Halibut, for instance, is a firm, but not meaty, textured fish with a very mild flavor that is neutral enough to be cooked with a variety of ingredients, from earthy herbs to sweet tomatoes. Grouper, snapper, bass, cod, flounder, and sole are other examples of mild fish. On the other hand, bluefish, which has more pungent fish oils, is generally cooked with simpler flavors. Other oily, strong-flavored fish include salmon, tuna, mackerel, and sardines.

HOW TO BUY THE BEST FISH

For fish and shellfish, freshness is imperative, since both start to deteriorate minutes after they're pulled from the water. Ask your fishmonger when and where the fish was caught, and pay attention to how the fish looks and smells. If you are buying a whole fish, look for glossy and clear eyes and bright red gills. The skin should feel slippery, but not slimy, and the scales should be firmly attached (unless the fishmonger has already removed them). Your thumbprint on a fish fillet should not leave a mark; the flesh should bounce back. A good fillet will look moist, never gray or "filmy." Smell, of course, is another indicator of quality. Never buy fish or shellfish with a strong "fishy" odor. It's natural for seafood to have a briny smell, but anything more is a bad sign. Similarly, the fish market should smell clean, not overly "fishy."

FRESH VS. FROZEN

Fish that is labeled as fresh has probably recently come off a fishing boat or from a fish farm, been prepared for sale at a cannery or processing plant, then shipped to market. Even if you live close to an ocean, this whole process can take anywhere from 24 hours to a week. If the fish has been well iced, refrigerated, and handled gently, it will keep well until it is delivered to the store. If you don't have a reliable fresh source, frozen fish is often your best option, even if it has lost some of its texture. Fish is usually frozen immediately after it is caught or brought to a cannery, ensuring that it will be fresher when you defrost it than it would have been if shipped unfrozen over a long distance.

SHELLFISH

Mussels, clams, and oysters should have tightly closed shells, or they should snap closed when you tap them. Lobster are always sold (and cooked) while still alive. Look for lobsters that are lively, and keep in mind that bigger doesn't always mean better. A 1- to 1¼-pound lobster is likely to be sweeter and more tender than an older lobster that weighs 2 pounds or more. Shrimp is almost always sold frozen or defrosted. Of course, fresh shrimp usually taste best, especially when you peel and devein them yourself, but depending on where you live, frozen shrimp may be your only option. If that's the case, look for those labeled "flash frozen" on the bag. Shellfish are usually steamed or boiled, although they can also be cooked in a variety of ways, including grilling, broiling, and frying, and are also often enjoyed raw.

A WORD ON LABELS

When most people lived on or near farms and regularly saw cows and pigs roaming the fields and chickens squawking around the coop, they had a good idea about how their food was raised. Today, however, when most meat, poultry, and seafood is purchased in grocery stores, tracking the original source of our food is increasingly difficult. What's more, industrial farming techniques continue to raise a host of environmental and ethical concerns.

In most midsize to large American grocery stores or supermarkets, you're confronted with a wide variety of choices in the meat and seafood sections. You'll find meats and poultry labeled "organic" and "natural," grass-fed beef and grain-fed beef; conventional chicken and free-range chicken; and wild salmon and farmed salmon, to list just a few. The prices of all of these selections also vary considerably. Untangling these designations can be daunting. What is the best? What is most healthy for you and your family? And what is worth the extra money? As with any food you buy, quality is paramount for taste. If you purchase meat that has been fed well, and raised and butchered humanely, it will probably also taste better. This is why you should buy the best-quality meat that you can afford. Look for organic meats whenever possible, and at the very least, meats that are labeled "natural" or "free-range."

More expensive, higher-quality cuts of meat don't have to break the bank—especially if you consider eating smaller portions. In many parts of the world, meat is used more as a flavor booster than a central part of the meal. In this country, the USDA recommended portion sizes for meat, poultry, and fish is a 3-ounce serving. If you fill out meals with more vegetables and whole grains, you'll find that you should be able to afford to buy very high-quality meats.

To understand what labels such as "organic" and "natural" mean, take a look at conventional and industrial farming and the kinds of meats these practices produce. Conventionally raised livestock are often kept in overcrowded living conditions. Many of these animals are also fed a diet that is not natural—nor suitable—to their delicate systems. The overcrowding and improper diet result in diseases, which in turn means these animals are often treated with antibiotics. Meanwhile, the economic push to produce meat faster drives farmers to pump livestock with growth hormones. These poor living conditions not only result in a poor quality of life for the animals but also in environmental pollution and foods that are much less healthful or flavorful. Farming methods that are "organic," "natural," and "free-range" all depart from these conventional methods in varying degrees. Following is a list of terms to help you make the most informed choices:

Certified Organic The USDA sets standards for organic meat and poultry. Animals must be fed 100 percent organic feed, kept free of hormones and antibiotics, and treated in more humane ways than conventional livestock. For example, cattle must have access to pasture (although the length of time is not specified), and other animals must have access to the outdoors and sunlight. Farms must also be inspected for compliance.

Natural Meats labeled "natural" are often confused with those labeled "organic," but they are not the same. Foods labeled "natural" are not subjected to the stringent regulation that USDA Certified Organic foods are (although, according to the USDA, new regulations are forthcoming). Producers that use "natural" on the label often follow some or many of the practices followed by Certified Organic producers, but not all of them. There are three criteria that must be followed for meats to be labeled "natural": the meats must be minimally processed; they must have no added food colorings, preservatives, or flavors; and producers must define what they mean by "natural" on the label. This is why you might find a package of "natural" chicken labeled as "antibiotic-free."

Local In recent years, there has been a widespread movement toward eating locally grown foods. The definition of "locally grown" can vary widely, but it is often thought of as foods grown or raised within 100 miles of where you live. Buying locally is a good way to support small, local farms, and also one of the best ways to ensure that you know what you're buying. If you go to your farmers' market, for example, you'll probably be able to speak to someone who was directly involved in raising the animals, and who should be able to explain how the farm operates.

Grass fed vs. grass finished Cattle and sheep labeled "grass fed" are raised grazing in pastures. But many are moved to feedlots a few months before slaughter and fed a grain-based diet to give them much more marbling. One of the disadvantages to feeding cattle grain is that it is not a natural diet for these animals, and can cause them to develop illnesses that make antibiotics a necessity. "Grass-finished" cattle are left to roam on pasture until they are brought to the slaughterhouse. Because there is no official USDA regulation of these labels, "grass fed" is often used as a catchall term for animals that have been finished with grass or grain (since both have technically been fed grass at some point). If the label says "grass fed," ask your butcher to clarify what it means.

Nature veal Veal comes from calves and young cows (usually male dairy cows), and is prized for its extreme tenderness, light color, and delicate flavor. Perhaps more than for any other meat, it is very important to know how and where the veal that you buy was raised. Some people feel that eating veal is unethical, because the animals are slaughtered at approximately four to six months of age. Yet, in reality, most pigs and sheep are also slaughtered at the same age to produce pork and lamb. Perhaps it's more important to consider the living conditions of the young animals. Many calves raised for veal live a very dismal life. They are raised in cramped crates (where they lack enough room to turn around), and are fed a formula diet. This diet, combined with the lack of movement, makes the meat very tender and light in color. In recent years, many organic farms, and even conventional farms, have changed the way they raise calves for veal. Some conventional nonorganic farms allow the calves to move freely with others in stalls and to eat a cereal- and milk-based diet. Organic veal calves are often allowed to roam in open pasture and feed off grass and milk, and they are not treated with hormones or antibiotics. Calves that are allowed to move freely, in either a stall or out in open pasture, will have meat that is slightly pink, and much more flavorful. Veal that is raised in this manner is labeled with a variety of names, including "nature," "suckled," "red," "pink," "rose," "pastured," "meadow," "grass-fed," and "free-range." To be sure of what you are getting, ask your butcher where the veal in the case came from and how it was raised. If he can't tell you, it's probably not any of the types noted.

Free range/free roaming The USDA defines "free range" or "free roaming" animals as "being allowed access to the outside." This does not necessarily mean that all chickens labeled "free range," for example, are allowed to peck at their food in a wide open farmyard or on a grassy hill. Some birds may get out of doors only for a few hours a day, if at all. For this reason, try to find out how the bird was raised—by purchasing poultry either from a local farm that you know or from a company that you trust.

Heritage This term is often used for historic or endangered breeds of livestock and poultry. Yet the description is most commonly used (and most clearly defined) for turkeys, which must officially meet three criteria to qualify as "heritage": the birds must be able to mate naturally (industrially farmed turkeys are often prevented from doing so); they must be able to withstand life outdoors and have a long, productive lifespan; and they must have a slow growth rate, in order to develop strong skeletal structures (heritage turkeys reach a weight that is marketable after about 28 weeks).

Wild vs. farmed fish As the name suggests, fish labeled "wild" are caught in oceans and rivers, where their living conditions are not controlled. Farmed fish are raised in a controlled atmosphere—usually in pens in ponds, or sometimes in the ocean. When purchasing either farmed or wild-caught fish, it's wise to consider a few specific environmental and health issues.

For wild fish, as an example, overfishing is a serious concern. Some fish are being caught more quickly than they can reproduce, resulting in endangered populations (and loss of livelihood for fishermen). At the same time, pollution—particularly mercury from coal-burning utility plants—has compromised the healthfulness of all fish that swim in rivers, lakes, and oceans. When mercury—a naturally occurring heavy metal—is released as emissions into the atmosphere, it falls back down to Earth. Mercury in this form is not all that dangerous when ingested, because the body does not easily absorb it. But when mercury comes into contact with water, bacteria chemically changes it into methylmercury, which is quite toxic because it is easily absorbed into the body. Fish absorb the methylmercury through foods that they eat, and then pass it along to humans via consumption. Nearly all fish have trace amounts of methylmercury in their systems, but the fish that are at the top of the food chain—those that are larger and that eat other fish—absorb more. These fish pose a bigger threat to humans who eat them. Methylmercury can cause neurological damage in fetuses, young children, and even adults. Recommendations for the amount of fish you should eat change often. Visit Oceans Alive's website (www.oceansalive.org) for the most up-to-date information on consumption advisories for seafood.

Farmed fish, on the other hand, comes with its own set of health issues. Some farmed fish are fed pellets that contain PCBs, a group of chemicals that are known carcinogens. The fish that eat the pellets will in turn have high levels of PCBs. To date, the FDA has not found sufficient evidence to issue guidelines.

One of the most likely times you'll be faced with a choice between purchasing wild or farmed fish is with salmon. Much of the salmon you'll find in grocery stores is farmed. Wild salmon tends to be pricier, and has a complex, more intense flavor than farmed salmon, which is fattier and mellower. Although both types of fish are a rich source of beneficial omega-3s, the fatty acids that may protect against heart disease, sustainably caught wild salmon is your best choice in this case.

The recommendations for eating wild or farmed fish change often, making it hard to keep track of which should be bought and which should be avoided. The Monterey Bay Aquarium Seafood Watch (www.mbayaq.org/cr/seafoodwatch.asp) maintains a detailed guide that rates the sustainability of nearly any fish you can buy.

COOKING TEMPERATURES

The USDA recommends specific temperatures for cooking beef, pork, lamb, and poultry. The numbers are designated to protect consumers from pathogens such as salmonella, *E. coli*, and many others, which can cause food-borne illnesses. Safety experts and professional cooks say that adhering to the USDA's standards is imperative when preparing meat for young children, pregnant women, older individuals, and anyone with weakened immune systems. But when it comes to cooking for healthy adults, many chefs feel comfortable diverging from the USDA guidelines and cooking most meats—except ground meat—to lower temperatures for the sake of better flavor and texture. That difference is anywhere from 5 to 30 degrees lower than the USDA's standard, depending on the type of meat, level of doneness, and whether resting time is taken into account.

A meat thermometer is essential for determining when meat has finished cooking—and to keep it from being under- or overcooked. This simple, inexpensive tool allows you to cook meat and poultry to the exact stage of doneness that you desire, without cutting into it and losing precious juices. The preference of many chefs is an instant-read model. These are available with either an analog or digital display, and they produce a reading in just a few seconds. Moreover, they can be calibrated easily. A few other things to keep in mind:

■ Get in the habit of calibrating your thermometer often to ensure that it's accurate. Stand it in ice water or boiling water; if it doesn't read 32° or 212°F, respectively, adjust it. If the thermometer cannot be calibrated, note the difference whenever you cook.

■ For roasts, insert the thermometer into the thickest portion of the meat; avoid hitting bone, as it may yield a false reading. For whole poultry, turn the bird so its neck cavity faces you, and insert thermometer through the thigh, near the socket (but, again, do not touch the bone).

■ For steaks, chops, and other small cuts, insert a thermometer through the side and into the middle, not from the top down. This is because the point on the thermometer that reads temperature is about 2 inches up the side.

■ Allow for carryover time. Meat continues to cook outside the oven, rising 10 to 15 degrees during a rest, depending on size. A roast beef, for example, cooked to 125° to 130°F per roasting guidelines (see chart, opposite) will rise several degrees to reach medium-rare. Resist any urge to cut into the meat until you've allowed it to rest sufficiently.

GENERAL STORAGE GUIDELINES

Storing To keep the juices from meat, fish, and poultry from dripping onto other foods in your refrigerator—thereby risking cross-contamination and the spread of food-borne illnesses—keep meats wrapped in their original packaging and store them in a nonreactive glass bowl or on a rimmed metal baking sheet. Plastic is porous and will absorb odors and flavors, so plastic containers should be avoided when storing raw meats. Store on the bottom shelf of the refrigerator.

Defrosting The safest way to defrost meat is in the refrigerator in its original packaging in a nonreactive pan or bowl (so that juices do not drip onto other foods). Defrosting in the refrigerator can take a while, especially for larger pieces of meat (such as turkeys and roasts), so allow for this extra time when planning a meal. If you need a quicker method, the USDA also recommends placing meat in a leakproof plastic bag and submerging the bag in cold water. The water should be changed every 30 minutes, and the meat cooked immediately after it has thawed.

MEAT TEMPERATURES CHART

MEAT DONENESS	USDA GUIDELINES *Before Resting*	PROFESSIONAL KITCHENS *Before Resting*
BEEF		
rare	—	115°–120°
medium-rare	145°	125°–130°
medium	160°	140°
medium-well	—	150°
well-done	170°	155°–160°
ground beef	160°	160°
PORK		
medium	160°	138°–145°
well-done	170°	160°
ground pork	160°	160°
LAMB		
rare	—	115°–120°
medium-rare	145°	125°–130°
medium	160°	140°
medium-well	—	145°–150°
well-done	170°	150°–155°
ground lamb	160°	160°
POULTRY		
whole bird, thighs, legs, wings, ground poultry	165°	165°
chicken breasts	165°	160°

How to Cut Up a Chicken

When cutting a chicken into parts, let the bird be your guide. The parts will separate at the joints with little effort. Chicken is commonly cut up into six, eight, or ten parts. To create six parts, cut off the legs and wings and then separate the breast from the back and split into halves. To create eight parts, continue by separating the legs into drumsticks and thighs. For ten parts, divide the breast into quarters.

1 First remove the legs and wings: Place the chicken, breast side up, on your work surface. Gently pull the leg away from the body, then slice through the skin between the breast and thigh. 2 Pull the leg outward until the thighbone pops out of its socket. 3 Cut along the backbone around the ball and socket, pulling the leg away to detach. Repeat with remaining leg. 4 Lay the breast on its side, and pull away the wing until the joint is exposed; cut between the joint and the breast to remove the wing. (If you want to remove the wing tips, simply pull them away and

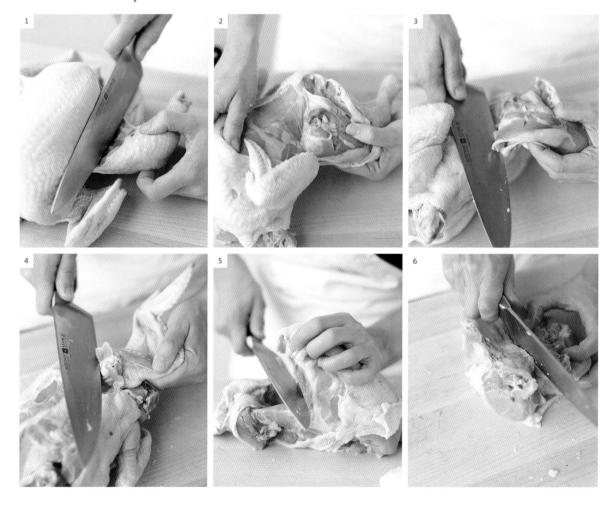

slice through the joint.) 5 Then separate the breast from the back: Lift up the breast, and using a knife or poultry shears, slice between the rib cage and shoulder joints. Slice through the rib cage on both sides of the bird. Cut down between those bones, trimming through any sinews, to separate the two sections. 6 To split the breast in half, start by placing the breast skin side down. Split the keel bone with heel of knife, then slit closely along the breastbone with a knife. 7 Then crack it open with your hands. (This step is optional, but makes the next step easier.) 8 Cut the breast in half with a knife or poultry shears. 9 To cut halves into quarters (you will need to do this for the fried chicken on page 269), cut in half diagonally through the bone. 10 To divide the leg: Turn the leg skin side down, and cut along the white fat line to separate the thigh from the drumstick. 11 You should end up with 8 to 10 parts, as shown here, depending on whether you cut the breast into quarters (like the one pictured on the right).

How to Bone a Chicken Breast

This technique is also called making a suprême—a deboned chicken breast half—because it is considered to be the best (supreme) part of the bird. Save the bones for making stock.

1 Lift up layer of fat from top of breast and pull to remove. Slice off the tough gristle from the center. 2 Locate the wishbone and insert tip of knife under to loosen. 3 Use your fingers to pull out the bone. 4 Slice along either side of the bone in the center (called the keel bone). 5 Work the knife gently along the rib cage to remove the meat from the rib cage. 6 Once both halves have been separated, trim away the slender fillet from each.

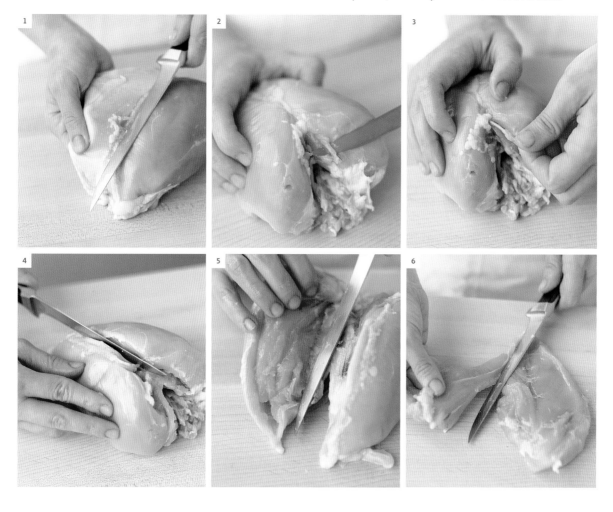

How to Spatchcock a Chicken

This technique is similar to butterflying (see page 115), but is specific to preparing a whole chicken or other small bird, such as quail, for grilling or broiling.

1 Set the chicken on a clean work surface, breast side down. Use sharp kitchen shears to cut along both sides of the backbone to remove it. 2 Flip the chicken over, then press down firmly on the breastbone with your palm to flatten.

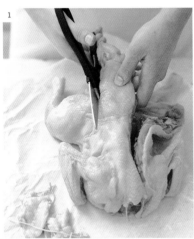

How to Truss a Chicken

Chicken does not always need to be trussed before roasting, but it will help ensure that the bird cooks evenly and maintains its form for serving.

1 With tail closest to you, and holding one end of twine in each hand, center and run kitchen twine around neck of chicken, passing it over drumsticks, then under their joints. 2 Cross twine over joints; tighten to bring them together. 3 Wrap one end of twine all the way around tail end; tie securely.

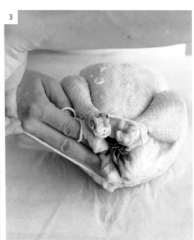

How to Bone a Leg of Lamb

Before you begin, remove the layer of fat and membrane (known as the "fell") from the surface of the lamb, being careful not to cut into the meat. A boned leg of lamb can then be butterflied (opposite) for grilling or stuffing and rolling for roasting.

1 Insert the knife at the tip of the pelvic bone, then slice down along the bone, working the knife around the bones and joints to free as much meat as possible. 2 Pry open meat to expose the bone. 3 Cut the meat from the tip of the bone, at the starting point. 4 Now slice along the shank bone to separate the meat. 5 Then lift the bone and cut around the joint to remove, first on one side. 6 Then continue cutting on other side to completely sever the bone from the meat.

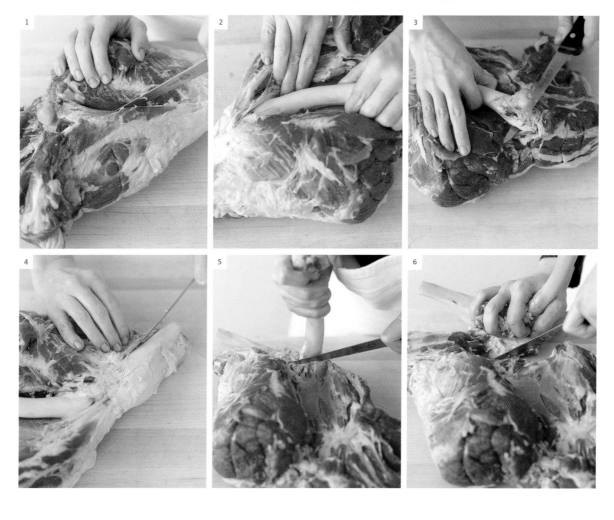

How to Butterfly a Leg of Lamb

1 Starting at one side of removed bone, make a horizontal cut, slicing outward through the meat in short strokes and leaving about 1 inch intact at outer edge. Then unfold meat (like opening a book) so it lies flat. Repeat with other side. 2 Trim off excess fat, then pound to even thickness (not shown).

How to Make Pork Medallions

Thin, boneless cuts of pork (and chicken or veal, called cutlets) cook more evenly when pressed (or pounded) to an even thickness. Pork (as opposed to chicken breast meat) can be sliced into somewhat uniform pieces, so it does not require as much pressure to make them perfectly even.

1 Using your fingers and a slicing knife, pull and slice off silver skin from tenderloin. 2 Slice tenderloin crosswise into 1-inch pieces, then place the pieces between two sheets of plastic wrap. Press gently with the palm of your hand until the medallions are desired thickness (usually ⅛ to ¼ inch).

How to French a Rack of Lamb

Although this is one of the more complicated techniques, it is worth learning so you can do it yourself rather than relying on the butcher. This method can be applied to veal and pork roasts, too; save any meat trimmings for making stock.

1 Position the knife about an inch from the "eye" (the meat visible at the end of the rack) and cut along the length of the rack, all the way down to the bone. 2 Using your fingers and the knife, pull away and separate the fat from the bones. 3 Slice through the center of the other (untrimmed) section. 4 Then slice and pull away the thick layer of fat and meat from the thicker (shoulder) end, working from the center out to the edge. This step will

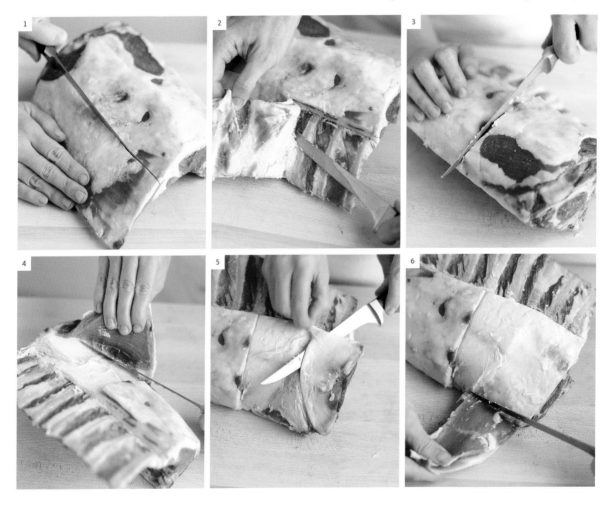

help the rack cook more evenly. 5 Slice off excess fat from the trimmed side. 6 Pull back and remove the trimmings. 7 Trim off excess fat from the other end of the loin. 8 Insert the tip of the knife at one of the ends of the loin and cut away the thick nerve that runs along the length of the rack. 9 Make a cut ½ inch from the eye along the length of the rack. 10 Turn the lamb over and cut along the same lines, then slice down the center of each bone to score the thin membrane, allowing the meat to separate more easily. 11 Pull the meat and fat from the bones, and scrape off any remaining fat with the knife. 12 The rack should now look like this, with the bones exposed on one side.

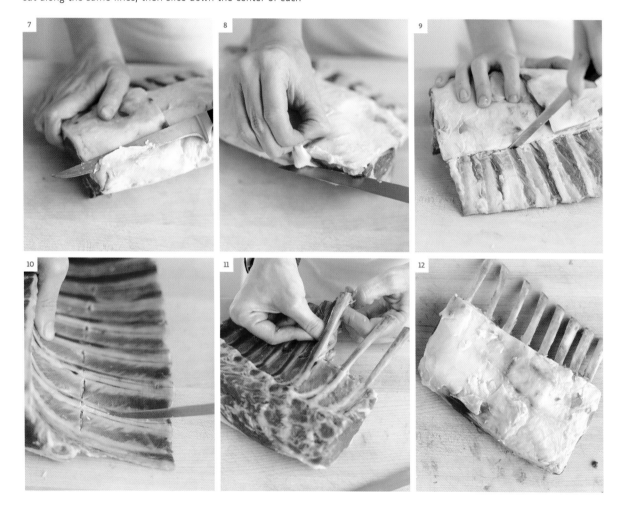

How to Trim a Beef Tenderloin

When buying beef tenderloin, look for one that feels soft, not hard, which indicates an excessive amount of fat at the surface (and consequently less meat for your money after all the fat has been trimmed). Use a very sharp knife and work carefully to avoid removing anything but the fat, gristle, and membrane. Save any meat trimmings for making stir-fries.

1 Starting at the narrow (tail) end, remove the fat by slicing with a sharp knife and pulling with your fingers. 2 Continue trimming off the excess fat as you work along the meat, being careful not to tear the flaps of meat near the thicker (head) end. 3 Remove the sinewy membrane, called the silver skin, which is extremely tough; angle the knife against the membrane, not the meat, and carefully slice off the silver skin in strips. 4 Place the meat with the fatty side facing up. Pull away the "chain" (which contains the thick white gristle that connects the loin to the bone) and cut to remove. 5 If desired, slice off the loose piece of meat at the tail end (this is optional but will help the meat cook more evenly). Remove remaining silver skin (not shown).

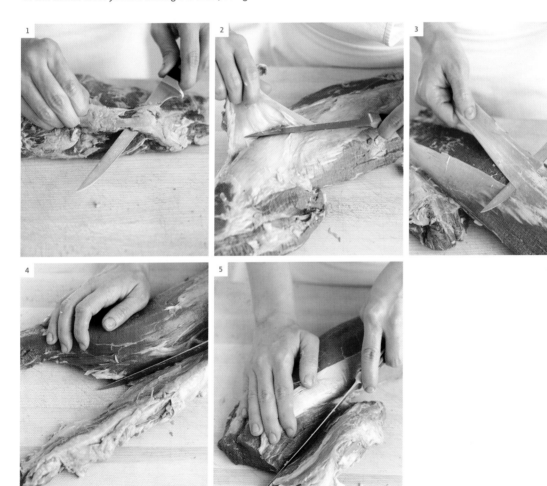

How to Tie a Roast

Once you get the hang of it, this method is actually faster to do, but if you prefer, you can simply cut equal lengths of twine and wrap each piece around the meat at equal intervals.

1 Tuck the tail end under (this is to help make the ends more equal in thickness for more even cooking). 2 Cut a long piece of kitchen twine (it should be long enough to tie the entire roast). Starting with the tail end, wrap twine around the meat and tie to secure. 3 Now form the twine into a loop around your thumb and fingers, twisting it to make an X about 2 inches from the first tie. Spread the loop and pass over the end. 4 Pull to tighten around the meat. Continue in this manner until the tenderloin is tied in even intervals from end to end. 5 Once you've reached the other end, turn over meat. Working in the opposite direction, loop the extra twine around each tie, until you reach the end of the tenderloin. 6 Turn the meat back over and tie a knot at the first intersection.

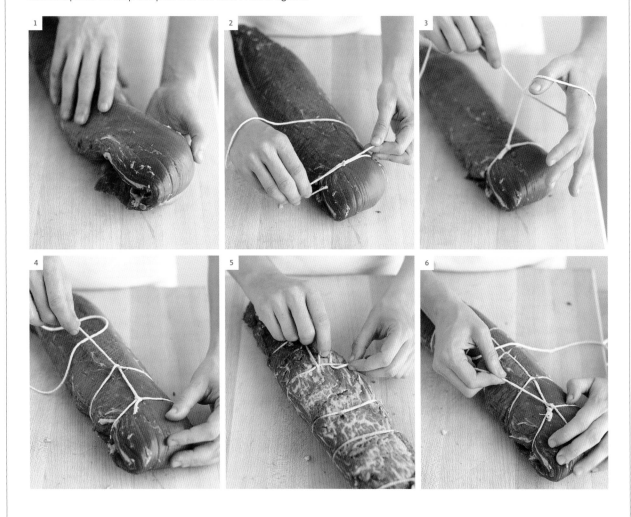

How to Fillet a Flat Fish

The technique used to fillet fish depends on the type of fish. Flat fish, including flounder, sole, and turbot, can be made into two or four fillets. The method shown in steps 1 through 5 produces four fillets and is good for using with larger fish. Smaller flat fish can be filleted as shown in the last photo to create two full fillets.

1 Make a slit across the base of the tail. Use kitchen shears to trim the fins from the sides, belly, and back (as shown, opposite). 2 Make a slit from head to tail on one side of center ridge. 3 Insert knife under tail end and run knife along the center bone to the head to separate flesh, lifting it as you go; angle knife toward the bone and make small cuts for more control, working from the center out. Repeat on other side. Turn fish over and repeat steps 1 through 3. 4 Lay fillet skin side down and cut to remove the roe sack, if necessary. 5 Trim off outer edge from each fillet. 6 To fillet a smaller flat fish: Starting at tail end, insert knife into an outer edge and slice flesh from the bones, all the way to the head. Lifting fillet as you work, continue slicing across width of fish along the bones to remove top fillet in one piece. Repeat with other side.

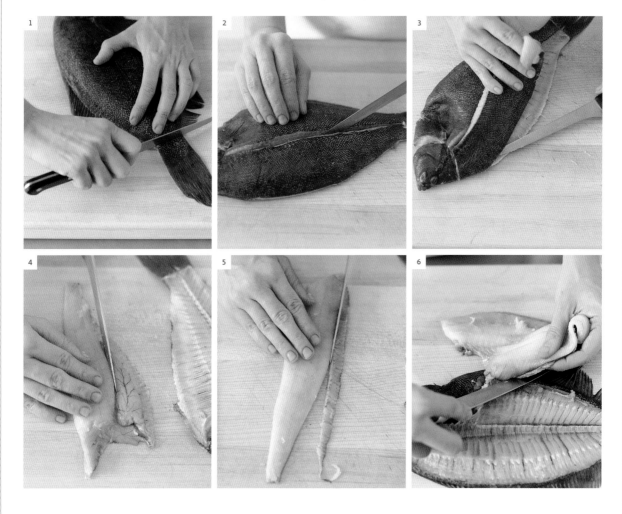

How to Fillet a Round Fish

Round fish are typically fabricated into two fillets, one from each side of the fish. The method below — the up and over technique — is for hard-boned fish such as bass, snapper, and grouper. You will need a knife with a flexible blade. For soft-boned fish, such as salmon and trout, you can simply slice down the length of the fish, keeping the blade against the backbone, in one smooth movement (don't use a sawing motion).

1 Use kitchen shears to trim fins from sides. 2 Snip off the fins from top and back. 3 Cut through the belly and around the gill plate (do not separate head completely). 4 Insert the knife behind the head and slice down the length of the fish, along the backbone, angling knife toward bone to keep the blade as close to the bones as possible. 5 Lift up the flesh and continue slicing to separate it from the bones, all the way across the body. This is called "up and over," since you need to cut around bones. 6 Place the fillet skin side down on your work surface and trim. Turn over fish and repeat on the other side.

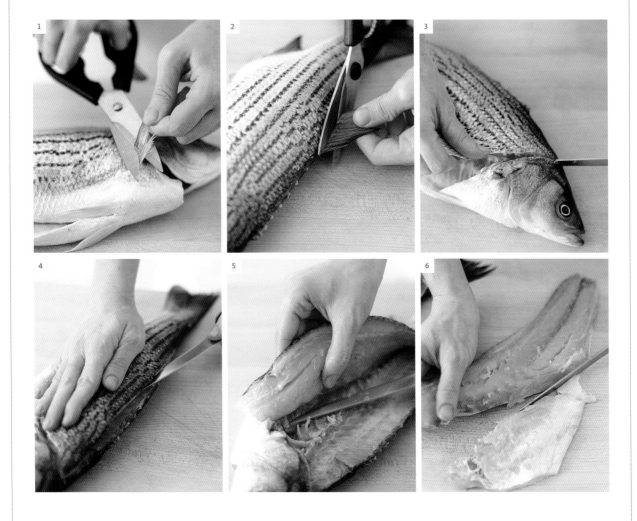

How to Peel and Devein Shrimp

Like other shellfish, fresh shrimp should be purchased the day you plan to use them, since they do not keep well. The flesh should smell like salt air and have a firm texture. Avoid using any shrimp that are grainy or have black spots.

1 Holding shrimp by the tail, peel shell from inside curve with your fingers, leaving tail intact (or remove, if desired). 2 Gently run a paring knife from head to tail along the center of the back to expose the vein. 3 Use the knife to remove the vein in one piece. 4 To butterfly shrimp, slice open the shrimp, from head to tail, leaving tail intact, then spread open flesh. (You will need to do this to make the stir-fry on page 265.)

How to Clean Soft-Shell Crabs

When possible, buy crabs that are still alive, and only on the day you plan to cook them. They should be kept in the coldest part of the refrigerator, wrapped in plastic or wet newspaper, until ready to be cooked.

1 Holding the crab with one hand, use kitchen shears to snip off the eyes and mouth (cut about ¼ inch behind the eyes). 2 Scoop out the soft matter just behind this cut. 3 Lift up the apron (the flap of shell on the belly) and cut or twist off. 4 Lift the shell on each side of the body and scrape off the gray gills (and discard). Rinse crab lightly before using.

How to Roast

Roasted meats are at the center of most holiday meals and celebrations; think of roasted spring lamb for Passover and Easter, Thanksgiving turkey, and Christmas goose. This isn't surprising if you consider that in ancient times spit-roasting, or skewering a whole or part of an animal, then rotating it slowly over an open fire, was the cooking method of choice for ceremonial occasions. The extremely hot, dry heat of spit-roasting browns the meat, creating a rich crust that's packed with flavor. Although we now primarily roast in ovens, meat can develop the same savory browned crust as when it is spit-roast, while still retaining the juicy meat inside. Because oven-roasting is straightforward and adaptable, the technique is a good first lesson in meat, fish, and poultry cookery. And the comforting and familiar roast chicken is an excellent starting point; you'll find the recipe on page 127.

Successful roasting relies on high heat to brown the meat or skin, but this presents a conundrum: the heat can dry out or burn the exterior before the interior is cooked. Roasting at a more moderate temperature will help retain the juices, but it won't brown the meat. There are a few ways around this. For larger roasts, such as turkey and prime rib, it helps to brown the crust first in a hot oven, then turn down the heat to cook the meat more slowly. Roasts with higher fat contents, such as duck, however, should be placed in the oven at a lower temperature to help render the fat; turning the heat up during the last ten minutes will crisp the skin. Other roasts are cooked at a constant, very high temperature, without pre-browning or any shift in temperature. A whole fish, for example, will stay moist and get crisp skin when roasted this way. Whichever method you use, the most important point to keep in mind when roasting is this: Check the internal temperature of the roast at about three-quarters of the total suggested cooking time, then keep checking at fairly frequent intervals (five to ten minutes) afterward. There is no turning back from an overcooked roast.

Smaller cuts are usually pan-roasted—browned on the stovetop, then often finished in a hot oven—to develop the crust. Thick chops, chicken breasts, fish fillets, and small game birds, such as Cornish hens and squab, all turn out very nicely when pan-roasted. Pan-roasting is fast and you can cook portion-size cuts for just a few people, making this an ideal method for simple weeknight meals.

Because roasting shows off the pure flavors of whatever you are cooking, the quality of your ingredients is critically important: it will have a direct impact on the taste. Look for USDA-graded Prime or Choice cuts, which have more marbling, and will consequently remain moist as they cook. The best cuts for roasting are tender, such as those from the loin or sirloin, because these cook quickly. Tougher cuts, which have a lot of connective tissue, don't cook well in high heat, since the collagen doesn't have enough time to melt. To roast successfully, they need to be cooked at a lower temperature, and may have to be enhanced by various methods. Fat is sometimes added to leaner cuts through barding (wrapping the meat in strips of bacon or other fats) or larding (inserting fat directly into the meat); for more on these techniques, see page 126.

The recipes in this section will teach you how to roast meat, fish, and poultry, of course, but that's not all. Most recipes contain "mini lessons" that demonstrate how to make a roast even more delectable, whether with added flavorings, such as rubs and stuffings, or through cooking techniques, such as baking in salt.

ROASTING VS. BAKING

Invariably, there is confusion regarding the difference between baking and roasting, since both take place in the oven. The simplest answer is that baking is done at a lower temperature and won't produce the same browned crust that roasting does. For the most part, *baking* is a term reserved for bread and pastries, and some vegetables, including potatoes. *Roasting* incorporates nearly everything else.

EQUIPMENT: ROASTING PANS

■ A sturdy pan is crucial. It should have a heavy bottom that won't buckle from the heat of the oven and be stovetop safe so that you can make gravy or other pan sauces in it. Disposable aluminum pans are too flimsy to support the weight of most roasts, making them not just impractical but also dangerous. Roasting pans with comfortable handles are very useful for holding turkeys, ham, and other large roasts, which can be a little unwieldy.

■ The roasting pan should be sized appropriately to whatever you are cooking; make sure there are a few inches to spare on all sides. If the pan is too big, the juices will spread over the bottom and evaporate, burning the residue into an acrid mess that will ruin any potential pan sauce. At the same time, a pan that is too small or too high-sided can prevent the roast from cooking evenly.

Best Cuts for Roasting

BEEF

Any of the following roasts can be cut into smaller pieces to serve fewer people.

☐ **Prime rib roast** A whole roast is 7 ribs. For easy serving, purchase a boneless roast with the ribs tied back on, which will add flavor but can be removed more easily after cooking than a bone-in roast. This cut is also called a standing rib roast, half standing rib roast, and a rolled rib roast.

☐ **Shell roast**

☐ **Tenderloin** When cut into steaks, this cut is called filet mignon.

VEAL

☐ **Rack of veal** For an elegant presentation, French the bones (see pages 116–117), or have the butcher do it, and tie the meat into a cylindrical roast. Two racks tied in a circle make a crown roast.

☐ **Top round**

☐ **Boneless loin of veal**

LAMB

☐ **Bone-in or boneless leg of lamb** A boneless cut can either be tied, or stuffed and then tied.

☐ **Rack of lamb** This cut can also be prepared as crown roast; see rack of veal.

☐ **Any roast from the loin,** particularly from the center. The boneless saddle of lamb is a particularly good candidate for roasting.

PORK

☐ **Crown roast**

☐ **Bone-in loin**

☐ **Fresh ham**

POULTRY

☐ **Whole bird**

☐ **Bone-in and boneless pieces (pan roasted)**

FISH

☐ **Whole fish with firm texture,** such as red snapper and bass. Fillets tend to dry out in the oven.

■ Large (10- to 12-inch) cast-iron (or other heavy) skillets are a good option for a whole chicken or pork loin because they conduct heat evenly and are well-proportioned to the size of the roast.

■ The sides on large roasting pans can be as high as 3 inches, but 1 to 2 inches high is better for cooking smaller roasts. Many professional chefs prefer commercial-grade aluminum rimmed sheet pans, available at kitchen supply stores, for roasting (these should not to be confused with regular baking sheets, which are much thinner). These pans are low-sided to allow for even browning, and are particularly effective for roasting vegetables. One caveat: Don't roast meats that produce an abundance of pan drippings (such as duck) on a sheet pan, since the juices can spill over the sides.

OTHER EQUIPMENT TO CONSIDER

■ A roasting rack. Whether you use a roasting rack or not is a matter of preference. Racks are either V-shaped or flat, and they elevate the meat above the bottom of the pan. Lifting the meat off the bottom will keep it from stewing in its own juices and fat, which can result in meat that is soggy or greasy (and limit the amount of pan juices needed to make a good gravy). If you don't have a rack, you can always improvise (and add flavor) by laying the roast on a bed of thickly sliced onions or other vegetables. Remember that whatever ingredients you use will impact the flavor of your pan sauce; thus, a bed of onions will produce gravy that tastes strongly of onions, and so forth.

■ Kitchen twine is useful for tying roasts. See page 119 for instructions on tying, or ask the butcher to tie the roast for you.

■ An instant-read thermometer (for more on thermometers, see page 108) is crucial for monitoring the internal temperature and, thus, the degree of doneness.

■ Some cooks rely on a bulb-baster to keep the meat moist, although a large metal spoon can be used just as effectively to ladle drippings back over the meat.

■ For making gravy, a fat separator—which looks like a measuring cup with a spout—makes it easier to pour off the fat that rises to the top of the pan drippings.

■ A carving knife is a good investment. Sharpen it before every carving, so that you don't damage the texture of the roast when you cut into it. If you don't have a regular carving knife, a serrated knife, which dulls less quickly, will work in a pinch.

RESTING A ROAST

There's more to preparing a tender, juicy roast than the specific cut and the temperature at which to cook it. The last, crucial step is to let the meat rest. The meat will continue to cook after it is removed from the oven, and the internal temperature can rise anywhere from 10 to 15 degrees. For this reason, taking the meat out when it is 10 to 15 degrees below the desired finished temperature should prevent it from overcooking. Most roasting recipes (including those in this book) will take into account this carryover cooking when recommending a temperature at which to remove a piece of meat from the oven. After this initial rise in heat, the meat will start to cool, which will firm up the texture and help redistribute the juices. Cutting into the meat too soon can cause the juices to seep out and collect on the cutting board, leaving the meat dry. A good rule is to rest smaller roasts about 10 minutes, larger ones such as prime rib for 20 minutes before serving.

HOW IT WORKS
The golden brown crust on roasts and other meats is often erroneously referred to as "caramelized." Caramelization occurs when simple sugars (sucrose molecules) are heated above 330°F, which produces the brown hues ranging from amber to chestnut that sugar-heavy foods take on. But foods that are composed of more than just sugar, such as meat, actually gain their burnished tone and rich flavor from another chemical process, called the Maillard reactions, named for Louis Camille Maillard, the French chemist who first documented them in 1910. When carbohydrate molecules (sometimes sugars, but not always) and amino acids (part of the food's proteins) are exposed to temperatures above 250°F, they combine, resulting in the creation of hundreds of new flavors. These flavors can include the bitter notes in roasted coffee and chocolate, the subtle sweetness of a crusty loaf of bread, and the intense savory crust of a well-browned roast.

BRINING
Poultry and pork are naturally low in fat and can easily dry out in intense heat, but brining before cooking will help keep these foods plump and juicy. (See the Perfect Roast Turkey recipe on page 149 for an example.) Brining works best for dry-heat cooking methods, including roasting and grilling. Simply put, brine is a solution of salt and water; sometimes flavorings such as sugar, garlic, lemon rind, herbs, and spices are also added. When meats soak in brine—whether for an hour or two or a couple of days (as some recipes for turkey and other large roasts recommend)—they remain much more succulent once cooked. To understand this process, imagine a whole chicken in a pot of brine. As the bird soaks, the salt interacts with the meat proteins and increases the meat fiber's capacity to hold moisture. In turn, water from the brine is absorbed into the fibers. Once the chicken is

cooked, it will be more flavorful (from the salt, sugar, and other seasonings) and juicier (from the trapped liquid) than it would be if roasted without brining first.

LARDING AND BARDING
These two age-old techniques are other delicious ways to produce a juicy roast.

■ Larding is a method of adding fat—typically lardons, or small strips of lard or fatback—to lean or very tough cuts of meat before roasting. The practice was used much more commonly when meats were tougher than what is commercially produced today. The added fat helps to tenderize the meat and keep it juicy while also imparting flavor. Often, the fat is seasoned with herbs or spices before being injected (literally) with a special tool called a larding needle. A somewhat less involved technique is simply to insert lardons (usually bacon) into slits in the surface of the meat.

■ Originally used with older cuts of meat that had become too dry to absorb any basting liquids during roasting, barding typically involved wrapping meat in fatback. The fatback would melt in the oven, infusing the meat with moisture (and flavor, though that was secondary). Today, barding relies less on straight fat and more on bacon and other cured meats, such as pancetta and prosciutto. Because the meat will not "sear" in the oven when its surface is not exposed to the heat, cuts to be barded are first seared on the stove, then rubbed with herbs before being wrapped (see page 135).

OTHER TIPS FOR SUCCESS
■ Let your roast come to room temperature before you begin cooking. This means letting it sit out for one or two hours. Don't try to take shortcuts here, or you will end up with meat that is unevenly cooked throughout.

■ Season the roast well before cooking to allow the flavors to develop properly. Meat that is generously salted before cooking will taste more complex than meat that is salted once it's out of the oven (which will just taste salty).

■ The challenge of making a roast for any cook—new or experienced—is to not overcook it. Be sure to rely on a couple of well-calibrated thermometers: the oven thermometer and an instant-read thermometer (see page 108).

■ And finally, remember to check the internal temperature early, using an instant-read thermometer, to account for carryover cooking, and to let it rest for the appropriate amount of time before you begin carving.

> ## *Roasting Recipes*

PERFECT ROAST CHICKEN Serves 4

Few dishes are as gratifying to prepare (and eat) as a simple roast chicken. Every cook should have this technique in his or her repertoire. It may seem like an easy feat, but making the best roast chicken—with crisp, golden skin and tender, juicy meat—takes some dexterity. The challenge lies in the bird itself, with the lean breast meat requiring less time to cook than the richer, fattier legs. Moreover, there's the goal of achieving the proper degrees of crispness, color, flavor, and moistness. Many recipes require you to turn and baste the chicken as it cooks, or to start at a lower temperature (presumably to allow the inside to cook through), then finish at a higher temperature (to crisp the skin). The technique

Roast Chicken Tips

> Buy the freshest, plumpest chicken you can find.

> Make sure the chicken is completely dry, inside and out, before you begin (any moisture turns to steam in the oven, which keeps the skin from turning crisp and brown).

> Season generously with salt and pepper to build flavor.

> Truss, or tie, the legs together, so the chicken cooks evenly (and holds its shape for a pretty presentation).

in this recipe relies on "fast and high" roasting, whereby the chicken is cooked in a hot (450°F) oven for the entire time.

Keep in mind that roast chicken is infinitely adaptable, and consider this recipe as the starting point for creating your own variations. Building flavor can be accomplished in many ways. You can stuff the cavity with fresh herbs, such as thyme, sage, or savory; citrus slices; or other aromatics, such as garlic or onion. Or make a rack of sliced onion, then place the bird on top. Spreading butter over the skin makes it even more brown and crisp; tucking butter and herbs under the skin *fig. 3.1* has a similar effect and adds another flavor component. (These steps will also lend much flavor to the pan sauce.) You can roast potatoes, carrots, parsnips, or other vegetables along with the chicken for a practically effortless one-pan dish. Also, you may want to roast two birds, side by side (leaving room between for ample browning); with a roast chicken in the refrigerator—it will keep for days—other dishes are within easy reach. Shred the meat to toss into green salads or to add to soups, casseroles, or pasta dishes. Or combine it with mayonnaise for a sandwich filling.

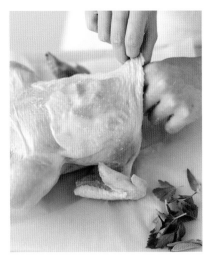

fig. 3.1 PLACING HERBS AND BUTTER UNDER THE SKIN

For chicken
1 FRESH WHOLE CHICKEN *(about 4 pounds)*
  COARSE SALT AND FRESHLY GROUND PEPPER
1 LEMON, *cut into ¼-inch rounds*
4 SPRIGS ROSEMARY
3 GARLIC CLOVES, *crushed*
2 TABLESPOONS UNSALTED BUTTER, *room temperature*

For pan sauce
½ CUP DRY WHITE WINE OR BASIC CHICKEN STOCK *(page 41)*
1 TABLESPOON UNSALTED BUTTER

Prepare chicken Heat oven to 450°F. Remove giblets and liver from cavity; discard (or reserve for another use). Let chicken rest at room temperature 1 hour. Trim excess fat from cavity [1]. Rinse chicken thoroughly under cold water, inside and out, then pat dry [2], making sure the cavity is as dry as possible. Season cavity with salt and pepper, then stuff with lemon, rosemary, and garlic [3]. Rub skin with 2 tablespoons butter [4]. Truss chicken according to directions on page 113 (or tie legs together with twine). Season all over generously with salt and pepper.

Roast Place chicken in a large ovenproof skillet [5] or small roasting pan (filled with a rack, if desired; see page 125). Roast until an instant-read thermometer inserted into thickest part of thigh (avoiding bone) registers 165°F [6], 50 to 55 minutes. Transfer chicken to a platter. Let rest 10 minutes.

Make pan sauce Spoon and discard fat from juices in pan [7]; pour accumulated juices in chicken cavity and plate into pan. Place pan over medium-high heat. Pour in wine [8] or stock to deglaze pan, stirring and scraping up browned bits with a wooden spoon. Cook until reduced by half, then pour through a small fine sieve into a liquid measuring cup [9]. Return to skillet and add 1 tablespoon butter, swirling pan until melted and incorporated.

Carve and serve Carve chicken as directed on page 130, and serve with pan sauce.

Roast Chicken, Step by Step

How to Carve a Chicken

Similar to roast turkey, a whole chicken is a welcome sight at the table, but sometimes you may want to serve the chicken already carved. Here's a way to cut up the chicken so that each serving includes both white and dark meat. Slicing the breast meat into smaller strips ensures there is enough to go around; or you could simply slice the breasts in half on the diagonal.

1 Place chicken breast side up. With kitchen shears or a chef's knife, cut through skin between breast and thigh. Gently pull leg away to expose joint. With scissors, cut through joint to free the whole leg. 2 Cut off wings at joints. 3 With a chef's knife, slice each breast half from bone, working knife along contour of rib cage. 4 Wriggle drumstick to find where it meets thigh, or try to locate with tip of knife. Cut through joint with a firm, downward motion. 5 Slice breast meat crosswise to desired thickness.

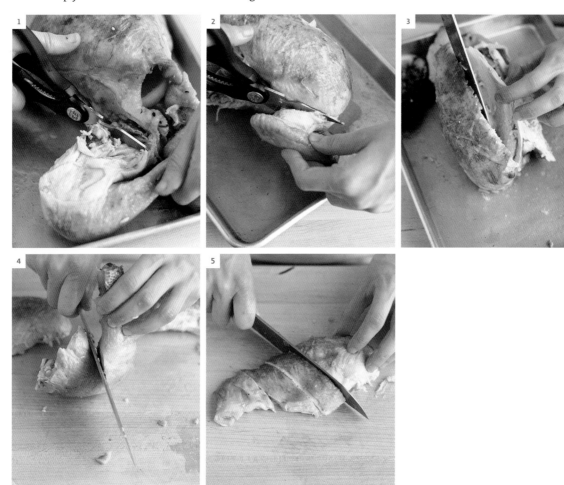

PAN-ROASTED CHICKEN Serves 4

Portion-size cuts of meat or chicken take a relatively short amount of time to cook through (as opposed to, say, a whole chicken or leg of lamb), so you can't rely on the high temperature of the oven to sear the surface of the meat to a golden brown. (In other words, it would take longer for the meat to brown on the outside than to cook through on the inside.) Instead, the meat is first seared on the stove. This recipe is for chicken breast halves (with the skin left on during cooking for added flavor and to keep the meat from drying out), but the method can be used to cook thick pork or lamb chops; skin-on fish fillets, such as bass, salmon, and snapper; or even steaks, such as porterhouse or T-bone, which take too long to cook entirely on the stove. Pan-roasting is frequently practiced in restaurants, as it allows chefs to get a nice crust on the meat and then quickly finish it in the oven.

Choose quick-cooking vegetables and other accompaniments, such as the grape tomatoes here, so that everything is ready at once.

1 PINT GRAPE TOMATOES

16 LARGE BLACK OLIVES, SUCH AS KALAMATA, *pitted and halved*

3 TABLESPOONS CAPERS *(nonpareil), drained and rinsed*

3 TABLESPOONS OLIVE OIL

4 SKIN-ON BONELESS CHICKEN BREAST HALVES *(about 6 ounces each), rinsed and patted dry*

COARSE SALT AND FRESHLY GROUND PEPPER

Prepare sauce Heat oven to 475°F. Toss tomatoes, olives, capers, and 2 tablespoons oil together in a bowl.

Sear chicken Season both sides of chicken with salt and pepper. Heat a large ovenproof skillet over high heat, about 1 minute. Add remaining tablespoon oil and heat until shimmering. Place chicken in skillet skin side down, and cook until deep golden brown *fig. 3.2*, about 4 minutes. Use tongs to flip chicken, then add tomato mixture to skillet.

Roast Transfer skillet to oven and roast chicken until cooked through and tomatoes have softened, 15 to 18 minutes.

Serve Transfer everything to a platter, or divide chicken among plates and spoon some tomato mixture over the top.

fig. 3.2 SEARING THE CHICKEN

PEPPERCORN-CRUSTED BEEF TENDERLOIN Serves 8 to 10

Tenderloin is widely considered one of the best sections of beef for roasting; it becomes meltingly tender during cooking. It's also one of the more expensive cuts, so you'll want to take care to cook tenderloin properly. Fortunately, this is spectacularly easy to do. The tenderloin is first seared on the stove, but this step is optional. (The roast will be just as delicious if it's not seared, but many people prefer the look—and texture—of a nicely browned crust.) If you decide not to sear the roast, you will need to increase the cooking time a bit. Just keep checking the temperature of the meat, until it registers 125°F.

1 WHOLE BEEF TENDERLOIN *(about 4 pounds, and 3 inches in diameter), trimmed and tied, pages 118–119; or have your butcher do this for you)*

OLIVE OIL

1 TABLESPOON PLUS 1 TEASPOON COARSE SALT

1 TABLESPOON WHOLE GREEN PEPPERCORNS, *coarsely ground*

Prepare beef Heat oven to 475°F. Let tenderloin rest at room temperature 1 hour. Pat meat with paper towels to dry, then lightly coat all over with oil. Sprinkle evenly with the salt and ground peppercorns, gently pressing to help them adhere *fig. 3.3*.

Sear beef Set a cast-iron griddle (or large roasting pan) over two burners and heat over high until hot. Carefully rub griddle lightly with oil (if using a roasting pan, add enough oil to barely coat the bottom of the pan) and heat until hot

Ingredients

Green peppercorns have a subtle fruity flavor, but black peppercorns can be substituted. Or you can coat the tenderloin evenly with a coating of finely chopped fresh horseradish, minced garlic, or chopped sturdy fresh herbs such as rosemary and thyme. These ingredients will scorch over high heat, so rub them on after the meat is seared, but before it goes into the oven (let cool briefly, or the meat will be too hot to handle).

fig. 3.3 SEASONING THE BEEF

fig. 3.4 SEARING THE BEEF

but not smoking, then place the tenderloin on the griddle and sear on all sides, about 3 minutes per side *fig. 3.4*. Use tongs to transfer beef to a rack set in a rimmed baking sheet.

Roast Roast until an instant-read thermometer inserted into thickest part registers 125°F for medium-rare, 20 to 30 minutes. Let rest 10 minutes.

Carve and serve Transfer tenderloin to a carving board and slice to desired thickness (about ½ inch is a nice size) before serving.

ROASTED PORK LOIN Serves 6

Lean, tender cuts of pork such as the loin are often roasted on the bone, which adds flavor and helps prevent the meat from drying out during cooking. Boneless pork is also delicious when roasted, so long as you avoid overcooking—a common refrain throughout any lesson on roasting—and build in flavor through various techniques, such as barding with pancetta (page opposite). Because the exterior of the pork will not "sear" in the oven when covered in pancetta, it needs to be browned first on the stove, then rubbed with herbs.

To roast the pork without barding, do not sear it first on the stove; the initial high heat of the oven will promote sufficient browning. To ensure a flavorful outcome, season generously with salt and pepper, then rub with some olive oil along with the herbs. Or make small slits in the top of the loin and insert slivers of garlic in each (known as "larding" with garlic, rather than the traditional fatback or lard; this technique is demonstrated in the leg of lamb recipe that follows).

1 BONELESS PORK LOIN (*about 2 pounds*)
   COARSE SALT AND FRESHLY GROUND PEPPER
1 TABLESPOON FINELY CHOPPED ROSEMARY, PLUS 1 WHOLE SPRIG
   OLIVE OIL
12 OUNCES PANCETTA, *very thinly sliced (about 20 slices)*

Sear pork Heat oven to 450°F. Let pork rest at room temperature 1 hour. Pat pork dry with paper towels, then season lightly with salt (don't oversalt, as the pork will be wrapped in pancetta) and pepper. Heat a large cast-iron skillet over medium-high, then add enough oil to barely coat the bottom of the pan and heat until hot but not smoking. Sear pork until brown on all sides, turning with tongs as each side browns [1], 6 to 8 minutes total. Remove from pan and let cool about 15 minutes (if you try to wrap pork while it's very hot, the pancetta will slip off). Pour (or spoon) off excess fat from pan.

Wrap in pancetta Rub pork all over with chopped rosemary. Lay six pieces of kitchen twine on a clean work surface, putting four in one direction (these will wrap around the pork crosswise so should span the length of the roast) and two across them. On top of the twine, arrange about 12 slices of pancetta, overlapping them slightly, in a rectangle (it should be about 1 inch larger on all sides than the pork). Place pork on pancetta [2] and lay remaining pancetta slices on top, again overlapping them slightly, to completely cover pork. Lay the rosemary sprig on top. To wrap, use the twine to secure them, tying first from end to end and then around [3]. (This will make the roast more compact for more even roasting and hold pancetta in place.)

Roast Return pork to the skillet and then place in the oven. Roast, basting occasionally with pan juices, until an instant-read thermometer inserted in the thickest part registers 138°F, about 40 to 50 minutes. Remove from oven and let rest for 10 minutes.

Carve and serve Remove twine. Slice pork to desired thickness, and serve.

Ingredients

The cooking times provided here are for a 2-pound boneless pork loin that is about 8 inches long and 4½ inches in diameter. Adjust the roasting time accordingly for thinner or thicker loins.

Pancetta, or Italian cured bacon, lends a distinctive flavor to the roast pork, although any type of bacon can be substituted. Have your butcher layer the pancetta slices between sheets of paper to keep them from sticking together; thin slices work better (up to a point— too thin and they will disintegrate under the intense heat of the oven).

You could roast cipollini onions, or some fruit in the same pan for serving alongside; prunes, apricots (and other stone fruit), apples, and pears all pair wonderfully with pork.

> ## Barding a Roast

Lamb Tip

If the vegetables are ready before the lamb is finished cooking, transfer to a platter and keep warm. If the lamb is ready first, return vegetables to the oven while lamb is resting.

fig. 3.5 TRIMMING LAMB

ROAST LEG OF LAMB Serves 8 to 10

Until fairly recently the best lamb was a luxury that could be found only in spring. Today, modern farming techniques make such lamb available year-round, although many of us still keep to tradition, preparing a roasted leg of lamb on Easter or Passover. The term "leg of lamb" generally refers to the hind leg and hip of the animal. Though the cut can be pricey, it is very straightforward to prepare, even for the novice home cook.

For this recipe, the lamb is "larded" with slivers of garlic along with fresh rosemary and thyme, to infuse it with flavor. The pan sauce is flavored with Dijon mustard and red wine, then thickened with a paste of equal parts softened butter and flour. This classic thickener is called beurre manie, and is often used to thicken stews and braises, including the cider-braised pork on page 183.

1 LEG OF LAMB *(about 6 pounds)*

3 TO 4 GARLIC CLOVES, *thinly sliced (you will need at least 50 very thin slivers)*

25 ROSEMARY LEAVES, *plus 1 whole bunch for pan (reserve 1 tablespoon leaves)*

25 SMALL SPRIGS THYME, *plus 1 whole bunch for pan*

4 TABLESPOONS EXTRA-VIRGIN OLIVE OIL

   COARSE SALT AND FRESHLY GROUND PEPPER

4 ONIONS, *peeled and quartered*

8 SMALL CARROTS, *peeled and halved lengthwise if thick*

6 MEDIUM STALKS CELERY, *peeled and halved crosswise*

12 NEW POTATOES, *halved if large*

2 TABLESPOONS ALL-PURPOSE FLOUR

2 TABLESPOONS UNSALTED BUTTER, *room temperature*

½ CUP DRY RED WINE

2 TEASPOONS DIJON MUSTARD

1 CUP BASIC BROWN STOCK *(page 50)*

fig. 3.6 MAKING SLITS IN LAMB FOR LARDING

Prepare lamb Heat oven to 500°F. Trim lamb of excess fat *fig. 3.5*. With the tip of a sharp knife, make about 50 1-inch slits all over lamb *fig. 3.6*. Place a sliver of garlic and a rosemary leaf or small sprig of thyme in each. Rub 1 tablespoon oil over bottom of roasting pan; cover with herb bunches. Place lamb on top. Season lamb with salt and pepper *fig. 3.7*. Cover with plastic wrap; let rest at room temperature 1 to 2 hours.

Roast Toss vegetables with remaining 3 tablespoons oil to lightly coat, and season with salt, pepper, and reserved 1 tablespoon rosemary leaves. Surround lamb with some vegetables, without crowding pan, then spread remainder on a rimmed baking sheet. Roast lamb and vegetables 20 minutes; turn vegetables and reduce heat to 375°F. Roast until meat thermometer inserted near center of lamb, avoiding bone, registers 130°F, for medium-rare 40 to 55 minutes. Transfer lamb and vegetables to a platter; let rest 20 minutes.

Make sauce Knead flour and butter together. Pour off fat from pan; place pan over medium heat. Add wine; boil to reduce by half. Add mustard and stock. Stir; reduce slightly. Strain into a saucepan; simmer. Add butter mixture in small pieces, whisking constantly. Remove from heat; season with salt and pepper.

fig. 3.7 SEASONING LAMB

Carve and serve Arrange lamb on a platter, surrounded by vegetables. Serve sauce on the side. Holding shank (small) end so lamb is at a 45-degree angle, use a sharp knife to slice the meat thinly parallel to the bone, always slicing away from you. Use long strokes rather than a sawing motion for the prettiest pieces. Turn lamb over and slice off meat in the same manner, working carefully around the shank bone (as there is more sinew there).

OVEN-ROASTED POTATOES

Potatoes make a delicious accompaniment when roasted with the meat, soaking up some of the flavorful juices and forming a crisp, golden crust. Before putting the roast in the oven, halve and peel 3 pounds russet potatoes. Place in a large pot of water and bring to a boil. Salt generously and cook potatoes for 5 minutes, then drain well. Score lines lengthwise in potatoes using the tines of a fork (see above). Then roast the meat as directed, adding potatoes to roasting pan after the meat has been in the oven 15 minutes. Drizzle with olive oil if there is not enough in bottom of pan to lightly coat potatoes. Proceed with recipe, roasting the meat with potatoes for another 15 minutes before reducing heat to 350°F; roast until meat is cooked through, turning potatoes after 30 minutes.

PRIME RIB ROAST Serves 8

Prime rib, or standing rib roast, has long been a mainstay at the holiday table (where it is often paired with Yorkshire pudding, a British specialty made from the pan juices and a simple batter of flour, eggs, and milk). As it is expensive, prime rib should be handled with extra care. It is imperative that you have an instant-read thermometer for determining the internal temperature; if allowed to cook too long, the meat will no longer be a rosy pink inside, the optimal color for any high-quality roast. Remove the roast when still rare, as it will continue to cook as it rests, rising as much as 10 degrees in 20 minutes.

Rubbing meat (as well as chicken and fish) with herbs, spices, and a bit of oil will add tremendous flavor. Here, the beef is coated with a mixture of bay leaves, sage, and orange zest, all familiar holiday flavors. Allowing the meat to "marinate" in the rub overnight deepens the flavor even more. A similar result is achieved by simply salting the meat a day or two before roasting, whereby the salt will have penetrated the meat much like a brining solution (page 126).

Larger roasts such as prime rib, crown roast, and a whole turkey are started at a high temperature (450°F) to sear the meat, then the temperature is lowered after 30 minutes to prevent the outside from burning before the meat is cooked through. The exterior won't develop a crust right away, but the initial high heat gives the outside a head start so that it will be perfectly browned in the end.

For rub

15 DRIED BAY LEAVES, *crumbled*

⅓ CUP COARSELY CHOPPED FRESH SAGE LEAVES, *plus several whole leaves for garnish*

½ CUP EXTRA-VIRGIN OLIVE OIL

COARSE SALT AND FRESHLY GROUND PEPPER

⅓ CUP FINELY GRATED ORANGE ZEST *(from 2 to 3 oranges)*

For roast

1 THREE-RIB PRIME RIB OF BEEF *(about 7 pounds), trimmed and frenched*

Prepare meat Stir together crumbled bay leaves, sage, the oil, 1½ teaspoons salt, and the orange zest in a small bowl. Season with pepper. Rub herb mixture all over the beef *fig. 3.8*, coating evenly. Refrigerate overnight, covered. About 2 hours before you plan to cook the beef, remove it from the refrigerator. Place beef, fat side up, in a roasting pan and allow it to come to room temperature. Meanwhile, heat the oven to 450°F.

Roast Cook beef for 30 minutes, then reduce temperature to 350°F and continue roasting until an instant-read thermometer inserted into meat (away from bone) registers 115°F to 120°F (for rare), about 1 hour to 1 hour 15 minutes longer. Let rest 20 minutes.

Carve and serve Slice meat away from ribs, cutting along the bones [1]. Then, slice meat crosswise to desired thickness [2]. Serve, garnished with whole sage leaves.

Ingredients

Prime rib is available at butcher shops and many large supermarkets. Ask for the first cut, which comprises the first three ribs in the short end of the beef, and have the butcher trim the roast and French the bones for you. The word "prime" in the cut's name is not to be confused with the Prime designation of quality from the USDA (page 101).

fig. 3.8 RUBBING WITH HERB MIXTURE

Carving a Rib Roast

SALT-BAKED FISH Serves 4 to 6

The effect of salt-baking is similar to baking (or rather steaming) in parchment paper (*en papillotte;* see page 215): the salt absorbs steam and becomes a hard shell when baked, creating a vacuum inside that seals in flavor and moisture (without making the fish taste overly salty). As when cooking *en papillote,* you can layer the fish with aromatics—lemons and herbs as in this recipe, or ginger, scallions, and lemongrass for Asian flavors—for more complexity.

Since the skin will not have crisped in the oven, you will need to remove it before serving the fish. Before doing this, you might want to invite your guests into the kitchen for a glimpse of the fish in its salt crust (it's an impressive sight) and perhaps to assist you in cracking it open.

fig. 3.9 MIXING SALT CRUST

1 WHOLE FISH *(2 to 3 pounds), such a red snapper or sea bass, scaled and cleaned*

3 POUNDS KOSHER SALT

4 LARGE EGG WHITES

½ BUNCH FRESH THYME, PLUS 2 TABLESPOONS LEAVES

2 LEMONS, *sliced into ¼-inch-thick rounds*

½ BUNCH FLAT-LEAF PARSLEY

4 DRIED BAY LEAVES

Prepare fish Heat oven to 450°F, with rack in center. Rinse fish thoroughly inside and out (until no traces of blood remain). Pat dry with paper towels.

Prepare crust In a large bowl, stir together salt, egg whites, and thyme leaves to combine thoroughly *fig. 3.9*. Pack enough of the salt mixture into the bottom of a 13-by-9-by-2-inch baking pan so it is ½ inch deep. Arrange half of the lemon rounds, the parsley, thyme sprigs, and bay leaves on top of salt to follow the shape of the fish, then tuck the remainder into the fish cavity. Place the fish on top. Pour the remaining salt mixture over fish, then spread it with your fingers to completely cover the body *fig. 3.10* (the tail may stick out of the pan).

fig. 3.10 PATTING CRUST ON FISH

Roast Place in oven and roast for 15 minutes per pound, or 30 minutes for a 2-pound fish. (One way chefs check for doneness is to insert a metal skewer through the salt crust and into the fish in the thickest part, then hold it to the chin, just under lower lip, for 15 seconds; if the metal feels very warm, the fish is ready.) Remove pan from oven and allow the fish to rest 5 minutes.

Serve Gently but firmly tap on the crust with a spoon, then gently break away. Transfer fish to a cutting board. Holding the skin at the tail end with one hand, carefully insert a knife under skin, then run the knife along the length of the fish to remove the skin, being careful not to tear the flesh. Trim the edges to make even, as desired. Lift fish in pieces, discarding bones, and serve.

ROASTED WHOLE FISH

To roast a whole fish (without a salt crust), heat oven to 450°F and rinse and pat dry fish as directed above. Score skin in serving-size portions. Place fish in a roasting pan or rimmed baking sheet; drizzle with olive oil, and season with salt and pepper. Stuff cavity with herbs and lemon slices (as above). Roast 10 minutes per inch of thickness (flesh should flake slightly when done). Serve drizzled with oil and fresh lemon juice.

ROAST RACK OF LAMB Serves 2

Rack of lamb is a good candidate for roasting, as the bones and external layer of fat guarantee that the meat will be flavorful and incredibly juicy. That layer of fat, however, requires more than the heat of the oven to sear, so the lamb is first browned on the stove, just on the one side. Rather than the more traditional mustard and herb crust, this rack is coated with yogurt, which adds subtle flavor and tang. The coating also contains bread crumbs, parsley, mint, lemon, garlic, and olive oil, all of which lend other flavor components as well as visual and textural contrast. For a more straightforward but still delicious version, simply rub the lamb with olive oil and season well with salt and pepper before roasting.

For coating

¾ CUP LIGHTLY PACKED FRESH FLAT-LEAF PARSLEY LEAVES

½ CUP LIGHTLY PACKED FRESH MINT LEAVES, *plus whole sprigs for garnish*

   FINELY GRATED ZEST OF 1 LEMON

1 GARLIC CLOVE

⅓ CUP EXTRA-VIRGIN OLIVE OIL

½ TEASPOON COARSE SALT

¾ CUP FRESH BREAD CRUMBS *(from 3 slices of bread, crusts removed)*

For lamb

1 EIGHT-RIB FRENCHED RACK OF LAMB *(1½ to 1¾ pounds), chine bone removed (for easier carving)*

   COARSE SALT AND FRESHLY GROUND PEPPER

   OLIVE OIL

1 TABLESPOON PLUS 1 TEASPOON PLAIN GREEK-STYLE YOGURT

Prepare coating Heat oven to 400°F. Let lamb rest at room temperature 1 hour, covered with plastic wrap. Puree parsley, mint leaves, lemon zest, garlic, olive oil, and salt in a food processor until smooth, scraping down sides of bowl as necessary. Transfer to a bowl and stir in bread crumbs.

⟩ Searing and Coating Rack of Lamb

Prepare lamb and sear Trim all but ¼ inch fat from lamb, then pat dry with paper towels. Season all over with salt and pepper. Heat a large (12-inch) sauté pan over medium-high until hot, then add enough oil to just coat the bottom of the pan and heat until shimmering. Place lamb in pan fat side down, and sear until browned [1], without turning, 2 to 3 minutes. Remove lamb from pan and let cool 10 minutes. Pour off excess fat from pan.

Coat lamb and roast Use an offset spatula to spread yogurt evenly over browned (fat) side only [2], then top with bread-crumb mixture, pressing gently with your fingertips [3] to adhere. Return to pan, coated side up. Roast until an instant-read thermometer registers 125°F (for medium-rare) when inserted through the eye (or midpoint of one side) of the rack, 18 to 24 minutes. Let rest 10 minutes to allow temperature to rise and juices to redistribute.

Carve and serve Slice rack between bones *fig. 3.11* and serve, garnished with mint sprigs.

fig. 3.11 CARVING ROAST

ROAST DUCK Serves 2

This roasting technique is unique to duck. For the skin to turn crisp, the thick layer of fat that covers the breast needs to be rendered. That's the reason for the slow roasting at a low temperature (300°F as opposed to 450°F for chicken). This allows the duck enough time in the oven to render the fat before the breast meat has finished cooking, producing a duck with crisp, golden skin. To offset its richness, duck is often coated with a tangy glaze. In this recipe, the classic *duck à l'orange,* which put French-style duck on the American map, has been updated with a glaze that combines the flavors of pomegranate, honey, and orange.

For duck
1 WHOLE PEKIN DUCK *(5½ to 6 pounds)*
   COARSE SALT AND FRESHLY GROUND PEPPER

For glaze
¼ CUP MILD-FLAVORED HONEY
¼ CUP POMEGRANATE MOLASSES
2 TABLESPOONS FRESH ORANGE JUICE

For garnish
1 ORANGE AND 1 LEMON, *each cut into eighths*
   FLAT-LEAF PARSLEY SPRIGS *(optional)*

Prepare duck Heat oven to 300°F. Remove neck, heart, gizzards, and any excess fat from cavity and cut away excess skin from the neck area. Rinse duck under cold water and dry thoroughly inside and out. With a very sharp knife, score the skin over the breast in a crosshatch pattern. Cut diagonally into the skin, making sure not to cut into the flesh. Prick the skin with the tip of the knife all over [1], especially in the fattiest areas (this will ensure the best rendering for crisp skin). Season with salt and pepper inside and out. Tie legs together with kitchen twine [2] and fold wing tips behind duck's back.

ABOUT DUCK

Most duck sold in supermarkets is Pekin duck. These ducks were brought to Long Island, New York, from China in the late 1800s, and as a result the area became renowned for duck production. Today, the majority of ducks bred for meat are Pekin and are raised in the Midwest; duck labeled Long Island–style is the same variety.

Muscovy ducks are larger and have a stronger flavor than Pekin ducks, and their livers are often used to make fois gras. Likewise, moulard ducks—which are a cross between Muscovy and Pekin ducks—are often bred for fois gras. Mallard ducks are a wild breed, but are occasionally raised on farms. All of these breeds are much less common than the Pekin duck, and are usually available only at specialty shops.

"Magret" is a term used for the breast meat of a duck raised for fois gras—usually a mallard or moulard duck. In French, *magret* means "the lean portion from a fat duck." Magret is delicious when it is cooked so that the fat renders and the skin becomes crisp, but the meat remains medium rare.

⟩ **Roast Duck, Step by Step**

Roast Place duck breast side up on a V-shaped rack set in a deep roasting pan and roast 1 hour. Remove duck and prick the skin over the breast and the fatty deposits around the thigh area with a sharp knife [3], then turn it over, so breast side is down, and roast for 1 hour more, spooning fat out of pan as needed. Turn duck over again and prick skin in any spots that aren't rendering as quickly as the others, then roast another hour. Prick the skin, turn breast side down, and roast until almost all of the fat has rendered from under skin and duck is cooked through, about 1 hour more. (Total roasting time should be about 4 hours.)

Meanwhile, make glaze Combine honey, pomegranate molasses, and orange juice in a small saucepan and bring to a boil. Reduce to a simmer, and cook until thick and syrupy, about 5 minutes.

Glaze duck and crisp skin Once duck has finished cooking, increase oven temperature to 400°F, turn duck breast side up, and roast 10 minutes. Brush with some of the glaze, and continue to roast until the skin is golden brown and crisp, about 5 minutes more (keep a careful eye through this step because the sugar in the glaze can burn quickly). Let the duck rest for 10 minutes.

Caramelize fruit Heat a skillet over medium-high heat. Brush orange and lemon wedges with some of the remaining glaze and cook until caramelized, about 3 minutes per cut side.

Serve Transfer duck to a platter and surround with caramelized fruit (for squeezing over the duck). Garnish with parsley, if desired. Or carve (see instructions opposite) and then slice thinly; divide among plates, and serve with caramelized fruit.

How to Carve a Duck

Carving a duck employs a method similar to that for chicken (see page 130), in that you want to separate the various parts —legs, thighs, and breast —to extract the most meat, without leaving any behind on the backbone.

1 Place the duck on a carving board, breast side down. Slice down the length of the backbone on both sides. 2 Turn over duck and slice down the breast, following the breastbone. 3 When you get to the thigh bone, sever the joint. 4 Remove the half in one piece. 5 Sever joint between leg and thigh. 6 Separate the breast from the leg quarter and slice breast in half.

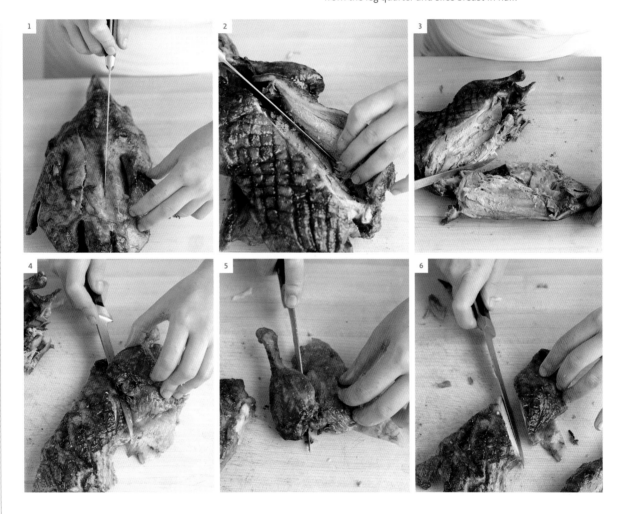

PERFECT ROAST TURKEY Serves 12 to 14

It's a safe bet that every cook will be called upon to roast a turkey at some point in his or her life. Since it's usually a once-a-year endeavor, there's not much room for practice. Instead, rely on proven methods and plan carefully. This is one instance where making sure you have the right equipment (a pot large enough to hold the brining turkey, plus a spot in the refrigerator to place it; a heavy roasting pan; cheesecloth for "basting" the bird as it cooks; and an instant-read thermometer) and sufficient time (a day for brining and then at least 5 hours for bringing the bird to room temperature and cooking it) is crucial. Also, take care of as much as possible in advance, such as preparing the stuffing the day before and refrigerating it overnight, while the turkey is brining. Then it will be much easier when the time comes to focus on the task at hand: roasting the perfect turkey.

Brining the meat ensures that the turkey will be tender and juicy. The brining solution contains aromatics for more flavor, but you could forgo those and simply use a mixture of salt, sugar, and water. For food safety reasons, it's essential that you let the brine cool completely before adding the turkey. Before being put in the oven, the brined bird should sit at room temperature for 2 hours; once it's out of the oven, let it rest for 20 minutes. For a moister bird, cook to 165°F; when taking the temperature, remember that the roast will continue to cook after being removed from the oven.

One more safety note: Never stuff a turkey ahead of time. Warm stuffing should not be put into a turkey until just before roasting. If the stuffing contains warm ingredients, such as sautéed onions or celery, get it into the bird and into the oven as soon as possible. Chilling warm stuffing before cooking it in a turkey is not as safe because the stuffing will, through cooling and heating, spend too much time at temperatures at which bacteria thrive (between 40 and 140°F).

For brine

- 6 QUARTS WATER
- 1¾ CUPS COARSE SALT, *plus more for seasoning*
- 1 CUP SUGAR
- 3 MEDIUM ONIONS, *peeled and coarsely chopped*
- 3 LEEKS, *white and pale-green parts only, coarsely chopped and washed well (page 32)*
- 3 CARROTS, *peeled and coarsely chopped*
- 3 CELERY STALKS, *coarsely chopped*
- 3 DRIED BAY LEAVES
- 6 SPRIGS THYME
- 6 SPRIGS FLAT-LEAF PARSLEY
- 1 TABLESPOON WHOLE BLACK PEPPERCORNS

For turkey

- 1 FRESH WHOLE TURKEY *(18 to 20 pounds), rinsed and patted dry, giblets and neck reserved for gravy*
- ½ CUP (1 STICK) UNSALTED BUTTER, MELTED, PLUS ¼ CUP (½ STICK), *room temperature*
- 1½ CUPS DRY WHITE WINE, *such as Sauvignon Blanc*
- COARSE SALT AND FRESHLY GROUND PEPPER
- CHESTNUT STUFFING *(page 156)*

Ingredients

A fresh turkey is preferable to a frozen one, but if you have to resort to frozen, here's how to defrost it properly: Leave it in its original wrapper, and place it breast side up on a rimmed baking sheet (to catch any juices) in the refrigerator. Be sure to plan ahead. Allow 1 day of thawing per 4 pounds of turkey.

For garnish
> LADY APPLES, FRESH SAGE LEAVES, AND WHOLE CHESTNUTS *(optional)*

For serving
> PERFECT GRAVY *(page 154; optional)*

Prepare brine Combine 2 quarts of the water with remaining brine ingredients in a medium saucepan, and bring to a boil, stirring until salt and sugar have dissolved completely. Transfer to a large pot (at least 5-gallon capacity) and add remaining 4 quarts water. Let cool completely.

Brine turkey Lower turkey, breast first, into the brine. Cover and refrigerate 24 hours. Remove from brine and pat dry with paper towels. Let stand at room temperature for 2 hours. Meanwhile, heat oven to 425°F with rack in lowest position.

Prepare cheesecloth Stir together melted butter and wine in a medium bowl. Fold a very large piece of cheesecloth into quarters so that it is large enough to cover breast and halfway down sides of turkey. Immerse cloth in butter mixture [1] and let soak.

Stuff turkey Place turkey, breast side up, on a rack set in a large roasting pan. Fold wing tips under [2] and season cavity with 1 teaspoon each salt and pepper, then fill loosely with stuffing [3]. Tie legs together with kitchen twine [4]. Fill neck cavity loosely with stuffing, and fold neck flap under, securing with tooth-picks. Pat turkey dry and rub all over with softened butter [5] and generously season with salt and pepper.

Roast Remove cheesecloth from butter mixture, squeezing gently over bowl to remove excess liquid. Reserve butter mixture for brushing. Lay cheesecloth over turkey [6]. Place turkey, legs first, in oven and roast 30 minutes, then brush cheesecloth and exposed turkey parts with butter mixture and reduce temperature to 350°F. Continue roasting, brushing every 30 minutes, for 1½ hours more (tent with foil if browning too quickly). Discard cheesecloth and rotate pan. Baste turkey with pan juices and continue to roast, rotating pan halfway through, until skin is golden brown and an instant-read thermometer inserted into the thickest part of thigh (avoiding bone) registers 165°F. This will take 1 to 2 hours more (start taking temperature after 2½ hours total cooking time).

Serve Transfer turkey to a platter and garnish with apples, sage, and chestnuts, if desired. Set pan with drippings aside for making gravy, if desired. Let turkey stand at room temperature at least 30 minutes before carving (see instructions on pages 152–153).

Perfect Roast Turkey, Step by Step

How to Carve a Turkey

The best way to hold the turkey steady on a carving board is to use your hand instead of the carving fork. A carving fork, while useful for arranging the meat once it is carved, will pierce and tear the flesh and doesn't provide the same grip. Do not use a serrated blade to cut, as it will also tear the flesh. With scissors, cut through the trussing, taking care to remove all of the string.

1 Remove the legs: Holding the tip of the drumstick with one hand, slice down through the skin between the leg and breast. 2 Pull the leg away from the breast, popping out the joint that attaches. Insert knife at joint, and cut to sever leg. Repeat on other side. 3 Separate drumstick from each thigh, cutting through joint. 4 Slice the thigh meat from the bone to remove. 5 Slice the thigh meat into pieces of desired thickness. 6 Slice open the neck cavity with an oval incision that allows you to

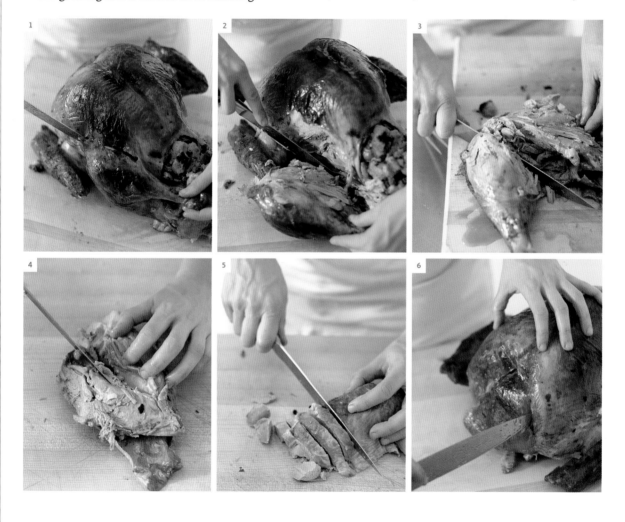

remove the stuffing with the skin intact. 7 Use a long-handled spoon to scoop out the stuffing from the body cavity; transfer it to a bowl for serving. 8 Place the knife horizontally at the bottom curve of the bird's breast, and slice in toward the rib cage to create a "guide cut" (not shown). Slice again down alongside the rib cage at the top. Be sure to cut carefully. 9 Cut vertically through the breast meat to create medallion slices, being careful to preserve some of the skin on each slice. Repeat steps 8 and 9 on the other side of the breast. (Alternately, remove the breast in one piece and cut into slices of desired thickness. 10 Place the knife at the first wing joint, insert the knife point, and twist it to sever the wing. Repeat with the other wing.

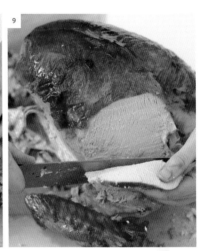

PERFECT GRAVY Makes about 4 cups

To make this delicious gravy, you will need to first make a flavorful stock with the reserved turkey giblets and neck (you can do this while the turkey is roasting). Also, reserve 3 tablespoons of the pan drippings from the turkey roasting pan (after the turkey has been removed to a platter), as well as the pan itself. Pour remaining drippings into a gravy separator and let stand until fat has risen to the top, about 10 minutes, or pour into a glass measuring cup and discard the fat that rises to the top.

For stock

RESERVED GIBLETS AND NECK FROM TURKEY
3 TABLESPOONS UNSALTED BUTTER
2 CELERY STALKS, *coarsely chopped*
1 MEDIUM CARROT, *coarsely chopped*
1 LEEK, *white and pale-green parts only, coarsely chopped and well washed (page 32)*
1 MEDIUM ONION, *peeled and coarsely chopped*
3 SPRIGS THYME
3 SPRIGS FLAT-LEAF PARSLEY
1 SPRIG ROSEMARY
1 FRESH OR DRIED BAY LEAF
5 WHOLE BLACK PEPPERCORNS
1 QUART WATER

For gravy

¾ CUP DRY WHITE WINE
3 TABLESPOONS ALL-PURPOSE FLOUR
COARSE SALT AND FRESHLY GROUND PEPPER

Make stock Trim fat and membranes from giblets, then rinse giblets and pat dry. Melt butter in a medium saucepan over medium-high heat. Cook celery, carrot, leek, and onion, stirring fairly often, until they begin to brown, 7 to 10 minutes. Reduce heat to medium. Add giblets, neck, herbs, peppercorns, and the water. Cover and bring to boil, then reduce heat to medium-low. Cook, uncovered, until reduced to about 3 cups, 50 to 60 minutes. Pour mixture through a fine sieve into a clean medium saucepan and keep warm over medium-low heat. Roughly chop giblets and shred meat from neck with a fork (discard other solids).

Deglaze roasting pan Place reserved roasting pan over two burners. Add wine and bring to a boil, stirring with a wooden spoon to loosen any browned bits on bottom of pan [1]. Remove from heat.

Make gravy Heat reserved 3 tablespoons pan drippings in a medium sauce-pan over medium heat. Add the flour, whisking briskly to combine [2], then continue whisking, cooking until mixture is fragrant and deep golden brown, about 9 minutes. Whisking vigorously, slowly add hot stock [3] and bring to a boil, then reduce heat to a gentle simmer. Stir in reserved deglazing liquid, defatted pan drippings [4], and giblets and neck meat [5]. Season with salt and pepper. Simmer, stirring occasionally, until the gravy has thickened to the consistency of heavy cream [6], about 20 minutes. Strain through a fine sieve into a saucepan (discard solids) and keep warm over low heat. Season with more salt and pepper just before serving.

Perfect Gravy, Step by Step

CHESTNUT STUFFING Serves 10 to 12

You will need to dry the bread cubes overnight; transfer them to resealable plastic bags until you're ready to make the stuffing, up to one day more. (You could also dry them in a 300°F oven for 20 to 30 minutes, if necessary.)

2 LOAVES GOOD-QUALITY WHITE BREAD, *cut into ¾-inch cubes (about 20 cups)*

1½ POUNDS (4 CUPS) FRESH CHESTNUTS

¾ CUP (1½ STICKS) UNSALTED BUTTER

4 SMALL ONIONS, *peeled and cut into ¼-inch dice (about 3 cups)*

1 BUNCH CELERY, *cut into ¼-inch dice (about 4 cups)*

3 TABLESPOONS FINELY CHOPPED FRESH SAGE

5 CUPS BASIC CHICKEN STOCK *(page 41)*

3 CUPS COARSELY CHOPPED FRESH FLAT-LEAF PARSLEY

1 TABLESPOON COARSE SALT

FRESHLY GROUND PEPPER

fig. 3.12 SCORING CHESTNUTS
BEFORE PEELING

Dry bread cubes Spread bread cubes in single layers on baking sheets. Let dry overnight at room temperature, uncovered.

Peel chestnuts Bring a large saucepan of water to a boil. Score chestnuts on the bottom with an X *fig. 3.12*, then boil until soft, about 20 minutes. Drain and let cool slightly, then peel and quarter.

Make stuffing Melt butter in a large skillet over medium heat. Add onions and celery and cook, stirring frequently, until translucent, about 10 minutes. Add sage and cook 3 minutes. Stir in ½ cup stock and cook until reduced by half, about 5 minutes. Transfer onion mixture to a large bowl. Add remaining 4½ cups stock, reserved chestnuts and bread cubes, and the parsley; season with salt and pepper and toss to combine. Proceed to stuff the turkey according to Perfect Roast Turkey recipe (page 149). If not stuffing turkey, transfer to a buttered 17-by-12-inch baking dish. Cover with parchment-lined foil and bake at 350°F for 25 minutes, then remove foil and continue baking until heated through and top is golden brown, 30 minutes more.

STUFFED TURKEY BREAST Serves 6 to 8

Instead of stuffing and roasting a whole turkey, you can use the same two components to create an equally delicious—and arguably more elegant—dish that cooks in less time. This recipe borrows a method commonly used with a breast of veal or leg of lamb (it can be applied to a whole chicken, as well). First, the meat is boned and butterflied, then slathered with a flavorful filling, rolled up into a log (called a *ballottine* in French culinary terminology), and roasted in the oven. This technique actually helps avoid some common roasting pitfalls. Butterflying the meat first makes it an even thickness throughout, and rolling it around a savory filling helps compensate for the lack of bone (bones hold on to moistness during cooking, as well as impart flavor). The *ballottine* is still quite dense, however, so there is a risk of drying out the outer layer before the inside is cooked through. That's why it gets covered in the (first removed and then

replaced) layer of skin, then wrapped and tied in a tight cheesecloth bundle and rubbed with a generous amount of butter before roasting. Removing the bird at 155°F and letting it rise to 165°F upon resting is one last step that keeps it from overcooking. The end result? Tender turkey meat surrounded by crisp, brown skin, and a perfect portion of stuffing in each neat slice.

The Italian-inspired stuffing is made with sausage, rosemary, and dried sour cherries, a refreshing alternative to cranberries but with a similar sweet-tart flavor.

1 BONELESS TURKEY BREAST HALF *(2½ to 3 pounds)*

   COARSE SALT AND FRESHLY GROUND PEPPER

   SAUSAGE AND SOUR-CHERRY STUFFING *(page 158)*

6 TABLESPOONS (¾ STICK) UNSALTED BUTTER, *room temperature*

Butterfly turkey Heat oven to 400°F. Use a slicing knife and your fingers to remove skin from breast *fig. 3.13*, reserving skin. Turn the breast over (so the side that had the skin is facing down) and lay it flat on the cutting board. Holding the blade of the knife parallel to the board, about halfway down, slice into the thickest portion of the breast. Cut along the length of the breast, but not all the way through. Unfold so the turkey opens like a book. Remove the tough piece of cartilage. Cover with a piece of plastic wrap and pound with a meat mallet [1] until the turkey is a uniform thickness (about ½ inch). Season with salt and pepper [2].

Stuff turkey Spread stuffing evenly (about ¾ inch thick) over turkey, leaving a 1-inch border [3]. Starting with one short end, roll into a log [4], completely enclosing the stuffing, and wrap the reserved skin around the breast, over the seam [5]. Season all over with salt and pepper. Roll in a piece of cheesecloth [6] and secure both ends with kitchen twine [7]. Tie twine around the roast in four evenly spaced intervals [8], then rub butter evenly all over cloth [9].

Roast Roast on a rimmed baking sheet until an instant-read thermometer inserted in the middle registers 155°F, 40 to 50 minutes. Let rest for 10 minutes (the internal temperature should rise to 165°F).

Slice and serve Remove cheesecloth and twine, then place turkey on a cutting board and slice crosswise about ¾ inch thick.

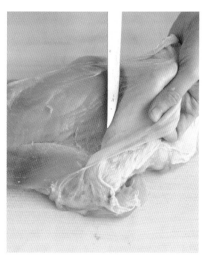
fig. 3.13 SKINNING TURKEY BREAST

SAUSAGE AND SOUR-CHERRY STUFFING
Makes about 2 cups

2 CUPS CUBES FROM A LOAF OF ITALIAN RUSTIC BREAD *(trimmed of crust)*
2 TABLESPOONS OLIVE OIL
1 SMALL RED ONION, *peeled and very thinly sliced (¾ cup)*
2 SMALL GARLIC CLOVES, *minced*
COARSE SALT AND FRESHLY GROUND PEPPER
6 OUNCES SWEET ITALIAN SAUSAGE (ABOUT 1½ LINKS), *casings removed*
⅓ CUP (2 OUNCES) COARSELY CHOPPED DRIED SOUR CHERRIES
1 TEASPOON FINELY CHOPPED FRESH ROSEMARY
⅓ CUP BASIC CHICKEN STOCK *(page 41)*
3 TABLESPOONS COARSELY CHOPPED FRESH FLAT-LEAF PARSLEY

Toast bread Heat oven to 400°F. Spread bread in a single layer on a rimmed baking sheet and toast, stirring occasionally, until golden brown, about 10 minutes. Let stand until cool.

Make stuffing Set a large skillet over medium-high heat until hot, then heat the oil. Add onion and garlic and season with salt and pepper. Cook, stirring occasionally, until onion is translucent, about 3 minutes. Add sausage and cook, breaking it up with the back of a spoon, until cooked through, about 3 minutes. Stir in cherries and rosemary and cook 1 minute more. Pour in stock and stir to combine, then stir in bread, making sure all parts are moistened with liquid. Remove from heat and stir in parsley. Adjust seasoning as desired, before proceeding with Stuffed Turkey Breast recipe (page 156).

Stuffed Turkey Breast, Step by Step

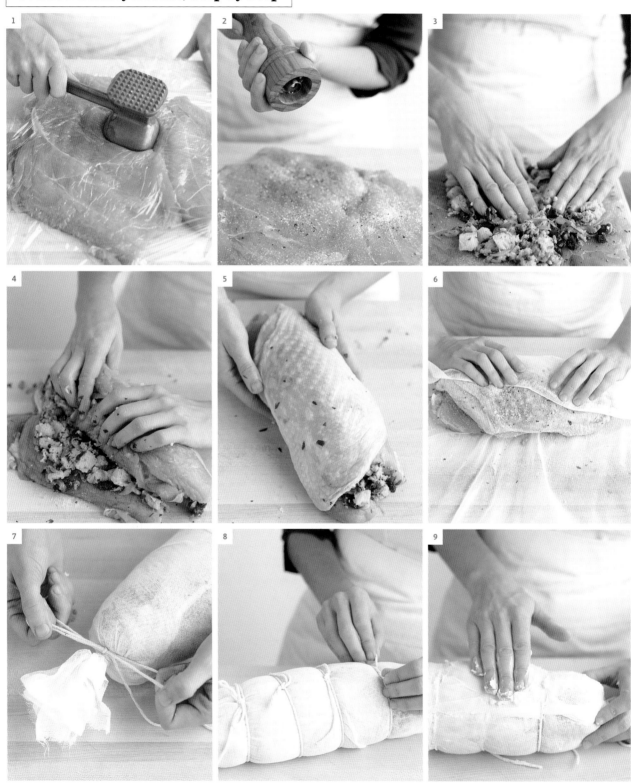

How to Grill

Few culinary activities are as gratifying as cooking over an open fire. Perhaps it has to do with being outdoors and feeling less restricted than in the kitchen. Or it could be the enticing aromas, sizzling sounds, and distinctive marks of the food itself. Whatever the case, and whether you call it a cookout or a barbecue, there's no more pleasant way to entertain than to share a freshly grilled meal with family and friends in the backyard. And all you really need to learn to be successful at grilling is how to gauge (and first build, if using a charcoal grill) a live fire. Then you can accomplish all manner of grilling recipes.

Like roasting, grilling is a dry-cooking method, but rather than relying on the heat of an oven, you cook the food over hot coals or a gas flame. The radiant heat of the grill sears the meat—shrinking the muscle fibers on the outermost layer—and imparts a hearty, smoky flavor as the meat cooks. All specialty grilling equipment and secret flavoring sauces aside, there's really nothing more to it than that. Once you've built your fire (or flipped the switch on a gas grill), you're ready to start grilling.

DIRECT VS. INDIRECT HEAT
Whether you grill over direct or indirect heat depends on what you are cooking. Some aficionados consider the time it takes for the food to cook as the deciding factor; a general rule of thumb is to use direct heat for meats that cook in 20 minutes or less, indirect for anything that takes longer. One of the challenges of grilling, just like other dry-heat methods, is making sure that the meat has a chance to cook all the way through before it becomes charred or overdone on the outside. Choose direct heat for tender, smaller cuts such as burgers, steaks, kebabs, pieces of fish, and sausages, and indirect heat for larger pieces such as whole chickens and turkeys (or bone-in pieces), whole fish, or large fish fillets (such as a side of salmon). Tougher cuts, such as brisket and ribs, are also cooked using indirect heat, but the temperature is much lower than that used for poultry and fish, and the technique is known as barbecuing (for more, see page 176).

Creating direct heat on a gas grill is simple: Set all burners on high for 15 minutes, then reduce to medium for cooking For indirect heat, light the outside burners (for about 15 minutes, to preheat) and place food in the center. Keep the lid down when cooking with indirect heat, except to baste or to take the internal temperature of the food. For details on creating direct and indirect heat on a charcoal grill, see How to Set Up a Charcoal Grill, page 163.

CHARCOAL VS. GAS GRILLS
There are devoted advocates of charcoal and gas grills, and advantages and disadvantages of both types. Charcoal grills take more time to start than gas, but many grilling devotees prefer the flavor and scent that charcoal imparts, caused when smoke envelopes the food. Most charcoal grills are freestanding, classically shaped like a large kettle. Use briquettes or hardwood lump charcoal (made of charred wood, which burns hotter and is better for direct-heat grilling). Avoid instant-light coals or liquid fire starters, both of which leave residual chemical flavorings on the food. Instead, start the coals in a chimney starter, a handled metal cylinder that holds the coals while lighting.

Cooks who choose gas-powered grills prefer the convenience of flipping a switch to turn on the flames. Gas grills are powered by propane tanks or piped-in natural gas. A barrier, such as lava rock or steel plates, separates the flame from the grate and helps disperse the heat. Smoke is created when drippings fall onto the barrier, but this smoke doesn't impart the same strong flavor as charcoal. Deluxe gas grills also come with warming drawers and side burners for steaming and boiling, making them convenient for people who like to cook and entertain outdoors regularly.

Best Cuts for Grilling

BEEF

☐ **Steaks from the loin,** including porterhouse, T-bone, filet mignon, and New York strip steak, which is alternately called shell steak, strip steak, New York sirloin, loin steak, and Kansas City strip.

☐ **Steaks from the rib,** including rib steak—which always comes bone-in—and rib eye, which is boneless.

☐ **Hanger steak** To ensure tenderness, cut the steak across the grain after cooking.

☐ **Flatiron steak** which is a tender cut from the chuck.

VEAL

☐ **Loin chop** After searing, cook thick chops over indirect heat.

☐ **Rib chop**

LAMB

☐ **Loin chops** After searing, cook thick chops over indirect heat.

☐ **Shoulder chops**

☐ **Baby rib chops**

☐ **Rack of lamb** Use indirect heat.

☐ **Butterflied leg of lamb**

PORK

☐ **Tenderloin**

☐ **Loin chops** After searing, cook thick chops over indirect heat.

☐ **Shoulder chops**

☐ **Rib chops**

POULTRY

☐ **Whole small birds,** including chickens. Cook the birds over indirect heat, or spatchcock them and grill over direct heat.

☐ **Bone-in or boneless pieces** Cook cutlets and paillards over direct heat, and bone-in breasts and other thicker pieces over indirect heat.

FISH AND SHELLFISH

☐ **Firm-fleshed fish,** such as tuna, salmon or bluefish, whole sea bass, striped bass, and red snapper. Delicate fish, such as flounder or sole, should be broiled, not grilled.

☐ **Clams, oysters, mussels**

TIPS FOR GRILLING SUCCESS

■ Whether grilling by direct or indirect heat, make sure that the rack is close enough to the coals or flames so that the radiant heat browns the meat, but far enough away so that the heat does not burn the meat.

■ Meat, fish, and poultry will cook more evenly if you bring them to room temperature before placing on the grill.

■ Don't crowd the grill or else foods won't cook evenly. Keep some space between items, and remember to leave an area open in case you need to move something there in the event of a flare-up.

■ Always transfer cooked foods from the grill to a clean platter; never use the platter on which you transported raw food to the grill.

■ Cut excess fat from steaks and poultry to minimize flare-ups—caused when fat drips onto the hot coals or gas fire. If flare-ups start to char the meat, or if the meat is starting to burn because the grill is too hot, simply move the pieces to the outer edge or to a cooler part of the rack, where the heat is less intense and the interior will have more time to cook.

OTHER GRILLING EQUIPMENT

Grilling is made much easier when you are equipped with a few basic tools, including:

■ Basting brush (preferably heatproof)

■ Spring-loaded, long-handled tongs

■ Large offset spatula

■ Wire brush for cleaning the grill

■ Instant-read thermometer

■ Long-handled lighter

GRILL PANS

You can approximate the results of cooking on a grill with a cast-iron or enameled cast-iron grill pan. These pans have ridges that add grill marks to meat and let the fat drip off. They will not produce the same kind of charring and flavor as an outdoor grill, but they are convenient and can be used year-round. You can also use your broiler when grilling is not an option.

GRILL TEMPERATURE GUIDELINES

The proper temperature of a grill is crucial. It's easy to determine the temperature of gas grills, since the burners can be controlled and many models are equipped with built-in thermometers. Charcoal grills can be a bit trickier to gauge, but simply placing your hand about 4 inches above the grate will tell you all you need to know. Here's a handy—and easy-to-remember—way to monitor the temperature of the grill:

- If you can hold your hand for 2 to 3 full seconds (count: one-one-thousand, two-one-thousand) before it becomes uncomfortable, the heat is high (375°–400°F)
- Count for 4 to 5 seconds and the heat is medium-high (350°–375°F)
- Count 6 to 8 seconds and the heat is medium (300°–350°F)
- Count 9 to 10 seconds and the heat is medium-low (200°–300°F)
- Count 11 to 14 seconds and the heat is low (under 200°F)

MARINADES, RUBS, PASTES, AND SAUCES

The rich browned crust on grilled and broiled meats is delicious in itself, but treatments such as marinades, rubs, pastes, and sauces can greatly enhance that flavor. (Brining is another popular flavor enhancer for foods that will be grilled; see page 126 for more on brining.)

Marinades Marinades are essentially oil, which helps baste the meat, and an acid—such as vinegar, citrus juice, yogurt, buttermilk, or wine. The acid in marinades tenderizes and adds moisture—similar to a brine—while the addition of seasonings improves flavor. Following a few basic rules will help ensure that you get the most from a marinade:

- Marinate in a nonreactive container, as the acid in the liquid will react with materials such as aluminum. Glass or stainless steel containers are good options; a heavy-duty resealable plastic bag also works well. Put the meat in the bag, pour the marinade directly into it, and seal. Turn the meat periodically to make sure it is coated evenly.
- Always rub marinade into the meat, including lamb and pork, to help it permeate. There's no need to do this with chicken or fish.
- Refrigerate food as it marinates; never let it sit out at room temperature for more than 1 hour.

- Marinate only for the recommended period of time, allowing meats to come to room temperature (in the marinade) before cooking. Soaking meat for an extended period won't necessarily equal better flavor, as it can take on an unpleasant texture. In fact, marinades that contain citrus juice, vinegar, tomatoes, or other highly acidic ingredients will quickly begin to chemically "cook" meats, particularly seafood (this is how ceviche is made, for example). Marinades that are less acidic, such as those made with yogurt or buttermilk, are generally left on longer to tenderize meat and chicken.
- Most recipes will give marinating times, but here are some general guidelines: (1) Marinate fish and shellfish for no more than 30 minutes (this is especially important for a highly acidic marinade); (2) Marinate chicken, pork, beef, and other meats for up to several hours in highly acidic marinades; less acidic marinades, such as buttermilk-based ones, can be used overnight.
- After removing meat, fish, or chicken from marinade, let excess drip back into container, and wipe off remaining liquid (which can cause flare-ups), along with any bits of herbs or other flavorings.
- Discard marinade after it's been in contact with raw meat or poultry, or boil marinade for several minutes before using to baste or as a dipping sauce (It's better to set some aside at the beginning before combining with meat). The liquid can pick up harmful bacteria from raw meat, fish, or poultry.

For marinade recipes, see page 173.

Rubs and Pastes Dry rubs consist of ground spices, often mixed with sugar, salt, and sometimes herbs. Mix a dry rub with oil, butter, or other moist ingredients, such as crushed garlic or ginger, and you have a paste. The flavors that rubs and pastes impart are much more intense than those from marinades. You need only apply the rub or paste to meat, poultry, or fish, then place in a resealable plastic bag in the refrigerator. Rubs and pastes are usually left on meats anywhere from 2 to 24 hours.

Rubs work particularly well for meats that will be cooked with indirect heat (direct heat can burn the sugar in these mixtures), as well as for fish (since fish cooks quickly enough so that the rub or paste won't burn).

For a recipe for Spice Paste, see page 173.

Sauces "Barbecue sauce" is a term that is used to encompass any sauce served with grilled meats, poultry, or fish. Such sauces contain acidic ingredients like vinegar and tomato, which help cut the fattiness in meats. Sauces should be put on the meat toward the end of grilling, to prevent them from burning. Since the meat will already basically be cooked, and the sauce is just to add flavor, brush meat about 5 minutes before you remove it from the grill or broiler.

For more on sauces, including a recipe for All-Purpose Grilling Sauce, see page 177.

How to Set Up a Charcoal Grill

Lighting Using a chimney starter is the best way to light a charcoal grill. Never use lighter fluid, as its odor and chemical components can penetrate your food. Place a few sheets of crumpled newspaper inside the bottom of the cylinder and fill to the brim with charcoal [1]. Light the paper in several places, which will in turn ignite the coals [2]. After 20 to 30 minutes, when the coals are ashy white, pour the coals in an even layer across the grate.

Creating direct and indirect heat For direct heat, spread the coals evenly over the lower grate. For indirect heat, pile coals on one side of the grill [3]; place meat on the other side. Keep the lid closed (with vents open) to trap heat inside. Or, arrange coals around a drip pan (such as a disposable aluminum pan) with food centered over pan. You will need to replenish the hot coals about every hour.

Cleaning grates Heat the grill about 10 minutes before each use to let the stuck-on bits of food burn off. Then scrub with a wire brush to free the grates of charred debris and residue [4]. Repeat after cooking. The stiff brass bristles rub off grime, while the steel blade tackles cooked-on bits and pieces.

Oiling the cooking surface To keep meat from sticking, use a heatproof silicone brush [5] to coat the grate with vegetable oil (or rub grate with an oiled rag or paper towels, holding with tongs). Apply the oil just before you place the meat on the grill; otherwise it may burn off before you start cooking.

Grilling Recipes

GRILLED STEAK Serves 2

The trick to perfect steak on the grill is simple: Make sure the grill is very hot, clean, and well oiled. In addition to the recipe for porterhouse below, you can successfully grill any of the cuts on the chart (opposite), including New York strip steak (shown above), using this method. Thicker cuts—1 to 2 inches—are typically best for grilling, as they will have a chance to absorb the flavor from the grill before being cooked through; too thick, however, and they will burn before reaching the proper internal temperature.

Grilled vegetables, such as onion and tomato slices, make delicious accompaniments—and are practical, too, since the grill is already heated. The only embellishment you might need is a pat of flavorful compound butter. (For more on compound butters, see page 166.) If you want to serve your grilled items with perfect crosshatch marks, place the most presentable side of the meat down first and let it cook long enough for the distinctive lines to burn into the food (usually 2 to 3 minutes, depending on the heat of the fire or coals). Turn the food 90 degrees for the crosshatch marks. For pristine grill marks, flip the meat just once. Thinner cuts shouldn't require much time to cook after you flip them to their opposite side. Never press down on burgers or steaks with a spatula—this will compress the meat and you'll lose some of the juices that make these meats succulent.

SUNFLOWER OR OTHER NEUTRAL-TASTING OIL, *for grill*

1 PORTERHOUSE STEAK *(2½ pounds, 1½ to 2 inches thick), room temperature*

COARSE SALT AND FRESHLY GROUND PEPPER

COMPOUND BUTTER *(page 166)*

LET STEAK REST AT ROOM temperature 1 hour. If necessary, tie steak for even cooking [1]; wrap kitchen twine around the outside edge, tying ends to secure.

Heat grill to medium-high (see Grill Temperature Guidelines, page 162). When it is hot, scrub with a grill brush and sweep lightly with oil. Season both sides of steak generously with salt and pepper and place on grill [2]. Cover, and grill over direct heat, rotating after 2 minutes for cross-hatch marks, until marked in spots, 3 to 4 minutes per side, flipping once. Move to indirect heat and continue cooking 7 to 8 minutes more per side, flipping once, for medium-rare (125°F on an instant-read thermometer) [3]. Remove from grill and let rest 10 minutes. Remove string with kitchen shears. Top steak with a pat of compound butter, and serve immediately.

GRILLED STEAK TIMES
(for medium-rare preparation)

FILET MIGNON
WEIGHT: 8 ounces (1¾ inches thick)
GRILLING TIME: 7–8 minutes per side, direct medium heat

NEW YORK STRIP
WEIGHT: 16 ounces (1½ inches thick)
GRILLING TIME: 5–6 minutes per side, direct medium heat

RIB EYE
WEIGHT: 10 ounces (1½ inches thick)
GRILLING TIME: 5–6 minutes per side, direct medium heat

HANGER STEAK
WEIGHT: 10 ounces (½ inch thick)
GRILLING TIME: 4–5 minutes per side, direct high heat

SKIRT STEAK
WEIGHT: 8 ounces (½ inch thick)
GRILLING TIME: 4–5 minutes per side, direct high heat

SIRLOIN
WEIGHT: 1½ pounds (1 inch thick)
GRILLING TIME: 7–8 minutes per side, direct medium heat

Grilling a Porterhouse Steak

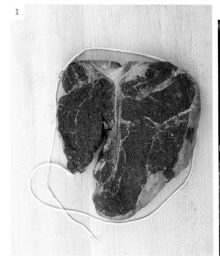

1

2

3

FLAVORING COMPOUND BUTTER
Practically any herb can be blended with butter; here are some common ones to use, along with other flavorful additions. Clockwise from top right: grated lemon zest (fine strips are shown in center), dill, rosemary, olives, capers, garlic, flat-leaf parsley, and oregano.

Compound Butter

The name belies the simplicity of this flavor enhancer, readily made by blending herbs and other aromatics with softened butter. It is most classically affiliated with steaks and chops, but compound butter can be used almost any time in place of plain butter. Try some on poached, steamed, or grilled fish or vegetables; feel free to experiment with different herbs and other flavorings. Compound butters will keep for up to 1 week in the refrigerator or up to 2 months in the freezer (thaw in the refrigerator before using); slip the parchment-wrapped cylinders into resealable plastic bags before storing. Or, chill the logs until firm, then slice off rounds and freeze individual portions. If you plan to serve the butter soon after it's made, simply scrape it into ramekins or other small serving dishes instead of forming it into a log (cover with plastic and refrigerate until needed).

> 1 CUP (2 STICKS) UNSALTED BUTTER, *room temperature*
> 1 TABLESPOON FINELY CHOPPED FRESH CHIVES
> 2 TEASPOONS FINELY CHOPPED FRESH THYME
> 1 TABLESPOON FINELY CHOPPED FRESH FLAT-LEAF PARSLEY
> 1 TEASPOON COARSE SALT

IN A MEDIUM BOWL, stir together all ingredients with a flexible spatula [1] until well combined. Place butter mixture on the center of a sheet of parchment paper [2], then loosely fold paper in half toward you and roll back and forth to form butter into a log. Then, while pulling parchment taut, push with a straightedge, such as the rim of a baking sheet [3], to mold into a neat cylinder, pressing hard to remove any air pockets. Wrap parchment around butter, then twist ends to seal and tie with twine. Refrigerate until firm, about an hour. (Alternatively, transfer butter to ramekins for individual servings.)

Compound Butter, Step by Step

ROSEMARY-OLIVE BUTTER

Substitute 2 tablespoons chopped rosemary and ¼ cup chopped oil-cured olives for the herbs and salt.

DILL-LEMON BUTTER

Substitute 2 tablespoons coarsely chopped dill and finely grated zest from 1 lemon for the herbs.

ORANGE-OREGANO BUTTER

Substitute 2 teaspoons finely grated orange zest and 1 tablespoon finely chopped oregano for the thyme and parsley.

CAPER-LEMON BUTTER

Reduce butter to 4 tablespoons (½ stick) and mix with 2 tablespoons each coarsely chopped fresh flat-leaf parsley and salt-packed capers (rinsed well and drained), 1 tablespoon finely grated lemon zest, and 1 minced garlic clove (about 1 teaspoon).

GRILLED SPATCHCOCKED CHICKEN Serves 5

A flattened, or spatchcocked, chicken will cook more quickly and evenly than when left intact. The parts that take the longest to cook (legs and wings) are conveniently on the edges (meaning they are exposed to more heat), while the quicker-cooking breast is in the center (where it is insulated a bit from the heat).

The origin of the term *spatchcock* is debatable, but one theory has it that it derives from "dispatch the cock," apparently shorthand for "prepare the chicken for roasting over a spit." No matter its past, cooks today understand that to spatchcock a chicken is to remove the backbone and open it like a book. While most commonly used for chicken that will be grilled or broiled, the method also works well for roasting. To further promote even cooking, the flattened chicken is weighted with a foil-wrapped brick while it grills, a technique borrowed from an Italian dish known as *pollo al mattone* ("chicken under a brick").

Brining helps keep the meat tender and juicy, and glazing adds another layer of flavor and promotes browning. In this recipe, citrus marries the brine and glaze, but you can forgo the glaze and make a brine solution of only salt, sugar, and water. A good ratio is 1 cup of coarse salt (never table salt, which will cause the meat to taste too salty) and ½ cup sugar to 1 gallon of water. For best results, brine the chicken for at least 1 hour and no more than 3 hours (any longer and the meat can develop an unpleasant texture).

For brine

FINELY GRATED ZEST OF 1 ORANGE

FINELY GRATED ZEST OF 1 LEMON

3 TABLESPOONS SUGAR

½ CUP COARSE SALT

2 TEASPOONS WHOLE BLACK PEPPERCORNS

2 GARLIC CLOVES, *crushed and peeled*

4 CUPS WATER

4 CUPS ICE CUBES

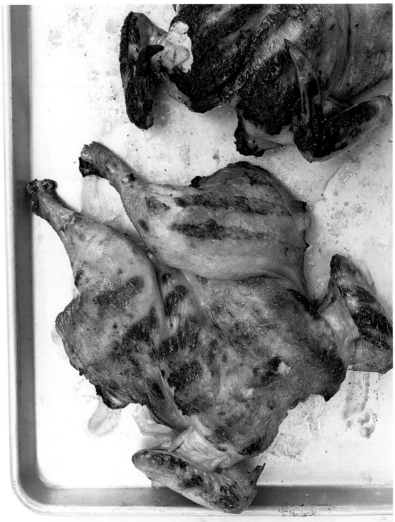

GRILLED SPATCHCOCKED CHICKEN

For chicken
   1 WHOLE CHICKEN *(about 3 pounds), spatchcocked as directed on page 113*

For glaze
   ¼ CUP HONEY
   3 TABLESPOONS FRESH ORANGE JUICE
   3 TABLESPOONS FRESH LEMON JUICE

For grill
   SUNFLOWER OR OTHER NEUTRAL-TASTING OIL

Make brine In a large pot, cook zests, sugar, salt, peppercorns, garlic, and the water over high heat, stirring occasionally, until salt and sugar have completely dissolved. Remove from heat, add ice cubes, and stir until completely cooled.

Brine chicken Submerge the chicken in the cooled brine, skin side down, and allow it to soak, covered, for 1 hour at room temperature or up to 3 hours in the refrigerator.

Meanwhile, make glaze Whisk together the honey and citrus juices in a small bowl.

Grill chicken Heat grill to medium-low (see Grill Temperature Guidelines on page 162). When it is hot, scrub with a grill brush and sweep lightly with oil. Remove chicken from brine and pat dry. Set on grill, skin side down. To flatten chicken during cooking, rest a small baking sheet on top of chicken and place two foil-wrapped bricks (or other heatproof weights) on the baking sheet *fig.3.14*. Grill until skin side is golden brown and releases easily from grate, 8 to 10 minutes. Flip chicken with tongs and brush with some glaze, then cover grill and cook until an instant-read thermometer inserted in thickest part of thigh (avoiding bone) registers 165°F, about 10 to 15 minutes more, brushing with glaze two more times. Transfer to a carving board, skin side up, and let rest for 5 minutes.

Serve Carve chicken as shown on page 130, and serve.

fig. 3.14 WEIGHTING CHICKEN
ON THE GRILL

GRILLING A WHOLE CHICKEN

When cooking a whole (not spatchcocked) chicken on the grill, the challenge is to allow it enough time to cook through before the skin becomes too crisp and charred. The solution is to wait to crisp the skin at the end. Heat grill to high, and start with the chicken over indirect heat, breast side up; cover grill, and cook for 50 minutes to 1 hour. The internal temperature of the legs should register 165°F. If not, cover the grill and continue cooking until it does (check every 5 minutes or so). Then flip chicken, breast side down, and grill over direct heat to crisp the skin, about 2 minutes, rotating the chicken 90 degrees after a minute so the skin will cook evenly. Remove from grill and let rest on a carving board for 5 to 10 minutes before carving and serving.

GRILLED CHICKEN PARTS

Like a whole chicken, individual chicken parts are prone to drying out on the grill if overcooked (160°F for breasts, 165°F for legs). Just be mindful of the times below, and take off each part as it is done. To keep meat moist, leave the skin on or, before cooking, brine chicken pieces for 1 to 3 hours in the refrigerator in a mixture of ¼ cup sugar, ½ cup coarse salt, 8 cups water, and the herbs of your choice. You could also rub them with Spice Paste (page 173) before grilling, or brush them with All-Purpose Grilling Sauce (page 177) about 5 minutes before you take them off the grill. And, of course, you can leave out those treatments altogether and simply season the chicken with salt and pepper. Heat grill to medium-high; pat dry chicken. First sear over direct heat, then finish over indirect (medium) heat. Split breasts require 30 to 35 minutes total, legs 18 to 22, thighs 15 to 20, and wings 11 to 13.

GRILLED BUTTERFLIED LEG OF LAMB Serves 6 to 8

Butterflying a leg of lamb produces a more uniform thickness, furthered by pounding, so the meat cooks evenly from end to end. It also creates more surface area for grilling, so that more of the meat takes on a charred taste. In this recipe, the lamb is marinated to infuse it with herbal flavors, but you could simply season it with no more than salt and pepper before grilling.

3 POUNDS BONELESS LEG OF LAMB *(about ½ half leg), butterflied as directed on page 115*

2 RECIPES FRESH HERB AND GARLIC MARINADE *(page 173)*

SUNFLOWER OR NEUTRAL-TASTING OIL, *for grill*

COARSE SALT AND FRESHLY GROUND PEPPER

Prepare lamb and marinate Cover lamb with plastic wrap. Pound lamb with a meat mallet until it is slightly thicker than 1 inch all over. Reserve ½ cup marinade. Place lamb in a large resealable plastic bag and add remaining marinade, then force out air and seal [1]. Massage the lamb a bit to coat it thoroughly. Set bag on a baking sheet (in case of leaks) in the refrigerator and marinate lamb 8 to 24 hours, turning bag occasionally.

Grill Remove lamb from bag and wipe off and discard as much marinade as possible so surface is dry. Let lamb rest at room temperature 1 hour. Meanwhile, heat grill to medium-high (see Grill Temperature Guidelines, page 162). When it is hot, scrub with a grill brush and sweep lightly with oil. Season lamb on both sides with salt and pepper. Grill (press down with tongs initially to make sure the lamb is evenly in contact with grill [2]) until charred in spots, 5 to 6 minutes, rotating the lamb 90 degrees halfway through. Flip the lamb, then brush with some reserved marinade [3] and cook until an instant-read thermometer inserted in the thickest part registers 125°F, again rotating it 90 degrees halfway through. This will take 5 to 6 minutes more. Let lamb rest 5 minutes.

Serve Slice lamb and serve with remaining reserved marinade on the side.

Grilled Butterflied Leg of Lamb, Step by Step

THYME, SHALLOT, AND LEMON

SPICE PASTE

INDIAN YOGURT

SPICY HOISIN

FRESH HERB AND GARLIC

ROSEMARY BALSAMIC

EXTRA CREDIT
Marinades

Sometimes all that's desired is to give meat a light coat of oil and some salt and pepper before grilling it. If it is of superior quality, the meat will need no further enhancement. But the grilling season is long, so the procedure could do with a little variety. Marinades (and spice pastes) act as tenderizers and flavor enhancers; reserve some for brushing on the meat as it comes off the grill, or to serve on the side for drizzling. (For more information about marinades, see page 162.)

MARINATING TIME GUIDELINES
Shellfish: 20 minutes
Fish fillets: 30 minutes for thin and flaky, 1 hour for thick and fatty
Beef, chicken, game, lamb, and pork: 6 to 24 hours

FRESH HERB AND GARLIC MARINADE
This marinade is especially good with chicken and lamb, imparting bright flavor and helping to keep the meat moist.

Whisk together 1 cup **extra-virgin olive oil**, 1 cup coarsely chopped **mixed fresh herbs** (such as oregano, thyme, savory, flat-leaf parsley, and rosemary; chop extra and reserve for garnish), 12 coarsely chopped **garlic cloves**, finely grated zest of 2 **lemons**, 1½ teaspoons **coarse salt**, and 1 teaspoon **freshly ground pepper** in a nonreactive dish. Makes enough for 2½ pounds meat or fish plus more for brushing. Refrigerate until ready to use, up to 1 day.

THYME, SHALLOT, AND LEMON MARINADE
This French-style marinade pairs nicely with almost anything, particularly shellfish and fish fillets.

Whisk together 3 tablespoons **fresh lemon juice**, 3 tablespoons **dry white wine**, 2 tablespoons **extra-virgin olive oil**, leaves from 1 bunch **fresh thyme** (12 to 15 sprigs), 2 thinly sliced **shallots**, and 1 **lemon**, sliced into ¼-inch rounds in a shallow nonreactive dish. Makes enough for 2 pounds of meat or fish. Refrigerate until ready to use, up to 1 day.

ROSEMARY BALSAMIC MARINADE
This goes remarkably well with steak.

Whisk together ½ cup **balsamic vinegar**, 2 tablespoons **extra-virgin olive oil**, 6 coarsely chopped **garlic cloves**, 6 coarsely chopped **rosemary sprigs**, and ½ teaspoon **freshly ground pepper** in a shallow nonreactive dish. Makes enough for 2 pounds of meat. Refrigerate until ready to use, up to 3 days.

SPICY HOISIN MARINADE
This Asian-inspired marinade pairs perfectly with pork— turning into a sticky, spicy, sweet glaze when cooked—but can also be used with chicken or beef.

Whisk ¼ cup **soy sauce**, ¼ cup packed **dark brown sugar**, 2 tablespoons **sherry vinegar**, 2 tablespoons **fresh orange juice**, 2 tablespoons **hoisin sauce**, 2 tablespoons **freshly grated ginger**, 2 minced **garlic cloves**, 2 **scallions** (white and green parts thinly sliced; chop 1 extra for garnish), 1 tablespoon **dry mustard**, 1 teaspoon **crumbled dried chile** or red pepper flakes, and finely grated zest of 1 **orange** in a nonreactive bowl. Cook meat as desired, basting with marinade during first half of cooking to create a glaze. Makes enough for 2½ pounds of meat. Refrigerate until ready to use, up to 3 days.

INDIAN YOGURT MARINADE
When making Pan-Fried Chicken Cutlets (page 269), increase the coriander seeds to 2 tablespoons and the fennel seeds to 2 teaspoons.

Toast 1 tablespoon plus 1 teaspoon **coriander seeds**, 1 teaspoon **fennel seeds**, 2 teaspoons **mustard seeds**, and 2 **green cardamom pods** in a dry skillet over medium heat until they darken slightly and become fragrant, about 1½ minutes. Grind to a fine powder in a spice grinder (or clean coffee grinder), then puree in a blender with 6 coarsely chopped **garlic cloves**, 2 teaspoons **coarse salt**, finely grated zest and juice of 2 **limes**, 4 coarsely chopped small **fresh chiles** (about 2 tablespoons), 1 coarsely chopped medium **white onion** (about 1 cup), and ½ cup **plain yogurt** to form a smooth paste. Transfer to a nonreactive dish. Makes enough for 1 pound of meat. Refrigerate until ready to use, up to 3 days.

SPICE PASTE
This garlicky paste, made with dark-brown sugar and spicy chile powder, imparts much flavor as well as color to grilled meat, including the ribs on page 176.

In a bowl, mix together 2 tablespoons each **paprika, ancho chile powder**, and **dark-brown sugar**; 1 tablespoon plus 1 teaspoon **coarse salt**; 2 teaspoons **dried oregano** (preferably Mexican); a pinch of **ground cinnamon**; 5 minced **garlic cloves**; and ¼ to ½ cup sunflower or other neutral-tasting **oil**. Refrigerate until ready to use, up to 2 days. Makes enough for 2 to 3 pounds of meat.

GRILLED SIDE OF SALMON Serves 6 to 8

Many cooks prefer to grill larger cuts of fish rather than smaller fillets, since the extra heft helps to trap in moisture and flavor. This recipe calls for a large piece from a side of salmon to be grilled on a bed of citrus and herbs, which helps keeps the fish from sticking to the grate. Instead of a crisp skin, you'll get plenty of bright flavors from the aromatics. Use this method to grill other types of fish, too, whether whole sides or smaller fillets (even skinless ones). The herbs can vary; dill, marjoram, parsley, and thyme are all particularly lovely with fish.

SUNFLOWER OR OTHER NEUTRAL-TASTING OIL, *for grill*

4 LEMONS, *sliced into ¼-inch rounds*

2 ORANGES, *sliced into ¼-inch rounds*

1 SMALL BUNCH FRESH BASIL

½ BUNCH FRESH OREGANO

1 PIECE WILD SALMON, *3 pounds, 2 to 2½ inches thick, preferably center-cut*

COARSE SEA SALT AND FRESHLY GROUND PEPPER

Prepare grill Heat the grill to medium (see Grill Temperature Guidelines, page 162). Once it is hot, scrub grates with a grill brush and lightly sweep with oil.

Grill fish Make a bed for the fish by first arranging the lemon and orange slices on the grate and then scattering the herbs on top [1]. Lay the salmon skin side down over the herbs and season with sea salt and pepper [2]. Cover the grill and cook salmon 20 to 30 minutes, depending on desired degree of doneness.

Serve Use two large spatulas [3] to carefully transfer the salmon, citrus, and herbs to a large platter or board. Serve hot, room temperature, or cold (cover with plastic wrap and refrigerate up to 24 hours).

Ingredients

A 3-pound piece of salmon is just right for this method. Anything larger may be unwieldy. If you can find only larger sides, have the fishmonger cut away the excess weight from the tail.

Sea salt, such as Maldon or fleur de sel, is best for seasoning fish and shellfish.

> Grilled Side of Salmon, Step by Step

BARBECUED BABY BACK RIBS Serves 4 to 6

Grilling baby back ribs is an exercise in patience, requiring low and slow heat to break down the tough connective tissue for a tender result (similar to what happens for braising; see pages 180–181). This method is called barbecuing, created by maintaining a constant stream of hot smoke over, rather than directly under, the ribs. To do this, the coals are heaped on one side and the ribs placed on the other *fig 3.15*; the opened vents, positioned over the ribs, draw the heat from the coals to the ribs. The temperature of the grill should be carefully monitored so that it never gets higher than 300°F; a basic oven thermometer set near the ribs will prove indispensable here. To cool it down quickly, open the lid.

> SPICE PASTE *(page 173)*
> 2 RACKS BABY BACK RIBS *(1½ to 2 pounds each)*
> SUNFLOWER OR OTHER NEUTRAL-TASTING OIL, *for grill*
> ALL-PURPOSE GRILLING SAUCE *(recipe follows)*

Marinate ribs Rub paste evenly over ribs and wrap well in plastic. Let marinate in the refrigerator for 6 to 12 hours.

Prepare grill Open the bottom vents and fill a chimney starter to the top with charcoal briquettes and allow them to burn until all are coated with a fine gray ash. Scrub grates with a grill brush and sweep lightly with oil. Push charcoal to one side of the grill and set the ribs on the opposite side. Rest an oven

ABOUT BARBECUE

The terms *grilling* and *barbecuing* are often used interchangeably, but there is an important (if little known) distinction between the two techniques. Barbecuing uses indirect heat at a very low temperature—even lower than indirect heat grilling—to slowly cook food with a combination of heat and smoke. The slow and low heat of barbecuing is ideally suited for large, tougher cuts of meat, such as whole briskets and racks of ribs. Grilling, on the other hand, uses a more intense direct heat that browns the meat, but that doesn't add the depth of smokiness that distinguishes true barbecue.

thermometer near the ribs. Cover the grill, then open the vents and position them over the ribs (this draws heat from coals to ribs).

Grill ribs After 20 minutes, check on the temperature inside the grill. The thermometer should read 275°F to 300°F (open lid, if necessary, to lower temperature). Let the ribs cook like this for a total of about 2 hours, turning them over and rotating 90 degrees every 30 minutes and adding more coals after 1 hour. If the ribs seem to be getting too dark too soon, tent them with foil. After 2 hours, the ribs should be cooked through (to test doneness, lift and hold the rack with tongs — they should bend and start to break away at the bend point) and nicely charred in spots; if not, continue cooking and check frequently until they are ready (this could take up to about 30 minutes more). Brush ribs with some sauce and cook 15 minutes more. Transfer ribs to a platter and let rest 5 minutes before serving with remaining sauce.

ALL-PURPOSE GRILLING SAUCE Makes about 3 cups

As its name implies, this sauce is extremely versatile — you can brush it on chicken (whole or parts), ribs, steak, even vegetables. A small amount of butter is added at the end for a smooth finish; feel free to leave it out, especially if you're using the sauce with a particularly fatty piece of meat.

2 TABLESPOONS SUNFLOWER OR OTHER NEUTRAL-TASTING OIL

1 MEDIUM YELLOW ONION, *cut into small dice*

3 GARLIC CLOVES, *crushed and peeled*

1½ CUPS TOMATO JUICE

1 CAN (8 OUNCES) TOMATO SAUCE

½ CUP DISTILLED WHITE VINEGAR

½ CUP WATER

2 TABLESPOONS UNSULFURED MOLASSES

1 TABLESPOON ANCHO CHILE POWDER

1 TEASPOON MUSTARD POWDER

2 TABLESPOONS WORCESTERSHIRE SAUCE

2 TABLESPOONS PACKED DARK-BROWN SUGAR

½ TEASPOON TOASTED CUMIN SEEDS, *finely ground*

½ TEASPOON DRIED OREGANO, *preferably Mexican*

1 TEASPOON COARSE SALT

¼ TEASPOON FRESHLY GROUND BLACK PEPPER

1 JALAPEÑO CHILE, *halved lengthwise (remove ribs and seeds for less heat)*

2 TABLESPOONS UNSALTED BUTTER, *room temperature (optional)*

HEAT THE OIL in a medium saucepan over medium heat. Cook onion until softened, stirring occasionally, about 3 minutes; add garlic and cook until fragrant. Add remaining ingredients except butter; stir several times to blend. Bring to a simmer; partially cover and cook over low heat until thick, about 1 hour.

Remove and discard jalapeño. Puree sauce (with butter, if desired) in a food processor or blender until smooth. Serve warm or at room temperature. The sauce can be refrigerated in an airtight container up to 1 week.

fig. 3.15 GRILLING OVER INDIRECT HEAT

Equipment

A 22-inch round charcoal grill is ideal for grilling ribs, as it will allow enough room for both hot and cool spots created by the charcoal. An 18-inch grill will also work, but you will need to start with fewer briquettes and to replenish them more frequently during cooking. Either way, they must be tended to with a watchful eye. Although it burns hotter than briquettes, hardwood lump charcoal can be used instead: Fill a chimney starter three-fourths full and add a handful of coals every 20 minutes; if the temperature in the grill rises too high, wait about 30 minutes before adding more coals. The trick is to know when the coals are starting to burn out, which can cause a significant decline in temperature; adding more coals at the right time will help maintain steady heat.

PICO DE GALLO

FIG AND PORT CHUTNEY

TOMATO PEACH
CHUTNEY

TOMATILLO SALSA

LEMON AND OLIVE RELISH

PEAR CHUTNEY

> EXTRA CREDIT
> ## Salsas, Chutneys, and Relishes

Whether plainly seasoned or rubbed with a fiery paste, grilled meat, chicken, and fish can be enhanced by fruity salsas, chutneys, and relishes with contrasting tastes, textures, and temperaments. The salsas and relish are best served the same day; chutneys will keep for a week or two in the refrigerator. Let cool completely before storing.

PICO DE GALLO

Toss together ½ small **white onion**, cut into small dice, 4 **plum tomatoes**, cut into small dice, 3 finely chopped **jalapeños** (remove seeds and ribs for less heat), ¼ cup coarsely chopped **cilantro**, 1 minced **garlic clove**, 2 tablespoons **fresh lime juice**, and 1 teaspoon **coarse salt** (or more to taste). Let sit at room temperature for 1 hour before serving to allow the flavors to meld. Makes 4 cups.

LEMON AND OLIVE RELISH

Cut 1 **lemon** (unpeeled; preferably organic) into ½-inch dice. Trim away peel and white pith from 7 more lemons and suprême these (page 34). Heat ½ cup **extra-virgin olive oil** in a saucepan over medium-low heat. Cook 1 medium **red onion**, diced, and reserved diced lemon until onion is translucent, about 4 minutes, stirring occasionally. Stir in ¼ cup plus 2 tablespoons **sugar** and cook until it melts, about 30 seconds. Cool 5 minutes, then scrape into a medium bowl and add the lemon segments and 4 ounces pitted and chopped **Niçoise or Gaeta olives**. Season with **coarse salt** and **freshly ground pepper** (about a half teaspoon each) and gently stir enough to combine but without breaking up the lemon sections too much. Let cool at least 30 minutes before serving. To make a mixed citrus relish, replace some of the lemon with lime or orange segments. Makes 2 cups.

TOMATILLO SALSA

Heat oven to 350°F, then heat a large skillet over high heat. Husk and rinse 1½ pounds **tomatillos**, then cook until nicely charred, about 6 minutes, turning them over about halfway through. Transfer pan to oven and cook until tomatillos soften slightly, about 10 minutes. Meanwhile, roast 1 **jalapeño** over a gas burner, turning with tongs as each side blisters and blackens. When cool enough to handle, slice jalapeño in half lengthwise (scoop seeds from one half for less heat, if desired). Combine jalapeño with ½ bunch **cilantro**, 1 coarsely chopped **onion**, and 2 teaspoons **coarse salt** in a blender. Add half the tomatillos and puree until smooth, then pour into a bowl. Let the other half cool slightly and coarsely chop (slightly larger than ¼ inch). Scrape into the bowl and stir to combine, then taste and add more salt as desired. Makes 3 cups.

TOMATO PEACH CHUTNEY

Heat 2 tablespoons **sunflower or other neutral-tasting oil** in a medium sauté pan over medium heat, then add 1 thinly sliced small **onion**, 2 thinly sliced **garlic cloves**, 2 teaspoons peeled and thinly sliced **fresh ginger** (from a ½-inch piece), and ½ teaspoon **coarse salt**. Cook, stirring occasionally, until onion is translucent, about 3 minutes. Add ¼ cup **sugar**, 1 **dried bay leaf**, 2 **peaches** (cut into ½-inch dice), and 1 **tomato** (also cut into ½-inch dice). Bring to a boil, then reduce heat and simmer, partially covered, until fruit is tender but not falling apart (the chutney should have a loose jamlike consistency), 15 to 20 minutes. Stir in 1 tablespoon **white vinegar** and season with **coarse salt** and **freshly ground pepper**. Makes 1½ cups.

FIG AND PORT CHUTNEY

Combine 5 ounces **dried black figs**, quartered (about ¾ cup), 5 ounces **dried white figs**, quartered (about ¾ cup), 1 **cinnamon stick**, 2 strips (1 by 2 inches) **lemon rind**, 2 **dried bay leaves**, 2 cups **ruby Port**, ½ cup **water**, 1 tablespoon **sugar**, 4 tablespoons (½ stick) **unsalted butter**, and ¼ teaspoon each **coarse salt** and **freshly ground pepper** in a pot and bring to a boil. Reduce heat and simmer, partially covered, until the liquid has reduced and the chutney has a loose jamlike consistency, 45 to 60 minutes. Makes 1½ cups.

PEAR CHUTNEY

Combine 3 **Bosc pears**, cored and each cut into 12 wedges, 1 thinly sliced small **red onion**, 2 tablespoons julienned peeled **fresh ginger** (from a 1-inch piece), 2 thinly sliced **garlic cloves**, 1 **jalapeño**, halved lengthwise (remove seeds for less heat) and cut into julienne, 1 dried **bay leaf**, 1 teaspoon **coarse salt**, 1 cup **rice-wine vinegar**, and ½ cup packed **dark-brown sugar** in a saucepan and bring to a boil over medium-high heat. Reduce heat and simmer, partially covered, until chutney has a loose jamlike consistency, 30 to 35 minutes. Makes 2½ cups.

LESSON 3.3
How to Braise and Stew

Braising and stewing are a busy cook's faithful friends. These cooking methods don't require much hands-on time; nor do they rely on special equipment or skills. Yet both techniques produce hearty, consistently delicious dishes that belie their ease. And because they work best with cuts of meat that are generally inexpensive, they are good building blocks for beginning cooks, since mistakes are not quite as disheartening as when made with more costly cuts.

The term *braise* has its roots in the Old French word *brese*, meaning "ember," and the Germanic *bhreu*, roughly translated as "boil" or "bubble," and originates from a time when cooks took advantage of the dying embers of their kitchen fires by tucking a covered pot filled with meat and vegetables into the coals. The most significant difference between braising and stewing is that meat, fish, and poultry for stews is cut into 1- to 3-inch pieces (depending on the recipe) and the cooking liquid entirely covers what's in the pot, while most braised meats are cooked in larger pieces and only partially submerged in the braising liquid. Just as in the past, today most braises and stews are cooked for a long period of time at a low temperature.

The best cuts for braising and stewing come from harder-worked muscle groups—the leg, shoulder, breast, and neck areas—of the animal, which are more flavorful. These cuts also have more collagen and intramuscular fat than tender cuts, which helps keep the meat moist. As the juices from the meat mingle with the aromatic vegetables, seasonings, and cooking liquid, a wonderfully rich sauce develops, coaxing a depth of flavor from the tough cuts that no other cooking method can equal. Brisket, chuck, and rump roasts tend to be good for braising, as well as for stewing. Look for cuts with a lot of fat marbled in them. The heavily worked thighs and legs of poultry also braise well.

EQUIPMENT

All you need for most braises and stews is a heavy pot with a tight-fitting lid to keep the cooking liquid from evaporating. When braising, the pot should be just big enough to snugly hold the meat and liquid. A vessel with too much surface area will allow the liquid to condense on the sides and won't leave enough liquid simmering around the meat and vegetables. Make sure the pot you use is stovetop and oven safe, so that you can use it for browning and oven braising, if necessary. Many cookware manufacturers sell specialty braiser pans, but any sturdy stainless steel pan or enameled cast-iron Dutch oven with a lid will do. Most of the braises and stews in this book were cooked in enameled cast iron, but if you have a pot made of copper, which conducts heat beautifully, by all means use it.

BRAISING LIQUIDS

Braises and stews most often begin with a mirepoix (for more on mirepoix, turn to page 41), but their flavor also depends on the cooking liquid. Nearly any liquid can be used—the most common are stock, broth, wine, beer, and water. If using stock, remember that homemade is always preferable to canned; the store-bought variety can cause your reduced braising or stewing liquid to taste excessively salty, and won't have the thickening power of gelatin-rich homemade stock. Once you've mastered the technique, you can experiment with other cooking liquids, just as you can substitute other seasonings and mirepoix.

The key to attaining fork-tender meat is to keep the liquid in your pot at a simmer, For braises, keep the cooking liquid as high as one-third to one-half of the way up the side of the meat, fish, or poultry; for stews, the liquid should cover the meat. As the cooking liquid and meat juices simmer, the liquid will naturally reduce, which will thicken the sauce and intensify the flavor. If your liquid reduces too much while cooking, add a little more liquid to the pot.

Best Cuts for Braising and Stewing

BEEF

☐ **Chuck** Look for a well-marbled cut from the center section with a little exterior fat.

☐ **Blade roast** This cut comes from the shoulder section, and is alternately called a shoulder roast or cross rib.

☐ **Brisket** Often divided into two cuts, the best piece of brisket for braising is the first cut; it should be well-marbled and have ¼ to ½ inch of exterior fat. Brisket is best for braising, not stewing.

☐ **Short ribs**

☐ **Bottom round** Look for the first cut; the last cut is too tough. The bottom round is particularly good for stewing.

VEAL

☐ **Any cut from the shoulder** Look for a solid piece with no jagged edges.

☐ **Shank** Traditionally used in the Italian dish osso buco.

LAMB

☐ **Any cut from the shoulder,** which is sometimes called the neck.

☐ **Shanks** These are best for braising, not stewing.

PORK

☐ **Any cut from the shoulder** (the shanks are best for braising, not stewing).

☐ **Spare ribs** These are best for braising, not stewing.

POULTRY

☐ **Bone-in or boneless thighs and legs**

☐ **Whole bird cut into pieces**

FISH

☐ **Any firm-fleshed fish that won't fall apart while cooking** Mild-flavored white fish, such as red snapper, bass, halibut, porgy, pompano, and monkfish, are particularly good for braising and stewing. More strongly flavored fish, such as tuna and salmon, can also be braised.

HOW IT WORKS

Braising and stewing are cooked by water convection, which means that the molecules in the hot water transfer their energy to the cooler meat that is being braised or stewed. This means that the heat in the pot will never rise above the boiling point, 212°F at sea level. Meats won't brown at this low temperature, which is why it is usually important to sear the meat on the stovetop first. A good sear will add a rich flavor to the sauce. As it cooks, the internal temperature of the meat rises and the juices eventually seep through the seared outer layer, mixing with the cooking liquid. At this point, if you open the pot, you'll probably find that the meat looks compact and shriveled, and is noticeably smaller than when you first put it in. Some people mistakenly assume that they've overcooked the meat at this point and take it out of the oven. But the meat is still in the process of cooking to a tender finish. As it continues to braise, the cooking liquid will seep back into the meat, infusing it with moisture. When the meat is done, you can stick a fork into its thickest part with little resistance. If you are not sure, be patient and continue cooking. You will know it has reached the right consistency when it is silky, can be shredded easily, or is falling off the bone (if there is one).

THICKENING AGENTS

Many braises and stews benefit from thickeners other than collagen. These include simply adding flour to sautéing vegetables before adding the liquid and browned meat to the pot, and adding more complex thickeners, such as roux (flour cooked in fat, usually butter) or beurre manié (equal parts flour mixed with softened butter) later in the process. To make an even richer stew, some recipes, such as the veal stew on page 205, call for more than one thickener, each added at separate points. In that recipe, a primary thickener is added about an hour after the stew starts cooking, and then a liaison of egg and cream is added when the stew is almost finished. Lighter stews can be thickened with pureed vegetables or dried fruit toward the end of cooking. And some stews and braises, especially shellfish and fish stews, are not thickened at all. The ingredients in seafood stews, such as cioppino and bouillabaisse, cook together for only a few minutes, and the cooking liquid ends up brothlike rather than thick.

> ## *Braising Recipes*

PORK SHOULDER BRAISED IN HARD CIDER Serves 8

This recipe employs many classic techniques of braising. To finish the sauce, the liquid is first reduced (a common thickening method) and then a secondary thickener called a beurre manié, a mixture of flour and butter, is added. Beurre manié can be added to most any sauce that seems to need a bit more body. And since the flavor of pork pairs well with apples, hard cider is used to braise the meat. For variation, the standard French mirepoix of onion, carrot, and celery is replaced with parsnip, celery root, and leek.

If you don't have a pot with a tight-fitting lid, cover your pot with aluminum foil lined with parchment paper and then the lid (you can even use the lid from another, similar-size pot or pan). Check 30 minutes after placing the pot in the oven to make sure that the liquid is gently simmering; if not, raise the temperature by 25 degrees, return the liquid to a boil on top of stove, and return the pot to the oven to finish cooking. (If vigorously boiling, decrease temperature by 25 degrees.)

For sachet d'epice
- 3 FRESH THYME SPRIGS
- 3 FRESH FLAT-LEAF PARSLEY SPRIGS
- ½ TEASPOON WHOLE BLACK PEPPERCORNS

For browning pork
- 3 POUNDS PORK SHOULDER
- COARSE SALT AND FRESHLY GROUND PEPPER
- OLIVE OIL

For aromatics
- 1 SMALL LEEK, *white and pale-green parts, finely chopped and washed well (page 32) (½ cup)*
- 3 GARLIC CLOVES, *peeled and minced*
- 1 SMALL PARSNIP, *peeled and cut into ½-inch dice (½ cup)*
- ½ SMALL CELERY ROOT, *peeled and cut into ½-inch dice (½ cup)*

For braising pork
- 4 CUPS HARD CIDER
- ½ CUP BASIC CHICKEN STOCK *(page 41), or more if needed*

For garnish vegetables
- 3 MEDIUM LEEKS, *white and pale-green parts, halved lengthwise and washed (page 32)*
- 3 MEDIUM PARSNIPS, *peeled and halved lengthwise*
- 1½ SMALL CELERY ROOTS, *peeled and cut into 1-inch wedges*

For sauce
- 1 TABLESPOON UNSALTED BUTTER, *room temperature*
- 1 TABLESPOON ALL-PURPOSE FLOUR
- ¼ CUP HEAVY CREAM *(optional)*
- 2 TEASPOONS GRAINY MUSTARD, *plus more for serving*

Ingredients

Pork shoulder (also called pork butt) is available bone-in or boneless; you can use either for this preparation.

Hard cider, or fermented apple juice, is a popular beverage in England and parts of France (notably Brittany and Normandy), where (like wine and beer) it is also used in cooking. If you prefer a nonalcoholic substitute, use a combination of chicken stock and sparkling apple cider (no more than half cider, or the dish will be too sweet) instead.

Heavy cream is stirred into the sauce at the end to add richness, but you can omit it if you like.

184

fig. 3.16 MAKING BEURRE MANIÉ

Make sachet d'epice Wrap the thyme, parsley, and peppercorns in a small piece of cheesecloth and tie with twine to form a sachet.

Brown pork Heat the oven to 400°F. Use paper towels to pat pork dry, then season generously with salt and pepper. Heat a large Dutch oven or other pot with a tight-fitting lid over high heat for 2 minutes, then add enough oil to barely coat bottom of pot and heat until shimmering. Cook the pork until well browned on all sides [1], turning with tongs once each side is seared (remember not to move the meat too soon or it will not brown properly and will stick to pot; wait until it releases easily). This will take a total of 12 to 15 minutes; reduce the heat if the bottom of the pot is getting too dark (you want browned, not burnt, bits for flavoring the sauce). If, after removing the pork, you see burned bits, wipe out the pot and add more oil before proceeding. (Or deglaze pot with a little water, bringing it to a boil and scraping up the browned bits; then pour off liquid and bits.)

Cook aromatics Reduce heat to medium and add the leek, garlic, parsnip, and celery root. Season with salt and pepper. Stir frequently and cook until leek is translucent [2], about 2 minutes.

Braise pork Return pork to pot, and pour in 1 cup cider. Bring to a boil, and deglaze pot, scraping up browned bits from bottom. Add remaining 3 cups cider [3] and the stock along with the herb sachet [4]. (The liquid should come about halfway up the sides of the pork; add more stock if it doesn't.) Bring to a boil on top of the stove. Cover, and put in the oven. Reduce oven temperature to 325°F. Cook until the pork is very tender (it should offer little resistance when pierced with a knife), 2 to 2½ hours, turning over with tongs about halfway through so the meat cooks evenly.

Finish braising with garnish vegetables Transfer the meat to a plate and strain the braising liquid through a fine sieve [5], pressing on the solids to extract as much liquid as possible (discard solids). Return the liquid and the pork to the pot and add the garnish vegetables, nestling them into the liquid (the liquid should almost reach top of vegetables) [6]. Bring to a boil on the stove then return to oven and cook until vegetables are tender, about 30 minutes [7]. Lift out the vegetables and arrange them on a serving platter. Transfer pork to another plate. Cover both and keep warm near the stove.

Finish sauce Make a beurre manié: rub the softened butter together with the flour *fig. 3.16* until completely incorporated. Pour off and measure the cooking liquid remaining in the pot; you should have about 2 cups. Return it to the pot and boil until reduced to 1 cup [8], about 6 minutes. Whisk in the beurre manié [9] and continue whisking until the liquid comes to a boil, then lower heat and simmer for 1 minute (to remove the raw starchy taste). Turn off the heat and stir in the cream (if using) and mustard.

Serve Use a fork to shred the meat into large chunks. Transfer to platter with vegetables. Serve with sauce and more mustard on the side.

Braised Pork Shoulder, Step by Step

Pot Roast Tip

It's easier to get beautiful slices
of roast the day after it has been
braised. If you plan to make it ahead,
hold off on adding the garnish
vegetables until the next day. Allow
the roast to cool completely in the
braising liquid, then refrigerate in
the covered pot overnight. When
you are about ready to serve, remove
the cold meat from the liquid and
slice. Heat the liquid, strain, and
return to the pot. Cook the garnish
vegetables until tender, then
add the meat slices and heat until
warmed through.

Equipment

Use a Dutch oven that is just slightly
larger (about an inch all around)
than the roast, since the meat will shrink
during cooking.

POT ROAST Serves 8

Like many favorite comfort-food dishes, pot roast was born of frugality. Here was
a dish based on inexpensive cuts of meat and basic root vegetables, cooked
together in the same pot, that could be stretched to make meals for days to come.
Many fans of pot roast think it tastes even better the next day, so it's also a good
make-ahead option for a big gathering. This particular recipe calls for less liquid
than other, more typical braises; here, the water will reach only about 1 inch up
the sides of the roast, instead of halfway. With less liquid in the pot, you'll need to
watch it more carefully, and turn the roast more frequently, but you probably
won't need to reduce the sauce in the end or add much thickener (only a tablespoon or so of flour).

A common frustration of many new cooks—and even some experienced ones—
is that their pot roast turns out stringy or dry. It could be that the meat is too lean,
causing it to dry out quickly; this is why it's important to buy a cut with fat marbled
throughout the flesh. A loose-fitting lid might also be the culprit, because the

cooking liquid will have evaporated. The cooking liquid should remain at a constant, gentle simmer, rather than a rapid boil—lower heat melts the collagen into gelatin more effectively. It might seem counterintuitive, but a dry or stringy pot roast could also result from undercooking, not overcooking, the meat. In fact, one of the beauties of braising is that it occurs at such a low temperature that it's fairly difficult (and takes quite a long time) for the meat to overcook.

For browning meat

3 TO 4 POUNDS CHUCK ROAST, *tied (page 119, or have your butcher do this for you)*

COARSE SALT AND FRESHLY GROUND PEPPER

SUNFLOWER OR OTHER NEUTRAL-TASTING OIL

For aromatics

1 TABLESPOON OLIVE OIL

1 LARGE ONION, *peeled and thinly sliced (1½ cups)*

1 MEDIUM CARROT, *peeled and coarsely chopped (¾ cup)*

1 CELERY STALK, *coarsely chopped (¾ cup)*

2 GARLIC CLOVES, *peeled and thinly sliced*

1 DRIED BAY LEAF

¼ TEASPOON WHOLE BLACK PEPPERCORNS

3 SPRIGS FRESH THYME

For braising meat

1 TABLESPOON ALL-PURPOSE FLOUR, *plus more if needed*

2 TABLESPOONS RED-WINE VINEGAR, *plus more if needed*

1¼ CUPS WATER

For garnish vegetables

¾ POUND TURNIPS *(about 3), peeled and cut into 1½-inch wedges*

¾ POUND NEW POTATOES *(about 12)*

¾ POUND CARROTS *(4 to 5 medium), peeled and cut into 3-inch lengths (halve thick ends lengthwise, then cut into 3-inch lengths)*

Brown meat Pat meat dry with paper towels, then season on all sides with salt and pepper. Heat a Dutch oven pot over high heat for 2 minutes. Then add enough oil to barely coat bottom of pot and heat until shimmering. Sear the meat until golden brown, turning to cook all sides evenly, about 8 minutes. Don't be tempted to turn the meat too soon, or it will tear; instead, wait until it easily releases from the pot. Once it is nicely browned all over, remove it from the pot. If there are lots of blackened bits on the bottom of the pot, wipe it clean with a paper towel, or deglaze with a little water and then discard.

Cook aromatics Reduce the heat to medium. Add the olive oil and all of the aromatics, and cook, stirring fairly often, until the onion is translucent, 2 to 3 minutes. You may need to increase the heat after a minute or two if the onion isn't softening, but only slightly. If the garlic or onion begins to burn, add a little water and stir up the browned bits from the bottom of the pan.

Braise meat Sprinkle the flour into the pot *fig. 3.17*, and stir to coat everything evenly; cook the flour just long enough to remove the starchy taste without taking on any color, about 30 seconds. Add vinegar and water, and bring to a boil. Deglaze pot, scraping up browned bits from bottom. Put the roast in the pot;

Ingredients

Tougher cuts of meat, such as chuck roasts, are best for pot roast. Ask your butcher to recommend the best cut. Also, ask for the roast to be tied, as this will help it maintain its shape during cooking.

This recipe calls for turnips, new potatoes, and carrots, but almost any root vegetable can be used. What you want is something that will add substance to the dish, since it is designed to be a meal in one pot. Others to try include parsnips, pearl onions, and any of the other varieties of potatoes (sweet potatoes, like carrots, will add a dash of color, too). Cooking times may vary.

fig. 3.17 THICKENING WITH FLOUR

the water should come only about 1 inch up the sides of the meat. Reduce the heat so the liquid is simmering, not boiling, and cover the pot tightly with the lid. While the meat is braising, turn it every 30 minutes; the meat should be almost tender (a sharp knife inserted in the center should meet little resistance) after 2½ to 3 hours. Remove the meat from the pot. Strain braising liquid through a fine sieve, pressing on the solids to extract as much liquid as possible (discard solids).

Finish braising with garnish vegetables Return the roast and the strained liquid to the pot. Nestle the garnish vegetables around the roast, submerging them a bit in the liquid (the liquid should almost reach top of vegetables). Bring the liquid to a boil, then simmer until the vegetables are tender, 15 to 20 minutes. The meat should be very tender by now and give no resistance when pierced with a knife. (The meat will be firm enough to slice; if you want it to be falling-apart tender, cook 30 minutes more.)

Finish sauce Transfer the meat and vegetables to a serving platter, leaving the sauce behind (there should be about 1 cup). Cover and keep warm near the stove. If the sauce is too thin, heat until reduced (but be mindful of the saltiness, since the more the sauce is reduced the saltier it will taste), or thicken it with a bit more flour, whisking until smooth. Add a small amount of vinegar if necessary to balance the flavors. Let roast stand for about 20 minutes, then slice to desired thickness. Spoon some sauce over pot roast and vegetables to moisten and serve with remaining sauce on the side.

WINE-BRAISED SHORT RIBS Serves 8

This recipe makes good use of a bone-in cut that takes very well to braising. The ribs are marinated overnight in red wine to give them a deep flavor, then the marinade is reduced to a sauce that glazes the meat. You will need to start with more liquid than in other braising recipes, to avoid having to turn the ribs frequently during cooking, but this leaves excess liquid that must be reduced separately later, before it can be used for glazing (all that reducing is advantageous, since it concentrates the flavors for a rich and unctuous sauce). To do this, use a technique called *depouillage*, whereby the pan is placed off-center over the burner as the liquid simmers, allowing the impurities to collect on one side for easy skimming and discarding.

For browning meat
> 5½ POUNDS BONE-IN SHORT RIBS *cut 3 to 3½ inches long*
>> COARSE SALT AND FRESHLY GROUND PEPPER
>> SUNFLOWER OR OTHER NEUTRAL-TASTING OIL

For aromatics
> 2 MEDIUM YELLOW ONIONS, *peeled and cut into 1½-inch pieces*
> 2 CELERY STALKS, *cut into 1½-inch pieces*
> 3 MEDIUM CARROTS, *peeled and cut into 1½-inch pieces*
> 4 GARLIC CLOVES, *smashed and peeled*

Equipment

A 6-quart Dutch oven will be just large enough to hold the ribs comfortably as they braise. To finish them in the sauce, you'll need a large straight-sided sauté pan, or any other pan large enough to hold them in a single layer.

Ingredients

Ask your butcher to cut the short ribs into 3-inch pieces, first cutting between the ribs to separate (not across several ribs at once). Basic Brown Stock (page 50) is called for but you could use Basic Chicken Stock (page 41).

For marinating meat
- 1 BOTTLE (750 ML) RED WINE, *such as Côtes-du-Rhône*
- 2 DRIED BAY LEAVES
- 5 WHOLE BLACK PEPPERCORNS
- 6 LARGE SPRIGS FRESH THYME

For braising meat
- ½ CUP GLACE DE VIANDE *(optional)*
- 5 TO 8 CUPS BASIC BROWN STOCK *(page 50)*

Brown meat Pat ribs dry with paper towels, then generously season on all sides with salt and pepper. Heat a Dutch oven over medium-high heat for 2 minutes, then add enough oil to barely coat bottom of pan and heat until shimmering. Working in batches so as not to crowd pan, sear ribs until deep brown all over, turning with tongs, about 1½ minutes per side. Transfer ribs to a plate and continue searing the rest, adding more oil as needed. Once all of the ribs have been removed, pour off all but about 2 tablespoons of oil from pot.

Cook aromatics Reduce heat to medium and add the onions, celery, carrots, and garlic. Stir occasionally, until beginning to turn golden, about 5 minutes.

Marinate meat Deglaze the pot with a cup of the wine, stirring to incorporate the browned bits from the bottom, then pour in the rest of the wine. Once it is simmering, remove the pot from the heat and return the ribs, submerging them partially in the liquid. Add bay leaves, peppercorns, and thyme *fig. 3.18*. Let cool

fig. 3.18 MARINATING THE RIBS

fig. 3.19 SKIMMING THE BRAISING
LIQUID

Equipment

A large straight-sided skillet (with a 3-quart capacity) will be large enough to hold all of the ingredients for braising. Make sure it has a tight-fitting lid, as rabbit (especially the loin) is particularly prone to drying out. You can also use a Dutch oven.

completely, then cover and marinate in the refrigerator for at least 8 hours (or up to overnight), turning the ribs once to ensure they marinate evenly.

Braise ribs Heat oven to 300°F. Set pot over medium heat. Add glace de viande, if using, and pour in enough stock (5 to 8 cups) to come almost to top of ribs. When stock comes to a boil, cover and place pot in oven. Check after 30 minutes. If it isn't bubbling, raise the oven temperature by 25°F. Continue braising until the meat gives little resistance when pierced with a sharp knife, about 2½ hours. Lift out the ribs with tongs or a slotted spoon and arrange in a single layer in a large straight-sided sauté pan.

Reduce braising liquid Raise oven temperature to 350°F. Strain the braising liquid through a fine sieve into a clean pot (you should have about 5 cups) and discard the solids. Bring to a rapid simmer, setting the pot slightly off center over one of the burners so that one side of the liquid is bubbling more fiercely than the other; this allows the impurities to collect on the other side, making it easier to skim them from the surface *fig. 3.19*. Simmer (and occasionally skim) until you have about 1½ cups of liquid, 20 to 30 minutes, adjusting the heat as necessary to maintain a steady simmer.

Glaze ribs Pour the reduced liquid over the short ribs (it should come about halfway up the sides) and spoon some over the tops. Bake, uncovered, for 20 to 25 minutes, basting every now and then, until the ribs are glistening with glaze and the surrounding liquid is syrupy.

Serve Set the ribs on a serving platter and spoon the sauce around the ribs, or serve on individual plates.

ORANGE BRAISED RABBIT Serves 4

This is an example of a shorter braise, but the result is much the same as for longer-braised dishes—tender, succulent meat that falls off the bone. Although rabbit is very popular in France and elsewhere, it is not as familiar in the United States, so feel free to substitute chicken legs or thighs (or a combination); breast meat is too lean for braising. Olives, orange, and rosemary lend this dish assertive flavors; it is best served over creamy Perfect Soft Polenta (page 419), and accompanied by a simple watercress (or other bitter green) salad.

For browning rabbit
- 1 FRESH WHOLE RABBIT *(about 2¾ pounds), cut into 5 pieces (4 legs and 1 saddle, which is boned; have the butcher do this for you)*
- COARSE SALT AND FRESHLY GROUND PEPPER
- 1 OUNCE FATBACK, *cut into two 5-by-½-by-¼-inch strips (optional); see note, opposite*
- 1 SPRIG ROSEMARY, *for saddle, plus another sprig for braising*
- OLIVE OIL

For aromatics
- 1 TABLESPOON OLIVE OIL
- 2 MEDIUM ONIONS, *peeled and cut into 1-inch wedges (leave stem end intact)*
- 3 GARLIC CLOVES, *peeled and thinly sliced*
- PINCH OF RED PEPPER FLAKES
- PINCH OF GROUND CINNAMON

Ingredients

Fresh rabbit can be found at butcher shops and some specialty markets; call ahead to order, since it might not always be in demand, and have the butcher fabricate it for you and bone the saddle.

This dish can be made with 3 pounds of bone-in, skin-on chicken thighs (in which case you wouldn't need the extra rosemary sprigs or fatback). The cooking time should be about the same.

Fatback, or salted pork fat, is available from most butchers; pancetta can be substituted. You can leave it out, but the rabbit won't be as flavorful.

For braising rabbit
½ CUP DRY WHITE WINE
½ TEASPOON FINELY GRATED ORANGE ZEST
1 CUP FRESH SQUEEZED ORANGE JUICE *(from 2 oranges)*
¾ CUP GREEN OLIVES, *preferably Sicilian, pitted*

For serving
1 NAVEL ORANGE, *cut into wedges*

Prepare rabbit Lay the boned saddle skin side down on a clean work surface and season with salt and pepper. Lay fatback strips down the center end to end and then a sprig of rosemary *fig. 3.20*. Season generously with salt and pepper. Wrap the flaps of the saddle over to enclose, and secure with twine.

Brown rabbit Season rabbit pieces on both sides with salt and pepper. Heat the skillet over medium-high heat for 1 minute, then add enough oil to barely coat bottom of pan and heat until shimmering. Cook the rabbit pieces (in

fig. 3.20 PREPARING SADDLE PIECE

batches if necessary to avoid crowding the pan) until well browned, starting with the skin side down and letting them sear before turning (to prevent the meat from tearing). This will take 4 to 5 minutes per side. Reduce heat if the bottom of the pan is getting too dark. (If there are burned bits after all the rabbit has been cooked, deglaze the pan with a little water and discard liquid and bits.)

Cook aromatics Reduce heat to medium and add the oil, onions, and garlic. Lightly season with salt and pepper, if desired. Cook, stirring occasionally, for 2 minutes, then stir in the red pepper flakes and cinnamon. Continue cooking and stirring until onions are translucent, about 3 minutes more.

Braise rabbit Heat oven to 200°F. Deglaze pan with the wine, scraping up any brown bits from bottom, and continue boiling until the liquid is slightly reduced, about 1 minute. Stir in the orange zest and juice, olives, and remaining sprig rosemary. Arrange the rabbit pieces skin side up in a single layer (they should fit snugly). Bring to a boil, then lower the heat to a simmer. Cover tightly and cook until the saddle is just cooked through, about 30 minutes. Transfer saddle to an ovenproof platter, cover and keep warm in the oven. Continue cooking legs until very tender, with meat almost falling off the bone, 10 to 15 minutes longer. Transfer legs to the platter.

Finish sauce Boil the braising liquid in the pan until it thickens and turns syrupy, 6 to 7 minutes.

Serve Remove the rosemary sprig from the sauce and from the saddle; discard. Slice saddle piece crosswise into 1-inch pieces. Arrange one of the legs with a couple of saddle slices on each plate, then spoon some of the olives, onions, and sauce over the rabbit. Garnish with orange wedges.

BRAISED FISH WITH FENNEL AND TOMATO Serves 4

This type of quick braising is similar to shallow poaching (page 210): An aromatic liquid is first simmered to allow the flavors to deepen, then simmered with fish, which takes on some of its character. Also, as with some poaching methods, the braising liquid becomes the sauce. Match the fish and aromatics wisely so as not to overwhelm one or the other. A fish such as salmon is easy to partner; its pronounced taste won't be flagged by aggressive flavors, such as rosemary or curry powder. Milder-tasting fish, such as grouper, halibut, sea bass, and striped bass, require more subtle companions, like the fennel, tomatoes, and lemon in this recipe. All of these fish are moist and firm-fleshed, ideal for braising.

3 TABLESPOONS EXTRA-VIRGIN OLIVE OIL, *plus more for drizzling*
1/3 CUP DRY WHITE WINE
1/4 CUP WATER
1 MEDIUM FENNEL BULB, *halved, cored, and thinly sliced lengthwise*
2 MEDIUM TOMATOES, *cored and coarsely chopped (1½ cups)*
3 TO 4 GARLIC CLOVES, *peeled and thinly sliced*
4 THIN LEMON ROUNDS
COARSE SALT AND FRESHLY GROUND PEPPER
4 SKINLESS FILLETS FIRM-FLESHED FISH, *such as grouper, halibut, sea bass, or snapper*

Ingredients

Buy four fillets of the same size (4 to 5 ounces each) so they cook at the same rate. A 1½-inch thickness is ideal, allowing the fillets to cook evenly inside and out. Much thicker and the exterior could toughen before the center has cooked.

If the skin on your lemons is not too bitter (check by tasting a washed one), you may want to leave it on; this will help the slices hold their shape. Otherwise, remove the rind before slicing.

Prepare braising liquid Pour the oil, wine, and water into a large (13-inch) skillet, then add the fennel, tomatoes, garlic, and lemon slices. Season with salt and pepper. Cover and bring to a boil over high heat, then simmer over moderate heat until the tomatoes begin to fall apart and the fennel softens, 12 to 15 minutes.

Braise fish Sprinkle both sides of the fish with salt and pepper and arrange the fillets in the pan, partially submerging them in the sauce. Cover and simmer until the fish is opaque throughout, 6 to 8 minutes (or 8 to 10 for thicker fillets).

Serve Spoon some of the braising sauce into a shallow bowl, then top with fish. Drizzle with olive oil and sprinkle with pepper.

> ## *Stewing Recipes*

BEEF AND STOUT STEW Serves 8

This stew is a variation on the well-known French favorite, boeuf bourguignon, also made with mushrooms and onions; here, stout replaces the red wine, but you could make the stew with either. There are a few steps that help enrich the flavor of this dish, all of which are classic in making some stews. First, lardons are cooked to render their fat for use in subsequent steps (they are added to the stew at the end, too). Next, the beef is browned and the pan deglazed to incorporate all of the tasty bits. Then, a bit of Dijon mustard is stirred into the aromatics. For even richer flavor, you can add about a half cup of glace de viande (page 52) along with the stock. The stew is thickened with a small amount of flour and by simple reduction; that's why the lid is kept partially askew while the stew simmers, to allow some moisture to escape.

Buttery noodles make a perfect accompaniment, as they soak up some of the flavorful broth, while julienned carrots and freshly grated horseradish add fresh flavors—and a little textural contrast—to the otherwise rich dish.

For browning beef

6 OUNCES SLAB BACON *(or 6 thick strips bacon), cut into 1-inch lardons (see note, right)*

SUNFLOWER OR OTHER NEUTRAL-TASTING OIL

3 POUNDS BONELESS CHUCK, *cut into 2-inch pieces*

COARSE SALT AND FRESHLY GROUND PEPPER

3 TO 4 CUPS BASIC BROWN STOCK *(page 50), or Basic Chicken Stock (page 41)*

For aromatics

1 MEDIUM ONION, *peeled and coarsely chopped (1½ cups)*

4 LARGE GARLIC CLOVES, *peeled and finely chopped (2 tablespoons)*

12 OUNCES CREMINI MUSHROOMS, *trimmed, wiped clean, and halved*

For the stew

2 TABLESPOONS ALL-PURPOSE FLOUR, *plus more if needed*

1 TABLESPOON DIJON MUSTARD

7 SPRIGS FRESH THYME

3 SMALL DRIED BAY LEAVES

2 CUPS STOUT *(see note, right)*

For garnish vegetables

1 POUND NEW POTATOES OR FINGERLINGS, *halved lengthwise (quartered, if large)*

12 OUNCES CIPOLLINI ONIONS, *blanched and peeled (page 31)*

COARSE SALT AND FRESHLY GROUND PEPPER

For serving

½ CUP GRATED FRESH HORSERADISH ROOT *(grated on the small holes of a box grater)*

1 TABLESPOON WHITE VINEGAR

1 POUND EGG NOODLES, *cooked according to package instructions*

1 TO 2 CARROTS, *peeled and cut into fine julienne (about 1 tablespoon per serving)*

2 TABLESPOONS COARSELY CHOPPED FRESH DILL

Ingredients

Whenever possible, buy slab bacon rather than packaged slices. Slab bacon can be sliced as needed for each recipe (especially helpful when making lardons), and the leftovers can be easily frozen (either whole or sliced) in airtight freezer bags.

Stout is a dry, very dark beer with a toasty flavor that some say has a hint of coffee. There are many types available, most originating in England or Ireland (notably Guinness). You will need 16 ounces for this recipe. A robust red wine, such as Burgundy or Cabernet Sauvignon, can be used instead.

MAKING LARDONS

Sautéed bits of slab bacon, called lardons, are classic flavor builders and are often used as a garnish for salads and soups. To make lardons, cut the slices into strips about ½ inch by 2 inches, or dice into cubes. The bacon will shrink substantially when cooked. Cook the lardons in a couple of tablespoons oil over medium heat until brown and crisp, 5 to 10 minutes (or as described in the recipe). Transfer to paper towels to drain.

Cook lardons In a large stockpot, combine the bacon and just enough oil to cover bottom of pot (about 2 tablespoons). Cook over medium heat, stirring occasionally, until the bacon just turns crisp and brown, about 7 minutes. Remove bacon with a slotted spoon [1], drain on paper towels, and pour off the rendered fat from the pot and reserve. (If necessary, wipe the pot with paper towels to remove any burned bits from the bottom before proceeding.)

Brown meat Pat beef dry with paper towels, then season generously with salt and pepper. Return about 2 tablespoons bacon fat to the pot and set it over high heat. Cook the meat in batches to avoid crowding the pot, leaving ample room between pieces, and turn it as it cooks so that all sides are browned [2]. Each batch should take a total of 3 to 4 minutes; as soon as it's ready, transfer the batch to a large bowl and then continue with the next one. You may need to add more fat if the pot becomes too dry during cooking. Once all of the meat has been cooked, pour off the fat and reserve. Pour in 1 cup stock, and bring to a boil over

Beef Stew, Step by Step

high heat. Deglaze pot, scraping up browned bits from the bottom. Pour this over the meat in the bowl.

Cook aromatics Return all of the reserved bacon fat to the pot (if necessary to coat bottom of pot, add 1 to 2 tablespoons oil), and set it over medium-high heat. Cook the onion and garlic until translucent, about 3 minutes, stirring fairly constantly. Stir in the mushrooms and cook until they begin to soften, about 2 minutes. (If the bottom of the pot is turning too dark, or the onions begin to stick, stir in about ¼ cup stock.)

Simmer stew Once the vegetables have softened, stir in the flour and mustard, and cook, stirring, 1 minute. Return the beef to the pot, along with any juices that have accumulated in the bowl, and the herbs. Pour in 2 cups stock and the stout (liquid should just cover meat) [3]. Bring the liquid to a full boil before reducing the heat so the stew is at a simmer. Partially cover pot, and simmer until the meat is tender (it should pull apart easily with a fork), about 1½ hours, skimming and discarding fat occasionally [4].

Cook garnish vegetables Put the potatoes and onions in the pot [5]. If necessary, add more stock so everything is covered for even cooking. Simmer, partially covered, until potatoes are just tender when pierced with a knife, about 25 minutes [6]. You'll need to give the pot a good stir every now and then. Once the vegetables are tender, stir in the lardons. Season with salt and pepper.

Serve Stir together the grated horseradish and vinegar. Place egg noodles in wide shallow bowls, then ladle the stew on top and garnish with carrots, dill, and the horseradish mixture.

BOUILLABAISSE Serves 6

Although it may seem like a complicated restaurant dish, bouillabaisse has simple origins in the French seaport city of Marseille, where there is an abundance of freshly caught seafood (and an aversion to waste). Julia Child defined it as a "fisherman's soup, made from the day's catch," or from its leftovers. What it actually consists of depends on whom you ask. A pot will typically have at least four types of fish (some insist on no fewer than seven) and a roster of regional ingredients, notably fennel, garlic, saffron, tomatoes, orange zest, and olive oil. Purists would insist on using fish only from the local (Marseille) waters and absolutely no shellfish, while others take a more liberal approach, improvising here and there but basically sticking to the same formula. Most everyone agrees on the required accompaniments: rouille and croutons made from a crusty baguette. The process for making the stock, which is similar to a classic fish fumet (page 55) but with Mediterranean flavors, takes little time; since it gives the finished dish its rich flavor, don't skimp on this step.

Rouille is a variation of mayonnaise (page 95), with spices, garlic, and fish stock for added flavors as well as bread for a rustic texture. It has a tawny color from the addition of saffron (hence its name, which means "rust" in French).

Bouillabaise Tips

To make the stock ahead of time, wait to buy the fish you will use in the stew and ask your fishmonger for scraps of similar fish to use in the stock. Then freeze the stock in tightly sealed containers for up to 2 months and thaw in the refrigerator before proceeding. Or make the stock as instructed (with the fish that will be served in the stew), let cool, and refrigerate overnight in a covered container.

If you're making the stock ahead of time, you can also make the rouille (since it calls for some of the stock, or you could use water instead). Cover and refrigerate overnight, then let it come to room temperature before serving.

BOUILLABAISSE

Equipment

You'll need to use a pot that is large enough to hold all of the ingredients, with about 3 inches to spare on top. (If you're not sure, pile the raw ingredients together in the pot before cooking.)

To strain the stock, line a fine sieve with cheesecloth; you'll have to do this step twice, each time with clean cheesecloth. Or pass the stock mixture through a food mill fitted with a coarse disk, then through a cheesecloth-lined sieve.

Ingredients

It's not so important which type of fish you choose, but rather that the fish is as fresh as can be, and that you have a variety, anywhere from four to seven types. Preferably the variety will include contrasting tastes (mild and briny) and textures (firm and flaky). The ones listed here are suggestions; buy whatever is fresh at your local fish market.

Traditional recipes for bouillabaisse do not contain any shellfish, but now many versions do. Cockles, which are similar to small clams, cherrystones, or littlenecks, would make a lovely addition, as would mussels.

Pernod, an anise-flavored apéritif, reinforces the flavor of the fennel. Pastis is equally appropriate.

For stock

6 POUNDS ASSORTED FRESH WHOLE FISH, *such as porgy, red snapper, branzino, pompano, striped bass, cod, or monkfish, cleaned and skinned (see note, opposite)*

¼ CUP PERNOD, *plus more for seasoning (optional)*

COARSE SALT AND FRESHLY GROUND PEPPER

2 LEEKS, *white and pale green parts, cut into 1-inch half-moons (about 2 cups) and washed well (page 32)*

1 CELERY STALK, *coarsely chopped (about ½ cup)*

1 MEDIUM FENNEL BULB, *trimmed, cored, and coarsely chopped*

½ MEDIUM ORANGE, *zested with a peeler (page 34)*

1 CAN (28 OUNCES) WHOLE PEELED TOMATOES, *drained and coarsely chopped (or 2 cups chopped peeled fresh tomatoes; see pages 381–382)*

1 CUP DRY WHITE WINE

1 DRIED BAY LEAF

10 CUPS WATER

For rouille and croutons

1 BAGUETTE, *3 slices (½ inch thick) cut off and crusts removed, cut into ½-inch cubes for the rouille, the rest sliced into ¼-inch-thick rounds for the croutons*

3 TO 5 GARLIC CLOVES *(depending on taste preference), peeled*

PINCH OF SAFFRON

¼ TEASPOON CAYENNE PEPPER

1¼ TEASPOONS COARSE SALT

1 LARGE EGG YOLK

1 CUP EXTRA-VIRGIN OLIVE OIL, *plus more for brushing on croutons*

For stew

½ TO ¾ TEASPOON SAFFRON

1 POUND FINGERLING POTATOES, *large ones sliced in half lengthwise*

Prepare fish Follow the instructions on pages 120–121 to fillet the fish (or have the fishmonger do this, giving you the head and bones); then skin the fillet (see right). You should end up with 3 to 4 pounds of fish fillets and 2 to 3 pounds of bones and heads. Cut the bones crosswise into 4-inch pieces and the fish into 2- to 3-inch pieces (make them uniform so they cook evenly). For the marinade, stir together 2 tablespoons Pernod, ½ teaspoon salt, and ¼ teaspoon pepper; pour over the fish, turn the pieces to coat, then cover and refrigerate for 1 to 3 hours, turning the fish again halfway through. (Do not marinate longer than 3 hours or the texture of the fish will start to deteriorate.)

Make stock Combine the fish bones and heads, leeks, celery, fennel, orange zest, tomatoes, remaining 2 tablespoons Pernod, wine, bay leaf, and the water in a large stockpot [1]. Bring to a boil, then reduce heat so the liquid is at a simmer, and cook for 30 minutes, skimming the foam from the surface with a ladle every so often. Strain the stock by pouring it through a cheesecloth-lined sieve, pressing on the solids with the ladle [2] to extract as much liquid as possible from fish heads and bones (this will add body to the stock). Discard the solids, and strain the stock again (using clean cheesecloth) to remove any remaining solids, without pressing this time. Set the stock aside in a clean pot. Reserve ½ cup stock for rouille.

Make rouille and croutons Ladle the reserved stock over the bread cubes and let soak for 10 minutes, then squeeze the bread with your hands (save the broth in case you need to thin the rouille). Puree garlic in a food processor or a blender, then add bread, saffron, cayenne, salt, and egg yolk, and puree until combined. With the motor running, add the oil in a slow, steady stream *fig. 3.21*, mixing until the sauce is emulsified. If it seems too thick—it should be spreadable like mayonnaise—you can thin it with some of the reserved stock. Meanwhile, heat the oven to 350°F. Brush the tops of the croutons lightly with oil, and toast until lightly browned, about 10 minutes.

Finish stew When you are about ready to serve, return the stock to the stove and add the saffron and potatoes [3]. Bring to a boil, then reduce heat, and cook at a rapid simmer for 10 minutes. Continue simmering until the potatoes are fork-tender, about 5 minutes. Add the fish from the marinade to the pot [4]. Cook over low heat (the stock should be at a gentle simmer) until the fish is just cooked through and opaque throughout [5], about 5 minutes. Remove each piece

SKINNING A FILLET
Lay fillet skin side down. Holding the tail of the fish in one hand, insert a slicing knife with a flexible blade between the skin and flesh. Keeping the knife at a 45-degree angle and cutting toward the skin, slice from tail to head to remove skin; you may need to move the knife from side to side slightly as you cut. You might also need to stop every now and then to get a firmer grip on the slippery skin (or hold with a paper towel).

fig. 3.21 **MAKING ROUILLE**

of fish as soon as it is ready. Taste, and season broth with salt and pepper and a splash (or two) of Pernod, if desired.

Serve Ladle broth and potatoes into bowls, and divide fish evenly among servings. Spread some of the croutons with rouille for floating on top, and serve the remaining croutons and rouille on the side. If desired, you can stir some rouille into the broth at the table.

Bouillabaise, Step by Step

CHICKEN CURRY Serves 6

Curry paste, the flavor base for many Indian stews, often begins with a puree of onion, garlic, and ginger, which is sautéed with spice blends (masalas) until golden brown and caramelized. There are countless varieties of curry pastes in Indian cooking, and the one in this recipe is among the most basic and traditional. The spice blends used in Indian curries are first either toasted in a dry pan or sautéed in oil; in both methods, the heat stimulates the oils in the spices—you'll know they are ready when they are fragrant (keep a very close eye on them, to prevent burning). Once you've mastered the technique, you can make a variety of curries using fish, shrimp, beef, lamb, goat, or one or more vegetables, such as cauliflower or peas and potatoes.

For garam masala

  1 CINNAMON STICK, *broken into 1-inch pieces*
  2 WHOLE CLOVES
  1 TABLESPOON CORIANDER SEEDS
  1 TABLESPOON FENNEL SEEDS
  ½ TEASPOON WHOLE ALLSPICE

For paste

  3 MEDIUM YELLOW ONIONS, *peeled and coarsely chopped (3½ cups)*
 10 TO 12 GARLIC CLOVES, *peeled and thinly sliced*
  1 PIECE (4 OUNCES) FRESH GINGER, *peeled and coarsely chopped*
  3 TABLESPOONS SUNFLOWER OR OTHER NEUTRAL-TASTING OIL
  1 TABLESPOON CUMIN SEEDS
  1 TABLESPOON BLACK OR BROWN MUSTARD SEEDS
  2 TABLESPOONS TOMATO PASTE

For stew

  1 QUART BASIC CHICKEN STOCK *(page 41)*
  1 TEASPOON TURMERIC
  6 FRESH CURRY LEAVES *(optional)*
  2 DRIED BAY LEAVES
  3 SMALL DRIED RED CHILES, *finely ground*
     COARSE SALT
 10 CHICKEN THIGHS *(about 3½ pounds), cut in half through the bone (or left whole)*
  2 MEDIUM RUSSET POTATOES, *peeled and cut into ½-inch dice*
  ½ CUP CHOPPED CILANTRO, *plus sprigs for garnish*

For serving (optional)

     COOKED BASMATI RICE *(page 412)*
     PLAIN YOGURT
     LIME WEDGES

Ingredients

Don't be put off by the number of ingredients called for, since many of them are quickly assembled to make classic spice blends and pastes from scratch. If you want to take a short cut, use store-bought garam masala (about ¼ cup). Be aware, though, that the flavor will not be nearly as pronounced (and will tend to taste too strongly of cloves).

Fresh curry leaves and Indian cinnamon sticks can be found at Indian (and some Asian) food markets or from online purveyors. Curry leaves are optional, but the flavor will be more authentic with them.

Make garam masala Gently toast the spices in a dry sauté pan over medium heat [1] until they are fragrant. Let cool slightly, then grind spice to a fine powder in a spice grinder or clean coffee grinder. You should have about ¼ cup.

Prepare paste Puree the onions, garlic, and ginger in a blender until smooth. Set a Dutch oven or other heavy pot pot over medium heat. When it is hot, add the oil, cumin seeds, and mustard seeds [2] and stir constantly with a wooden

CHICKEN CURRY

spoon until fragrant and starting to turn golden brown, and mustard seeds begin to pop, 30 to 60 seconds. Stir in the onion paste [3] and cook until caramelized, about 45 minutes. During this time, you'll need to stir only occasionally in the beginning, but as the moisture evaporates you'll need to stir more and more frequently and, at the end, fairly constantly to keep it from turning too dark [4]. Once the paste is ready, stir in the garam masala and tomato paste [5] and continue cooking and stirring for another 5 minutes.

Make stew Pour in the stock and deglaze pot, stirring vigorously to incorporate the paste mixture [6]. Add turmeric, curry leaves, bay leaves, and ground chiles, and season with salt. Bring to a boil, then reduce to a simmer and cook, stirring occasionally, until the stock has reduced slightly (and the flavors have melded), about 45 minutes. Add the chicken and potatoes, submerging them in the liquid as much as possible. Simmer until the chicken is tender (but not falling off the bone) and cooked through (prick the meat to make sure the juices run clear) and the potatoes are tender (they should still hold their shape but offer little resistance when pricked with a sharp knife). This will take about 30 minutes more.

Serve Add the chopped cilantro and stir to combine. Garnish stew with cilantro sprigs, and serve with rice, yogurt, and lime wedges, as desired.

Making Curry Paste

VEAL STEW WITH ARTICHOKE HEARTS, FAVA BEANS, AND PEAS Serves 4

This "white" stew borrows a nonbrowning method commonly used in making blanquette de veau, one of the canons of French cuisine. In that dish, a stew of veal, onions, and mushrooms is blanketed in a creamy sauce. The meat is never browned (hence the term "white stew"); the stock is thickened with a roux and, traditionally, a secondary thickener called a liaison, made with egg and cream, making it exceptionally rich. This recipe, however, opts for springtime produce over the usual vegetables and makes the liaison optional (you can omit the egg and just stir in the cream, without tempering). To make a classic blanquette de veau, see the variation that follows.

For sachet d'epice

- 3 SPRIGS FLAT-LEAF PARSLEY
- 2 SPRIGS THYME
- 1 DRIED BAY LEAF
- 1 GARLIC CLOVE, *crushed and peeled*
- 1 SMALL ONION, *peeled and thinly sliced*
- 1 MEDIUM CARROT, *sliced 1 inch thick*
- 1 MEDIUM CELERY STALK, *sliced 1 inch thick*
- ¼ TEASPOON WHOLE BLACK PEPPERCORNS

For stew

- 1 POUND FRESH FAVA BEANS, *shelled (to yield 1 cup)*
- COARSE SALT
- ¼ CUP DRY WHITE WINE
- 2 POUNDS BONELESS VEAL SHOULDER, *cut into 1½-inch cubes*
- 6 CUPS WATER
- 3 LARGE FRESH ARTICHOKE HEARTS, *prepared as directed on page 305, and each cut into sixths*
- 1 POUND FRESH GREEN PEAS, *shelled (to yield 1 cup)*

For sauce

- 4 TABLESPOONS (½ STICK) UNSALTED BUTTER
- ¼ CUP ALL-PURPOSE FLOUR
- 1 LARGE EGG YOLK *(optional)*
- ¼ CUP HEAVY CREAM

For serving

- COARSE SALT AND FRESHLY GROUND PEPPER
- JUICE OF 1 LEMON, *or to taste*
- COARSELY CHOPPED FRESH DILL OR PARSLEY

Ingredients

This stew is best made in spring when all the ingredients are in season, but in a pinch, substitute frozen peas, fava beans, and even artichoke hearts, adding all at the end, just to heat through.

Prepare sachet d'epice Place the aromatics on a large piece of cheesecloth, gather the edges to enclose, and tie with kitchen twine *fig. 3.22*.

Blanch favas Prepare an ice-water bath in a large bowl for shocking the beans (which stops the cooking and preserves their color). Drop the fava beans into a large pot of boiling salted water until bright green and just tender, about 2 minutes. Lift out the peas with a slotted spoon (or a spider) and plunge into the ice-water bath. Once they are thoroughly cool, drain and peel off the tough outer skins.

fig. 3.22 MAKING SACHET D'EPICE

Cook veal and artichokes Pour the wine into a large saucepan and bring to a boil, then reduce the heat and simmer for 1 minute (to cook off some of the alcohol). Add veal, water, and 1 teaspoon salt. Bring to a boil and skim the foam from the surface with a slotted spoon (veal produces more surface foam than other meats, so this step is important). Add herb sachet and reduce heat to a low simmer. Cook, uncovered, 1 hour, skimming the surface frequently. Add artichokes to the pot, submerging them partially in the liquid. Cook until the artichokes and veal are tender when pierced with the tip of a sharp knife, 20 to 30 minutes more, adding peas during last 3 minutes of cooking. Remove the sachet and squeeze out the liquid into the pot. Then strain the contents of the pot through a fine sieve into a bowl or large measuring cup, reserving veal, artichokes, and peas. You should have about 3 cups liquid.

Thicken sauce Wipe out the pot and return it to the stove. First, make a roux by melting the butter over medium heat until foamy, swirling the pan to melt

▷ Making Velouté and Thickening with a Liaison

evenly, then whisk in the flour [1] and cook, whisking constantly, 1 minute. Next, make a velouté by whisking the reserved liquid into the roux [2] and bringing to a boil (again, always whisking), cooking until the mixture is smooth. (Classic culinary teaching would have you whisk cold stock into a hot roux, or vice versa, to prevent the sauce from forming lumps, but that isn't necessary as long as you whisk diligently.) Reduce heat and simmer 10 minutes.

Make liaison (optional) Whisk together the egg yolk, if using, and heavy cream [3], then temper by gradually whisking in a cup of the velouté [4] (this will allow the egg to gently heat so it doesn't curdle). Now whisk everything back into the pot [5] and cook over gentle heat until the sauce thickens enough to coat the back of the spoon, 1 to 2 minutes. (If you prefer, omit the egg and whisk the cream directly into the velouté in the pan.)

Serve Return the veal, artichokes, and peas to the pot along with the peeled favas and cook gently to heat through, stirring [6]. Season with salt and pepper. Add lemon juice and chopped dill or parsley to taste.

BLANQUETTE DE VEAU
Omit fava beans, peas, and artichokes. Once the veal has cooked for 1 hour and 20 minutes, melt 2 tablespoons unsalted butter in a medium saucepan over medium-high heat. Add 8 ounces small white button mushrooms and 6 ounces blanched and peeled pearl onions (page 31), tossing to combine. Pour in ¼ cup stock from the stew and cook, stirring occasionally, until the vegetables are cooked through and the stock has reduced to a syrupy glaze, about 9 minutes. Finish with the liaison, then return veal to the pot along with the vegetables.

LAMB TAGINE Serves 4 to 6
This North African stew is named for the traditional dish it is cooked in. A tagine is a clay pot that consists of a shallow round base and a cone-shaped lid designed to allow all the moisture to flow back down into the base during cooking. The stews known as tagines are often thickened (and flavored) with dried fruits; the recipe here contains dried apricots, but prunes, raisins, and dates are also common. In France, tagines are often accompanied by couscous; while flatbread is more typical in Morocco.

This is a nonbrowned stew, similar to the veal stew on page 205, though far simpler to prepare.

For aromatics
- 2 PINCHES SAFFRON
- 3½ CUPS WATER
- 1 LARGE ONION, *peeled and finely chopped (about 1½ cups)*
- 2 GARLIC CLOVES, *peeled and finely chopped (1 tablespoon)*
- 2 TABLESPOONS MINCED PEELED FRESH GINGER *(from about a 2-inch section)*
- 3 TABLESPOONS SUNFLOWER OR OTHER NEUTRAL-TASTING OIL
  COARSE SALT
- 1 DRIED BAY LEAF
- 2 PIECES (EACH 1 INCH) CINNAMON STICK
  FEW PINCHES RED PEPPER FLAKES

Equipment

This recipe is prepared using a 6-quart Dutch oven or other heavy pot with a tight-fitting lid. If you want a more authentic preparation, make it in two tagines (each measuring 9¾ by 2½ inches), dividing ingredients evenly among them. Look for tagines at specialty cookware shops or online.

For stew
2½ POUNDS LAMB STEW MEAT, *preferably bone-in lamb pieces from the neck or shoulder, cut into 2- to 3-inch pieces*

6 OUNCES DRIED APRICOTS, *preferably Turkish*

For serving
FRESH FLAT-LEAF PARSLEY, *coarsely chopped*

½ CUP SLICED ALMONDS, *toasted (optional)*

HARISSA *(optional)*

Ingredients

Use bone-in lamb (from the neck or shoulder) for the most delicious results, as the bones help keep the meat moist during cooking and impart flavor and texture. The pieces should be similar in size (2 to 3 inches) so they cook at the same rate.

Harissa is a fiery blend of hot chiles, garlic, spices, and olive oil that is often used to embolden stews and other North African dishes. It is available in Middle Eastern markets, specialty stores, and some large supermarkets.

Lamb Tagine Tips

> You can prepare all of the ingredients for the stew while the saffron sits in the water for 10 minutes.

> Toast the almonds in the heated oven just before putting in the tagine (since they cook at the same temperature).

Prepare aromatics Heat the oven to 350°F. Stir the saffron into the water in a small saucepan and set aside for 10 minutes, then heat just to a simmer (saffron is not soluble in oil, so you must soak it first in water to release the flavor). Mix together the onion, garlic, ginger, oil, and 1 teaspoon salt, then transfer the mixture to a Dutch oven, spreading to form an even layer. Add bay leaf, cinnamon stick, and red pepper flakes, then pour in the simmering saffron water.

Cook stew Add the lamb, and season with more salt. Cover and cook in the oven until lamb is almost tender (it should meet slight resistance when prodded with a fork), about 1 hour and 30 minutes. About halfway through, skim the fat from the surface and turn the lamb pieces over so they'll cook more evenly.

Finish stew Add the apricots to the pot, submerging them in the liquid, then continue cooking (covered) until the fruit is almost falling apart and the sauce has thickened. This will take 30 to 40 minutes, so start checking after about 25 minutes or so; if the liquid doesn't seem to be thickening by this point, remove the lid for the rest of the cooking time. (You can also mash some of the apricots into the sauce to help it thicken.) Discard bay leaf and cinnamon sticks. Taste and season with more salt, as needed.

Serve The stew can go right to the table from the oven; pass the parsley and toasted almonds and harissa, if desired, in individual bowls on the side. Or, spoon the stew into serving bowls and sprinkle the garnishes on top.

LAMB TAGINE

LESSON 3.4

How to Steam, Poach, and Simmer

The beauty of steamed, poached, and simmered foods lies in their clarity. These gentle techniques coax essential flavors from delicate fish, shellfish, poultry, and meats, all without overpowering them. Because they are wet-cooking methods, they produce foods that are exceptionally moist and tender throughout, with pure flavors, unadulterated by much more than subtle hints from the cooking liquid. It's precisely that purity that makes steamed, poached, and simmered foods so versatile and delicious.

Because they require little (if any) fat, these cooking methods are among the most healthful. As part of a multilayered meal, steamed, poached, and simmered dishes can help balance the textures and flavors of richer foods; this is how they are treated in Chinese cuisine, for example, where at least one steamed dish appears as part of nearly every meal to provide contrast to fried, roasted, or more strongly seasoned foods.

Yet despite their reputation as so-called spa cuisine, steamed and poached foods are far from bland or uninteresting. A perfectly poached chicken breast, for example, is delicious without any embellishment, but the cooking method allows some opportunity to subtly accentuate flavors with a choice of aromatics and cooking liquids. The same chicken breast can also serve as a component of another dish such as pot pie, or in a composed salad with a creamy herbed dressing. Steamed lobster is equally delicious when served simply, with drawn butter and lemon, and in other preparations, like a lobster roll. If you think of these foods as clean slates, or starting points for a host of recipes, you begin to understand the appeal and importance of the cooking techniques.

ABOUT STEAMING
Steamed foods are suspended over simmering liquid, usually in a steamer basket, and cooked by hot vapor. Their clear flavors are also considered to be cleansing to the palate. Because steam transfers heat more efficiently than boiling water or hot air, steaming is among the quickest cooking methods. This is also why steam shooting from a kettle of boiling water feels much hotter than the heat in a 400°F oven. The steam—which hovers around 212°F—will likely burn your hand, while the heat from the oven will not.

Some of the best cuts for steaming are tender, uniformly even fillets of fish, boneless chicken breasts, and shellfish. The pieces need to be relatively thin because steam heats only the surface of the meat quickly, then this heat moves much more slowly to the center of the meat. Thicker pieces tend to overcook on the outside while the interior remains underdone.

Another way to steam is to wrap foods such as fish or poultry in parchment paper (this classic French preparation is known as *en papillote*), and place the tightly sealed packet in the oven, where the food cooks in its own juices (and perhaps a little extra liquid). Aromatics such as herbs, ginger, scallions, sliced onion, and lemon wedges, as well as other thinly sliced or shredded vegetables, can also be enclosed in the parchment packets and steamed along with the fish or poultry. Although not essential, a bit of oil or butter can be included; compound butters (page 166) are especially good, since they add both richness and flavor. The bundles make lovely individual servings that can (and should) be unwrapped at the table, allowing their wonderful aromas to be released as you and your guests dig in.

ABOUT POACHING
To poach, submerge foods fully or partially in barely simmering liquid. The water is at the proper poaching temperature, which ranges from 160°F to 185°F, when small air bubbles start to form at the bottom of the pot and just a few bubbles break the surface of the water. Similar to steaming, poaching is also best for tender cuts such as fish, poultry pieces, and certain cuts of pork and veal (as in the Italian classic *vitello tonnato*).

There are two methods for poaching (depending on the size and thickness of the food to be poached):

Shallow poaching involves partially submerging food in simmering liquid, and cooking by a combination of the hot liquid and the steam rising into the covered pan. The foods are generally thin, delicate, and quick to cook. The liquid is often reduced to make a sauce to serve with the dish. Beurre blanc (page 223), a French sauce made of reduced cooking liquid whisked with butter (and sometimes cream), is commonly served with shallow poached fish.

Deep poaching calls for completely submerging the food in the cooking liquid, and the liquid is often then served as a broth with the meal. Larger fillets are often deep poached, as are whole fish such as salmon (page 229).

ABOUT SIMMERING

Simmering is similar to deep poaching, except that the water is a few degrees hotter, between 185° and 200°F. The bubbles that break the surface are small and rise more frequently, and are concentrated around the edges of the pot. Although you can take the temperature of the water with an instant-read thermometer, it's best to develop a sense of what the water looks like at these different temperatures. The water should never come to a full boil, as this would cause the meat or fish to toughen before being cooked through. Even in well-known boiled dishes—Pot-au-Feu, the classic French "boiled" dinner as an example (page 235)—the food is actually simmered.

The higher temperature of simmering is suited to slightly tougher cuts—similar, in fact, to the meats that are appropriate for braising or stewing. For example, short ribs and brisket, both great cuts for braising, are simmered to make Pot-au-Feu. These cuts have a lot of connective tissue that breaks down better in the hotter simmering liquid than they would at a lower poaching temperature.

EQUIPMENT

For steaming: A variety of tools can be employed for steaming, some designed specifically for the task and others improvised. Whatever vessel you use, make sure it's big enough so that the vapor can circulate around the food. If the steamer is too small, the food will not cook as quickly or evenly.

■ Metal steamer baskets and pot inserts have small holes that let vapor surround all sides of the food. A steamer basket has plates that contract or expand to fit the size of different pots, while a pot insert is shaped like a pot and has handles for easy lifting.

■ The multilevel bamboo basket is very common in Asian cooking. Its advantage is that multiple foods can be cooked simultaneously in the tiered baskets. Foods that need more time to cook—such as vegetables—are placed in the bottom basket, closer to the heat source, while more delicate foods—such as fish—are placed in the top tiers (see the recipe for Steamed Salmon with Peas, page 213). A bed of leafy greens such as lettuce or cabbage is usually placed on the bottom of each basket to keep foods from sticking to the bamboo; aromatic herbs can also be used, and can impart additional flavor.

■ A metal colander with small holes will work in a pinch, as long as it has a pedestal to keep the bottom out of the cooking liquid, and you use a lid that covers the pot completely so steam doesn't escape.

■ Whole fish can be steamed on a plate placed on a wire rack in a roasting pan; covering the pan with foil lined with parchment paper will keep the steam from escaping (see the recipe for Steamed Whole Fish on page 220).

For poaching and simmering: You don't need much more than a sturdy pot, but there are some points to consider.

■ The food, liquid, and aromatics should fit comfortably in the pot.

■ The lid should partially cover the pot so you can keep an eye on the water to make sure it isn't boiling. In place of a lid, you can use a round of parchment paper cut to fit the pot. The parchment will trap some steam but let enough escape to keep the water from boiling.

■ When deep poaching and simmering, use a skimmer or slotted spoon to remove any froth or foam that rises to the top of the water.

■ A slotted spatula is ideal for lifting delicate foods such as fish.

TEMPERATURES OF POACHING, SIMMERING, AND BOILING WATER

Poaching temperature: 160°–185°F

Simmering temperature: 185°–200°F

Boiling temperature: 212°F

Best Cuts for Steaming, Poaching, and Simmering

BEEF
- ☐ **Short ribs** This cut is alternately called flanken.
- ☐ **Chuck** Look for a center cut.
- ☐ **Bottom round** Look for the first cut; the last cut is too tough for simmering.

VEAL
- ☐ **Shank**
- ☐ **Shoulder**
- ☐ **Top round**

LAMB
- ☐ **Shank**
- ☐ **Any cut from shoulder**

PORK
- ☐ **Shank**
- ☐ **Any cut from shoulder**

POULTRY
- ☐ **Whole chicken**
- ☐ **Breast**

FISH AND SHELLFISH
- ☐ **Cockles, mussels, clams**
- ☐ **Lobster, crab, shrimp**
- ☐ **Whole fish**
- ☐ **Fillet of fish** Can be a firm or delicate fish, depending on the technique.

COOKING LIQUIDS AND SAUCES

The liquids used for steaming generally impart very little flavor to the meat; for this reason, water is used most often. One exception is shellfish, which is frequently steamed in white wine, a light stock, or even beer; the liquid is combined with the juices of the seafood to make a sauce, such as for mussels. A number of aromatic herbs and other ingredients, such as citrus, can be added to the liquid for flavor.

For poaching or simmering, water, wine, or stock—vegetable, fish, chicken, or beef (white)—can be used. Choose one that will not overpower the flavors of whatever you're cooking. For example, delicate fish is often shallow-poached in a fish stock, such as fish fumet (page 55) or dashi (a Japanese stock made of kombu seaweed and bonito flakes; see the recipe on page 60). Wine is good paired with richer-tasting fish such as salmon. The flavor of chicken can be enhanced with a good homemade chicken stock. For deep poaching, the traditional choice is often Court Bouillon (page 231), a classic broth made with aromatic vegetables, such as carrots, leeks, onions, garlic or fennel, and sometimes white wine.

The liquids used for deep poaching and simmering not only impart flavor but also take on the flavors of whatever foods are cooked in them, so they can often be used to make great broths. Save the liquids to serve with your meal (strain, then garnish with julienned vegetables) or to use later to make a soup or to incorporate into another dish such as a braise or stew.

HOW IT WORKS

It's hard to go wrong with steaming, poaching, and simmering. Since the temperature of the water won't rise above 212°F—the boiling point—it's impossible to burn foods cooked this way, but you do have to beware of overcooking or undercooking. The cooking times and temperatures for each cut of fish, meat, or poultry depend primarily on its internal fat (marbling) and connective tissue. A chicken breast, for example, which is lean and has little connective tissue, will turn tough and rubbery if cooked for too long. On the other hand, cuts that are tougher and that have more connective tissue (such as the short ribs and brisket in Pot-au-Feu) should be cooked for a longer time so that the collagen will have time to melt. (This is also why stewed and braised dishes must simmer for hours before the meat becomes fork-tender.) If you end up with meat that is tough or rubbery, you've probably cooked it for too long or not long enough. Next time, keep a close eye on tender cuts, test them often, and take them out just when they've cooked through. (And keep just as close an eye on the water, which should never reach a full boil.) When cooking tougher cuts, such as brisket or short ribs, don't be shy about letting them simmer just a little bit longer—the extra time can actually make them more tender.

> ## *Steaming Recipes*

STEAMED SALMON WITH PEAS Serves 1

Bamboo steamers are tiered, allowing you to cook more than one item at a time and make a meal out of assorted components, such as the salmon and vegetables in this recipe. General rules of steaming apply no matter which implement you use. For instance, when steaming fish or other proteins, place any aromatics (such as the dill used here) directly underneath them. You could also add the aromatics to the steaming liquid (instead of or in addition to). Adding wine, vinegar, or lemon (or other citrus) juice to the steaming liquid is another way to subtly boost flavors. As with many steamed foods, this dish is equally delicious when served hot, cold, or at room temperature, making it a perfect meal for busy weeknights. The lemon yogurt sauce is a lovely accompaniment, especially when the fish is chilled before serving.

½ CUP DRY WHITE WINE

½ CUP WATER

2 LARGE LETTUCE LEAVES, *for lining the basket*

2 SPRIGS DILL

1 SALMON FILLET *(each about 7 ounces and 1 inch thick)*

COARSE SALT AND FRESHLY GROUND PEPPER

1 SMALL GREEN-CABBAGE LEAF, *for the "cup"*

½ POUND FRESH ENGLISH PEAS, *shelled (to yield ½ cup)*

½ TABLESPOON UNSALTED BUTTER, *cut in half*

¼ CUP PLAIN YOGURT

1 TEASPOON FRESH LEMON JUICE

Prepare steamer basket Bring wine and water to a simmer in a large skillet or wok. Meanwhile, line the top of a small steamer basket with 1 lettuce leaf and a dill sprig. Season both sides of the salmon fillet with salt and pepper and place on top of the lettuce, then place remaining dill sprig over fish. Place the remaining lettuce leaf in the bottom basket and then top with cabbage "cup." Place the peas in the cup. Dot peas evenly with butter and season with salt.

Steam fish and peas When the liquid in the skillet is boiling, set the basket with the peas in the skillet, rest the salmon basket on top *fig. 3.23*, then secure the bamboo lid tightly in place. Steam until peas are just tender and bright green and fish is evenly opaque throughout, 7 to 9 minutes (you'll have to remove the top basket to check).

Meanwhile, make sauce Whisk together yogurt, lemon juice, and salt to taste. Serve salmon, cabbage, and peas immediately, with yogurt sauce on the side.

Ingredients

Frozen peas can be substituted for fresh; thaw them under cold running water before steaming to ensure they cook at the same rate as the fish.

Equipment

A bamboo steamer is best; to serve 2 people, multiply the ingredients by 2 and place everything in a larger basket. Or serve 4 by steaming 2 large baskets side by side, in 2 simmering pots of water. If you use a metal steamer basket, you will need to cook the items separately, so plan accordingly.

fig. 3.23 PREPARING STEAMER BASKET

STEAMED FISH EN PAPILLOTE Serves 4

Preparing foods en papillote, which loosely translates to "wrapped in paper," is actually another way to steam food, even though it takes place in the oven rather than on the stove. It is most commonly used for fish fillets but is also well suited to shellfish and leaner cuts of chicken, such as boneless breast halves. This French technique always manages to impress, the pretty little packages resembling gifts, one for each guest. When the packets are slit open—ceremoni- ously, at the table—their fragrant aromas are released all at once, hinting at the tastes to come. These bundles are ideal for entertaining, but cooking en papillote has other advantages, too. The packets can be assembled a few hours ahead of time (covered with plastic wrap and refrigerated on a baking sheet) and then tucked into the oven once your guests arrive. And, like other steaming methods, it doesn't require much added fat; instead, the sealed parchment

Ingredients

Firm-fleshed fish varieties with plenty of flavor work best with the caper butter in this recipe; try halibut, salmon, or striped bass.

Since they can be rinsed, salt-packed capers will actually taste less salty than those packed in brine and have a pure caper taste. Use nonpareil capers whenever possible.

traps in all that wonderful moisture and flavor. In this recipe, a compound butter helps bring all the components together while adding richness to the dish.

Forming the packets is easy—no special skills required. The shape isn't as important as making sure the edges are tightly sealed. You can fold the parchment into envelopes, wrap it into bundles, or form it into bags, but half-moon packets are the classic shape. The traditional technique begins by cutting paper into a heart shape, but this one starts out as a simple rectangle.

4 SKINLESS FIRM-FLESHED FISH FILLETS, *such as bass, halibut, or salmon (each about 1½ inches thick)*

COARSE SALT AND FRESHLY GROUND BLACK PEPPER

2 CUPS TRIMMED SPINACH LEAVES *(from 1 bunch)*

CAPER-LEMON BUTTER *(pages 166–167)*

2 LEMONS, *one sliced into ⅛-inch rounds, the other cut into wedges*

Steamed Fish en Papillote, Step by Step

Prepare parchment packets Heat the oven to 400°F. Lightly season fish on both sides with salt and pepper. Cut four pieces of parchment paper (each measuring 12 by 17 inches) and lay them on a clean work surface. Fold each in half crosswise; then open, and lay flat. Divide spinach leaves among parchment, mounding it on one side of the fold. Divide the compound butter in half, then divide one of the halves among the four packets, spooning it on top of the spinach; top each with 2 lemon slices [1]. Lay a fillet on top of the lemons and spoon remaining compound butter on fish [2]. Fold over parchment [3] and then form the half-moon packet: beginning at one of the corners [4], make small overlapping pleats all the way around [5] to seal the edges completely [6].

Steam packets Transfer packets to a rimmed baking sheet, and cook in the oven until parchment puffs up, about 12 minutes (8 minutes per inch of thickness for firm-fleshed fish).

Serve Immediately place a packet on each of four plates and use kitchen shears to cut open the packets at the table. Serve with lemon wedges.

STEAMED MUSSELS WITH WINE AND SAFFRON Serves 4

Steaming a pot of shellfish is actually quite simple—and quick. It requires just a small amount of aromatic liquid, such as the wine used in the recipe below, which imparts flavor to the shellfish while also mixing with the flavorful liquid released from the shellfish, resulting in a delicious broth. And the shells serve as a "steamer basket," keeping the shellfish from being submerged in the liquid. A dry white wine is used as the steaming liquid; other good choices would be beer or water (you could even forgo adding liquid and steam the mussels in a covered pot until they open, as they have enough liquid in their shells, then sprinkle with salt and pepper). Here some aromatics are sautéed before the liquid is added to enhance its flavor before adding the mussels. In Belgium and France, mussels are traditionally accompanied by piping hot French Fries (page 333), but a crusty loaf of bread is always welcome.

3 POUNDS FRESH MUSSELS

1 LARGE PINCH OF SAFFRON *(about 30 threads)*

¾ CUP DRY WHITE WINE

2 TABLESPOONS UNSALTED BUTTER

2 MEDIUM SHALLOTS, *thinly sliced (about ½ cup)*

2 GARLIC CLOVES, *thinly sliced*

COARSE SALT AND FRESHLY GROUND PEPPER

2 MEDIUM TOMATOES, *coarsely chopped (about 2 cups)*

¼ CUP COARSELY CHOPPED FRESH FLAT-LEAF PARSLEY

Clean and debeard mussels Holding mussels under cool running water, scrub with a stiff sponge (or vegetable brush); then debeard: Grip the tough fibers extending from shell *fig. 3.24* and pull to remove (discard beards).

Prepare cooking liquid Steep the saffron in the wine for 10 minutes [1]. (Saffron is soluble in water, not fat, so it won't release its color or flavor if added directly to the butter.) Meanwhile, melt the butter over medium-high heat in a

Ingredients

Wild mussels will have a more pronounced taste than farmed mussels, but can be more challenging to clean (they are worth the extra effort). When buying, avoid those with cracked shells or a strong odor. It's best to buy mussels the day you plan to cook them; store on a damp cloth in the refrigerator, in a covered container.

fig. 3.24 DEBEARDING MUSSELS

shallow stockpot. Once it's foamy, add the shallots, garlic, and ½ teaspoon salt. Cook until shallots are transparent and garlic is soft [2], about 3 minutes, stirring every so often to keep the garlic from scorching. Pour in the wine and saffron [3], then add the tomatoes [4] and return to a simmer, stirring once or twice.

Steam mussels Add the mussels and cover tightly. Cook until all the mussels open [5], about 6 minutes, stirring once about halfway through. Discard any unopened mussels. (If using wild mussels, strain broth through a cheesecloth-lined sieve to remove any sand, if necessary.) Taste the broth and season with salt and pepper.

Serve Sprinkle with parsley before ladling the mussels and broth into bowls.

Steamed Mussels, Step by Step

STEAMED MUSSELS WITH
WINE AND SAFFRON

CLAMS IN HERBED BROTH

CLAMS IN HERBED BROTH Serves 4

This is another example of the basic method of steaming shellfish in a small amount of liquid, rather than in a basket set over the liquid. The broth below is given even more depth (and wonderful color) with a last-minute addition of herb oil; butter lends it a bit of richness. To soak up the flavorful broth, serve crusty bread on the side. You could also serve the clams and broth over long-stranded pasta, such as linguine or spaghetti.

1 CUP LOOSELY PACKED FRESH FLAT-LEAF PARSLEY LEAVES

½ BUNCH FRESH CHIVES, *coarsely chopped (about ½ cup)*

¼ CUP FRESH DILL

½ CUP LOOSELY PACKED FRESH BASIL LEAVES

½ CUP EXTRA-VIRGIN OLIVE OIL

1½ CUPS FISH FUMET *(page 55)*

Ingredients

Any small clams, such as cherrystone, littleneck, or Manila (ask for the littlest ones) will do, or you could substitute mussels or cockles.

Instead of the fish fumet, you could use Basic Chicken Stock (page 41), strained Court Bouillon (page 231), or even water for steaming.

fig. 3.25 REMOVING OPENED CLAMS

3 DOZEN FRESH SMALL CLAMS, *such as littleneck or small Manila, picked over (discard any with broken shells) and scrubbed well with a stiff sponge (or vegetable brush) under cool running water*

3 TABLESPOONS UNSALTED BUTTER

COARSE SALT AND FRESHLY GROUND PEPPER

Make herb oil Pulse parsley, chives, dill, and basil a few times in a food processor to coarsely chop. Pour in the oil and pulse until it is combined and the oil is a vibrant shade of green. You may need to stop and scrape down the sides with a rubber spatula a few times to incorporate all the herbs. Cover, pressing plastic wrap directly on surface to prevent discoloration, and refrigerate until ready to serve (to help keep it from turning brown), up to 3 hours.

Steam clams Bring the fish fumet to a boil in a medium stockpot over high heat. Once it is at a rolling boil, add the clams and cover with a tight-fitting lid. Allow them to steam until all clams have opened, 6 to 7 minutes (discard any that remain closed). Use a spider or slotted spoon to transfer the clams to serving bowls *fig. 3.25*.

Finish broth Strain the broth remaining in the pot through a cheesecloth-lined sieve to remove any sand. Wipe the pot with paper towels, then pour the strained broth back in and return to a boil. Whisk in the butter and about half the herb oil, whisking to combine. Season with salt and pepper.

Serve Ladle the broth over the clams and serve with more herb oil on the side.

SLICING GINGER INTO JULIENNE
To cut fresh ginger into julienne, first peel with a paring knife or a small spoon, then cut into a neat rectangle. Slice as thinly as possible, cutting across the grain to prevent the ginger from becoming stringy in the dish. Then stack the slices and cut into very thin strips.

STEAMED WHOLE FISH Serves 4

In many Asian cuisines, a common way to steam whole fish (usually surrounded by aromatics) is on a plate that is customarily set in a very large wok. The plate captures the juices that collect during cooking and create a flavorful broth. You can set the platter in a roasting pan if the fish is quite large, but use a wok if yours will accommodate. You'll have about a cup of broth after the fish has finished cooking, so use a platter deep enough to hold it. Then, be sure to drizzle some over each serving. Set out bowls of steamed rice and bok choy or wilted spinach along with more Asian fish sauce, a traditional table condiment.

1 FRESH WHOLE FIRM-FLESHED FISH, *such as red snapper, black bass, striped bass, or flounder (2½ to 3 pounds and about 2½ inches at the thickest part), cleaned and scaled (ask your fishmonger to do this)*

2 LARGE LEMONGRASS STALKS (2 ounces), *woody ends removed, split lengthwise*

¼ CUP LOOSELY PACKED FRESH CILANTRO LEAVES, *plus sprigs for garnish*

1 PIECE (2 INCHES) FRESH GINGER, *peeled and cut into julienne to yield ¼ cup*

1 TO 2 LIMES, *zested (2 tablespoons) and each lime halved*

2 GARLIC CLOVES, *thinly sliced lengthwise*

4 SCALLIONS, *julienned*

2 TABLESPOONS ASIAN FISH SAUCE (such as nam pla)

Prepare fish Fit a wire rack in the bottom of a large roasting pan (17½ by 12 inches) and add about 1 inch of water (it should come just below the top of the rack). Place pan over two burners on stove and bring to a boil over medium-high heat. Meanwhile, rinse fish well inside and out, scraping off any loose scales,

and pat dry. Rest the fish on a shallow platter large enough to hold the fish. Tuck the cilantro, half of the lemongrass, and a third of the ginger inside the cavity. Scatter the remaining lemongrass and ginger along with the lime zest, garlic, and half the scallion over the top of the fish and around the platter. Squeeze half of 1 lime over the fish and drizzle with fish sauce. (Reserve remaining scallion for garnish.)

Steam fish Set the platter on the rack in the pan and cover the pan tightly with parchment-lined foil *fig. 3.26*. Steam over medium-high heat until the fish is cooked throughout, about 10 minutes per inch of thickness (25 minutes for a 2½-inch-thick fish). Test by inserting a sharp knife into the flesh near the backbone; the flesh should be opaque and offer little resistance.

Serve Remove the foil and lift the platter from the pan, being careful not to spill the juices. Garnish with scallion and cilantro and serve immediately.

fig. 3.26 STEAMING WHOLE FISH

> ## *Poaching Recipes*

SHALLOW-POACHED FISH FILLETS Serves 4

Thin fillets require a more delicate touch than larger pieces and whole fish, which typically have enough heft (and bones) to remain intact when poached by the method described on page 210. So while those meatier pieces of fish are generally deep poached, thin fillets are only partially submerged in the cooking liquid. For shallow poaching, the type of fish needs to be of the quick-cooking, flaky variety. The poaching liquid (called *cuisson* in French culinary terms) is usually reduced to make a pan sauce to serve with the fish. The first step in making a cuisson is to sweat an aromatic, such as shallots, to build flavor. An acidic liquid, such as wine, vinegar, or citrus juice, is added to brighten that flavor and to help ensure that the sauce has the desired consistency. This recipe uses a combination of white wine and citrus juices.

You could simply reduce the poaching liquid until it has more body and serve it as is, or enrich it with a bit of cream or butter. This recipe turns the cuisson into beurre blanc, one of the classic sauces of French cuisine, and then emboldens it with more kumquats for color, flavor, and texture. Two sauce variations for shallow poached fish follow.

For poaching fish

- 4 OUNCES KUMQUATS, *halved*
- 1 TABLESPOON UNSALTED BUTTER
- 1 MEDIUM SHALLOT, *minced*
- ½ CUP DRY WHITE WINE
- ½ CUP FRESH TANGERINE JUICE *(from 2 to 3 tangerines)*
- 4 MEDIUM FISH FILLETS SUCH AS TURBOT, SOLE, OR FLOUNDER
  (each about 4 ounces and ¼ inch thick), or substitute 8 small fillets
- COARSE SALT

For beurre blanc

- 6 TABLESPOONS (¾ STICK) UNSALTED BUTTER, *well chilled and cut into small cubes*
- 6 KUMQUATS, *thinly sliced*
- FRESHLY GROUND PEPPER

For garnish

- 2 TABLESPOONS CHIFFONADE OF MINT *(page 21), plus whole leaves*

Prepare poaching liquid Gently squeeze the kumquats over a measuring cup to release juice, then add kumquats. Melt butter in a large skillet over medium heat. When it is foamy, sweat the shallot until it is softened [1] but not taking on any color, about 2 minutes. Add wine, tangerine juice, and kumquats (and juice) and bring to a simmer [2].

Poach fish Fold thin ends ("tails") of fish fillets under a little so the fillets have a more uniform thickness. Season with salt, then gently slide the fillets into the simmering liquid. The fish will not be completely covered with liquid but should be in a single layer [3]. Cover with a parchment-paper round and reduce heat so the liquid is barely moving (just under a simmer). Poach until fish is opaque throughout and flaky to the touch. (Check after 1 minute, but it may take up to 5 minutes.) Use a slotted fish spatula (or other long spatula) to transfer fish to a platter [4]. Cover with parchment paper and set in a warm spot until ready to serve.

Make beurre blanc Pour the cooking liquid through a fine sieve to strain out the solids, pressing on the fruit to extract as much liquid as possible [5]. Return liquid to the skillet and boil over moderate heat until reduced to about 3 tablespoons, 2 to 3 minutes. Turn off heat and gradually add the butter, whisking in a few cubes at a time [6]. If butter is not melting, return pan to moderate heat and swirl to hasten melting. Whisk until each addition is incorporated before adding more. When all of the butter has been added, stir in the sliced kumquats. You should have about ½ cup sauce. Season with salt and pepper.

Serve Drizzle beurre blanc over the poached fish, and garnish with mint.

Ingredients

Fresh orange juice can be used instead of tangerine; one navel orange should yield about ½ cup of juice.

When buying the fish, look for flat fillets that are the same size so they cook evenly. Mild, delicate fish, such as sole, turbot, and flounder, are good options for shallow-poaching. Flounder fillets are often very thin and require less time to cook through; check after 30 seconds.

MAKING A PARCHMENT ROUND
To cut a piece of parchment that will fit neatly inside a skillet (or round cake pan), begin with a square piece about the same size as your pan. Fold the square into quarters, then fold so two creased sides meet to form a triangle. Fold same way again; repeat until widest end is one inch wide. Place sharpest point at pan's center. Mark outer edge just inside rim of skillet, then cut to size and unfold.

LEMONGRASS-ORANGE BEURRE BLANC

When preparing the poaching liquid, sweat 1 stalk lemongrass (woody ends trimmed and discarded, remainder smashed and minced) and ½ teaspoon finely grated orange zest with the shallot (omit kumquats) and substitute orange juice for the tangerine. Then, after poaching the fish and straining the cuisson, follow the directions for making the buerre blanc (again omitting the kumquats). Garnish servings with suprêmed oranges (see page 34), omitting mint.

BEURRE ROUGE

When preparing poaching liquid, add 1 tablespoon tomato puree along with wine (omit juice and fruit); reduce and finish with butter as described (omit mint).

Shallow-Poached Fish Fillets, Step by Step

POACHED CHICKEN BREAST Makes 2 breast halves

Poaching chicken breasts on the bone results in more flavorful and juicy meat than poached boneless breasts. It's also harder to overcook the meat. The aromatics used in the poaching liquid below are designed to add flavor to the chicken, but Basic Chicken Stock (page 41) can be used to similar effect.

Poached chicken has myriad uses: add shredded chicken to soups, casseroles, pot pies, and Mexican dishes such as enchiladas, burritos, and quesadillas, or to all kinds of green salads. This one's a particular favorite: Cut the chicken in to 1-inch pieces and toss with chopped tomatoes and cucumbers, torn fresh basil leaves, shredded Romaine, and a creamy dressing, such as Green Goddess (page 359).

- 2 BONE-IN, SKIN-ON CHICKEN BREAST HALVES
- ¼ TEASPOON WHOLE BLACK PEPPERCORNS
- 3 SPRIGS FLAT-LEAF PARSLEY
- 1 SPRIG THYME
- 1 DRIED BAY LEAF
- 1 MEDIUM CARROT, *peeled and cut crosswise in half*
- 1 MEDIUM STALK CELERY, *cut crosswise in half*
- 1 TEASPOON COARSE SALT
-   UNSALTED BUTTER

Poach chicken Place chicken in pot just large enough to hold it with about 3 inches of room on top. Add water to cover by 1 inch. Add peppercorns, parsley, thyme, bay leaf, carrot, celery, and salt [1]. Bring water to just under a simmer over medium-high heat (bubbles should start forming around edges of pot and rising to surface, but there should be no bubbles in center of pot). Reduce heat to medium-low to keep temperature constant (it should be between 170°F and 180°F). Cook, skimming foam from surface as necessary [2], until an instant-read thermometer inserted in the thickest part of the breast registers 160°F [3], 15 to 18 minutes after the liquid reaches the right temperature.

Strain and cool Transfer chicken to a heatproof bowl. Strain liquid and pour over poached chicken [4]; let cool in liquid (this will keep the chicken moist and tender). When chicken is cool, or you are ready to serve it, separate meat from bones [5], discard skin and bones. Slice chicken against the grain into 1-inch pieces [6], if desired.

Poached Chicken Breast, Step by Step

POACHED CHICKEN BREAST AND SPRING VEGETABLE SALAD Serves 4 to 6

A composed salad of marinated seasonal vegetables becomes a main course when fortified with sliced poached chicken. Not only is this an economical way to stretch a meal, it is practical in other ways, too. For starters, many of the components can be prepared (and refrigerated) ahead, and when served as shown, guests can select the ingredients they prefer. This salad offers an array of spring-time's fresh bounty, including asparagus, new potatoes, leeks, and artichokes, all gently cooked just until tender. You can adapt this formula to take advantage of whatever is in season throughout the year.

POACHED CHICKEN
BREAST

SPRING VEGETABLE
SALAD

12 OUNCES SMALL NEW POTATOES, *scrubbed well*

    COARSE SALT

 2 POACHED CHICKEN BREAST HALVES

 1 POUND STEAMED ASPARAGUS *(see page 294)*

    LEEKS VINAIGRETTE *(page 305)*

    MARINATED ARTICHOKE HEARTS *(page 305)*

    BUTTERMILK HERB VINAIGRETTE *(page 359)*

Cook potatoes Cover potatoes in a medium saucepan with water by 1 inch and add 2 teaspoons salt. Bring to a boil, then reduce to a simmer and cook until tender when pierced with tip of knife, about 15 minutes. Drain well and let cool.

Compose salad and serve Arrange chicken on a platter, and asparagus, potatoes, leeks, and artichokes on another. Drizzle some dressing over the potatoes and asparagus. Sprinkle chicken and potatoes with coarse salt, if desired. Serve platters with a bowlful of dressing on the side.

DEEP-POACHED FISH FILLETS Serves 4

This is the standard technique for poaching most thick (at least 1 inch) fish fillets or steaks, such as halibut or salmon. Similar to braising, the fish is gently simmered in a flavorful liquid, only in this method the fish is completely covered in liquid. (To poach thinner fillets, follow the shallow-poaching method on page 210, as they may overcook if deep poached.) The cooking time will depend on the thickness of the fillet; plan for 4 to 5 minutes per inch. In this recipe, halibut fillets are poached in chicken stock enhanced with a few aromatics and then served in their cooking liquid (a manner of serving called "à la nage").

Equipment

This fish is poached in a medium saucepan but a large straight-sided skillet can be used instead. You want the fillets to fit in a single layer in the pan, with a little space between.

2 LEMONS

3 TO 3½ CUPS BASIC CHICKEN STOCK *(page 41)*

3 GARLIC CLOVES, *peeled*

4 SPRIGS FRESH THYME

10 WHOLE BLACK PEPPERCORNS

4 FISH FILLETS, *such as halibut or grouper (each 4 to 6 ounces and about 1 inch thick)*

COARSE SALT

EXTRA-VIRGIN OLIVE OIL, *for drizzling*

Prepare poaching liquid Use a vegetable peeler to remove 6 strips of zest from 1 or 2 of the lemons (page 34). Then juice the lemons and combine the zest and juice with the stock, garlic, thyme, and peppercorns in a medium saucepan. Bring the liquid to a boil, then reduce to a simmer.

Poach fish Season fish on both sides with salt, then carefully lower into the pot. It should just be covered by liquid (add more stock if necessary). Return the liquid to just under a simmer (it should barely move, with bubbles rising from the bottom but breaking before the surface). Cook until fish is opaque throughout and firm to the touch, about 4 minutes (or slightly longer for firmer fish) *fig. 3.27*. Use a slotted fish spatula to transfer the fish to a platter. Tent loosely with parchment-lined foil to keep the fish warm.

Strain broth Pass poaching liquid through a cheesecloth-lined sieve into a bowl, reserving lemon zest and thyme, and return to the pot. Bring it to a full boil, then immediately turn off the heat.

Serve Divide broth among wide, shallow bowls; gently set a fillet in each. Garnish with reserved zest and thyme, and drizzle with oil. Serve immediately.

POACHED WHOLE SALMON Serves 12

When poaching a large whole fish, place it in cool liquid first and then slowly bring the liquid to the proper temperature to result in an even texture inside and out. Adding the raw fish to hot liquid would cause the outside to overcook before the inside is cooked. Court Bouillon (page 231) is the traditional poaching liquid for seafood, imparting gentle flavors to the fish without being the least bit overpowering. For the prettiest presentation, remove the skin from the fish while it is still warm, as it will slip off more easily than when cold.

A whole fish is always an impressive sight at the table, but even more so when poached and then wrapped in thin ribbons of cucumber, the plump pink fish in stark contrast to the bright-green ribbons.

2 RECIPES COURT BOUILLON *(page 231, cooking for 30 minutes), unstrained and cooled to room temperature*

1 WHOLE SALMON *(about 7 pounds and 2½ to 3 inches thick), cleaned, fins and gills trimmed, rinsed well (have the fishmonger do this)*

1 ENGLISH CUCUMBER

1 BUNCH EACH WATERCRESS AND UPLAND CRESS, *for garnish*

CUCUMBER, CRESS, AND CAPER SAUCE, *for serving (page 231)*

LEMON WEDGES, *for serving*

Ingredients

Grouper, sea bass, striped bass, and salmon are worthy substitutes for (and slightly firmer than) the halibut shown here, but they may take slightly longer to cook. If you can't find skinless fillets, remove the skins after poaching; they will come off more easily when the fish is still warm.

For a fish with Asian flavors, replace the lemon, thyme, and peppercorns in this recipe with sliced fresh ginger and a little soy sauce (keep the garlic), then garnish with cilantro sprigs.

fig. 3.27 DEEP-POACHING FISH FILLETS

Ingredients

The salmon is garnished with a mixture of watercress and Upland cress (a member of the mustard family with a sharp, spicy flavor), which are also used in the accompanying sauce. You can find Upland cress (also called English cress or garden cress) at farmers' markets, or use all watercress instead.

POACHED WHOLE SALMON

Equipment

A poacher is just the right size and shape for cooking a large whole fish, such as the salmon in this recipe. For smaller whole fish, a roasting pan fitted with a wire rack can be used instead.

To make the paper-thin strips of cucumber that appear to wrap around the fish, a mandoline is the best tool. A Japanese-style mandoline, such as Benriner, is inexpensive and sold at most kitchen supply shops. A vegetable peeler can be used instead, but it will not be able to produce the same uniform thickness as the mandoline.

Prepare poacher Pour the Court Bouillon into a fish poacher and set the poacher over two burners on the stove. Lower the rack so it rests on the vegetables (in the court bouillon), then lay salmon on rack (trim the tail if necessary to fit inside). Add enough cool water to cover the fish completely; or, if only a small bit of fish is showing, you can cover it with a piece of parchment paper (cut to fit inside poacher).

Poach fish Bring the liquid to a simmer over medium-high heat, then immediately reduce heat to medium-low. Check temperature with a candy thermometer and adjust heat so it is between 165° and 180°F (very few bubbles will break the surface but there should be steam coming from the surface). Poach salmon, adjusting heat as necessary to maintain the proper temperature, until an instant-read thermometer inserted into the thickest section registers 130°F (fish will continue cooking off heat). You can also test by inserting a knife into the flesh along the backbone; the flesh should still be slightly translucent and offer little resistance. The cooking time should be about 5 minutes per inch of thickness (once liquid has reached a simmer). Remove poacher from heat and allow it to cool until you no longer see any steam, about 1 hour. Lift the rack with the salmon from the poacher and set it over a large pan (or the sink) to allow the salmon to drain until just cool enough to handle, about 30 minutes.

Prepare fish for serving Transfer salmon to a clean work surface. Use your fingers and a paring knife to pull and scrape off the skin from the top side of the fish *fig. 3.28*. Use the back of the knife to scrape off any brown areas from the surface. Using two large spatulas, carefully slide the salmon onto a serving platter. At this point, the salmon can be covered with plastic wrap and refrigerated for up to 4 hours.

Serve Slice the cucumber lengthwise into very thin strips. Arrange the strips diagonally across salmon, spacing them about 1 inch apart, and tuck the ends underneath so they appear to wrap around the fish. Garnish with watercress. Separate into pieces and serve sauce and lemon wedges on the side.

fig. 3.28 SKINNING THE FISH

COURT BOUILLON Makes 3 quarts

With its clean taste and light body, Court Bouillon is used to poach fish, shellfish, and lean white meats such as chicken and veal, when you want to impart only subtle flavor. It can be as simple as a few aromatics steeped in water or more complex with a fruity white wine or other acidic ingredients, such as vinegar or lemon juice. As with stocks, you should feel free to improvise with whatever is in your vegetable bin (or garden, if you have one). The ingredients called for here are common, but you can leave out some or replace them with other mild-tasting herbs or vegetables. The goal is to avoid overpowering the food that will be poached in the liquid.

2 MEDIUM CARROTS, *peeled and cut into ½-inch pieces*

1 MEDIUM CELERY STALK, *cut into ½-inch pieces*

1 LEEK, *cut into ½-inch pieces and washed well (page 32)*

1 LEMON, *thinly sliced*

3 QUARTS WATER

2 TABLESPOONS WHITE WINE VINEGAR OR ½ CUP WHITE WINE

2 DRIED BAY LEAVES

2 SPRIGS THYME

½ TEASPOON WHOLE BLACK PEPPERCORNS

COARSE SALT

COMBINE EVERYTHING in a large stockpot, adding salt as desired (be careful not to oversalt at this point; you can always add more at the end). Bring to a boil, then lower the heat and simmer 15 to 30 minutes, depending on desired intensity of flavor. Strain through a fine sieve to remove solids, if desired; cool completely before using or refrigerating in airtight containers, up to 2 days.

CUCUMBER, CRESS, AND CAPER SAUCE

Peel and finely chop 1 English cucumber, then toss with 1½ teaspoons coarse salt and 1 tablespoon each Champagne vinegar and small (nonpareil) capers that have been rinsed and drained. Set aside for 5 minutes, then stir in 1 cup sour cream and ½ cup finely chopped cress (use half watercress and half Upland cress, if you can find it). Season with freshly ground pepper and more salt. Serve immediately, or cover and refrigerate up to 4 hours before serving. Makes about 2¼ cups.

> EXTRA CREDIT
> ## *Confit*

This rich, indulgent dish actually has its roots in culinary common sense. The word *confit* is French and means "to conserve" or "to preserve." It refers to a method of curing pieces of duck or other meat with salt; slowly cooking them in their own, rendered fat; and then storing them, encased in that fat, protected from air and light. The effect is very similar to poaching, only with fat rather than another cooking liquid. For hundreds of years, it was a highly effective way of keeping meat without refrigeration. There are alternative storage methods today, of course, but the silky texture and incomparably rich flavor of confit makes this dish worth the effort even now.

Today, the word *confit* appears in reference to all sorts of dishes. There are lemon, onion, and tomato confits, among many others. In those cases, the word is used loosely to describe a food that is slowly cooked, usually in oil or other fats.

A true confit, though, is typically made of duck, goose, or pork. It's a good use of otherwise less desired cuts, such as duck legs and thighs, as opposed to breasts. And though the process involves a large amount of fat and can seem rather messy, it's actually very easy to do. You begin by curing the meat; be sure to allow adequate time (at least a day) for this before cooking. Rub a mixture of salt and seasonings over the meat, and refrigerate for at least 24 hours; this will add flavor and remove excess moisture. For the cooking, many recipes call for a combination of lard and other fat; for duck, however, use duck fat exclusively, as lard adds a hint of pork flavor that some find undesirable. The meat should be submerged in melted fat and cooked at a very low, constant heat until it's cooked through and meltingly tender.

Once the cooking is complete and the meat comes to room temperature, it should be chilled, covered completely by fat. (Traditionally, any cool, dry place, such as a root cellar, would do, but today, the refrigerator is preferred.) Then keep it chilled until the right mood—or a moment of need—strikes. When you're ready to serve the confit, remove it from the fat and crisp it on the stove or in the oven. Serve hot or warm, in salads, as part of cassoulet (page 403), over beans or lentils, or as a meat course with potatoes and vegetables. You might also enjoy the unctuous meat as a filling for stuffed pasta, such as ravioli (page 374).

DUCK CONFIT Serves 6

4½ POUNDS DUCK LEGS AND THIGHS, *attached (6 leg and thigh combinations)*

3 TABLESPOONS COARSE SALT

1 TABLESPOON FRESH THYME LEAVES

1 TEASPOON JUNIPER BERRIES, *crushed with a rolling pin*

3 BAY LEAVES, *crumbled*

6 GARLIC CLOVES, *smashed and peeled*

7 CUPS (2½ POUNDS) DUCK FAT

Cure Trim fat from legs and thighs, leaving skin intact over meat, but removing excess [1]. In a bowl, combine duck with salt, thyme, juniper berries, bay leaves, and garlic [2], and rub salt mixture all over the duck to cover completely. Cover and refrigerate at least 24 hours and up to 2 days.

Ingredients

You'll need a large amount of duck fat to make the recipe; look for it at specialty food purveyors such as D'Artagnan.

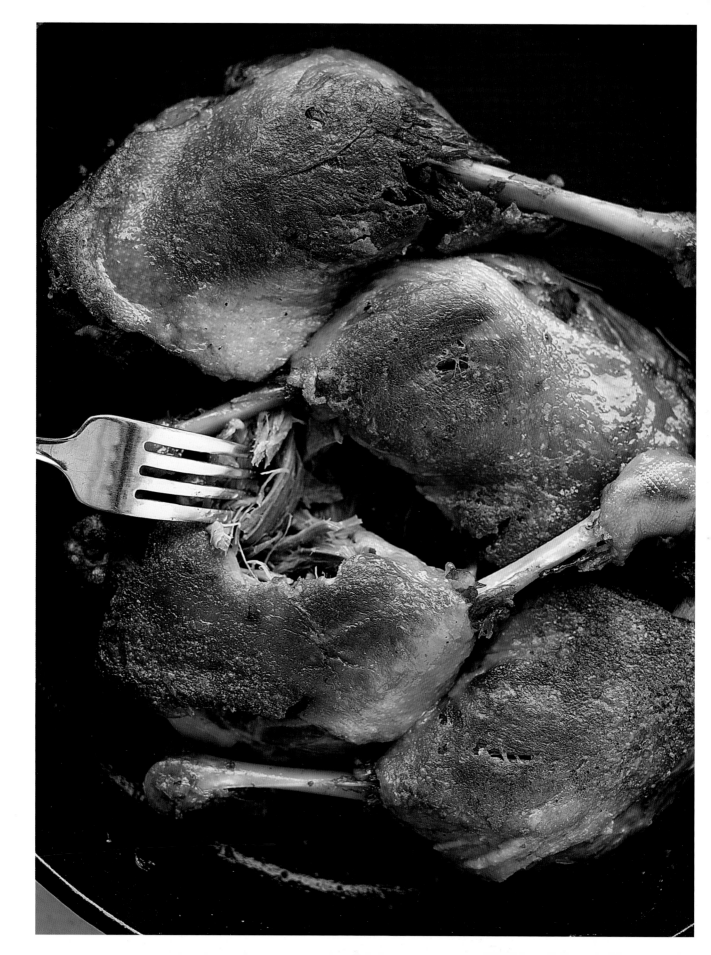

Poach duck Remove from refrigerator and rub off excess cure (reserve garlic). Melt duck fat over medium heat in a Dutch oven large enough to hold duck, with about 3 inches space at the top. Add garlic and then duck, skin side down, and heat until fat reaches about 200°F (test with a candy thermometer or electronic probe). The surface should look like it is gently boiling (but should not actually be at a boil). Adjust heat if necessary to keep temperature consistent throughout cooking. Cook until the fat is clear and a knife stuck into one of the legs slides out easily, 2½ to 3 hours.

Store duck Transfer the legs to several glass, stainless steel, or glazed stoneware containers. Strain fat, discarding any solids including garlic, and pour, still warm, over legs [3], making sure they are completely covered. Cool to room temperature, then refrigerate until ready to use, up to 3 weeks.

Heat and serve Remove desired amount of confit from fat, scraping off any excess, and keeping remaining legs covered with fat. Place skin side down in a cold cast-iron skillet or other heavy skillet. Place over medium-low heat and cover. Cook until skin is crisp, spooning off excess fat as it cooks, about 10 minutes. Carefully loosen skin with a thin-edge spatula, if necessary, and turn over. Cover and cook until warmed through, about 5 more minutes.

Making Duck Confit

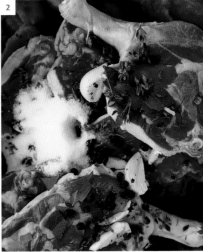

> ## *Simmering Recipes*

POT-AU-FEU Serves 8 to 10

Pot-au-feu (literally "pot on the fire") is sometimes described as the national dish of France. It certainly embodies one of that country's primary tenets of cooking: taking inexpensive and widely available ingredients and, with a bit of careful tending-to and extended cooking, turning them into a dish fit for a king. Calling it a one-pot dish, however, is a bit of a misnomer; sure, most everything is cooked in the same pot, just not at the same time (the potatoes are always cooked separately). What you end up with is a multifaceted meal that retains the taste of each of its components. If you want to follow tradition, serve the broth as a separate course, then present the sliced meat and vegetables on a platter. Choose among mandatory accompaniments—fresh horseradish, assorted mustards, cornichons (or gherkins), and sea salt—and be sure to offer toasted bread for spreading with the marrow scooped from the bones.

For first stage

- 4 POUNDS SHORT RIBS, *cut into 3-inch lengths (ask the butcher to do this for you)*
- 3 POUNDS VEAL BONES
- 1 BRISKET *(3 to 3½ pounds), trimmed of fat*
- 10 SPRIGS THYME
- 2 TEASPOONS WHOLE BLACK PEPPERCORNS
- 20 SPRIGS FRESH FLAT-LEAF PARSLEY *(stems and leaves)*
- 2 DRIED BAY LEAVES
- 5 GARLIC CLOVES *(unpeeled)*
- 2 MEDIUM YELLOW ONIONS *(unpeeled), halved lengthwise*
- 4 WHOLE CLOVES
- 2 MEDIUM CARROTS, *peeled and cut into 2-inch lengths*
- 3 CELERY STALKS, *cut into 2-inch lengths*
  COARSE SALT

For second stage

- 4 MEDIUM LEEKS, *halved lengthwise and well washed (page 32)*
- 12 SMALL CARROTS, *peeled and about 2 inches of tops intact, if desired*
- 10 MARROW BONES *(about 1½ inches thick)*
- 1 WHOLE CHICKEN *(about 3 pounds)*
- 2 MEDIUM TURNIPS, *peeled and quartered*
- 1 HEAD SAVOY CABBAGE, *outer leaves removed, cut through the root into 8 small wedges*
- 16 TINY NEW POTATOES *(1½ inches in diameter), or 8 lsarger ones, halved or quartered*
  COARSE SALT

For serving

- CROUTONS *(page 199)*
- GRAINY FRENCH MUSTARD
- CORNICHONS
- FLEUR DE SEL *(French sea salt)*
- FRESH HORSERADISH *(grated on the small holes of a box grater)*

Pot-au-Feu Tip

> You can make the first stage a day before serving and refrigerate the meat in one container, then strain the broth and store it in another. Proceed with the second stage the next day.

Ingredients

Any successful pot-au-feu should have a variety of meats; this recipe uses brisket and short ribs, but veal and oxtail are also common. Marrow bones are essential, but poultry is optional (and is classically used in its own dish, called *poule au pot*). Vegetables are just as important; carrots, cabbage, and turnips are traditional, as are onions often studded with cloves or charred to deepen their flavor.

Call your butcher ahead of time to reserve plenty of veal and marrow bones. You might also want to order the brisket in advance (and ask for it to be trimmed); ask for the second cut, as this is the more marbled part.

POT-AU-FEU

Prepare first stage Wrap the short ribs in a single layer of cheesecloth and tie with butcher's twine to form a neat bundle; this helps keep the meat on the bones during cooking and makes for easy removal when they're done. Place ribs in a very large stockpot along with the veal bones and brisket and add enough water to cover everything by about 1 inch (8 to 9 quarts should be enough). Set over high heat and bring to a simmer (this will take about 35 minutes), then continue simmering over moderate heat for 30 minutes, skimming any foam that rises to the surface.

Meanwhile, make a sachet by placing the thyme, peppercorns, parsley, bay leaves, and garlic on a large square of cheesecloth, then gathering the edges to form a bundle and tie tightly with twine.

In a small sauté pan over medium-high heat, char one onion half by placing it cut side down into the hot pan for about 5 minutes. Stick the cloves into the cut side of another onion half. Add all of the onion halves to the pot along with the carrots, celery, herb sachet, and 2 tablespoons salt. Return the liquid to a boil and then gently simmer until the meats are almost tender and cooked through, about 2 hours, skimming off surface foam as necessary. Add more water if necessary to keep the ingredients submerged at all times, but don't worry if they just start to show above the surface of the water. (Add as little water as possible, so as not to dilute the flavor.)

Move to second stage Remove the short ribs and brisket from the pot, and cover to keep warm. Then strain the broth through a fine sieve, pressing lightly to extract juices (discard the bones, sachet, and vegetables). You should have about 5 to 6 quarts broth. Return the broth to the cleaned pot and bring it back to a boil. Meanwhile, use twine to tie the leeks into one bundle and the carrots into another. Wrap the marrow bones in cheesecloth and secure with twine.

Submerge the chicken in the pot. Reduce heat and simmer for 15 minutes, then add the leeks, carrots, and marrow bones along with the turnips and cabbage. Continue simmering another 20 to 30 minutes or until chicken is cooked through and vegetables are tender, removing each as soon as it is ready.

Meanwhile, place potatoes in a medium saucepan and cover with water; add salt. Bring to a boil, then lower the heat and simmer until you can pierce the potatoes with a paring knife, about 15 minutes. Drain them in a colander and cover to keep warm.

Serve Thoroughly skim the fat from the surface of the broth, then carefully transfer the vegetables to a large serving platter. Cover with parchment-lined foil and keep warm. Remove the ribs and marrow bones from their bundles, and arrange ribs on the same platter (serve marrow bones on the side, with croutons and salt). Slice the brisket ¼ inch thick against the grain and arrange on the platter. Finally, add the whole chicken to the platter, and cover to keep warm.

Just before serving, ladle a bit of the broth over the meat and vegetables to moisten; pour the rest into a pitcher or bowls and pass at the table (save remaining broth for another use). Serve suggested accompaniments on the side.

ASSEMBLING THE INGREDIENTS FOR
POT-AU-FEU

Equipment

This dish requires a very large stockpot, one with at least a 16-quart capacity, to hold all of the ingredients. If you must, divide the ingredients between two smaller pots, but keep the chicken whole.

You'll also need plenty of cheesecloth and kitchen twine.

BOILED OR STEAMED LOBSTERS Serves 4

These lobsters need nothing more than drawn butter and lemons as companions at the table (preferably one covered with newspaper and set with bibs, lobster picks, and nutcrackers). Lobster also has an affinity for fresh herbs, such as tarragon, chervil, and parsley, any of which can be minced and stirred into the melted butter. Of course, some people think the best way to eat lobster is to pile it on a buttered, toasted bun (see recipe below). No matter how you plan to enjoy lobster, you'll need to extract the succulent meat; see the how-to (page 240).

COARSE SALT

4 LIVE LOBSTERS *(1½ pounds each)*

MELTED BUTTER

LEMON WEDGES, *for serving*

To boil Fill a large stockpot three-quarters of the way with cold water. Bring to a rolling boil and then add a generous amount of salt (the water should be very salty, to match the brininess of the ocean; at least ½ cup in a 4-gallon pot). Plunge 4 live lobsters, one at a time, headfirst into the water, and cook uncovered until they turn bright red. This will take anywhere from 8 to 14 minutes, depending on their size. Use tongs to remove them from the pot and transfer to a platter. Allow lobsters to rest for several minutes until they are cool enough to handle. Serve with butter and lemon wedges.

To steam Fill pot with enough cold water just to reach the bottom of the steaming basket (or an inverted colander). Cover and bring to a boil. Quickly arrange 4 live lobsters in one layer in the basket (or cook in batches). Steam until bright red, 15 to 17 minutes. Use tongs to remove lobsters from pot, then allow to rest for several minutes until they are cool enough to handle.

Ingredients

Purchase lobsters no more than a day before you plan to use them. They can be stored, with their claws banded, on moist seaweed (if your fish market provides it) or damp newspaper in an open bag in the refrigerator until you are ready to cook. (To avoid getting pinched, always hold a live lobster by its body, with the claws facing down.)

Look for lobsters that are not only alive but lively. Those that are 1½ pounds are ample enough for individual servings. Don't be surprised by their black or bluish-brown color; they will turn their characteristic red only after cooking.

Equipment

A large (at least 4-gallon) stockpot is needed to boil or steam 4 lobsters at once. Or you can use smaller pots to cook lobsters in batches. When steaming lobster, an inverted metal colander is a good substitute for a steamer basket.

LOBSTER ROLLS Makes 8

When you're using fresh lobster meat, the fewer the other ingredients, the better-tasting (and more authentic) the salad will be. Some people like to use only mayonnaise or melted butter, but a sprinkling of fresh herbs and lemon juice can also be delicious and not at all overpowering. Buttered toasted buns and a side of chips are musts—at least among purists.

TO MAKE THE SALAD, stir together 1½ pounds shelled lobster meat (from about four cooked 1½-pound lobsters), chopped into ½-inch pieces, with 2 tablespoons homemade mayonnaise (page 95) or good-quality store-bought. If desired, stir in ½ teaspoon finely chopped fresh chives and ½ teaspoon finely chopped fresh tarragon or chervil. Add 1 teaspoon fresh lemon juice (or to taste) and season with coarse salt (use sea salt, if you have some) and freshly ground pepper. Cover and refrigerate the salad, up to 2 hours.

Lightly brush outsides of 8 top-split hot-dog buns with 2 tablespoons melted butter, then cook on a hot griddle or in a heavy skillet until golden brown, about 1½ minutes per side. Spoon about ½ cup lobster mixture into each bun, and serve immediately.

How to Remove Lobster

Some people enjoy the green liver, or tomalley, from the lobster's carapace, or body; mix it with lemon juice or butter and spread it on crackers.

1 Remove lobster from pot with tongs; if you like, snip the tips of claws and let liquid drain out. Remove rubber bands. Let cool. 2 Twist claws with their knuckles from the body to loosen. 3 Pull claw from body, completely separating. 4 Grasp the head and tail and twist the tail from the joint where it meets the body.

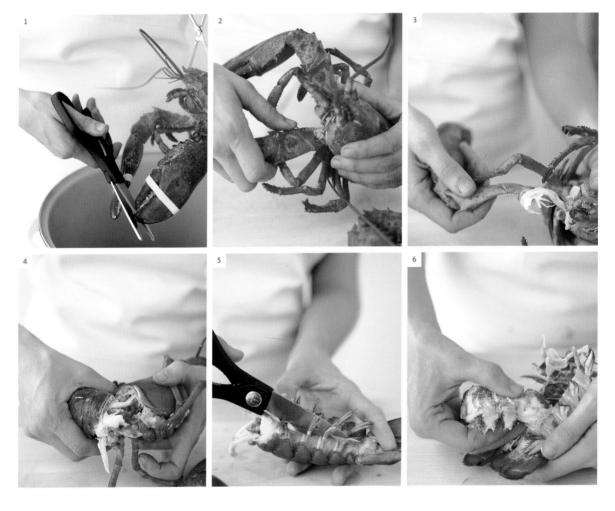

5 Use kitchen shears to slice down center of tail. 6 Open the sides of the tail apart to release the meat. Use your fingers to pull out the meat from the tail. 7 Separate knuckles from claws. Crack knuckles open and remove meat with small fork (not shown). Grasp the "thumb" from the claw and bend it back to snap it off. 8 Place the claw on its side on your work surface. Holding it with one hand, and using the back (dull edge) of a chef's knife, whack the claw several times to crack the shell without cutting into the meat. 9 Twist to open and then pull out the meat with your fingers.

SHRIMP BOIL Serves 2 to 4

Seafood boils are a mainstay of Southern cooking, the type of shellfish varying by region. Shrimp boils are most commonly associated with Low Country (South Carolina) cooking, while crawfish is a specialty of Louisiana. In most of these one-pot dishes, new potatoes and corncobs (and sometimes onion wedges and sausages) are first cooked in the pot, often on the grill, and the shellfish added at the end. Then everything is piled onto a platter and served with lemon wedges, melted butter, and hot sauce on the side.

Despite the name of the preparation, shrimp shouldn't actually be boiled (or even poached), since they will toughen if overcooked. And the point at which they turn from perfectly cooked to overcooked is very hard to detect when in boiling water. Here, the cooking water is spiked with a few simple aromatics, but you could use Old Bay Seasoning (follow the suggestions on the package for the amount) for classic peel-and-eat shrimp. Or replace the water with Court Bouillon (page 231). Serve chilled shrimp with cocktail sauce (recipe below) or as an ingredient in salads.

Ingredients

Cooking the shrimp in their shells will increase the flavor—and is necessary for peel-and-eat servings. But when used in salads or shrimp cocktail, the shrimp will have a neater appearance if peeled and deveined before cooking (the shells slip off easier when raw).

3 QUARTS WATER

2 MEDIUM CARROTS, *peeled and coarsely chopped*

1 MEDIUM CELERY STALK, *coarsely chopped*

1 LEMON, *half cut into wedges for serving, the other half juiced (reserve squeezed half)*

4 SPRIGS THYME

½ TEASPOON WHOLE BLACK PEPPERCORNS

  COARSE SALT

1 POUND LARGE (16 TO 20 COUNT) SHRIMP

COMBINE THE WATER with carrot, celery, lemon juice and reserved lemon half, thyme, peppercorns, and a generous amount of salt, in a large (5-quart) stockpot. Bring to a rolling boil, then add shrimp. When the water is almost at a boil again, which should take about 1½ minutes, the shrimp should be bright pink and curled; immediately remove the shrimp with a slotted spoon, and serve.

    If you plan on serving the shrimp cold, in shrimp cocktail or salad, immediately shock them in an ice-water bath to stop the cooking *fig. 3.29*. Peel and devein, if desired (page 122). Chill in the refrigerator, covered, until ready to serve, up to 1 day.

fig. 3.29 COOLING SHRIMP IN AN
ICE-WATER BATH

FRESH COCKTAIL SAUCE Makes about ¾ cup

Using the side of a chef's knife, mash 1 small garlic clove with ¼ teaspoon coarse salt to form a paste. Pulse 2 coarsely chopped medium tomatoes (1¾ cups) in a food processor until coarsely pureed. Transfer to a fine mesh sieve and let drain for 10 minutes, reserving liquid. Return tomatoes to food processor. Add 4½ teaspoons freshly grated horseradish (or to taste), ½ teaspoon finely grated lemon zest, 1 tablespoon plus 1 teaspoon fresh lemon juice, 1 teaspoon coarse salt, 1¼ teaspoons Worcestershire sauce (or to taste), 1½ teaspoons Tabasco sauce (or to taste), and the garlic paste. Pulse to combine. Add 2 tablespoons extra-virgin olive oil and process until combined. Add up to ¼ cup reserved liquid to mixture to adjust to desired consistency. Chill until ready to serve.

LESSON 3.5
How to Sauté and Fry

Quickness is key for sautéed and fried dishes. Take the word *sauté* itself: It means "to jump" in French—an apt description for the way food behaves in the pan. You should have everything ready to go and at the right temperature before you begin, so that you can remain focused during the actual cooking time. The goal is to produce foods that are golden and crisp on the outside and juicy within. Aside from getting the timing right, none of these techniques is terribly difficult. And mastering them will bring very satisfying—and speedy—rewards.

It may seem counterintuitive, but sautéing and frying are considered dry-heat cooking methods, since oil and other fats do not contain any water. They do lock in moisture, however, when they are heated high enough, so long as the heat remains constant. Start with oil (or any other cooking fat) that is too cold, and your fried foods will absorb too much of it and turn out greasy. Heat the oil too high before adding the food, and you'll end up with a burned crust surrounding an undercooked interior. Just as important is not overcrowding the pan, which can cause the food to steam rather than fry, and the temperature of the oil to drop significantly.

The terms may be used interchangeably, but there are distinct differences in the four techniques:

Sautéed foods are cooked in a sizzling-hot pan in just a small amount of butter, cooking oil, or other type of fat. The best cuts for sautéing are tender, portion-size, and of an even thickness. The method is well suited to cooking just a few pieces at once, since you can quickly prepare and serve without having to worry about keeping things warm between batches. For even cooking, the meat should first be brought to room temperature (30 to 60 minutes). Keep in mind that moisture is the enemy of sautéed foods and will cause them to steam rather than brown. So pat the meat completely dry and wait until just before cooking to season with salt (since salt draws out moisture). Many sautéed dishes are served with a pan sauce made from the drippings left in the pan; the pan is usually deglazed with a flavorful liquid, then the liquid reduced (to thicken) and finished with butter or cream and flavored with juices, herbs, or other seasonings.

Pan-searing uses high heat to seal in juices by forming a delicious crust. The trick to pan-searing is making sure the pan is hot enough. To test a pan for readiness, sprinkle a drop of water onto the pan; the water should sizzle or jump. The cooking fat (butter or oil) should be heated through, but should not burn. Add the meat; do not move it until a crust has formed. Use a spatula to turn the food; be sure not to tear the crust.

Stir-frying has long been associated with Asian cuisines, but the technique is popular with chefs and home cooks in other parts of the world as well. Stir-fried foods are cut into small, even pieces and cooked quickly in a little fat in a hot wok or high-sided skillet. The meats and vegetables that take the longest to cook are added to the pan first, followed by those that cook more quickly, so that everything is finished at the same time. Like sautés, stir-fried dishes are often served with a sauce made from the pan drippings.

Fried foods are cooked in fat over moderate to high heat, either by pan-frying or deep-frying. Pan-frying (also called shallow-frying) requires that foods are only partially submerged in fat; deep-fried foods, as the name suggests, are completely submerged in the cooking fat. Both pan-fried and deep-fried foods are usually coated with a breading or batter to create a deliciously rich and textured crust. The best cuts for frying are of uniform size and naturally tender, such as pieces of poultry, fish, and some shellfish. Beef is generally not a candidate for frying, although some steaks, usually tougher cuts from the round, are breaded and fried to create "chicken-fried" steak. Despite the large amounts of fat used, properly fried foods should absorb very little oil. A chicken that is cut into eight pieces and pan-fried, for example, should absorb less than 3 tablespoons of oil. The crust is where most of the fat from the cooking oil is retained, so if fat is a concern you can always take this layer off before eating and still enjoy the juicy meat (although most would agree you'd be losing the best part!).

Best Cuts to Sauté, Stir-fry, or Fry

Although sautéing, stir-frying, and frying are similar in technique, different cuts are appropriate for each method.

BEEF

☐ **Steaks from the loin,** including T-bone, porterhouse, and New York strip steak, which is alternately called a shell steak, strip steak, and Kansas City strip. Sauté or pan-sear.

☐ **Steaks from the rib,** including rib steak—which comes bone-in—or the rib eye, which is boneless. Sauté or pan-sear.

☐ **Tougher steaks,** such as the flatiron steak and flank steak. These steaks can be cut across the grain and into smaller pieces, which makes them easier to chew. Stir-fry.

VEAL

☐ **Boneless loin** Sauté.

☐ **Leg** Stir-fry.

☐ **Top round** Stir-fry.

☐ **Bottom round** Stir-fry.

LAMB

☐ **Baby lamb chops** Sauté.

☐ **Noisette** This cut is also called the boneless eye of the loin. Sauté.

☐ **Boneless leg** Stir-fry.

PORK

☐ **Boneless pork chop** This cut can come from the loin, shoulder, or rib. Sauté.

☐ **Fillet of pork** This cut comes from the tenderloin. Stir-fry.

☐ **Boneless loin** Stir-fry.

POULTRY

☐ **Boneless pieces** Sauté.

☐ **Small boneless pieces** Stir-fry.

Bone-in pieces Pan-fry.

FISH

☐ **Most fish** Sauté.

☐ **Delicate fish,** such as flounder. Bread and pan-fry or deep-fry.

☐ **Firm-fleshed fish** such as halibut, cod, and red snapper. Deep-fry.

☐ **Oysters and clams** Deep-fry.

☐ **Shrimp** Deep-fry or stir-fry.

EQUIPMENT

Sautéing A sauté pan is shallow and wide-mouthed, and has tilted sides that make it easier to toss items such as onions and other vegetables. Choose a pan made of a metal that conducts heat well, and with a heavy bottom. Cast-iron skillets are the best for searing steaks and chops, as you can get them very hot and they retain their heat. Make sure your pan or skillet is large enough for everything to fit comfortably, as the meat will not brown correctly if overcrowded. Otherwise, you'll have to cook in batches, which is not ideal for entertaining.

Stir-frying A heavy-gauge metal wok is best, although a large sauté pan is a reasonable substitute. The key is to get the pan really hot and to cook the ingredients as quickly as possible, keeping them moving the whole time to evenly distribute the heat. (Actually, for stir-frying, it's not the equipment that matters as much as the heat of the range. The reason stir-fries usually taste much better in restaurants and are relatively difficult to produce at home has less to do with the pan than with the fact that ranges in home kitchens can't reach the same high temperature as commercial ranges.)

Pan-frying Choose a pan with straight sides higher than those of a sauté pan, if possible, to hold more oil and contain spattering. Otherwise, the same principles apply: the pan should be heavy-gauge, able to withstand high temperatures, and big enough to hold the food in a single layer. For pan-fried chicken, a wide cast-iron skillet is the traditional pan of choice.

Deep-frying Deep fryers are incorporated into some specialty ranges and are also sold as stand-alone countertop appliances. Unless you plan on deep-frying frequently, however, a deep pot (at least 6 inches high) should suffice. Choose one that's heavy-gauge so that the bottom won't warp, but not so nice that you will worry about damaging the finish (very hot oil may cause pitting). Or designate a cheaper pot exclusively for deep frying; heavy-duty aluminum and cast-iron pots work well, and are usually inexpensive.

Other useful tools for these techniques include:

Thermometers A fry thermometer is essential for both pan-frying and deep-frying (or use a candy thermometer). Of the many types available, an analog model that clips to the side of the pot is most convenient. A digital thermometer with a stainless-steel probe that can be set into the oil is also good (but usually more expensive). An instant-read thermometer is crucial for testing the internal temperature of meats and poultry, such as fried chicken, without cutting into them.

A slotted spoon or metal skimmer: For transferring pan- and deep-fried foods from the pot to a paper towel–lined plate or work surface to drain.

Metal tongs: These help you turn foods while they fry. They are also good for retrieving foods from hot oil. Choose long-handled models, for safety.

Spatter guard: To protect your cooking surfaces (and your arms) from hot grease.

Wooden spoon: Choose one with a flat edge, for scraping the bottom of the pan when making pan sauce.

Metal wok spatula: The rounded edge of this utensil is designed to conform to the shape of a wok, so foods can be tossed about more easily while stir-frying.

ABOUT FRYING FATS

A variety of fats and oils can be used for sautéing and frying, but you should choose wisely when deciding between them. Consider these three factors: the oil's smoke point, its flavor, and any health concerns.

If you are using only a small amount of fat—say, for sautéing—olive oil and butter are best; they have low smoke points, and can impart nice flavors. They are more expensive than most neutral-tasting oils, however, so you might want to use a less expensive olive oil (save the most expensive extra-virgin oils for drizzling over salads and cooked foods). Clarified butter, which has been cooked to separate out the milk solids, has a much higher smoke point than regular butter, making it ideal for sautéing. See page 88 for how to make clarified butter.

Because vegetable oils (canola, grapeseed, peanut, safflower, and sunflower among them) generally have high smoke points and are mild (or neutral) in scent and flavor, they are often recommended for frying. There are health issues associated for a few of them, however. As a general rule, try to avoid blended vegetable oils and chemically extracted oils; oils that say "cold-pressed," "expeller-pressed," or "naturally pressed" on the labels are far better choices. Likewise, avoid hydrogenated oils or trans fats, which are solid at room temperature, and oils that are high in polyunsaturates, like corn and soybean oil. To play it safe, look for oils that are high in mono-unsaturated fats, which are rich in antioxidants; sunflower oil and safflower oil are excellent options.

All cooking oils have a limited shelf life, so check the expiration date. Also, label bottles with the date of purchase and discard anything you've had on hand for 12 months or more. Always smell and taste the oil before using. Rancid oil will have an unpleasant smell and a bitter taste. To prevent them from becoming rancid, store all vegetable and olive oils in a cool, dark place, never on a shelf near the stove or on top of the refrigerator.

FRYING TIPS

Home cooks often find that fried foods absorb too much oil. The best way to prevent this is to keep a vigilant eye on the temperature of the cooking oil by constantly monitoring your thermometer. This may require you to turn the burner up or down, depending on how the oil is reacting. Turn up the heat slightly to raise the temperature of the oil. Keep a few cups of room-temperature oil on hand to add to the frying oil as necessary if it gets too hot; the new oil will bring down the temperature quickly. And avoid crowding the skillet with too many pieces, which can also cause the temperature to fall too much.

As you use any cooking oil, its smoke point (or ability to withstand heat) will drop. If you are frying multiple batches, you can run into problems once the oil you are frying with is no longer fresh (usually by the third batch). The simplest solution is to have a second pan of oil ready to turn on when the oil in the first one is spent. Of course, this means you'll end up using more oil, but the food will cook cleanly and evenly in every batch.

Another problem occurs when pieces of coating fall off during frying; those floating bits blacken and degrade the cooking oil. Skim out any blackened bits after each batch, to keep them from sticking to successive batches. To keep the coating in place, avoid overcoating the food, as thick layers tend to fall off in the skillet. Let the excess marinade or egg wash drip off a piece of meat before you dredge it. Coat it completely, then shake off excess flour or bread crumbs.

Other guidelines to follow include:

■ Always prepare a paper towel–lined plate or other surface before you start frying, to drain fried foods and absorb any excess oil.

■ Never fill the pot or pan more than two-thirds with oil.

■ Keep fried foods warm between batches by setting in a low (200°F) oven.

ABOUT PAN SAUCES

Even the most moist and succulent sautéed meats can benefit from a flavorful pan sauce, and putting one together is extraordinarily easy. After the meat or fish is cooked and removed from the pan, add aromatics such as finely chopped onion or shallots. Deglaze the pan with a liquid, such as stock or wine (a good rule of thumb is about ¾ cup to serve four people). Use a wooden spoon to loosen any browned bits at the bottom, which will lend flavor to the sauce. Continue cooking until reduced by half, and then you can finish with a little cream or butter if you wish (remember: fat adds flavor), swirling it in until incorporated.

For any sautéed floured dish, such as chicken piccata (page 248), little bits of flour from the breading thicken and add texture to the sauce; finishing with butter provides additional body and sheen. Leaving out the butter would result in a lighter sauce, but it won't have the same luscious quality and velvety texture. Always add the butter after the liquid has reduced to the desired consistency, as you don't want to actually cook the butter, just gently heat. Also, if the butter is melted too fast, it will separate into pools; for a smooth, glossy sauce, swirl the pan off heat to slowly melt the butter. Fresh herbs (often parsley, but others work as well) can be added along with the butter to brighten the sauce.

ABOUT BREADINGS AND BATTERS

Batters and breading make crisp and flavorful crusts for fried meats, fish, and poultry. Because batters create fluffier, more delicate crusts than breading, they are more often used on fish, shellfish, and vegetables. Beer batter and tempura—a traditional Japanese preparation for shellfish and vegetables (page 335)—are both good examples. Battered coatings tend to get soggy if left sitting too long after cooking, so these foods are best served immediately after frying.

Breading, on the other hand, produces a more robust crust, and foods that are breaded can be made a few hours, or even a day, ahead of serving time. Some foods, like Buttermilk Fried Chicken (page 269), are marinated before being breaded to tenderize the meat and help the breading adhere. Other than that, breading can be as simple as dredging foods in flour, but any number of dry ingredients—like cornmeal, bread crumbs (including Japanese panko), herbs, toasted spices, shredded coconut, and ground nuts—can provide additional flavor and crunch. The flour you choose to dredge with can also impact the crust's texture. Wondra, a brand name for granulated flour that dissolves immediately in water, makes a delectably light breading for fish and poultry because it doesn't form clumps. (See the recipe for Sole à la Meunière on page 250 as an example.)

DEEP-FRYING AT HOME

Deep-frying produces a strong smell (and can create a bit of smoke), so to keep the odors (and smoke alarms) at bay, take these simple steps: open any windows in the kitchen; turn the stove fan on high; and cover the pot with a spatter guard. You might also want to keep a small fire extinguisher nearby in case of any flare-ups.

DISPOSING OF FRYING OIL

Even small quantities of oil can clog pipes, so never pour it down the drain. If there is just a little oil left in your skillet, soak it up with a few paper towels that you then drop into the trash can. If you have a large amount of used oil—say, a cup or two—you can pour it into a heatproof container with a tight lid and place it in the garbage. (Make sure the oil is cool before you transfer it from the pan.) If you place the container of oil in the freezer, it will help solidify the oil and eliminate the chance of its spilling while you throw it in the trash (this is also a technique that works well for the grease left in the skillet after frying bacon).

PUTTING OUT A GREASE FIRE

When oils or fats are heated too high they can spontaneously ignite. In this case, the first thing to do is to cut off the oxygen from the fire. The National Safety Council (www.nsc.org) recommends placing a tight-fitting lid directly over the pot or pan, so be sure to keep a lid next to your stove whenever you're frying. Also, keep a fire extinguisher in an accessible area in the kitchen, but away from heat, as the chemicals inside the canister may become less effective. A Class B fire extinguisher is specifically designed to put out oil and grease fires. Check the extinguisher regularly (about once a month) to make sure it's adequately pressurized.

Never put water on a grease fire. Water will only spread the oil, and thus the fire. Also, never transport the pan or pot with the fire in it outside. The oil is liable to spill over the sides of the pan, which can burn you and spread the fire to other parts of the house.

248

Sautéing Recipes

POUNDING CHICKEN CUTLETS
To ensure that the cutlets cook evenly, they should have a uniform thickness, usually around ¼ inch. Place the cutlets on your work surface, and cover with plastic wrap; use the smooth side of a meat mallet (or a heavy skillet) to pound until desired thinness.

CHICKEN PICCATA Serves 4

This simple yet timeless Italian dish demonstrates beautifully the process of sautéing: cutlets—most often chicken or veal—are dredged with flour, then sautéed in a mixture of olive oil and butter, a typical combination that is practical and flavorful. The flour encourages the chicken to form a light crust (and helps thicken the pan sauce), the butter helps it to brown, and the oil raises the smoke point so the butter doesn't brown too much before the chicken is cooked through. A simple pan sauce is the only accompaniment, and is designed to make good use of the tasty browned bits left in the pan from cooking the chicken.

¼ CUP ALL-PURPOSE FLOUR

COARSE SALT AND FRESHLY GROUND PEPPER

4 CHICKEN (OR VEAL) CUTLETS *(about ¼ inch thick)*

2 TABLESPOONS OLIVE OIL

3 TABLESPOONS UNSALTED BUTTER

3 TABLESPOONS DRY WHITE WINE

3 TABLESPOONS FRESH LEMON JUICE

2 TABLESPOONS SALT-PACKED CAPERS, *soaked in water 20 minutes, then drained, rinsed, and drained again*

1 TABLESPOON CHOPPED FRESH FLAT-LEAF PARSLEY

Dredge chicken Spread flour in a shallow dish; add ¾ teaspoon salt and ¼ teaspoon pepper and whisk to combine. Place chicken in seasoned flour [1], turning to coat thoroughly, then tap off the excess [2].

Sauté chicken Heat the oil and 1 tablespoon butter in a large skillet over

> ## Chicken Piccata, Step by Step

medium-high heat until butter starts to sizzle. Cook the chicken in batches, if necessary, to avoid crowding the pan (the cutlets should fit snugly in a single layer [3]) until golden and cooked through, 2 to 3 minutes for each side. The cooking time will depend on the thickness of the cutlet. Transfer the chicken to a platter. Pour out any excess fat from the pan.

Deglaze pan and make sauce Return pan to medium heat and add wine, scraping up any browned bits from the bottom of the pan with a wooden spoon. Cook until the liquid is reduced by half [4], about 30 seconds. (If the liquid is reducing too quickly—before all the browned bits have been incorporated—remove the pan from the heat.) Remove the pan from the heat. Add lemon juice, capers, and remaining 2 tablespoons butter [5] and swirl until melted and combined, then add parsley [6] and season with salt as desired.

Serve Immediately pour the sauce over the chicken, and serve.

SOLE À LA MEUNIÈRE Serves 2

As à *la meunière* means "in the manner of the miller's wife" in French, it's no surprise that this preparation often calls for the fish to be coated with flour before being sautéed, to promote browning.

1 WHOLE DOVER SOLE *(1 to 1½ pounds), trimmed and skinned*
COARSE SALT AND FRESHLY GROUND PEPPER
3 TABLESPOONS CLARIFIED BUTTER *(page 88)*
½ CUP WONDRA OR ALL-PURPOSE FLOUR
4 TABLESPOONS (½ STICK) UNSALTED BUTTER, *cut into tablespoons*
1 TABLESPOON CHOPPED FRESH FLAT-LEAF PARSLEY
1 LEMON, *halved*

Dredge Season both sides of fish with salt and pepper while heating the clarified butter in a copper oval sauté pan (or a large sauté pan) over medium heat. Pour flour onto a large shallow dish and press both sides of the fish into the flour, making sure it is fully coated. Shake off any excess flour.

Sauté Set the fish skin side up in the pan and sauté until golden brown underneath, about 4 minutes. Use a fish spatula (or two large, wide spatulas) to carefully flip the fish and sauté until the skin side is golden brown and cooked throughout (the flesh should flake with a fork and the thickest part of the fish should be opaque), about 3 minutes more.

Make sauce Drop the butter pieces into the hot pan, around the fish, and let it melt. Sprinkle parsley over fish. When butter is frothy, squeeze the lemon over it (so the juice runs into the butter) and immediately spoon this over the fish. (Alternatively, transfer fish to a platter and sprinkle with parsley before adding butter and lemon juice to the pan, swirling to combine.)

Serve Fillet fish and parcel portions onto plates, then spoon some more of the sauce on top, and serve.

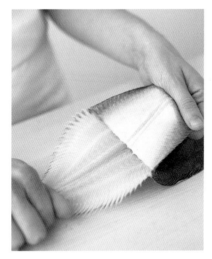

SKINNING DOVER SOLE
This recipe calls for removing the skin from one side only. Begin by snipping off the fins (see page 120). Next, make a small incision in the skin just above the tail. Hold the skin at the incision and then carefully peel back a small portion to make a flap. Holding the flap firmly in one hand and the tail firmly in the other, quickly pull the skin back toward the head to remove skin in one piece.

Ingredients

True Dover sole, which comes only from the waters of the Atlantic off the Dover coast of England, is difficult to find in the United States and fairly expensive. Gray sole and petrale sole (both of which are actually types of flounder), are perfectly fine. If you'd rather not trim the fish yourself, ask your fishmonger to do this.

Because clarified butter (page 88) has a higher smoke point than regular butter, it is the cooking fat of choice for sautéing delicate fish such as sole.

Wondra is a low-protein flour that has been processed so it dissolves instantly. (It is often called "instant flour" for this reason.) Since it is less likely to clump than all-purpose flours, it has long been a favorite among chefs for the ultralight coating it gives sautéed fish.

Serving Sautéed Dover Sole

1 Using a fish knife (or a large spoon), slice on one side of the backbone from head to tail to separate fillet, keeping knife at an angle (away from flesh) and against the bone; carefully slide knife under fillet to loosen (not shown). 2 Trim away outer edge of fillet with the knife. 3 Lift fillet with the knife and fork to remove. 4 Rotate fish and repeat above steps to remove the other top fillet. 5 Loosening with the knife as you work, lift off the bones to completely separate from the remaining flesh. 6 Lift to remove each of the bottom fillets, leaving the skin in the pan.

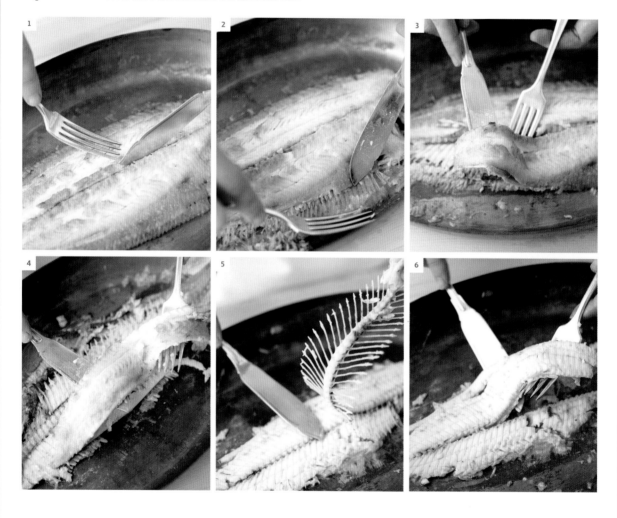

SAUTÉED CALF'S LIVER Serves 4

Liver is another good option for sautéing, since it cooks so quickly, inside and out. A simple dredging in seasoned flour is all that's required; soaking the liver in milk first will mellow its flavor and tenderize the meat. Be sure to pat the liver dry before coating; otherwise the flour will form clumps, which can fall off in the pan.

Liver and onions is a classic dish, and can be prepared by caramelizing some sliced onion (two onions would be plenty for four servings) in butter before browning the liver. Then finish by returning the onion to the pan just to heat through. Or serve with Tomato and Onion Confit (on page 306), as pictured above.

1 POUND CALF'S LIVER, *cut into ½-inch-thick pieces*

1½ CUPS WHOLE MILK

COARSE SALT AND FRESHLY GROUND PEPPER

½ CUP ALL-PURPOSE FLOUR

2 TABLESPOONS SUNFLOWER OR OTHER NEUTRAL-TASTING OIL, *plus more as needed*

TOMATO AND ONION CONFIT *(page 306), for serving*

Soak liver Place liver in a nonreactive (ceramic or glass) bowl and pour milk over. Refrigerate, covered, 3 hours (or up to overnight). Drain liver and discard milk. Pat liver dry with paper towels.

Dredge Spread flour on a plate and season with salt and pepper. Thoroughly coat liver with the flour mixture, shaking off excess *fig. 3.30*.

Sauté Heat a large (13-inch) sauté pan over medium heat, then add the oil and heat until shimmering. Cook (in batches, if necessary, to avoid crowding pan) until liver is firm (but not hard) and browned on the outside but still slightly pink in the center, 1 to 2 minutes per side. Repeat with remaining liver, adding more oil to the pan as necessary.

Serve Divide liver among plates and top with the confit. Serve immediately.

fig. 3.30 DREDGING THE LIVER

SAUTÉED SKATE WING Serves 4

Try this technique with any mild, flaky white fish, including sole, tilapia, or turbot, all of which work nicely with the sauce. Brown butter—or *beurre noisette,* created when butter is cooked until the milk solids turn golden brown—is one of those *à la minute* (cooked to order) sauces that should be a part of any home cook's repertoire, since it can be altered in countless ways. Nuts are classically paired with browned butter, as their flavors are complementary; citrus juice or wine balances the richness; and other ingredients, such as herbs, provide complexity.

Since this recipe is so quick to prepare, you need to have your *mise en place* at the ready before you heat the pan. Toast and chop the hazelnuts, suprême the citrus, and put salt, pepper, and flour in separate dishes (for seasoning and dredging the fish) set near the stove.

Ingredients

Skate is a type of ray fish, with flat pectoral fins (called wings) that give it a batlike appearance. The wings are the most desirable part of the fish, with a delicate, flaky texture. They are most commonly sautéed and served with brown butter and capers.

4 SMALL SKATE WINGS, *each cut into 2 equal pieces*

COARSE SALT AND FRESHLY GROUND PEPPER

½ CUP WONDRA OR ALL-PURPOSE FLOUR

¼ CUP SUNFLOWER OR OTHER NEUTRAL-TASTING OIL

4 TABLESPOONS (½ STICK) UNSALTED BUTTER, *cut into tablespoons*

⅓ CUP LIGHTLY TOASTED BLANCHED HAZELNUTS, *coarsely chopped*

4 SPRIGS THYME

1 TEASPOON FRESH LEMON JUICE

1 SMALL PINK GRAPEFRUIT, *suprêmed (page 34) and juice reserved (to yield 12 segments and 2 tablespoons juice)*

Dredge Heat a large sauté pan over medium-high heat as you season skate with salt and pepper and then dredge in flour, shaking off excess.

Sauté When pan is hot, add oil and heat until shimmering. Add skate pieces, working in batches to avoid crowding the pan, and sauté until fish is golden brown underneath, 1½ to 2 minutes. Carefully turn pieces over with a fish spatula and reduce heat to medium. Cook until fish is uniformly opaque and browned on the other side, about 1½ minutes more. Transfer to a plate and cover to keep warm.

fig. 3.31 **MAKING BROWNED BUTTER**

fig. 3.32 **FLAVORING BROWNED BUTTER
WITH NUTS AND HERBS**

Brown butter Wipe pan with paper towels and set over medium-low heat. Drop butter pieces into pan *fig. 3.31* and swirl constantly (to cook evenly) until butter is melted and golden brown, 30 to 60 seconds. Stir in thyme and citrus juices; the butter will spatter a bit. Add hazelnuts, then remove from heat *fig. 3.32*.

Serve Divide skate pieces among plates, arrange three grapefruit segments over each serving, and drizzle evenly with hazelnut brown butter. Serve immediately.

SAUTÉED PORK MEDALLIONS Serves 2 to 4

Not all sauté recipes start with dredging the meat in flour. Instead, this recipe demonstrates how meat can achieve a nice sear simply by relying on the high heat of the pan (and a little science, called the Maillard reactions; see page 126). To encourage browning, you must make sure the meat is dry, as moisture will hinder the process. First, pat the meat dry with paper towels and wait to salt it until just before cooking (since salt will draw the juices to the surface). The sautéed meat will leave golden-brown bits behind, so you'll want to deglaze the pan and incorporate them into a pan sauce. This one is made with a fragrant combination of brandy, shallots, apples, and raisins (all good partners for pork) and finished with cream, which thickens as it simmers, giving body to the sauce.

2 TABLESPOONS OLIVE OIL

1 MEDIUM PORK TENDERLOIN *(about 1 pound), formed into medallions as directed on page 115*

COARSE SALT AND FRESHLY GROUND PEPPER

2 TABLESPOONS UNSALTED BUTTER, *cut into pieces*

2 MEDIUM SHALLOTS, *halved lengthwise and thinly sliced crosswise*

1 APPLE *(such as Granny Smith or Fuji), peeled, cored, and cut into ½-inch dice*

3 TABLESPOONS RAISINS

2 TABLESPOONS TO ¼ CUP WATER

⅓ CUP BRANDY

⅓ CUP HEAVY CREAM

1 TABLESPOON CHIFFONADE OF SAGE *(page 21), plus small leaves for garnish (optional)*

Sauté Heat a large (13-inch) sauté pan over medium-high heat. Add the oil and heat until shimmering. Meanwhile, pat the medallions dry with paper towels and season both sides with salt and pepper. Cook (in batches if necessary to avoid crowding the pan) until golden brown, 1 to 1½ minutes per side. Transfer pork to a plate and cover to keep warm.

Make pan sauce Add butter to pan and reduce heat to medium. Add the shallots, apple, and raisins. Cook for 2 minutes, stirring occasionally so the apple browns evenly. Deglaze the pan with 2 tablespoons water, cooking and scraping up the browned bits from the bottom of the pan, until the water has evaporated. If after about 2 minutes the apple is not yet tender, add additional 2 tablespoons water and continue cooking a few minutes more. Pour in the brandy and cook until reduced by half, 30 to 60 seconds, then add heavy cream and any juices from the pork that have collected on the plate. Simmer until the sauce has thickened enough to coat the back of a spoon, about 1½ minutes. Stir in sage and season with salt and pepper to taste.

Serve Spoon pan sauce over medallions, garnish with small sage leaves, if desired, and serve.

PAN-SEARED STRIP STEAK WITH MUSTARD CREAM SAUCE Serves 2

Cooking steaks on the stove is fast and efficient. They require only a few minutes in a very hot skillet, which can then be deglazed to make a flavorful sauce (see variations below). Very little butter is needed to encourage the meat to form a nice crust; be sure to wait until the steaks release easily from the pan before turning them. For the quintessential bistro dish, serve the steaks with French Fries (page 333). Mashed or crushed potatoes (page 309) are also a natural accompaniment, as is Creamed Spinach (page 297).

For searing steaks

2 BONELESS STRIP STEAKS, *each 8 to 10 ounces and 1 inch thick, room temperature*

COARSE SALT AND FRESHLY GROUND PEPPER

1 TEASPOON UNSALTED BUTTER

For sauce

½ CUP VERMOUTH OR WHITE WINE

2 TEASPOONS DIJON MUSTARD

¼ CUP HEAVY CREAM

Sear steaks Heat a 10-inch cast-iron skillet over medium-high until it is very hot but not smoking, about 2 minutes. Season steaks on both sides with salt and pepper. Add half the butter to the pan and set one of the steaks directly on top [1]. Repeat with the remaining butter and steak. Without moving the steaks, sear until steaks release easily from pan and a golden brown crust has formed, about 2 minutes. Using tongs, hold steaks and sear both sides [2], about 3 seconds each, then turn steaks over and continue cooking until an instant-read thermometer reaches 115°F to 120°F for rare, 125°F for medium-rare, and 135°F to 140°F for medium [3]. Transfer steaks to a warm plate to rest.

Make sauce Remove pan from heat and carefully pour in vermouth [4] (it will spatter). Return skillet to heat. Deglaze pan, stirring up any browned bits with a wooden spoon, and cook until liquid is almost completely reduced, about 45 seconds. Stir in mustard and heat for 15 seconds. Add the cream and any juices

Pan-Seared Steak, Step by Step

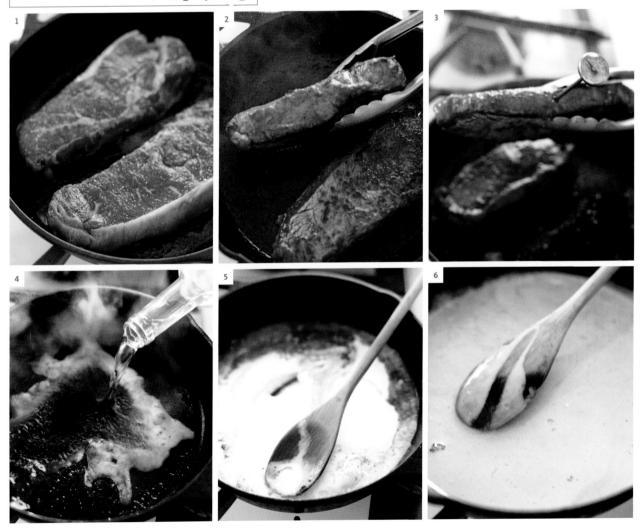

PAN-SEARED STEAK WITH
MUSTARD CREAM SAUCE

that have collected from steak, and stir to combine [5]. Cook until sauce lightly coats the back of a spoon [6], about 10 seconds. Season with salt and pepper.

Serve Place the steaks on dinner plates and pour the sauce over, dividing evenly, before serving.

PAN-SEARED STEAK WITH BALSAMIC SAUCE

Cook steaks as directed, adding 2 small sprigs of fresh rosemary to the skillet a few seconds before steaks have finished cooking, just to heat them slightly. Transfer steaks and rosemary sprigs to a warm plate to rest. Return skillet to heat and carefully pour in ⅓ cup balsamic vinegar. Deglaze pan, stirring up any browned bits, and reduce to a syrupy consistency, 15 to 25 seconds. Season with salt, add any juices that have collected under the steaks, and stir to combine. Remove from heat. Add 1 tablespoon unsalted butter, swirling to combine. Place steaks on plates and brush each with sauce, dividing evenly. Garnish with rosemary sprigs.

TESTING FOR DONENESS
With some experience, you can learn to gauge if a steak has reached the desired degree of cooking throughout by pressing on the thickest part with your finger. The softer the steak, the rarer it will be.

fig. 3.33 DEGLAZING PAN WITH
RED-WINE SHALLOT SAUCE

PAN-SEARED STEAK WITH RED-WINE SHALLOT SAUCE
Combine 1 cup dry red wine, such as Côtes-du-Rhône, and 1 large shallot, thinly sliced crosswise, in a small saucepan and bring to a boil over medium-high heat, then reduce heat to medium and simmer until reduced by half, 8 to 10 minutes. Cook steaks as directed above. After removing them from the pan, return skillet to medium-high heat. Once it is hot again, remove from heat and carefully pour in wine mixture (it will spatter). Return to heat and deglaze the pan, stirring with a wooden spoon to scrape up any browned bits *fig. 3.33*. Reduce heat and simmer until liquid is reduced by half, 1 to 2 minutes. Season with salt, add any juices that have accumulated on the plate, and stir to combine. Remove from heat and add 1 tablespoon unsalted butter, swirling to combine. Place steaks on plates and pour sauce over, dividing evenly.

PAN-SEARED SCALLOPS WITH
FENNEL PUREE Serves 12 as an hors d'oeuvre

Because scallops have a high moisture content, the risk in preparing them is that they will release their liquid in the pan and steam instead of sear. They also become tough and rubbery if overcooked. The trick is to heat the pan and oil sufficiently so the scallops brown quickly, without overcooking. Swirling the oil to completely coat the pan is crucial, as the heated oil will provide a slick surface that will prevent the scallops from sticking, but you should give the pan a good, strong jerk as soon as the scallops have been added, just in case. Succulent, sweet scallops have an affinity for anise-flavored fennel, and they look lovely resting on pools of silky fennel puree.

6 LARGE SEA SCALLOPS
COARSE SALT
SUNFLOWER OR OTHER NEUTRAL-TASTING OIL
¾ CUP FENNEL PUREE *(page 310), fennel fronds reserved for garnish*

Sear scallops If necessary, remove the small, tough muscle (called the adductor) found on the side of the scallops (often the fishmonger will have removed it), then slice each scallop in half horizontally so that you have twelve pieces. Heat a large skillet over high heat. Season scallops on both sides with salt. When pan is hot, add enough oil to coat bottom of pan (about 1 tablespoon), and swirl to coat evenly. Working in batches to avoid crowding pan, add scallops and quickly jerk the pan to keep them from sticking. Sear until lightly golden, about 45 seconds; with an offset spatula, turn over and cook until opaque throughout, about 30 seconds more (be careful not to turn too soon or the scallops may tear). Transfer to a plate lined with paper towels and cover to keep warm (if necessary). Repeat with more oil and remaining scallops.

Serve Heat fennel puree in a small saucepan over medium heat until warm. Spoon 1 tablespoon puree onto each of 12 small plates and top with a scallop slice. Garnish with fennel fronds, and serve.

DUCK BREAST WITH ORANGE GASTRIQUE Serves 2

Duck breast, long considered a delicacy in French cuisine, is exceptionally moist and tender when properly prepared. The breast is small enough to cook in a pan (rather than having to roast the whole bird) and it needs no flour or added fat to develop a crisp golden crust. You do need to follow a few special rules, however, as duck has quite a bit of fat under its skin.

Duck should always be cooked sufficiently to render out its fat, some of which is poured off and reserved for another use (such as roasting potatoes or sautéing vegetables). To render fat, the duck is cooked first on its skin side, then turned over to finish cooking through. The desired degree of doneness depends on whom you ask; some cooks insist that the breast meat should always remain pink, while others would have you cook it further (the USDA, for example, recommends cooking to 170°F). In the recipe that follows, the time given should result in a medium-rare (pinkish) interior after the duck has rested, so cook it longer if you prefer it more well done. The rich taste of duck makes it a fine partner for fruit, especially orange (think of the French standby, *duck à l'orange*). Here it is served with a sweet-and-sour sauce called *gastrique,* made by caramelizing sugar and then deglazing the pan with an acidic liquid, such as vinegar or citrus juice (this recipe uses both). This dish would pair particularly well with mashed or pureed turnips or sautéed bitter greens.

1 LARGE DUCK BREAST *(about 1 pound)*

COARSE SALT AND FRESHLY GROUND PEPPER

1 ORANGE, *zest of one half sliced into julienne (page 34), both halves juiced (to yield about ⅓ cup)*

½ CUP SUGAR

½ CUP BEST-QUALITY RED WINE VINEGAR

Render fat Using a sharp knife, trim away excess skin from the duck (leaving enough to amply cover the breast) and score the skin, first cutting diagonally in one direction and then the other in a crosshatch manner [1]. Cut all the way through the skin and most of the fat but avoid the flesh. Season both sides with salt and pepper and place in an unheated 10-inch skillet with the skin side down [2]. Cook over medium-low heat until a small pool of fat forms in the pan. Use tongs to turn breast over and then cook the other side 1 minute. Turn breast over again (skin side down) and pour out fat into a heatproof bowl. (Reserve fat for another use; allow it to cool before storing in an airtight container at room temperature.) Continue cooking duck until the skin is nicely browned and crisp, 10 to 12 minutes, spooning off and reserving excess fat as necesary.

Sauté Turn duck once more, skin side up [3] and cook until duck is medium rare, 8 to 12 minutes. It should register 125°F on an instant-read thermometer (insert into thickest part). Transfer to a wire rack set over a rimmed baking sheet to rest for 5 to 8 minutes. The duck will continue to cook slightly during this time.

Cooking Duck Breast

Make gastrique Bring a small pot of water to a boil. Add orange zest and simmer for 2 minutes, then drain. (This will remove some of the bitterness and also help soften the the zest.) Heat sugar in a small saucepan over medium heat without stirring [1]. Once the sugar has started to melt, swirl the pan (to redistribute the melted sugar so it caramelizes more evenly) and continue cooking until it is uniformly amber, about 5 minutes more. Pour in vinegar [2] and stir with a wooden spoon to combine, then continue simmering (and stirring every so often) until slightly reduced and syrupy, about 5 minutes. Pour in orange juice [3] and add zest [4]; simmer until reduced to a thick syrup [5] and a foam forms on top, about 5 minutes longer. Season with salt and pepper.

Serve Slice duck crosswise into ¼-inch-thick slices, fan out on serving plates, and drizzle with sauce before serving.

Making Orange Gastrique

> ## *Frying Recipes*

STIR-FRIED SHRIMP WITH
BLACK BEAN SAUCE Serves 2

Unlike other frying methods, stir-frying requires very high heat and very little fat. A wok is the best implement; it heats up quickly and to just the right temperature, and the shape promotes the brisk tossing about of food that is so characteristic of stir-frying. You can achieve similar results in a skillet as long as it's large enough to accommodate all the ingredients (with room for tossing): Set the pan over high heat until very hot, add the oil and shrimp (or other items), and then adjust the heat as necessary during cooking.

This method results in perfectly coated shrimp with lots of flavor, but there will not be much sauce for serving with rice (which is more authentic than heavily sauced renditions); if desired, double the amount of sauce ingredients.

Ingredients

Fermented black beans are dried soybeans that have been preserved in salt, and sometimes garlic and spices. They are available at Asian markets.

Shao-hsing wine is a traditional Chinese cooking wine brewed from pure grain, with a low level of alcohol. Sake or sherry can be substituted.

PEELING GINGER
Use the edge of a teaspoon to peel fresh ginger. Run the spoon along its length, working in and out of the crevices, using a firm but light touch so you remove only the papery coating, not the flavorful flesh beneath.

For sauce

    3 GARLIC CLOVES, *minced*
    1½ TEASPOONS UNTOASTED SESAME OR PEANUT OIL
    1 TABLESPOON FERMENTED BLACK BEANS, *rinsed and crushed with the back of a spoon*
    1½ TABLESPOONS MINCED FRESH GINGER
    1½ TABLESPOONS SHAO-HSING WINE
    2 TEASPOONS HOISIN SAUCE
    1½ TEASPOONS SOY SAUCE
    1 FRESH HOT CHILE, *such as Thai (also called bird), sliced very thinly crosswise (remove seeds for less heat)*
    1 SCALLION, *thinly sliced on the diagonal; reserve 1 tablespoon for garnish*

For stir-frying

    1 POUND LARGE SHRIMP (16 TO 20 COUNT), *peeled and deveined (page 122)*
    1 TABLESPOON CORNSTARCH
    3 TABLESPOONS PEANUT OIL

For serving

    PERFECT WHITE RICE *(page 407)*

Make sauce Whisk together sauce ingredients in a bowl and set aside.

Stir-fry Heat a wok on high for 2 minutes; it should be very hot (test by sprinkling in a bit of water, which should sizzle and evaporate upon contact). Toss shrimp with cornstarch to coat (don't do this too soon or the coating will get gummy). Pour the peanut oil into the wok and add shrimp, letting them sit for 5 seconds (press on them with a spatula for better searing) before quickly stirring a few times and again letting them rest another 5 seconds. Continue resting and stirring until the shrimp are bright pink and opaque and seared to a golden brown, 1 to 2 minutes longer. Pour in sauce, bring to a boil, and cook for 30 seconds (without stirring), then stir a few times to coat the shrimp thoroughly.

Serve Garnish with reserved scallion. Serve immediately, with rice.

STIR-FRY VARIATIONS

Sea scallops Follow recipe above, replacing shrimp with a dozen sea scallops (adductor muscle removed) and searing on each side for 20 seconds (without moving). Add sauce and proceed as directed.

Cubed pork Make the sauce as instructed above. Toss ¾-pound pork tenderloin, cut into 1-inch cubes, with cornstarch. Sauté pork until golden brown, stirring occasionally so that all sides brown evenly, about 4 minutes, then add sauce and proceed as directed.

Sliced pork Follow pork variation above, slicing ¾-pound pork tenderloin into very thin strips and sautéing just until they begin to turn golden, about 2 minutes. Then add sauce and proceed as directed.

WIENER SCHNITZEL Serves 4

Wiener schnitzel (German for "Viennese cutlet") is a time-honored Austrian dish believed to be inspired by the Italian methods of cooking cutlets known as Milanese or scaloppine. All of these are variations of the same technique: a cutlet (either veal, chicken, or pork) is coated with flour, then beaten egg, then bread crumbs before being pan-fried to a golden crisp. What distinguishes Wiener schnitzel from other sautéed meats is that the pan-fried cutlets pay a second visit to the pan for a last-minute dip into sizzling butter.

Because the cutlets are breaded in a three-step method, they have a wonderfully crisp crust. The method is ideal when pan-frying cutlets and other smaller pieces since they will be able to cook through in the same time the crust turns crisp and brown. The process is simple but each step has a purpose: The flour creates a dry surface for the egg to cling to, while the egg serves as the "glue" for the breading, and the crumb coating (such as bread crumbs, panko, or ground nuts) adds unbeatable texture and flavor. Pat or press the crumbs firmly onto the meat and gently shake off any excess.

¼ CUP ALL-PURPOSE FLOUR

COARSE SALT AND FRESHLY GROUND PEPPER

1 CUP FRESH BREAD CRUMBS

2 LARGE EGGS

4 VEAL CUTLETS, *each about 4 to 5 ounces and pounded to ¼ inch thick (ask the butcher to pound them for you)*

SUNFLOWER OR OTHER NEUTRAL-TASTING OIL, *for frying*

4 TABLESPOONS (½ STICK) UNSALTED BUTTER

2 TABLESPOONS FINELY CHOPPED FRESH FLAT-LEAF PARSLEY, *plus sprigs for garnish*

LEMON WEDGES, *for serving*

Bread cutlets Heat the oven to 200°F while you prepare the three components of the breading. Place flour in a shallow dish and whisk to combine with 1 teaspoon salt and ½ teaspoon pepper. In another shallow dish, whisk to combine bread crumbs with 1 teaspoon salt. Lightly beat eggs in a wide, shallow bowl. Pat cutlets dry with paper towels. Dredge one cutlet at a time in the seasoned flour, turning to coat, then shake off excess. Next dip in the eggs, again making sure to coat completely and to allow the excess to drip back into bowl. Then coat with bread crumbs, patting them firmly so they adhere but being careful not to coat too thickly. Place coated cutlets on piece of parchment paper [1] or a large baking sheet.

Pan-fry Heat ¼ inch of oil in a large skillet on medium heat until it is 350°F. Working in batches to avoid crowding pan [2], cook cutlets until golden brown on the bottom, 1 to 2 minutes. Flip with a flexible thin spatula [3] and fry until the other side is golden brown and cutlets are cooked through, 1 to 2 minutes more, monitoring temperature of oil to maintain 350°F. Transfer to a baking sheet lined with a double layer of paper towels and keep warm in the oven.

Wiener Schnitzel Tips

Choose a skillet that's large enough to accommodate a single layer of the cutlets without overcrowding, or cook in batches.

Heat oil, about ¼ inch deep, in the skillet on medium until a pinch of bread crumbs sizzles when dropped in. If the oil is not hot enough, the breading will absorb too much of it, become soggy, and possibly slide off.

Carefully turn the pieces of meat with a spatula or tongs.

Between batches, remove excess crumbs from the skillet with a slotted spoon to avoid burning.

Wiener Schnitzel, Step by Step

Finish Pour off and discard oil remaining in skillet, then wipe clean with paper towels. Working in batches again if necessary, melt the butter in the same skillet over medium heat until sizzling. Set pan-fried cutlets in the pan to coat one side with butter, then quickly flip to coat the other side. Place on paper towels to drain.

Serve Arrange the cutlets on a platter and sprinkle with chopped parsley. Garnish with parsley sprigs and serve with lemon wedges.

PAN-FRIED CHICKEN CUTLETS WITH INDIAN YOGURT MARINADE
For this variation on schnitzel, chicken cutlets get marinated overnight in Indian-spiced yogurt and then coated with panko (Japanese bread crumbs), which creates a lighter, crunchier crust than standard bread crumbs.

PLACE 4 CHICKEN CUTLETS (each 4 to 5 ounces and ¼ inch thick) in a shallow dish and pour 1 recipe Indian Yogurt Marinade (page 173) over, turning the chicken to thoroughly coat. Cover and marinate overnight in the refrigerator. When ready to proceed, remove cutlets from the marinade and wipe with paper towels to remove any marinade that might be clinging to them (you want them to be dry before dredging). Follow the above recipe to bread the cutlets, replacing the bread crumbs with 2 cups panko that have been lightly crushed by hand (and seasoned with salt). Fry the cutlets as directed above, cooking two at a time for about 2½ minutes per side. Omit the last step (do not return cutlets to the pan after frying) and serve with lime wedges, fresh cilantro, and thinly sliced onion.

PAN-FRIED CHICKEN CUTLETS WITH
INDIAN YOGURT MARINADE

BUTTERMILK FRIED CHICKEN Serves 4

Next time you want to welcome guests Southern-style, cook up a batch (or two) of crisp fried chicken. It's hard to imagine anything else that exudes both down-home appeal and true culinary wizardry. The recipe here is for one chicken, but you can easily double the ingredients to fry two.

Whenever you are preparing a mixture for dredging, start off by whisking together only half the amounts called for; then, if you find you need more, whisk together the rest. Many recipes call for more dredging ingredients than you'll need, and the excess must be discarded because it came into contact with raw meat. Or, you can whisk everything together, transfer some to the bowl for dredging, and then freeze any unused (and untainted) portion in a resealable plastic bag.

When pan-frying most foods, you do not want to crowd the pan. But fried chicken is an exception. Placing more pieces in the pan helps to stabilize the temperature of the oil during frying so that it does not spike as much or as quickly.

The chicken can be soaked in ice water overnight in a covered dish in the refrigerator to remove any blood or impurities; be sure to change the water a few times.

If you prefer a thicker crust, double dredge: coat the chicken in the flour mixture and let sit for 15 minutes, then dredge in the flour again, tapping off excess.

Ingredients

- Small chickens called fryers (2½ to 3 pounds) are tender and best for frying. Follow instructions on pages 110–111 for cutting a whole chicken into 10 parts; this includes cutting the breast pieces in half diagonally, as shown, to separate the thicker part from the thinner, quicker-cooking section. You can buy a cut-up chicken, but you'll pay more.

- Buttermilk lends the chicken a subtle tang. Because it contains lactic acid (which also has a tenderizing effect on proteins), it also helps the chicken remain moist and juicy.

- Cornmeal adds extra crunch to the coating.

- When frying the chicken, keep extra vegetable oil (room temperature) nearby; if the oil in the pan gets too hot, you can cool it down by adding some of this.

Equipment

A cast-iron skillet is the best pan for frying chicken, since it will conduct and hold heat more effectively than other types of skillets. If using a 10-inch pan, cook the chicken in two batches.

An instant-read thermometer is the most accurate way to determine whether the chicken parts are cooked through; to test, remove a piece of chicken from the oil and insert thermometer into the thickest section, away from the bone.

Wire racks are ideal for draining the chicken, after marinating and after frying (wash them well between uses to avoid contamination); set them on rimmed baking sheets to catch any drippings. Line the racks with paper towels for draining fried pieces; this will help absorb oil while also allowing air to circulate underneath to preserve crispness.

Use long-handled tongs to remove chicken from the marinade, dredge in the coating, and handle during frying.

For marinating

    1 WHOLE FRYER CHICKEN *(2½ to 3 pounds), cut into 10 parts (pages 110–111)*
    1 QUART LOW-FAT BUTTERMILK
      COARSE SALT
1½ TABLESPOONS DRY MUSTARD
    1 TEASPOON OLD BAY SEASONING *(optional)*
    1 TEASPOON CAYENNE PEPPER

For dredging

1½ CUPS ALL-PURPOSE FLOUR
    2 TABLESPOONS YELLOW CORNMEAL
      COARSE SALT AND FRESHLY GROUND BLACK PEPPER
   ¼ TEASPOON CAYENNE PEPPER

For frying

    VEGETABLE OIL *(about 3 cups to start, plus more if needed)*

Marinate chicken Arrange chicken snugly in a large shallow bowl or baking dish (or divide between two dishes). Whisk together the buttermilk and seasonings and pour over the chicken, making sure the parts are completely submerged. (Alternatively, divide the chicken and marinade evenly among large resealable plastic bags; rest the bags on a rimmed baking sheet to catch any leaks.) Cover tightly, and refrigerate for at least 3½ hours (or up to overnight).

Prepare for dredging About an hour before you plan to cook the chicken, remove the pieces from the marinade and allow them to drain on a wire rack set over a rimmed baking sheet [1]. (This allows the excess marinade to drip off and the remaining marinade to lose some of its moisture and become slightly tacky, so the coating will adhere better and produce a crisper crust. The chicken will also come to room temperature, allowing it to cook more quickly and evenly.) Meanwhile, whisk together the flour, cornmeal, and seasonings, and spread in a shallow bowl or pie plate.

Heat oil When you are ready to begin frying, pour just under ½ inch oil in a large cast-iron skillet, and bring the oil to 375°F over medium heat. (If you don't have a thermometer, try this test: drop a cube of white crustless bread into the oil; it should turn golden brown within 1 minute.) While the oil is heating, use tongs to dredge the chicken pieces [2]. Make sure they are thoroughly coated, shaking off the excess flour for a nice, even, lump-free crust. (You can also do this in a large resealable bag: scoop some of the flour mixture into the bag, then add a few pieces of chicken at a time; seal bag and shake to coat.) Set the dredged pieces on a baking sheet lined with parchment paper as you work.

Fry Heat oven to 200°F. Before beginning, set a wire rack in a rimmed baking sheet and set several layers of paper towels on top of the rack for draining the chicken. Working in batches, arrange the chicken pieces skin side down in the pan in a single layer. Remember to add enough pieces to fill the pan [3], without touching. After placing the chicken in the pan, the temperature of the oil will drop dramatically. Make sure to adjust the heat as needed to maintain a steady temperature of between 330°F and 340°F during frying, as this will help the parts cook evenly, inside and out.

BUTTERMILK FRIED CHICKEN

Cover the skillet during frying to help the chicken cook through evenly (and reduce spattering), peeking inside to check on the progress. (Using a probe-style thermometer allows you to monitor the temperature of the oil without lifting the lid.) Once the first side is crisp and golden, after 4 to 5 minutes, carefully turn the pieces. Be sure not to turn them too soon, or the crust will tear; they should release easily from the pan. Then cover the pan again and continue frying until the other side is crisp and the meat is cooked through (it should register 160°F for breasts, 165°F for thighs on an instant-read thermometer). This should take another 4 to 5 minutes, depending on the size of the pieces. Check each piece in the batch and remove it as soon as it is ready. Wings, drumsticks, and thinner breast pieces cook faster than the thighs and thicker breast pieces, so remove these first. Transfer to rack on prepared baking sheet and keep warm in the oven. Return the oil to 375°F before adding the next batch.

⟩ Fried Chicken, Step by Step

PAN-FRIED SOFT SHELL CRABS Serves 4 as a first course

Soft shell crabs are blue crabs that have shed their hard shells. But they are soft for only a very short amount of time; in another six to eight hours, if left in the water, their hard shells re-form. Their season is also brief, depending on the region. In the cold waters of the Chesapeake Bay (shared by Maryland and Virginia)—the most famous region for blue crabs—they are available only in the spring; those from the warmer waters of the Gulf of Mexico may be harvested for longer periods but in much smaller numbers. In parts of Asia, where there is a high demand, crabs have become available year-round.

½ CUP COCONUT MILK *(or milk or buttermilk)*

COARSE SALT AND FRESHLY GROUND PEPPER

¼ CUP ALL-PURPOSE FLOUR

¼ CUP CORNSTARCH

4 SOFT SHELL CRABS, *cleaned (page 123, or have your fishmonger do this)*
SUNFLOWER OR OTHER NEUTRAL-TASTING OIL, *for frying*
GREEN PAPAYA SLAW *(page 274), for serving*

Coat Heat oven to 200°F. Whisk together coconut milk, ½ teaspoon salt, and ¼ teaspoon pepper in a shallow dish. In another dish, whisk together flour, cornstarch, and ½ teaspoon each salt and pepper. Working with one at a time, place crabs in milk mixture and turn to coat completely. Lift crabs, allowing excess liquid to drip into bowl, then dredge in flour mixture, turning to coat both sides. Tap off excess flour mixture and set the crabs on a baking sheet as you work.

Pan-fry Line a baking sheet with a double layer of paper towels. Heat ¼ inch of oil in a large skillet over medium-high heat until shimmering. Add crabs (be

Ingredients

Soft shell crabs should be used within several hours (no longer than 6 hours) of purchase. Store them over a bed of ice in the refrigerator until you are ready to cook them.

careful, as their liquid can cause spattering), and cook until both sides are crisp and golden brown and flesh is cooked through (it should be firm to the touch), about 4 minutes per side. Do not try to flip the crabs too soon, as the crust needs time to form; they should release easily from the pan. Using a slotted spatula, transfer crabs to prepared baking sheet to drain.

Serve Divide the slaw evenly among four plates and top each with a crab.

GREEN PAPAYA SLAW Serves 4

Whisk together 2 tablespoons Asian fish sauce such as *nam pla*, 1 tablespoon plus 1½ teaspoons peanut oil, ¼ cup fresh lime juice, 1 tablespoon plus 1 teaspoon palm sugar, and 2 tablespoons tiny dried shrimp in a large bowl. Add 1 peeled and very thinly sliced shallot and 1 fresh Thai chile, thinly sliced crosswise, and let stand for 15 minutes, then add ½ green papaya, peeled, seeded, and julienned, and 1 peeled and julienned medium carrot and let stand for 15 minutes to 30 minutes longer. Tear 2 tablespoons fresh mint leaves and ¼ cup cilantro leaves; crush ¼ cup peanuts. Stir herbs and nuts into salad. Taste and adjust seasoning with additional fish sauce, lime juice, sugar, and chile so there is a proper balance of hot, sour, salty, and sweet. Serve immediately.

FRIED FISH Serves 4

Deep frying works best for smaller pieces of fish (and chicken), since they will cook through before the crust has a chance to darken too much. Most any type of coating will do, but beer batter is favored for its puffy yet sturdy crust. The beer's effervescence produces a lighter texture than those made with other liquids (such as buttermilk) and imparts subtle flavor, depending on the type of beer used (the dark beer used here will be more perceptible than lighter lagers). You can alter the flavor by whisking dried herbs (dill is great with fish), ground dried chiles, and other seasonings into the dry ingredients. This batter also makes a nice choice when coating shrimp, chicken tenders, and onion rings.

Pair the fish with French fries (page 333) and serve with malt vinegar and salt for authentic pub-style fish and chips. Or make Baja-style *tacos de pescado,* or batter-fried fish tacos (page 276).

For beer batter

2 LARGE EGGS

1 CUP MEXICAN DARK LAGER BEER, *such as Negra Modelo*

1½ CUPS CAKE FLOUR *(not self-rising)*

1 TABLESPOON COARSE SALT

For frying fish

VEGETABLE OIL, *for frying*

2 POUNDS SKINLESS FIRM WHITE FISH, *such as cod, haddock, fluke, orange roughy, or scrod, cut into 3-by-¾-inch pieces*

Make beer batter Whisk eggs in a small bowl, then gradually whisk in the beer. In a separate bowl, whisk together flour and salt. Slowly whisk wet

FISH TACOS

fig. 3.34 COATING FISH PIECES

fig. 3.35 REMOVING FRIED FISH

mixture into the dry ingredients, just until the batter is thick and creamy (it should have the consistency of pancake batter). For the crispest results, it's better to have a few lumps remaining than to overmix. Cover and refrigerate for at least 20 minutes (and up to 2 hours) before using.

Heat oil Preheat oven to 200°F and line a baking sheet with a double layer of paper towels. Pour 3 inches of oil into a large pot (at least 6 quarts and preferably cast-iron) and heat to 375°F on a deep-fry or candy thermometer over medium heat. (Using moderate heat will help reduce the risk of spiking, but it will take longer for the oil to reach the proper temperature than if starting out over high heat.)

Coat Once the oil is ready, begin coating the fish. Working in batches (about 12 pieces each so as not to crowd the pot), use tongs to dip fish in the batter to completely coat each piece and allow the excess to drip back into the bowl *fig. 3.34*.

Fry As soon as it is coated, use tongs to carefully lower the fish into the hot oil and fry until the crust is deep golden brown, 5 to 7 minutes. Turn the pieces once or twice to ensure that the crust browns evenly. Monitor the temperature at all times; it should remain between 350° and 375°F (add more room temperature oil if necessary to cool the oil quickly and adjust the heat). Use a spider or slotted spoon to remove fish and transfer to the lined baking sheet to drain *fig. 3.35*. Keep warm in the oven while you fry the remaining fish. After each batch is removed, skim oil of any loose bits so they don't burn and stick to fish, and return the oil to the proper temperature before adding the next batch.

Serve Once all the fish has been fried, serve immediately.

FISH TACOS Serves 4

The popular version of fish tacos—as opposed to those made with grilled fish, native to Mexico—is believed to have originated in Southern California, where there is a strong Mexican influence on cooking and plenty of coastline for reeling in fish. They are garnished with a variety of piquant salsas and relishes and usually crema, the Mexican equivalent of sour cream; these are topped with a sour cream–based sauce, spiked with smoky chipotle chiles.

WHISK 1 CUP OF SOUR CREAM in a small bowl until it is perfectly smooth, then whisk in fresh lime juice, chipotle sauce (or adobo sauce from canned chipotles), and coarse salt to taste.

Soften 16 (6-inch) corn tortillas according to instructions on page 85. For each taco, stack 2 tortillas on a plate and top with fried fish pieces, dividing evenly. Garnish with finely shredded green cabbage, cilantro leaves, and thinly sliced radishes. Drizzle sauce over tacos and serve with lime wedges.

Grinding and Binding

Grinding meat has long been a handy way to tenderize and make use of tougher, less pricey cuts; it also opens up a variety of surprisingly sophisticated culinary possibilities. You can buy ground meat, of course, or ask your butcher to do the grinding for you, but it's highly worthwhile to grind it yourself. Once you do, you'll find even your basic hamburgers are a cut above the ordinary, and more multilayered dishes, such as pâtés, suddenly become possible in your kitchen.

Grinding meat yourself is also safer, in many cases, in part because you can cook it promptly: since bacteria can spread more readily in ground meat than in whole pieces, knowing that meat hasn't been sitting around postchopping can give you some peace of mind. Also, since contamination can come from improper handling or equipment that hasn't been properly washed after previous use, grinding meat yourself gives you an added measure of confidence. (To be absolutely safe, of course, the USDA calls for cooking ground meat, no matter who grinds it, to an internal temperature of 160°F, in order to kill any bacteria.)

Cooking with ground meat is also about handling it correctly—as gently as possible—and knowing which binding agents, if any, you need to hold it together.

As for equipment, you can buy a basic meat grinder at a kitchen supply store, or look for a grinder attachment for a standing electric mixer.

THE VERY BEST BURGERS Serves 6

The hamburger might be an easy weeknight staple, but it can also be a gourmet creation worth serving to company—if prepared right. The best hamburgers begin with top-quality meat. Grinding it yourself is preferable to buying packaged meat because you have a lot more control over the cut and quality of the meat you use. Chuck, with at least 15 percent fat, produces a juicier, more flavorful burger than a leaner cut like sirloin. Start with a top-quality chuck roast from the butcher's counter. Doing your own grinding also allows you to determine the coarseness of the meat. The technique below was developed after much experimenting. Dividing the meat in half and grinding it two ways, one a bit coarse to keep the mixture juicy and not too dense, and one finer to help bind everything together, results in the very best burger. It's more work than opening a package and tossing patties into a pan, but the effort pays off in a big way.

GROUND BEEF FOR BURGERS

You can add whatever seasonings you like to the meat, but don't skimp on salt and pepper—a generous sprinkling of each is imperative. Handle the ground meat as little and as gently as possible—form it into patties with your hands, taking care not to press or condense the meat too much—since overworked meat will yield a tough burger. Make a slight indentation in the center of each patty; this will prevent a "ballooning" effect as it cooks, and help you resist the temptation to press it down with a spatula, condensing the patty and forcing delicious juices to be lost. Also, keep in mind that the meat will shrink while cooking. To ensure that your hamburger will be the same size as the bun, form the patties a half-inch larger in diameter than the size of the bun.

Finally, because ground meat cooks relatively quickly, chilling the burger before cooking (especially on the grill, as in the variation on page 279), will make it easy to achieve a burger with a rare, juicy center, if that's what you're aiming for. Chilling is also more convenient for entertaining, since the patties can be formed ahead of time and refrigerated and covered until needed.

2½ POUNDS BONELESS CHUCK ROAST

COARSE SALT AND FRESHLY GROUND PEPPER

¼ CUP SUNFLOWER OR OTHER NEUTRAL-TASTING OIL

3 TABLESPOONS UNSALTED BUTTER

6 HAMBURGER BUNS *(3½ inches), sliced in half*

SUGGESTED ACCOMPANIMENTS: LETTUCE, SLICED TOMATO AND ONION, PICKLE SLICES, CHEESE SLICES

Grind meat Chill the metal parts of a meat grinder or grinder attachment in the freezer for at least 1 hour prior to use. Cut chuck roast into ¾- to 1-inch cubes, removing and discarding any sinew or silver skin. Chill meat in freezer 15 minutes, covered with plastic wrap. Fit grinder with the largest die. Grind meat [1], making sure to work in small batches so as not to overwork the grinder. Remove and wash grinder attachment. Transfer half of ground meat mixture to a bowl; chill in the refrigerator. Fit grinder with the smallest die. On medium speed, pass remaining half of meat through grinder. Add to bowl and freeze 15 minutes. Using your hands, gently combine the two portions of meat.

Form burgers and chill Handling as little as possible, form meat into six equal patties, about 4½ inches in diameter and 1¼ inches thick [2]; make a slight indention in the center of each [3]. Chill, covered, 15 to 30 minutes. Season both sides of each burger generously with salt and pepper.

Cook burgers Heat a large skillet over medium-high heat for 2 minutes. Add enough oil to coat bottom of skillet and heat until shimmering. Working in batches if necessary to avoid crowding the skillet (the patties should be at least 2 inches apart), arrange burgers in skillet and cook for 3 minutes. Reduce

Forming the Very Best Burgers

THE VERY BEST BURGER

temperature to medium-low and flip burgers. Cook for an additional 2½ minutes for medium-rare, 4 minutes for medium, and 6 minutes for medium-well.

Serve Transfer to a platter and let rest for 3 minutes; cover to keep warm. Meanwhile wipe out pan with paper towels. Melt half the butter in pan, then add half the buns, cut sides down, and cook until lightly toasted. Repeat with remaining butter and buns. Serve burgers in buns, with suggested accompaniments on the side.

Variation To grill burgers, heat grill to medium (see page 162 for Grill Temperature Guidelines). Form burgers as above, seasoning well with salt and pepper. Grill over direct heat, 3 to 5 minutes per side for medium-rare. Alternatively, heat broiler and cook burgers about 4 inches from the heat source for the same amount of time.

COUNTRY PÂTÉ Serves 6 to 12

Making homemade pâté, of course, is all about grinding. Here again, you can always buy a ready-made pâté from a specialty store, but making your own allows you total command of the quality of the ingredients and the freshness of the finished product. This recipe is for a country-style pâté, which means that it's more rustic in texture and appearance than a smoother, mousse-like pâté. Country-style pâté usually includes chicken liver as well as pork and veal. The mixture is ground coarsely, and small cubes of meat, bits of fruit, and nuts—called garnishes—are folded in before the whole thing is packed into a terrine and baked. Maintaining the desired texture depends on making sure that all the ingredients—as well as the grinding equipment itself—are well chilled before you grind. Place everything in the freezer (the grinder for a half hour, the meat for fifteen minutes or so), so it's very cold, then grind the meats according to their fat content, starting with the fattiest, as these are most likely to lose their structure and become pasty if ground when warm. After baking the terrine in a water bath (bain marie), the final, vital step is weighting the pâté to compress it, eliminating excess moisture and fat and giving it a sliceable texture.

Once the terrine is compressed and well chilled, unmold it, then slice with a serrated knife, which will cut cleanly without marring the shape. Serve with its classic accompaniments: good bread, a flavorful grainy mustard, and cornichons.

For ground meat

1 TABLESPOON EXTRA-VIRGIN OLIVE OIL
3 MEDIUM SHALLOTS, *peeled and minced*
8 OUNCES SKINLESS FATBACK, *cut into small dice, chilled*
6 OUNCES CHICKEN LIVERS *(about 6), chilled*
5 OUNCES BONELESS PORK LOIN, *cut into small dice, chilled*
5 OUNCES BONELESS VEAL SHOULDER OR NECK, *cut into small dice, chilled*
3 OUNCES BEST-QUALITY COOKED HAM, *cut into small dice, chilled*

For garnishes

1 OUNCE FATBACK, *skin removed, cut into ⅓-inch dice*
2 OUNCES CHICKEN LIVER *(about 2), cut into ⅓-inch dice*
2 OUNCES BONELESS VEAL NECK OR SHOULDER, *cut into ¼-inch dice*
2 OUNCES BONELESS PORK LOIN, *cut into ¼-inch dice*
2 OUNCES BEST-QUALITY HAM, *cut into ¼-inch dice*
10 GRINDS FRESH BLACK PEPPER
PINCH OF ALLSPICE
PINCH OF FRESHLY GROUND NUTMEG
1 LARGE EGG
1 TABLESPOON COGNAC
1 TABLESPOON PORT WINE
¼ CUP GOLDEN RAISINS
¼ CUP PLUS 2 TABLESPOONS SHELLED, UNSALTED PISTACHIOS
COARSE SALT
2 DRIED BAY LEAVES

For lining mold

1¼ TO 1½ POUNDS THINLY SLICED BACON OR FATBACK

Equipment

You will need a 1½-quart terrine that is about 4 by 13 inches. The terrine is lined with bacon in the recipe below to add another layer of flavor; be sure there is adequate overhang on one long side of the dish, so you can wrap it over the top of the mixture, covering the entire surface.

Prepare ground meat Heat the oil in a medium sauté pan over medium-low heat. Add shallots and cook until translucent, stirring constantly to prevent browning, about 6 minutes. Place in a large mixing bowl to cool. Meanwhile, grind the meats on medium speed with the fine die [1], making sure not to put too much meat into the feed tube at once. Grind the fatback first, before it becomes too warm, followed by the chicken livers, then the raw meats. Grind the cooked ham last (it has the firmest texture and least amount of fat and will be able to grind well even though the grinder parts are no longer as cold).

Add shallots and garnishes Stir in the shallots, along with all of the garnishes, except the bay leaves. Add 2 teaspoons salt and mix to evenly distribute [2]. To test for seasoning, heat some oil in a small skillet and cook a small amount of pâté mixture thoroughly. Taste and adjust seasoning, if desired.

Prepare mold Heat oven to 400°F with rack in center. Line a 1½-quart, 4 by 13-inch terrine with bacon, slightly overlapping the pieces and leaving an overhang of about 4 inches on one side [3] (most likely you will need to use one whole piece and a half piece laid end to end, in order to have a piece long enough to line mold with desired overhang).

Fill mold Bring a medium pot of water to a boil while you fill the mold. Spoon some of the meat mixture in the bottom of the mold and press firmly into the corners. Continue with remaining meat, making sure to distribute it firmly and evenly as you work so there are no gaps or air bubbles. When all meat is in the mold, press to flatten meat evenly. Fold over bacon, beginning with the long sides first, then the short ends [4]. Arrange bay leaves on top. Cover with terrine lid.

Bake Place terrine in a roasting pan and add boiling water until the level reaches halfway up the sides of the terrine [5]. Bake until an instant-read thermometer inserted near the middle registers 165°F, about 1½ hours.

Compress pâté Cut a piece of cardboard to fit the interior of the terrine mold. Wrap cardboard tightly in aluminum foil. Remove terrine from roasting pan. Remove lid, and place terrine on wire rack set on a rimmed baking sheet. Place prepared cardboard on top of the terrine. Weight with canned items [6] or other heavy objects. (This will allow excess fat to spill over the sides of the terrine as the pâté compresses.) Refrigerate terrine for 8 hours. (Terrine can be refrigerated up to 3 days; remove cardboard and weight after 8 hours, then cover tightly with lid or plastic wrap.)

Unmold pâté Unmold terrine by inverting onto a platter or cutting board. If necessary, dip terrine in warm water and run a paring knife around edge to loosen before inverting.

Serve With a serrated knife, cut pâté into ½-inch-thick slices, and serve with toasted baguette slices, grainy mustard, and cornichons.

Country Pâté, Step by Step

4 Vegetables

VEGETABLES

VEGETABLES BRING VIBRANCY to the table. Their reds, greens, oranges, and yellows can enliven any dish. Of course, vegetables are also at the heart of a healthful diet. But integrating vegetables into your meals isn't just about wholesome living. The range of flavors and textures that they offer the home cook are nearly infinite. Cooking them properly will help them retain the bright colors and flavors that make them so appealing in the first place.

Despite the abundance of produce to choose from, many home cooks prefer to stay with what's familiar, both in terms of the vegetable and the cooking method (think baked potato). This chapter offers ways for you to feel comfortable trying something new. First, there's a guide to buying, storing, and preparing a range of vegetables—both common and more unusual varieties. Next, you will learn ways to cook vegetables to bring out their best qualities—you might be surprised to discover that there are more than a dozen versatile cooking methods. They include steaming, wilting, blanching, simmering, roasting, stir-frying, sautéing, frying, braising, and grilling. Master them, and you can approach nearly any vegetable—new to you, or a longtime favorite—with confidence, and build on these techniques to make delicious purees or mashes, gratins, and even salads.

A WORD ON SEASONALITY

Before deciding what to cook, take stock of the quality of vegetables available to you. Ideally, the choices you make should be determined by what is in season. This means you'll have abundant choices in summer and the early autumn, but it does not exclude the colder months, when certain types of leafy greens, root vegetables, and tubers are at their peak. Even if you do find out-of-season vegetables at the store—such as tomatoes or asparagus in the middle of winter—they will likely have been shipped a long distance, and are probably not as tasty as varieties that were picked nearby during their natural harvest. Furthermore, vegetables begin to lose nutrients after they are picked, so they will lose more vitamins the farther they have to travel.

There are, of course, times of the year when you just don't have access to local fresh vegetables. In this case, frozen varieties are a good option, since the vegetables are frozen immediately after being picked (look for organic ones, if possible); corn, peas, and spinach freeze particularly well. Or you might have to choose different cooking methods to coax flavors from less-than-perfect vegetables. Take tomatoes: in the heat of summer, when it's easy to find fragrant tomatoes fresh off the vine, you need little more than a pinch of salt to draw out their flavor. But in the winter, you may have access only to tomatoes that have little (if any) of their distinctive flavor. In that case, you might want to slow-roast them at a very low heat to concentrate their sweetness.

THE RIGHT TEXTURE

Simply holding a vegetable in your hand will tell you a lot about how fresh it is; in most cases, vegetables should feel firm and heavy for their size. This is because vegetables are composed mostly of fiber and water, the latter being what keeps them plump and crisp (and firm and heavy). As a vegetable loses its moisture, it feels softer and its skin begins to shrivel; the texture may become chewy or chalky. Never buy vegetables that are in this condition.

WASHING VEGETABLES

Vegetables fresh from your garden should be rinsed to remove grit and dirt, but produce that you purchase— from a grocery store or farmers' market—will likely need a more thorough cleaning. They may have been sprayed with pesticides, and almost certainly have had time to accumulate dust from sitting in bins as well as dirt and bacteria from being handled. So it's wise to wash it well before eating or preparing for use in cooking. Avoid washing vegetables with soap, which can leave residue behind. Instead, follow these guidelines:

■ Rinse under cold or cool water; hot water can damage more delicate vegetables. In most cases, use the strongest stream of running water that you can without damaging the food—this should remove a great deal of dirt and bacteria.

■ Soft-skinned vegetables, including tomatoes and zucchini, can be rubbed gently with fingers under running water, while those with firm surfaces, such as potatoes and carrots, should be scrubbed with a brush reserved especially for this purpose. A good scrubbing will also help to eliminate any waxy coating that may have been applied to produce such as cucumbers. If scrubbing doesn't remove the coating sufficiently, peel the vegetable.

■ When washing leafy greens, remove and discard the outermost layers, as they are usually the dirtiest and most likely to be contaminated if the produce has been treated with pesticides. Separate the rest of the leaves and place them in a basin or bowl of cool water. Swish them around to loosen any dirt, and let the leaves soak for a few minutes, then lift them carefully out of the water (the dirt will have settled to the bottom). Repeat until no sand or grit remains in the bottom of the bowl. It often takes two to three washings for spinach, basil, arugula, and lettuces. Use a salad spinner to dry them, or wrap leaves in clean kitchen towels and gently blot.

AVOIDING DISCOLORATION

Artichokes and other vegetables such as fennel and celery root turn brown when peeled or cut and exposed to air. Acidulated water helps prevent this. Before you start peeling or cutting, squeeze the juice of a lemon into a large bowl filled with cold water. Then place the vegetables into it as you work. When you are ready to proceed with the recipe, drain the cut pieces. When working with potatoes, soaking in cold water alone is sufficient to prevent discoloration (since this will also draw out some of their starchiness, it's not always desirable to do so).

UNDERSTANDING THE LABELS

Most vegetables sold in large grocery stores are grown conventionally, using pesticides and synthetic fertilizers. A number of other agricultural methods are more environmentally friendly and produce better-tasting and healthier foods. Still, it can be difficult to know what the distinctions, if any, are. Here are a few considerations to keep in mind:

Certified organic The USDA sets standards for organic fruits and vegetables, and monitors farms for compliance. Among a number of criteria, plants must be grown without pesticides or synthetic fertilizers. Although organic vegetables may not look as picture-perfect or be as large as conventionally grown types, they will (for the most part) taste better and be healthier for you.

Biodynamic The USDA does not set standards for biodynamic agriculture, but this farming practice follows many of the same principles as certified organics. In addition to the use of natural fertilizers and compost, biodynamic growing focuses specifically on soil fertility, utilizing the application of herbal and mineral combinations to compost and plant according to the astronomical calendar. This agricultural technique is particularly popular for the cultivation of wine grapes. Proponents of biodynamic viticulture believe that the practice produces better-tasting wines that express the specific vineyard's *terroir*—the French term indicating the particular flavors and scents of specific microclimates and soils.

Local Of course, there is no better way to eat locally than growing your own, but not everyone has this option. The definition of locally grown vegetables can vary, but many people see it as eating foods that are grown within 100 miles of where you live. Buying locally grown vegetables is an excellent way to purchase only what is fresh.

Heirloom These are old varieties that have been handed down through generations, and selected for their distinctive flavor rather than their long shelf life or resistance to blemishes (as many hybrids are). Heirloom-variety fruits and vegetables—such as some beans, melons, and tomatoes—are genetically diverse (similar to heritage animal breeds; see page 107).

Vegetable Buying Guide

The way a vegetable looks, smells, and feels is the best indicator of its quality. If you can, buy locally grown vegetables at peak season at farmers' markets or farmstands. Also, take your time when shopping. Handpick items instead of reaching for prepackaged cartons or bags, which often include smaller, inferior produce. After purchasing, take care not to bruise or damage vegetables on your way home, and keep them fresh by storing them properly; clean them when you are ready to use. Finally, choose the right preparation to maximize a vegetable's characteristic flavors and textures. Here's a primer on buying, storing, and preparing a variety of produce:

ARTICHOKES

Look for Compact, heavy vegetables with thick green leaves that squeak against one another when pulled off.

Avoid Brown, spreading, or cracked leaves are all signs of age. Avoid those with gray or black discoloration—a sign of bruising.

Storage Store, unwashed, in a plastic bag in the refrigerator up to 1 week.

Preparation See how-tos on pages 296 and 297.

Cooking methods Steam whole artichokes, poach or simmer hearts.

ASPARAGUS

Look for Choose bunches with tightly closed tips and no flowering. Stalks should be bright green and firm. Thickness is a matter of taste.

Avoid Stalks that are flattened, wrinkled, or that feel hollow.

Storage Place ends upright in a glass with an inch of water (or wrap in a damp paper towel), then wrap a plastic bag around the tips to keep moist. Refrigerate up to 4 days.

Preparation Cut or snap stalks off at the woody (sometimes white) end. Peel ends of thicker asparagus, if desired.

Cooking methods Steam, blanch, roast, grill, or stir-fry.

AVOCADOS

Look for Seek out Hass avocados, with bumpy, dark green to almost black skin. Buy firm ones and allow them to ripen at room temperature (they will be less likely to bruise from overhandling). When ripe, they should give to gentle pressure (pressing too hard will bruise the flesh).

Avoid Hollow feeling, or those with bruising or sunken spots.

Storage Store firm ones at room temperature to ripen. Place in paper bag to accelerate ripening. Once ripe, store in the refrigerator.

Preparation Slice in half and remove pit; cut flesh into cubes, and scoop out with a spoon; or scoop out flesh in one piece, then slice.

Cooking methods Avocados are eaten raw, in salads, on sandwiches, as a topping for tacos and soups, and integrated into dips (such as guacamole). Only occasionally cooked.

BEANS *including shell beans and string beans*

Look for Bright, firm beans, with no soft spots or wrinkles. String beans should snap when bent.

Avoid Wilted or rubbery pods, or those that are yellowing. Tough, leathery skin indicates overly mature beans.

Storage Tightly wrap in plastic bag and store up to 1 week in refrigerator.

Preparation Remove tip and tail ends of string beans, if desired. Remove shell beans from pods.

Cooking methods Boil, blanch, steam, or stir-fry.

BEETS

Look for Firm, round, and heavy beets, with bright color (deep red, yellow, or orange, depending on variety). Should have long and slender taproot. If sold with tops, leaves should be fresh and dark green.

Avoid Elongated beets with scaly patches near the top of root (which can be strongly flavored and tough). Wrinkled or wilted roots mean the beets have been exposed to the air too long.

Storage If beets have greens, discard the stems but keep the leaves, if desired, and store greens and roots separately in the crisper of the refrigerator for up to 3 days.

Preparation Scrub root well with vegetable brush; trim and wash greens.

Cooking methods Sauté greens; roast root (which helps retain juices), or boil. Peel after cooking.

BROCCOLI

Look for Bright green (or sometimes purplish green) florets, with compact clusters of buds. Stalks should be sturdy, but tender.

Avoid Open bud clusters (so that you can see the yellow flower within); any wilting or yellow color are signs of over maturity. Avoid specimens with slick or soft bud clusters, as they are sign of rot. Avoid stalks that are cracked at the bottom, brown, or slimy.

Storage Moisture will encourage spoilage. Store unwashed in an open or perforated plastic bag for up to 5 days.

Preparation Cut top into florets; peel stems and cut into pieces.

Cooking methods Steam, sauté, roast, or braise.

BROCCOLI RABE *alternate names: broccoli raab, rapini*

Look for Vibrant green leaves and plump stems. Smaller-leaved plants are younger (therefore milder-tasting) than larger-leaved specimens.

Avoid Bunches with yellowed leaves, flowering buds, or dry-ended stalks.

Storage Wrap in damp paper towel and keep inside a plastic bag in refrigerator up to 4 days.

Preparation Trim tough stems. Cut into bite-size pieces if desired.

Cooking methods Braise; or blanch, then sauté.

BRUSSELS SPROUTS

Look for Firm, dense heads with compact leaves that have a bright green color.

Avoid Yellowing sprouts or those with spots, blemishes, or signs of insects.

Storage Store in plastic bag in the refrigerator up to 3 days.

Preparation Trim bottoms, and remove any discolored or damaged outer leaves. Leave whole, cut into halves, quarters, or slices, or separate leaves.

Cooking methods Roast, boil, steam, sauté.

CABBAGE

Look for Firm, dense heads. The outer leaves that fit around the head should be red or green.

Avoid Heads with wilted or yellowing leaves, or signs of worm damage, which can penetrate to the center.

Storage Store, unwashed, in the crisper, in a sealed perforated plastic bag up to 1 week.

Preparation Slice in half and remove core, then slice, shred, or separate into leaves; or cut head into wedges, then slice off core.

Cooking methods Serve raw in salad (such as coleslaw); or steam, braise, roast, or sauté.

CARROTS

Look for Bright color, smooth skin, and firm texture. If tops are attached, they should be bright green and fresh looking.

Avoid Those with dry skin, cracks up the sides, or sprouts where tops were cut off.

Storage Greens will hasten spoilage, so cut them off. Wrap carrots in paper towels in resealable plastic bag and keep in refrigerator up to 1 week.

Preparation Scrub or peel. Cut as specified in recipe.

Cooking methods Serve raw (sliced or grated) in salads, steam, roast, or braise. Often a component of mirepoix and soffritto.

Vegetable Buying Guide *continued*

CAULIFLOWER

Look for Creamy-white or white florets. Head should feel compact and heavy.

Avoid Brown spots or wilting, which are signs of aging. Smudging or speckling is caused by insects.

Storage Moisture will encourage spoilage, and leaving out at room temperature can cause to become woody and fibrous. Store unwashed in open or perforated plastic bag in refrigerator up to 5 days.

Preparation Trim leaves and stem, then cut through head to separate florets; or turn upside down, remove and discard stem, and separate into florets.

Cooking methods Serve raw or blanched in crudité or steam, roast, or bake (in gratins).

CELERY

Look for Crisp, light green stalks with fresh-looking leaves.

Avoid Wilted, rubbery, or hollow-feeling stalks or leaf stems. Also avoid any bunches with brown, black, or gray discoloration on branches.

Storage Store in a plastic bag in the crisper up to 1 week.

Preparation Peel with vegetable peeler if fibrous.

Cooking methods Serve raw in crudités or salads, sauté, stir-fry, or braise. Often a component of mirepoix and soffritto.

CELERY ROOT *alternate name: celeriac*

Look for Small to medium roots that are very firm, with golden, knobby skin.

Avoid Large roots (which can be tough); those with slimy spots.

Storage Trim leaves and stems. Store root in a plastic bag in the crisper up to 1 week.

Preparation Use paring knife to remove skin.

Cooking methods Serve raw (grated or shaved) in salads, boil (for purees and soups), or slice and bake (for gratins).

CHARD

Look for Crisp stalks and tender, deep green, shiny leaves. The stalks and veins of red chard should be dark fuchsia. Rainbow chard is a mixture of red, white, pink, and yellow; stems should be vibrant.

Avoid Yellowing leaves or those with any sign of wilting, decay, or insects. Also avoid overly thick, fibrous stems.

Storage Store in a plastic bag in the refrigerator up to 3 days.

Preparation Separate leaves from stems. Stems that are trimmed and chopped crosswise can be cooked with leaves, although they will take a little longer.

Cooking methods Sauté, wilt (and cream), or steam.

COLLARDS AND OTHER HEARTY GREENS
including mustard and turnip greens

Look for Dusty-looking leaves that are firm and unmarred.

Avoid Wilted, yellowing, or slimy leaves.

Storage Store in a plastic bag in the refrigerator up to 3 days.

Preparation Remove and discard tough stems. Cut or tear leaves into pieces; chiffonade.

Cooking methods Sauté young leaves (cut into chiffonade); braise.

CORN

Look for Bright-green husks wrapped tightly around ears, with flowing, moist silk (not dried). Pull back husk; kernels should be small, shiny, firm, plump, and tightly packed.

Avoid Ears with wilted, yellowed, or dry husks; kernels that are very big, very small, or dry; or silk that is dried or slimy.

Storage Best if eaten immediately after picking. Shuck just prior to cooking; the husk helps protect the kernels. Keep in refrigerator up to 2 days.

Preparation Remove husk, as well as strands of silk.

Cooking methods Whole cob: steam or boil for 5 minutes, or grill in husk (silk removed). Kernels cut from cob: serve raw (if very fresh), or blanch (for salads and salsas), sauté, or roast.

CUCUMBERS

Look for Firm, unwaxed cucumbers without wrinkles or soft spots. Kirbys should be bright green, and no more than 6 inches long.

Avoid Cucumbers with withered ends, which can be tough and bitter tasting (and are also a sign of age or improper storage). Also avoid specimens that are very thick or have a dull, yellow color, or that have soft or slimy spots.

Storage Store unwashed and loosely wrapped in a plastic bag up to 1 week in the refrigerator.

Preparation Scrub, or peel, if desired.

Cooking methods Serve raw in salads, or pickle.

EGGPLANT

Look for Flesh should give a bit when gently pressed, with no hard spots. Skin should be shiny, not shriveled, wrinkled, or mottled. Stems should be green.

Avoid Those with brown or soft spots, or shriveled skin.

Storage Whole eggplant will keep up to a few days in a cool place.

Preparation Remove stem. Cut into slices or wedges, or leave whole. Peel or leave skin on. Sometimes salted to remove excess bitterness.

Cooking methods Roast, pan-fry, stir-fry, or grill.

FENNEL

Look for White or light-green bulbs with bright, fresh, licorice-scented greens.

Avoid Brownish or cracked bulbs or any with wilted greens.

Storage Store in paper bag in crisper up to 4 days.

Preparation Trim any brown spots. Shave or cut into wedges; keep in acidulated water to prevent discoloration.

Cooking methods Serve raw in salads, braise, or roast.

GARLIC

Look for White or purple papery skin; firm, plump bulb.

Avoid Yellowing skin or bulbs that are shriveled, feel hollow, light, or have brown spots, or those with green sprouts.

Storage Store in a cool, dark area in a bowl, away from other fruits and vegetables.

Preparation Break apart into cloves. Peel, or smash and remove skins. Slice, mince, or mash to a paste (see how-to on page 33).

Cooking methods Used as a flavor base for many dishes; can also be roasted or sautéed.

KALE

Look for Dark, fresh, crisp-looking leaves.

Avoid Yellowing leaves, or those with signs of wilting.

Storage Store in plastic bag in refrigerator for up to 3 days.

Preparation Remove and discard stems. Cut or tear leaves into bite-sized pieces; chiffonade.

Cooking methods Baby kale can be used in salads; shred mature kale and sauté, braise, or blanch and then sauté.

LEEKS

Look for Bright, crisp greens that extend from the root end. Roots should be firm and creamy white.

Avoid Tops with any sign of discoloration, wilting, or decay. Avoid roots with translucent, soft, or brown spots.

Storage Place in plastic bag in crisper up to 1 week.

Preparation Cut off dark green ends, wash white and light-green section well (see page 32 for how-to).

Cooking methods Sauté as flavor base for many dishes; braise; poach or simmer, then marinate in vinaigrette.

MUSHROOMS

Look for Firm texture and gills that are pink or tan.

Avoid Those that are slimy or have discolored or pitted caps.

Storage Store in paper bag (plastic will trap moisture and accelerate spoilage) in the refrigerator up to 3 days.

Preparation Use soft brush or paper towel to remove dirt, or briefly submerge in water, drain, and use immediately.

Cooking methods Sauté, stir-fry, roast, or grill.

Vegetable Buying Guide *continued*

OKRA

Look for Firm pods that are no bigger than 3 inches. Skin should be a little fuzzy and bright green.

Avoid Those that are soft, have blemished skin, that are too large (which can make them fibrous), or that have large seeds inside.

Storage Store in plastic bag in the refrigerator up to 3 days.

Preparation Trim off stem ends.

Cooking methods Stew or fry.

ONIONS

Look for Dry, papery skins and flesh that is full and firm.

Avoid Any with mold, discoloration, or soft spots, or ones in net bags (it's better to select them one by one).

Storage Store in a cool, dark, dry place for up to 3 weeks. Do not store with potatoes.

Preparation Peel, unless using in stock.

Cooking methods One of the most important vegetables for flavoring foods; also a component of mirepoix and soffritto. They can also be caramelized, braised, roasted, and grilled.

PARSNIPS

Look for Smaller roots that are firm and beige-white in color (should be shaped like carrots).

Avoid Spotted, wilted, or abnormally shaped roots, or those with soft areas.

Storage Store in resealable plastic bag (add damp paper towel for moisture, if desired) up to 1 week.

Preparation Trim ends and peel.

Cooking methods Roast, bake, steam, or boil (and mash or puree).

PEAS *including English peas, snap peas, snow peas*

Look for Bright, firm peas, with no soft spots or wrinkles. Snap and snow peas should snap when bent.

Avoid Wilted or rubbery pods, or those that are yellowing. Tough, leathery skin indicates overly mature peas.

Storage Best if eaten soon after picking. Otherwise, tightly wrap in a plastic bag and keep up to 1 week in refrigerator.

Preparation Remove garden peas from shells; remove strings from snap peas and snow peas.

Cooking methods Garden peas: Boil (and mash or puree), blanch, steam, or stir-fry. Snap and snow peas: Serve raw or blanch, sauté, or stir-fry.

PEPPERS

Look for Bell: choose very firm peppers, with taut skin; flesh should be thick, with vibrant color and bright-green stems. Chiles: Any variety you choose should be vibrant in color and have smooth skin.

Avoid Those with soft spots or wrinkles of any kind.

Storage Store in a paper bag in the crisper up to 5 days.

Preparation Bell: Remove stems, ribs, and seeds (unless roasting or grilling whole). Chiles: Remove stem, ribs, and seeds (unless more heat is desired).

Cooking methods Chopped bell peppers are used as a component in soffritto, and are often sautéed, stir-fried, roasted, and stuffed and roasted whole. Chile peppers can be roasted whole, or minced and used raw in salads and dips.

POTATOES

Look for Firm texture, without any soft areas or wrinkled skin.

Avoid Sprouting eyes, slits, or a green tinge. Also avoid buying potatoes in bags (it's better to select them one by one). Buy all one size to cook evenly.

Storage Store in a cool, dark place (long exposure to light can cause potatoes to turn green and bitter, which can be toxic) up to 1 month.

Preparation Peel, or scrub if skin is to be left on.

Cooking methods Bake, roast, boil (and puree or mash), grate and sauté, or fry.

SCALLIONS AND SPRING ONIONS

Look for Bright, fresh greens that extend from the root end. Roots should be firm and creamy white.

Avoid Tops with any sign of discoloration, wilting, or decay. Avoid roots with translucent, soft, or brown spots.

Storage Store in plastic bag in crisper for up to 4 days.

Preparation Trim root end. Can use white and light-green parts, or only dark-green parts if desired.

Cooking methods Chop and use raw in salads; grill or braise.

SHALLOTS

Look for Papery, dark tan skin and firm, slightly purple bulbs.

Avoid Bulbs with translucent, soft, or brown spots.

Storage Keep in mesh or paper bag in a dry, cool area for up to 2 weeks.

Preparation Peel, unless recipe states otherwise (can be roasted unpeeled).

Cooking methods Often used as a flavor component in mirepoix; sauté or roast.

SPINACH

Look for Bright green, tender, firm leaves.

Avoid Yellowing or wilted leaves, or those with slimy spots (a sign of rot). Avoid pre-bagged spinach.

Storage Wrap in paper towels and keep in plastic bag in the refrigerator up to 3 days.

Preparation Wash thoroughly in bowl of water to remove grit (see page 299).

Cooking methods Serve raw in salads; sauté, wilt (and cream), or steam.

SWEET POTATOES

Look for Relatively unblemished skin that is uniform in color and texture.

Avoid Those with soft spots, sprouts, or any holes in the skin, which can speed up decay.

Storage Sweet potatoes are more perishable than regular potatoes. Store in a cool, dark place for up to 3 weeks.

Preparation Peel if desired, scrub if leaving skins on.

Cooking methods Roast, bake, grill, fry, boil (and mash or puree).

TOMATOES

Look for Earthy, strong "tomato" smell; taut skin, firm flesh, deep and even color (greenish coloring at stem end on heirlooms is okay).

Avoid Pale, hard ones or those that are overly ripe; green or yellow markings around the stem in tomatoes, other than heirloom, indicate sunburn. Also avoid those with growth cracks (which will appear as brown scars).

Storage Store at room temperature. Ripe tomatoes should be used within a few days. Unripe tomatoes can be placed in a paper bag to accelerate ripening. Refrigerating tomatoes will give them an undesirable, mealy texture.

Preparation Blanch and peel, or leave skin on, and cut as desired with a serrated or very sharp knife.

Cooking methods Serve raw in salads and pastas; roast, or broil, stew, or make into sauce.

TURNIPS AND RUTABAGAS

Look for Roots that are heavy for their size and have smooth skin. Small roots are sweeter.

Avoid Shriveled roots, or those with rough skin. Large roots tend to be tough and woody.

Storage Store in perforated plastic bag in the crisper for up to 1 week.

Preparation Scrub young, thin-skinned vegetables, or peel larger ones.

Cooking methods Roast, boil (and mash or puree), braise, stew, or bake (in gratins).

WINTER SQUASH

Look for Heavy squash, with smooth, brightly colored, uniformly hard rind.

Avoid Those with soft spots, which is a sign of rot or rough handling.

Storage Store in a cool, dry place up to 3 weeks.

Preparation If removing rind, use a vegetable peeler or paring knife. Can roast in skin, then scoop out flesh for purees, mashes, and soups.

Cooking methods Roast, bake, boil (and mash or puree).

ZUCCHINI AND SUMMER SQUASH

Look for Firm, small to medium vegetables (less than 8 inches). Skin should be smooth and shiny (patty pan squash should be no bigger than 4 inches across).

Avoid Very large or bulbous squash, which tend to be watery or fibrous, and those with blemishes or punctures in the skin.

Storage Store in plastic bag in refrigerator up to 4 days.

Preparation Leave skin on, or peel with vegetable peeler.

Cooking methods Sauté, stir-fry, grill, fry.

How to Steam

Few techniques equal steaming for the bright, clean flavors and uniformly moist texture it imparts to vegetables. Not only are steamed vegetables low in fat (since they're not cooked with oil or butter), but they retain more vitamins than vegetables cooked by other methods. Naturally tender vegetables such as snap peas, asparagus, green beans, carrots, turnips, new potatoes, broccoli, and cauliflower are best for steaming. Cut them into uniform pieces so that they'll cook evenly. Sturdier vegetables, including artichokes, can also be steamed so long as they are properly trimmed first. Water is used most commonly, but stocks and broths impart delicate flavors. Incorporate herbs, citrus, and other aromatics for other subtle notes. Lemon juice, vinegar, and other acidic liquids will contribute bright flavors, though they can cause the color of green beans and asparagus to dull slightly.

Most vegetables should be steamed just until crisp-tender. To test, insert the tip of a paring knife into the thickest part; the knife should meet little resistance.

Bamboo steamers and metal inserts can be used interchangeably, with a few simple adaptations. Bamboo steamers sit right in the water, which should come 1 inch up the sides, and they have their own lids; metal inserts should sit above the water (the pot should have at least 1 inch of water to produce sufficient steam) and the pot will need to be covered during steaming. The vegetables should fit in a single layer in the basket; overcrowding will cause some to become overdone while leaving others underdone. An improvised steamer, such as a metal colander, can also be used as long as it sits above the cooking liquid and the pot's lid can be placed firmly over the top to trap the steam.

Steamed vegetables are delicious with nothing other than melted butter or a flavorful olive oil, but they can also be tossed with compound butter (page 166), yogurt, or crème fraîche, or served with the vinaigrettes (page 356–357) or with Hollandaise Sauce (page 96).

STEAMED ASPARAGUS AND BOK CHOY WITH SOY-GINGER VINAIGRETTE Serves 4 to 6

When steaming asparagus, choose thick stalks over pencil-thin ones, which cook quickly and can become limp. The cooking time depends on the thickness and freshness of the stalk, as well as your preference for firmer or more tender texture.

    1 POUND ASPARAGUS
    1 POUND BOK CHOY
      GINGER-SOY VINAIGRETTE *(page 357)*

Trim asparagus Line up stalks and cut off the tough ends *fig. 4.1*, which are usually white and woody, or snap off ends where they naturally break *fig. 4.2*.

Prepare steamer Place a bamboo steamer in a large pot or wok. Fill pot with 1 inch of water and bring to a rapid simmer.

fig. 4.1 CUTTING OFF ASPARAGUS ENDS

fig. 4.2 SNAPPING OFF ASPARAGUS ENDS

fig. 4.3 STEAMING ASPARAGUS

Steam vegetables separately Lay asparagus in the steamer, spreading in an even layer *fig 4.3*, then cover steamer and cook until asparagus is crisp-tender *fig 4.4* and bright green, about 5 minutes. Asparagus will keep cooking a little after it is taken off the heat, so be careful not to overcook. Steam bok choy in same manner, 2 to 3 minutes.

Dress and serve Transfer vegetables to a platter and drizzle with some vinaigrette. Serve immediately, or marinate in the vinaigrette for 30 minutes (or longer for more flavor, but the color of asparagus will change.)

fig. 4.4 TESTING FOR DONENESS

fig. 4.5 CUTTING OFF TOPS OF
ARTICHOKES

fig. 4.6 TRIMMING ARTICHOKE LEAVES

STEAMED ARTICHOKES WITH TARRAGON BUTTER Serves 4

Steaming is the classic way to cook globe artichokes. Their leaves become very tender and perfect for dipping one by one into melted butter (this one is flavored with fresh tarragon). The artichokes would also be delicious with Hollandaise Sauce (page 96), or crème fraîche and caviar.

For steaming artichokes

4 MEDIUM OR LARGE GLOBE ARTICHOKES *(about 2 pounds total)*
1 SPRIG TARRAGON
  COARSE SALT
4 THIN LEMON SLICES

For tarragon butter

¾ CUP (1½ STICKS) UNSALTED BUTTER
1 TABLESPOON FINELY CHOPPED FRESH TARRAGON LEAVES
  COARSE SALT

For serving

  LEMON WEDGES

Prepare artichokes Using a serrated knife, cut off top quarter of each artichoke *fig. 4.5*. Use kitchen shears to trim sharp tips of artichoke leaves *fig. 4.6*.

Remove any small leaves from bottoms of artichokes and trim stems so artichokes can stand upright.

Prepare steamer Fill a large pot with about 2 inches of water and add a sprig of tarragon and a pinch of salt. Set steamer basket in pot (make sure water doesn't seep through holes). Bring to a boil, then reduce to a rapid simmer.

Steam artichokes Stand artichokes upright in steamer and season with salt. Top each with a lemon slice *fig. 4.7*. Cover pot and steam until bottoms of artichokes are very tender when pierced to the center with the tip of a paring knife, 35 to 50 minutes. (Add more hot water if necessary to maintain level during cooking.)

Meanwhile, make butter Melt butter in a small saucepan over low heat, then stir in chopped tarragon and season with salt.

Serve Place an artichoke on each plate with some lemon wedges and serve warm tarragon butter on the side for dipping.

fig. 4.7 PREPARING ARTICHOKES FOR
STEAMING

LESSON 4.2
How to Wilt

Wilting is a type of steaming done directly in a pan rather than in a steamer basket or insert. This is a good technique for cooking tender, leafy greens, including spinach, chard, beet greens, and mustard greens, because it retains their bright colors. The greens are cooked using only the liquid clinging to their leaves from washing (no oil, butter, or other fats are used). You'll know the greens are wilted when they just begin to collapse and the vegetable's natural liquid is released. This liquid won't evaporate, so you may need to squeeze it out of the vegetable if using it in other preparations, such as a filling for stuffed pasta or pie. Also keep this technique in mind for preparing a simple side of cooked greens.

For particularly soft greens like spinach and escarole, plan on about two and a half pounds for four servings. Heartier greens, such as chard, will not lose as much volume, so start with about one pound.

CREAMED SPINACH Serves 4

Wilted spinach can be served on its own, dressed with oil and vinegar and seasoned with salt and pepper, or quickly warmed in a pan with olive oil, slivered garlic, and red pepper flakes. But it is also commonly used as a component of another dish; here it is mixed with a rich béchamel sauce to make the classic accompaniment to steaks and chops.

2½ POUNDS SPINACH

1 TABLESPOON UNSALTED BUTTER

1 TABLESPOON PLUS 1½ TEASPOONS ALL-PURPOSE FLOUR

1¼ CUPS MILK, PLUS MORE IF NECESSARY

COARSE SALT AND FRESHLY GROUND PEPPER

PINCH OF FRESHLY GRATED NUTMEG

Varieties of Leafy Greens

RUSSIAN KALE

KALE

SPINACH

TUSCAN KALE

DANDELION GREENS

RED CHARD

COLLARD GREENS

MUSTARD GREENS

SWISS CHARD

CREAMED SPINACH

fig. 4.8 REMOVING STEMS

Prepare spinach Remove tough stems from the spinach with your fingers *fig. 4.8*. Drop spinach into a large bowl of cold water and let sit for 1 minute, swishing the leaves a few times to loosen any grit. Lift spinach out of water, then pour water from bowl and rinse out any grit. Repeat until no more grit is visible in bottom of bowl. Once the spinach is clean, lift spinach from the water and gently shake leaves to remove most, but not all, of the liquid *fig. 4.9*.

Wilt spinach Place spinach in a large pot. (If all will not fit in the pot, add it in batches, covering pot for 30 seconds and then stirring to wilt each batch before adding more.) Cover and cook over medium-high heat, stirring occasionally, until wilted and bright green [1], 2 to 4 minutes. Drain in a colander.

Squeeze and chop When spinach is cool enough to handle, squeeze out as much liquid as possible [2], reserving liquid. Coarsely chop spinach [3].

Make béchamel Melt the butter in a medium skillet over medium heat, then whisk in the flour [4]. Cook, whisking constantly, until bubbling but not browning, 1 to 2 minutes. Gradually whisk in the milk [5], whisking until it is fully

fig. 4.9 WASHING SPINACH

incorporated while bringing it to a simmer. Cook until thickened, about 2 minutes, stirring with a wooden spoon (scrape across the bottom and around edge of pan to prevent scorching). Season with salt and pepper.

Combine spinach with sauce Add spinach [6] and stir to combine. If necessary, thin with more milk (up to ¼ cup) or some of the reserved spinach liquid. Add nutmeg and cook just to heat through.

Serve Transfer spinach to a bowl and serve immediately.

Creamed Spinach, Step by Step

MIXED BEAN CRUDITÉ

How to Blanch

Blanching, a classic chef's technique, is a simple way to capture the fresh flavor and color of vegetables. It involves very briefly cooking vegetables in boiling water to just a step or two beyond raw, preventing discoloration and retaining vitamins in the process. Shocking the vegetables by plunging into an ice-water bath, also called refreshing, stops the cooking and helps them stay crisp. In minutes, vibrant blanched produce, full of flavor, becomes a crisp-cool side dish, part of a salad, or a healthful snack.

Blanching is also useful when preparing vegetables that will eventually be finished in some way or another, either by sautéing with butter or oil and fresh herbs, or incorporated into a soup, stew, or risotto. This is a common technique in professional kitchens, where it is called par-cooking or par-boiling. When blanching for

Varieties of Fresh Beans and Peas

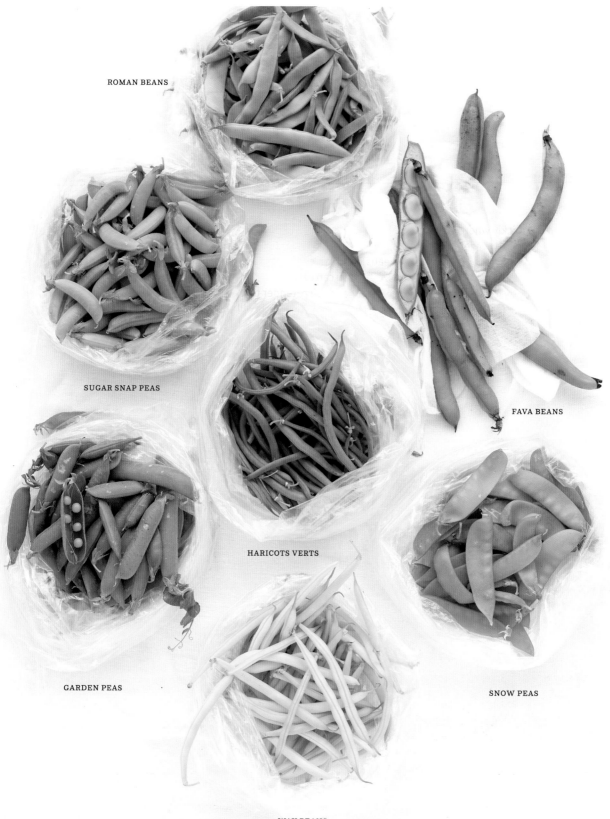

ROMAN BEANS

SUGAR SNAP PEAS

FAVA BEANS

HARICOTS VERTS

GARDEN PEAS

SNOW PEAS

WAX BEANS

this reason, cut vegetables to uniform size to ensure even cooking. Each type of vegetable should be blanched on its own to maintain the individual flavors (and to avoid discoloration). Green beans, broccoli, carrots, broccoli rabe, and sturdy greens, such as kale or mustard greens, are well-suited to par-boiling. Blanching is also the method used to loosen the skins of tomatoes, peaches, pearl onions, and fava beans, for easy peeling.

Perhaps the best reason for blanching is to make a platter of crudité (the French term for raw vegetables), so the vegetables are slightly more tender, flavorful, and colorful than when raw. Carrots, broccoli, cauliflower, green beans, snap peas, snow peas, and asparagus all benefit from being blanched before serving. The recipe that follows is for a variety of green beans, but you can adapt it to cook other vegetables.

To blanch vegetables, begin by bringing a large pot of water to a vigorous boil (so it boils again quickly when vegetables are added). Add a generous amount of salt for flavor. Then add vegetables in batches, cooking each one separately and starting with mild-tasting ones (green beans) and proceeding to stronger vegetables (broccoli). The cooking times will vary, but you can easily determine when each is ready by looking for a brightened color and crisp-tender texture (for example, a stalk of asparagus should resist slightly when bent). This will take between 45 seconds and 2 minutes, depending on the type of vegetable (broccoli will take longer than snow peas, for example) as well as your preference for crunchy or more tender texture. Remove with a slotted spoon and immediately plunge into an ice-water bath to stop the cooking and set the color.

MIXED BEAN CRUDITÉ Serves 6

Buy the freshest vegetables available and only during their peak season. The ones here are at their best in mid- to late summer.

- ½ POUND WAX BEANS
- ½ POUND ROMAN BEANS
- ½ POUND HARICOTS VERTS
- SALT
- CUCUMBER RANCH DRESSING (page 359)

Trim beans Snap off the ends of all the beans, leaving the "tail" on if desired.

Boil water Bring a large pot of water to a vigorous boil. Add a generous amount of salt.

Blanch and shock vegetables Cook beans and peas in separate batches, starting with the wax beans and ending with the haricots verts, just until color is brightened and they are crisp-tender (they should bend without snapping but not be at all limp), 45 to 60 seconds. Remove with a slotted spoon and immediately plunge into an ice-water bath.

Drain and chill Once beans have cooled completely, drain in a colander, shaking to remove as much excess water as possible. Spread them on a clean kitchen towel and gently pat away remaining moisture. Loosely wrap vegetables in the towel and chill for up to 2 hours.

Serve Arrange vegetables on a platter and serve with dressing, for dipping.

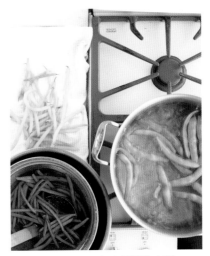

BLANCHING, SHOCKING, AND
DRAINING FRESH BEANS

LESSON 4.4
How to Simmer, Boil, and Poach

Boiled and simmered vegetables are cooked until just tender, and can be served simply in butter and herbs or incorporated into salads (such as potato salad), purees, and mashes. The two crucial rules to boiling are to not overcook your vegetables, and to season the water with salt (it should be as "salty as the sea," as most chefs learn in culinary school). You may be surprised how much flavor the vegetables will pick up from the liquid. Use a pot that is big enough to accommodate all of the vegetables; if you have more than your pot can easily hold, cook them in batches so that they cook evenly. (For example, a six- to eight-quart pot is ideal for one head of broccoli.) Use enough liquid to cover the food. Water is the most common boiling liquid, but stock (and even cream or milk) will add flavor. Reserve flavorful liquids, or water thickened by starchy potatoes, to incorporate into purees. In most cases, the water should be brought to a boil before vegetables are added. Potatoes are an exception (because of their density); they should be started in a pot of cold water and heated gradually, otherwise the exteriors can get mushy before the center has a chance to cook. Boil green vegetables uncovered to allow gasses that can discolor the leaves to escape. Keep a watchful eye on the pot and a paring knife at the ready; most vegetables should be tender (but never mushy), and potatoes and beets should still give a little resistance when pierced.

BOILED PARSLEYED POTATOES Serves 4

Potatoes are boiled for all sorts of reasons: to make mashed potatoes, or to slice or quarter for salads. But they are also delicious as is, as demonstrated by this simple side dish. The best potatoes for boil-and-serve are waxy types such as red potatoes or fingerlings; they will hold their shape better than starchy russets.

BOILED PARSLEYED POTATOES

2 POUNDS SMALL WAXY POTATOES, *such as red creamer, red bliss, or fingerlings; halved if large*

COARSE SALT AND FRESHLY GROUND PEPPER

2 TABLESPOONS UNSALTED BUTTER

2 TABLESPOONS COARSELY CHOPPED FRESH FLAT-LEAF PARSLEY

Boil Place potatoes in a large saucepan and cover with cold water by 1 inch. Add 1 tablespoon salt and bring to a boil over high heat, then reduce heat to a simmer. Cook until the tip of a paring knife inserted into center of potatoes meets only slight resistance, 15 to 20 minutes.

Drain and toss Drain potatoes in a colander and return to warm saucepan. Toss with butter and parsley, and season with pepper.

Serve Transfer to a serving dish and serve immediately.

LEEKS VINAIGRETTE Serves 4

In this classic French first course, the vegetables are first poached, then marinated in vinaigrette. For deeper flavor, the vegetables can be braised in stock instead of poached. The leeks are especially delicious when garnished with sieved egg yolk (called "mimosa" for its resemblance to the golden flower and most often used with asparagus). The leeks can also be combined with other components to create an elegant composed salad, such as the one on page 312.

1 SPRIG THYME

JUICE OF ½ LEMON

COARSE SALT

6 SMALL OR 3 MEDIUM LEEKS *(about 13 ounces), white and pale green parts only, halved lengthwise and washed well (or left whole if very small)*

LEMON VINAIGRETTE *(page 357)*

Poach leeks Bring 5 quarts water to a boil in a large pot with the thyme, lemon juice, and 2 teaspoons salt. Add leeks and reduce to a simmer, then cook until tender, 6 to 10 minutes (or 12 to 15 minutes if medium-size). Remove carefully with tongs and drain on paper towels.

Marinate Put leeks in a shallow dish and pour vinaigrette over. Let stand at room temperature for 30 minutes or refrigerate, covered, up to 1 week.

LEEKS VINAIGRETTE AND MARINATED
ARTICHOKE HEARTS

MARINATED ARTICHOKE HEARTS Serves 4

1 LEMON

4 LARGE GLOBE ARTICHOKES *(about 2 pounds total) or 10 baby artichokes*

COARSE SALT AND FRESHLY GROUND PEPPER

LEMON VINAIGRETTE *(page 357)*

Prepare artichokes Cut lemon in half and squeeze juice of half into a large bowl of cold water (this is called acidulated water, which will keep the cut artichokes from discoloring), then add one half to the water. Working with one artichoke at a time, snap off dark outer leaves until you reach ones that are mostly yellow. Use a paring knife to peel the dark parts from base and stem. Use a serrated knife to trim dark green top of artichoke until an inch to an inch and a half of the pale part remains. (If using baby artichokes, halve and add to acidulated water.) Scrape out purple leaves and fuzzy choke with a small spoon and discard. Cut artichoke into quarters or eighths through the stem (so the shapes stay intact). Rub exposed parts with lemon half and add to lemon water *fig. 4.10*.

Poach artichokes Place artichokes in a medium saucepan; add water to cover. Add salt and bring to a boil. Reduce to a simmer and cook until artichokes are tender when pierced with the tip of a knife, 8 to 12 minutes for large hearts (6 to 8 minutes for baby artichokes).

Marinate Transfer to a bowl and add vinaigrette. Let stand at room temperature for 1 hour or refrigerated, covered, up to one week.

fig. 4.10 PLACING ARTICHOKES IN
ACIDULATED WATER

OVEN-POACHED GARLIC
WITH THYME Makes 2 heads (plus 2 to 3 cups infused oil)

For this method, garlic is poached with oil, which becomes infused with the flavor of garlic and thyme. When lightly pressed, the cloves will pop out of their peels, and can be served with crusty bread, or spread onto the pastry shell of a savory tart before filling and baking. The oil can then be drizzled over vegetables before roasting, used in vinaigrettes or marinades, or brushed on crostini.

2 HEADS GARLIC, *top ½ inch cut off and discarded*
10 SPRIGS THYME
EXTRA-VIRGIN OLIVE OIL

HEAT OVEN TO 275°F. Place garlic cut sides down in a small heatproof saucepan and add thyme and enough oil to just cover. Transfer pan to oven and bake until garlic is soft, 1½ to 2 hours. Let garlic cool in oil, then transfer garlic and oil to an airtight container and refrigerate up to 2 weeks. Oil can be strained after a day or two (so it doesn't take on too much flavor) and refrigerated separately.

OVEN-POACHED GARLIC

TOMATO AND ONION CONFIT Makes 3 cups

Unlike most other vegetables, tomatoes release a lot of moisture as they cook, so there's no need to completely submerge them in the oil (or added liquid). It is this "cooking in its own juices" that makes this dish a "confit" (see page 232). Because this technique cooks out most of the moisture from the vegetables, it concentrates the sugars, for a sweet, jamlike condiment to serve with roasted, grilled, or sautéed meats (such as the calf's liver on page 253). While the confit cooks, stir very gently, or the tomatoes and onions may fall apart.

¼ CUP EXTRA-VIRGIN OLIVE OIL
2 POUNDS YELLOW ONIONS *(about 4 medium)*, thinly sliced *(about 10 cups)*
1 POUND CHERRY OR GRAPE TOMATOES *(red, yellow, orange, or a combination)*
1¼ TEASPOONS COARSE SALT

Sweat onions Heat oven to 275°F. Heat oil in a 4-quart Dutch oven over medium heat. Add onions and sweat until soft and translucent, about 8 minutes, stirring occasionally. Add tomatoes and salt and stir to combine.

Poach in oven Transfer the mixture to oven and cook (uncovered), gently stirring occasionally, until onions are light golden and completely tender (almost like a jam) and tomatoes are wrinkled but not mushy, 4 to 4½ hours. The confit can be allowed to cool and then stored in an airtight container for up to 2 weeks in the refrigerator.

TOMATO AND ONION CONFIT

PEA PUREE

CAULIFLOWER PUREE

WINTER SQUASH PUREE

CELERY ROOT PUREE

POTATO PUREE

EXTRA CREDIT
Vegetable Mashes and Purees

Mashing and pureeing can turn vegetables such as potatoes, squash, and peas into all manner of thick, nourishing, flavorful side dishes that have an appealing texture—whether creamy and fine or more rustic and coarse. Boiling is the preferred method for preparing vegetables for these methods, most likely to ensure that they are moist throughout, an essential prerequisite for achieving super-smooth and creamy purees. (Steamed vegetables yield a similar result, but boiling is a simpler technique that requires only a pot of water—or stock or milk, depending on the consistency of the vegetable and the desired flavor. Roasted vegetables can also be pureed, but the consistency tends to be less refined, though equally flavorful.)

fig. 4.11 **CRUSHING WITH A FORK**

fig. 4.12 **PUREEING WITH A RICER**

To make mashes and purees, first cook vegetables until tender, then mash or puree and mix with liquid (milk, cream, or reserved cooking liquid), butter or olive oil, and seasonings. Purees are more refined and are typically passed through a sieve, while mashes are coarser.

The trick to perfect mashes or purees lies in knowing which tool to use. For crushed vegetables, use the back of a fork fig. 4.11. For mashes, use an old-fashioned potato masher, a ricer, or a food mill fitted with the fine disk. To make purees, use a ricer for potatoes fig. 4.12, a blender or food processor for other vegetables, adding more liquid to achieve a perfectly smooth texture. Passing the puree through a sieve will produce the finest texture.

If the purees are too thin or runny, such as for vegetables with a high water content, like cauliflower and fennel, drain them in a sieve set in the sink, or cook over moderate heat until they reach the desired consistency, stirring frequently to keep them from scorching. This is also one way to reheat them after storing (you can also set the pot over—not in—a pan of simmering water).

GARLIC AND ROSEMARY
POTATO PUREE Makes 4 cups

Infusing liquid—cream, milk, or stock can all be used in this recipe—with herbs is a simple yet effective way to add depth of flavor to purees and other preparations (see the gratin on page 320). Garlic is a complementary flavor for potatoes; we boiled the cloves along with the potatoes to mellow their flavor, but you can use Oven-Poached Garlic instead (page 306). For a lighter-bodied puree, replace the cream with milk or stock, or use a combination. For a richer puree, reduce 1½ cups of heavy cream by half, then infuse with herbs.

¾ CUP HEAVY CREAM, *plus more for reheating (optional)*

1 TO 2 TABLESPOONS ROSEMARY LEAVES *(from about 2 sprigs)*

½ CUP (1 STICK) UNSALTED BUTTER

2 POUNDS RED OR WHITE POTATOES

2 GARLIC CLOVES, PEELED

COARSE SALT AND FRESHLY GROUND WHITE PEPPER

Infuse cream Bring cream and rosemary to a simmer in a small pot, then remove from heat and let steep 30 minutes. Strain through a fine sieve (to remove the herbs as well as any skin that might have formed) and clean pot, then return cream to pot. Add butter and heat over medium until melted, stirring to combine. Cover and keep warm (either over lowest setting on the stove or in a warm spot).

Meanwhile, boil potatoes Peel and cut potatoes into 1½-inch pieces, then place in a medium stockpot and cover with water. Add the garlic and a generous amount of salt and bring to a boil, then reduce to a rapid simmer. Cook until potatoes are very tender when pierced with the tip of a paring knife, about 15 minutes. Drain well, then return to pot and set over low heat, stirring until the potatoes are thoroughly dry.

Puree While potatoes are still hot, pass through a ricer or a food mill fitted with the fine disk. Stir in cream mixture and season with salt and pepper. If a finer texture is desired, pass puree through a medium-mesh sieve *fig. 4.13*, pressing on solids with a rubber spatula to extract as much puree as possible. Reheat over medium heat with a little more cream (or water), if necessary, before serving.

Variations For a rustic puree, pass the potatoes through the large disk of a food mill, and enrich with ¼ cup each of olive oil and butter (omit cream and rosemary). Finish by stirring in chopped flat-leaf parsley and freshly ground black pepper, if desired.

For mashed potatoes, crush the potatoes with a potato masher; add just enough cream and butter to achieve the desired consistency, mashing to combine *fig. 4.14*. Season with salt and white pepper.

fig. 4.13 PASSING PUREE THROUGH
A SIEVE

fig. 4.14 USING A POTATO MASHER

FENNEL PUREE Makes 1 cup

This recipe produces a puree that is smooth and creamy without adding any heavy cream. Instead, the vegetables are boiled in milk and then pureed with some of the reserved cooking liquid, resulting in a side dish with a pure vegetable taste. When pureeing in a blender, add only enough liquid to keep the blade spinning freely. The fennel puree is delicious with the seared scallops on page 260. It can also be thinned with some of the strained cooking liquid to form a soup.

> 2 MEDIUM FENNEL BULBS, *trimmed (reserve fronds for garnish, if desired) and chopped into 1-inch pieces*
>
> 3 CUPS WHOLE MILK, *or enough to just cover fennel*
>
> COARSE SALT AND FRESHLY GROUND WHITE PEPPER
>
> 2 TABLESPOONS UNSALTED BUTTER *(optional)*

Boil In a small pot, combine chopped fennel and milk. Bring to just under a boil over high heat, then immediately reduce to a simmer. Cover and cook until fennel is completely tender (it should not offer any resistance when pierced with the tip of a knife) but not falling apart, 20 to 25 minutes. Drain in a sieve, reserving liquid.

Puree Combine fennel and ¼ cup reserved liquid in a blender, and blend on high speed until smooth, about 4 minutes. Add more liquid a tablespoon or so at a time as necessary to keep the blender running smoothly.

Strain Transfer to a fine sieve set over a large bowl or liquid measuring cup and press with a rubber spatula to extract as much puree as possible. Discard remaining solids and rinse sieve thoroughly. Return puree to the sieve and set over a bowl to drain for 1½ hours longer.

Serve Transfer to a saucepan and cook over medium heat until warmed through. Stir in butter, if desired, and serve.

CAULIFLOWER PUREE

Trim 1 head cauliflower and cut into florets, then prepare as directed above (for fennel), seasoning with a pinch of freshly grated nutmeg along with salt and ground white pepper to finish. Makes about 1¼ cups.

CELERY ROOT PUREE Makes 2 cups

Because of their denser texture, root vegetables can be simmered in water instead of milk, then pureed with milk (or cream) and butter.

> 1 LARGE CELERY ROOT *(about 1¾ pounds), peeled and chopped into 1-inch pieces (5 cups)*
>
> COARSE SALT AND FRESHLY GROUND PEPPER
>
> 1 CUP WHOLE MILK
>
> 3 TABLESPOONS UNSALTED BUTTER

Boil Place celery root in a medium saucepan and cover with water. Add salt and bring to a boil, then reduce to a rapid simmer. Cook, partially covered, until very tender (it should offer no resistance when pierced with the tip of a paring knife), 15 to 25 minutes. Drain.

Heat liquid and butter Heat milk and butter in a small saucepan until butter is melted and mixture is hot.

Puree and strain Puree celery root with the milk mixture in a blender until smooth, about 2 minutes. Pass through a sieve, pressing on solids with a rubber spatula to remove as much puree as possible. Season with salt and pepper. If puree is too loose, cook, stirring, over moderate heat until desired consistency, before serving.

PEA PUREE Makes 1½ cups

To preserve their bright green color, the peas are shocked in an ice-water bath after boiling. You can skip this step if desired, but the puree will not have the same vibrancy. Frozen peas can be substituted for fresh; boil them for two minutes.

COARSE SALT

4 CUPS SHELLED FRESH GARDEN PEAS *(from about 4 pounds in pod)*

1 TABLESPOON EXTRA-VIRGIN OLIVE OIL

Boil and shock Prepare an ice-water bath. Bring 2 quarts of water to a boil, then add 1 tablespoon salt and the peas. Boil until tender and bright green, about 5 minutes. Reserve ½ cup liquid; immediately plunge peas into the ice bath. Drain well.

Puree Transfer peas to a blender. While blending, add oil in a slow, steady stream through the feed tube, and puree until very smooth, adding reserved liquid as necessary for desired consistency, about 2 minutes. Season with salt.

Strain Pass puree through a fine sieve into a clean pot, pressing with a rubber spatula to extract as much puree as possible; discard solids. Return to stove and heat over medium just to heat through, stirring constantly, before serving.

WINTER SQUASH PUREE Makes about 2 cups

Winter squash makes a very beautiful, fine-textured puree, and there is no need to strain it to finish.

2 POUNDS BUTTERNUT, KABOCHA, OR HUBBARD SQUASH, *peeled, seeded, and chopped into 1-inch pieces*

COARSE SALT AND FRESHLY GROUND PEPPER

4 TABLESPOONS (½ STICK) UNSALTED BUTTER

Boil Bring a medium pot of water to a boil, then add 1 tablespoon salt and the squash. Return to a boil, then simmer until very soft, about 10 to 15 minutes. Drain well.

Dry Return squash to pot and cook over low heat, stirring, to dry squash, 1 to 2 minutes.

Puree Transfer squash to a blender. Puree with butter until very smooth, about 2 minutes. Season with salt and pepper, and serve immediately.

LESSON 4.5
How to Roast and Bake

Roasting is one of the best ways to impart intense flavor to vegetables, producing crisp browned exteriors and tender, moist interiors. It's a favorite technique of many chefs, as it consistently produces such satisfying vegetable dishes. For best results, cut vegetables into uniform pieces to ensure even cooking. Lightly coat them with oil to add flavor and promote browning (and to keep them moist), and sprinkle with salt and pepper before cooking. Herbs and zest can also be used to season; if the oven is very hot or the cooking time is long, these should be added toward the end to keep them from burning (or use whole sprigs or stems, which can also be removed easily after roasting). Spread the vegetables in an even layer on a rimmed aluminum sheet pan, sturdy rimmed cookie sheet, or shallow roasting pan. Don't overcrowd the pan, or the vegetables won't brown properly.

The terms *roasting* and *baking* are often used interchangeably (as mentioned on page 124), yet for vegetables, baking usually refers to those that are cooked in the oven while left whole, rather than chopped first (think of a baked potato as opposed to roasted potatoes). Vegetables are also considered baked when they are hollowed out and stuffed with savory fillings. There are also gratins and tians; these baked vegetable dishes exemplify ways to (literally) build layers of flavor. The difference between the two is that a gratin contains cream or other liquid to bind all the vegetables, while a tian does not. Other than that, the technique is similar: Thinly sliced vegetables are neatly arranged in an overlapping fashion and then baked, with or without a bread-crumb topping, until golden and tender.

ROASTED AUTUMN HARVEST SALAD Serves 4 to 6

Just as a salad of chilled marinated vegetables feels right for spring, warm roasted vegetables make a splendid salad in the fall. The goal is similar for both: take seasonal produce, cook them to coax out their flavors and soften their texture, then toss each component separately in dressing before artfully arranging on a platter. You could even apply this formula to a summer salad of grilled vegetables, including eggplant, bell peppers, tomatoes, and zucchini.

The recipe calls for roasted shallots, parsnips, carrots, and beets, but other root vegetables would also be lovely, such as turnips, winter squash (butternut, acorn, or pumpkin), Brussels sprouts, or sweet potatoes and other tubers. Toasted spiced pepitas (hulled pumpkin seeds) are an entirely optional addition, yet they contribute welcome notes of heat and crunchy texture. Grated sharp Cheddar cheese would add protein and another layer of complexity.

For roasted vegetables

- ¼ CUP EXTRA-VIRGIN OLIVE OIL
- 8 BABY RED OR GOLDEN BEETS OR 4 MEDIUM BEETS, *scrubbed and trimmed*
- 8 SHALLOTS, *peeled and cut in half if large*
- 4 MEDIUM PARSNIPS *(about 1 pound), peeled and cut into 3-inch lengths (halve the thicker end pieces lengthwise)*
- 6 LONG CARROTS, *scrubbed well or peeled, halved lengthwise*

  COARSE SALT AND FRESHLY GROUND PEPPER
- 2 TABLESPOONS FRESH ROSEMARY LEAVES *(from 2 sprigs)*

Perfect Roasted Vegetables

For best results, roast vegetables in a single layer on a rimmed baking sheet, tossing them once or twice during roasting and rotating the pan for even cooking.

ASPARAGUS
Trim tough ends of stalks and toss with olive oil, salt, and pepper on a baking sheet. Roast at 450°F in a single layer until golden and tender, 20 to 25 minutes.

BEETS
Trim stems and roots; drizzle with olive oil and wrap in parchment-lined foil. Roast at 450°F until tender when pierced with the tip of a knife, about 1 hour 15 minutes (depending on size). Let cool slightly. Rub off skins with paper towels, wearing gloves to avoid staining hands.

BROCCOLI AND CAULIFLOWER
Peel and cut stems from a head of broccoli or cauliflower into 1-inch pieces; break head into florets. Toss with olive oil, salt, and pepper on a baking sheet. Roast at 450°F until tender and browned, about 25 minutes.

BRUSSELS SPROUTS
Trim Brussels sprouts and halve if desired. Toss with olive oil, salt, and pepper and roast at 450°F until golden brown and tender, 20 to 25 minutes.

CARROTS AND PARSNIPS
Peel carrots and toss on a rimmed baking sheet with olive oil, salt, and pepper. Roast at 450°F until tender and golden brown, 30 to 45 minutes (depending on size).

CORN
Roasting ears in their husks gives them an appealing smokiness. Slit husks and peel back; remove corn silk. Fold husks around corn; tuck in a few herb sprigs (thyme, oregano, or marjoram), a sprinkle of salt, and bits of butter. Tie with kitchen twine to secure, and roast in a baking pan at 450°F until tender, about 25 minutes.

FENNEL
Trim and cut bulbs into 8 wedges and toss with olive oil, salt, and pepper in a baking pan. Roast at 450°F, turning occasionally, until browned and tender, about 40 minutes.

MUSHROOMS
Toss whole mushrooms (shiitake, cremini, white button, or oyster) with olive oil, salt, pepper, and herbs (thyme, oregano, or savory). Roast at 450°F until golden brown and slightly shriveled, 20 to 25 minutes.

POTATOES
On a baking sheet, toss small potatoes with olive oil, salt, pepper (or crushed red pepper), and herbs (rosemary or thyme). Roast at 425°F until tender and browned, about 30 minutes. You can also roast russet potatoes the same way; cut them into wedges first.

SHALLOTS
Peel shallots and toss on a baking sheet with olive oil, salt, and pepper. Roast at 450°F until tender and caramelized, about 30 minutes.

SWEET POTATOES
Cut into wedges and toss with olive oil, salt, and pepper on a baking sheet. Roast at 450°F until tender and golden, 20 to 25 minutes.

TURNIPS
Peel and cut small turnips into wedges. Toss with olive oil, salt, and pepper on a baking sheet and roast at 450°F until tender and golden, 20 to 30 minutes.

WINTER SQUASH
Cut in half and remove seeds; cut squash into wedges or rings. Toss with olive oil, salt, pepper, and herbs (sage, rosemary, or thyme). Roast at 450°F until tender and golden, turning once, 35 to 40 minutes. If desired, drizzle with honey or maple syrup 10 minutes before finished. Also acorn squash can be cut in half; fill seed cavity with some butter and honey or maple syrup. Roast, basting with juices until golden and tender, about 40 minutes.

ROASTED AUTUMN
HARVEST SALAD

SPICED PEPITAS Makes 2½ cups
Heat oven to 350°F. Beat 1 large egg
white until soft and foamy in a
medium bowl. Combine ¼ cup sugar,
1 teaspoon coarse salt, ½ teaspoon
ground chile, ¼ teaspoon ground
allspice, ¼ teaspoon ground cumin,
and 1¾ teaspoons cayenne pepper,
and whisk into egg white. Stir in
2½ cups raw pepitas (hulled green
pumpkin seeds) until well coated.
Spread mixture in a single layer on a
rimmed baking sheet, and bake until
golden and fragrant and seeds are
almost completely dry, 10 to 15 minutes. Place pan on a wire rack to cool.
Spiced pepitas can be stored in an
airtight container at room temperature
up to 2 weeks. Pecans, walnuts,
cashews, or almonds may be substituted for the pumpkin seeds.

For salad
    2 BUNCHES ARUGULA, *trimmed and washed well (6 cups)*
      BASIC SHALLOT VINAIGRETTE *(page 356; substitute sweet cider for sherry vinegar)*

For garnish
      SPICED PEPITAS *(optional; recipe left)*

Roast beets Heat oven to 450°F. Place beets on a parchment-lined piece of
aluminum foil and drizzle with 1 tablespoon olive oil. Wrap in foil and bake
until beets are tender when pierced with the tip of a knife, 30 to 45 minutes
for baby beets and up to 1¼ hours for larger beets. Let stand until cool enough
to handle, then rub off skins with paper towels. Cut beets in half (or into
quarters or sixths if large).

Meanwhile, roast shallots, parsnips, and carrots Toss shallots, parsnips,
and carrots in a large bowl with remaining 3 tablespoons oil, then season with

salt and pepper. Spread in a single layer on a rimmed baking sheet and sprinkle with rosemary, tossing to coat. Roast until tender and golden, turning vegetables over once, about 30 minutes. Transfer to a bowl.

Prepare greens Wash arugula and dry thoroughly, then place in a bowl and cover with a damp kitchen towel (or damp paper towels). Refrigerate until needed (this will help crisp the leaves).

Toss vegetables and greens with vinaigrette Toss parsnips, carrots, and shallots with 2 tablespoons vinaigrette. Toss beets separately with 1 tablespoon vinaigrette (to prevent their color from bleeding). Toss arugula with 2 tablespoons vinaigrette and season lightly with salt and a pinch of pepper.

Compose salad and serve Line a serving platter with arugula and arrange vegetables on top. Serve pepitas on the side, if desired, or sprinkle over the top of salad. Serve salad immediately.

MARINATED ROASTED RED PEPPERS Serves 4 to 6

Bell peppers are roasted largely to remove the skins, which makes the vegetables supple and almost silky and perfect for marinating in a fragrant mix of oil, garlic, and basil. (This works for orange and yellow peppers, too, but not for green, because the skin is too thin.) Many recipes call for cutting the peppers into pieces lengthwise and roasting under the broiler, but it can be difficult to make the pieces flat enough to blacken evenly. It's easier to roast them right on the stove, over a gas burner, turning with tongs as each side blackens. Serve the marinated pieces as part of an antipasto with bread, cheese, olives, and cured meats, or toss them into pastas or over a pizza.

MARINATED ROASTED RED PEPPERS

   2 RED BELL PEPPERS
  ½ CUP EXTRA-VIRGIN OLIVE OIL
   3 TABLESPOONS BALSAMIC VINEGAR
   1 GARLIC CLOVE, *peeled and very thinly sliced lengthwise*
     COARSE SALT AND FRESHLY GROUND PEPPER
   1 TABLESPOON CHIFFONADE OF BASIL *(page 21)*

Roast Place bell peppers directly over a gas flame and cook, turning with tongs, until charred all over [1].

Steam and peel Transfer to a bowl and cover tightly with plastic wrap [2]. Let stand until cool enough to handle, about 10 minutes, then rub off skins with a paper towel [3]. (Do not run peppers under water, or you will wash away the flavor.) Remove seeds and veins and discard.

Marinate Slice peppers into 1-inch-wide strips. Transfer to a bowl and toss with oil, vinegar, and garlic. Season with salt and pepper, and toss with basil. Serve immediately, or refrigerate, covered, up to 3 days. If refrigerating, bring to room temperature and wait until just before serving to add basil.

Roasting Red Peppers

SLOW-ROASTED TOMATOES Makes 10 pieces

When slow-roasted in the oven, tomatoes develop a concentrated flavor with a dense yet chewy texture that is similar to that of sun-dried tomatoes but fresher. They are excellent alone or in salads, sandwiches, and pasta dishes. The length of time it takes to slow-roast tomatoes depends their size and freshness, but little effort is involved once they are in the oven except to check their progress every now and then, especially toward the end. (If they are darkening too quickly, reduce the temperature to 225°F.) The tomatoes will keep for one week in the refrigerator in a covered container. This recipe calls for beefsteak tomatoes, but you can successfully slow-roast plum tomatoes as well.

> 5 MEDIUM BEEFSTEAK TOMATOES, *halved crosswise*
> ¼ CUP PLUS 1 TABLESPOON EXTRA-VIRGIN OLIVE OIL, *plus more as needed*
> 2 TEASPOONS COARSE SALT
> ½ TEASPOON FRESHLY GROUND BLACK PEPPER
> 2 TO 3 GARLIC CLOVES, *thinly sliced*
> 3 TABLESPOONS FRESH THYME LEAVES

HEAT OVEN TO 300°F. Toss tomatoes in a large bowl with ¼ cup of the oil, or more if necessary (they should be thoroughly coated), then arrange cut side up on a parchment-lined baking sheet. Sprinkle evenly with the salt and the pepper and bake on middle rack for 45 minutes. Reduce heat to 250°F and continue baking until tomatoes are reduced in size and beginning to wrinkle around the edges, about 3 hours. Remove from oven and evenly distribute garlic and thyme on top of the tomatoes, then drizzle with remaining 1 tablespoon oil. Return to oven and continue baking until garlic is golden and tomatoes are dark around edges and shriveled but still soft, about 2 hours longer. Remove from oven; let cool before using or storing.

SLOW-ROASTED
TOMATOES

TOMATO PETALS

TOMATO PETALS Makes 24 pieces

This is a good way to use tomatoes that are less than perfect, as the baking intensifies their flavor, and honey enhances their sweetness. They make lovely accompaniments to meat, chicken, or fish, or use them when steaming *en papillote* (see page 215). The tomatoes can be refrigerated in an airtight container up to three days.

6 SMALL RIPE PLUM OR VINE-RIPENED TOMATOES

1 TEASPOON FRESH THYME LEAVES

1 TEASPOON HONEY

2 TABLESPOONS EXTRA-VIRGIN OLIVE OIL

COARSE SALT

Prepare tomatoes Heat oven to 275°F and prepare an ice-water bath. Blanch and peel tomatoes (page 381). Cut tomatoes in half and scrape out seeds, then cut halves in half. Transfer to a bowl and toss with the thyme, honey, oil, and salt to combine. Arrange in a single layer on a parchment-lined baking sheet.

Bake Bake until slightly shrunken and almost dry, about 2 hours. Check after 1 hour; if they are turning too dark, reduce temperature to 225°F. Remove from oven; let cool before using or storing.

Varieties of Peppers, Eggplant, and Tomatoes

HABANERO PEPPERS

HUNGARIAN WAX PEPPERS

RED AND GREEN BELL PEPPERS

EGGPLANT

POBLANO PEPPER

WHITE EGGPLANT

SERRANO PEPPER

JALAPEÑO PEPPER

JAPANESE EGGPLANT

GIANT RED MARCONI PEPPER

CHERRY TOMATOES

ITALIAN EGGPLANTS

ROMA TOMATOES

HEIRLOOM TOMATOES

BEEFSTEAK TOMATOES

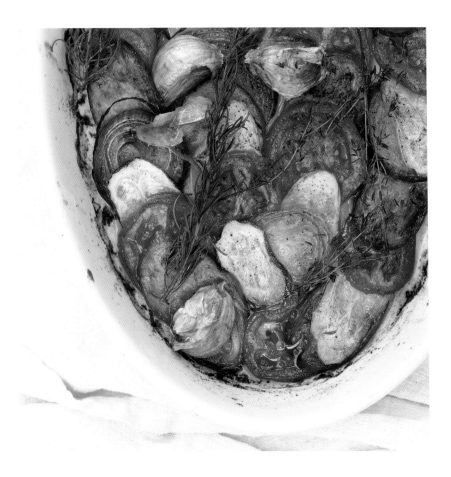

VEGETABLE TIAN Serves 6

A tian is a Provençal creation named for the traditional earthenware baking dish. Be sure to drizzle generously with oil to impart flavor and keep the vegetables from drying out (remember, there's no other liquid in a tian); you can spoon off excess oil after cooking.

⅓ TO ½ CUP OLIVE OIL

1 SMALL EGGPLANT *(about 6 ounces), thinly sliced crosswise on a slight diagonal*

1 YELLOW SQUASH OR ZUCCHINI *(about 6 ounces), thinly sliced crosswise on a diagonal*

4 PLUM TOMATOES *(about 1 pound), sliced lengthwise ¼ inch thick*

2 SMALL RED, WHITE, OR YELLOW ONIONS *(8 ounces), thinly sliced crosswise*

COARSE SALT AND FRESHLY GROUND PEPPER

SPRIGS OF HERBS, *such as thyme, rosemary, oregano, or marjoram*

1 HEAD GARLIC, *separated into cloves but not peeled*

Assemble Heat oven to 400°F. Coat the bottom of an oval baking dish or 9 by 13-inch baking dish with 2 tablespoons oil. Arrange vegetables in dish, alternating them and overlapping them *fig. 4.15*. Season with salt and pepper; drizzle with enough oil to coat generously, and scatter herbs and garlic evenly over the top.

Bake Bake 25 minutes, then baste vegetables with oil from pan and continue baking until tender and browned, about 20 minutes more.

fig. 4.15 ARRANGING THE VEGETABLES

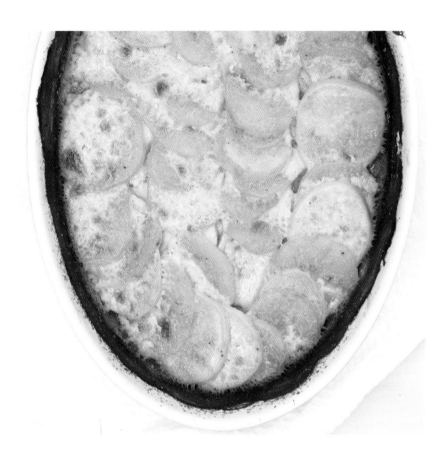

POTATO AND TURNIP GRATIN Serves 6

Heavy cream is the most traditional liquid in gratins, but milk or stock, or a combination, can replace half the cream for a lighter result. In this recipe, the liquid is infused with thyme to help its flavor disseminate more effectively since the vegetables will soak up the liquid; this step can be omitted but it does make a difference.

> 1 TO 2 TABLESPOONS UNSALTED BUTTER *(optional)*, plus more for baking dish
>
> 1½ CUPS HEAVY CREAM, *plus more if needed*
>
> 3 SPRIGS ROBUST HERBS SUCH AS THYME OR SAGE
>
> 2 POUNDS TOTAL POTATOES (PREFERABLY RUSSETS) AND TURNIPS, *peeled and thinly sliced*
>
> COARSE SALT AND FRESHLY GROUND PEPPER

Infuse liquid Heat oven to 375°F and butter a 2½-quart oval gratin dish or 9-by-13-inch baking dish. Bring cream and thyme to just under a boil in a small saucepan, then remove from heat and let stand 30 minutes. Strain through a fine sieve and discard solids.

Assemble Arrange the vegetable slices in an overlapping fashion in the baking dish, alternating them and seasoning with salt and pepper as you go. Dot with butter, if using. Pour cream over top (it should almost cover the vegetables; add up to ½ cup more if necessary) *fig. 4.16* and cover tightly with parchment-lined foil.

Bake Bake until vegetables are tender, about 45 minutes, then remove foil and bake until golden brown and bubbling, about 15 minutes more. Serve at once.

fig. 4.16 POURING CREAM OVER LAYERED SLICED VEGETABLES

LESSON 4.6
How to Sauté

Sautéed vegetables are cooked in a hot pan in just a small amount of oil or butter. The beauty of sautéing is that you don't actually need a lot of fat to create the flavor and color so distinctive to this method. Use a pan that is the appropriate size for the amount of vegetables you're cooking: too small and the vegetables will steam instead of browning; too big and they run the risk of burning. Heat the pan on high until hot; this will ensure that you need only a little fat to cook the vegetables and to keep them from sticking. Start by adding aromatics, such as onion and garlic, to the pan to build flavor. When sautéing a number of vegetables in one pan, cook those that will take the longest first. Thick or fibrous vegetables, such as carrots, can be parboiled before sautéing; kale, collards, and other tough leafy greens should be shredded or blanched beforehand.

SICILIAN-STYLE SAUTÉED GREENS Serves 4

In Sicilian cooking, raisins and nuts—often pine nuts, but almonds and walnuts are also common—are frequently used to lend sweetness to bitter greens and vegetables, including chard, spinach, and kale, as well as broccoli and cauliflower. They also add textural contrast to a dish of sautéed greens, as in this chard recipe. You can make a simplified version by omitting the shallots, nuts, and raisins, and starting at the point where you cook the garlic and red-pepper flakes in oil.

For greens
- 1 POUND SWISS CHARD

For nut mixture
- 2 TABLESPOONS EXTRA-VIRGIN OLIVE OIL
- 2 MEDIUM SHALLOTS *(or 1 small onion), thinly sliced*
- 1 GARLIC CLOVE, *minced*
- PINCH OF RED PEPPER FLAKES *(optional)*
- ⅓ CUP WHOLE ALMONDS *or pine nuts, coarsely chopped*
- ⅓ CUP RAISINS *(golden or dark), coarsely chopped, or other chopped dried fruit*

For sautéing greens
- 2 TABLESPOONS EXTRA-VIRGIN OLIVE OIL, *plus more for drizzling*
- 1 TABLESPOON UNSALTED BUTTER
- JUICE OF ½ LEMON *(1 to 2 tablespoons)*
- COARSE SALT AND FRESHLY GROUND PEPPER

Prepare greens Remove stems from chard. Fill a large bowl with cold water. Add leaves and let stand, swishing in water occasionally to loosen grit, for 1 minute. Lift greens out of water. Drain bowl and rinse out grit. Repeat until no grit remains in bottom of bowl when greens are removed, up to 4 more times. Repeat with stems. Slice greens crosswise into 1-inch-wide strips. Slice stems into ½-inch pieces *fig. 4.17*, cutting just enough to yield 1 cup (discard remaining stems).

Cook nut mixture Heat 2 tablespoons olive oil in a large skillet over medium heat. Cook shallots, garlic, and red pepper flakes (if using) until fragrant but not

SICILIAN-STYLE SAUTÉED GREENS

fig. 4.17 SLICING CHARD STEMS

brown, about 2 minutes, stirring frequently. Add nuts and raisins and cook [1], stirring, until fragrant and raisins have softened, about 2 minutes more. Remove from pan; set aside.

Sauté greens Heat 2 tablespoons olive oil in same skillet. Stir in the chard stems [2] and cook for 1 minute. Add greens one handful at a time, stirring to wilt slightly [3] before adding more, then cook until wilted and tender, 3 to 5 minutes. Add butter and stir until melted and combined. Squeeze lemon juice [4] over greens and season with salt and pepper.

Serve Return nut mixture to pan and stir into greens [5], then drizzle with a little olive oil, if desired, and serve immediately.

Sicilian-Style Sautéed Greens, Step by Step

SAUTÉED SNAP PEAS AND BABY TURNIPS Serves 4

This recipe uses a combination of steaming to soften the texture and brighten the color (especially helpful when cooking green vegetables), and sautéing in butter to increase flavor. The method is similar to blanching then sautéing, only in the same pan. This steam-sauté method can also be used to cook green beans, snow peas, green peas, asparagus, broccoli, and Brussels sprouts. In the recipe below, sautéed snap peas are combined with shaved raw baby turnips, which are slightly bitter and contrast nicely with the sweetness of the peas. Radishes would offer the same balance of taste and crunchy texture.

1 POUND SUGAR SNAP PEAS

2 TABLESPOONS UNSALTED BUTTER OR HERBED COMPOUND BUTTER *(page 166)*

3 TABLESPOONS WATER

COARSE SALT AND FRESHLY GROUND PEPPER

3 BABY TURNIPS, *scrubbed well, shaved paper thin on a mandoline*

2 TEASPOONS CHAMPAGNE VINEGAR

1 SCALLION, *dark-green part only, thinly sliced crosswise on the diagonal*

Trim peas Snap off tip of one end of a pea pod and pull string along the spine to remove, then repeat, working from other end. Repeat with all peas.

Steam-sauté Melt butter in a large skillet with a lid over medium-high heat. Add peas and toss to coat, then stir in water. Once water is at a boil, cover and cook until crisp-tender and bright green, about 2 minutes. Remove lid and continue cooking until any remaining liquid has evaporated (there shouldn't be much, if any) *fig. 4.18*. Season with salt and pepper, then cook for 30 seconds, just to allow the seasonings to infuse.

Add turnips Stir together turnips and vinegar, then add to pan and immediately remove from heat and toss to combine.

Serve Transfer to a platter and sprinkle with scallions. Serve immediately.

SAUTÉED SNAP PEAS AND BABY TURNIPS

fig. 4.18 SAUTÉING SNAP PEAS

Varieties of Squash

BUTTERNUT SQUASH

ACORN SQUASH

KABOCHA SQUASH

YELLOW SQUASH

ZUCCHINI

PATTYPAN SQUASH

ASIAN CUCUMBERS

SLICING CUCUMBER

KIRBY CUCUMBERS

ENGLISH CUCUMBER

SAUTÉED ZUCCHINI AND CORN Serves 4

This sauté makes good use of an abundance of summer vegetables, the small amount of cream adding a touch of richness without overwhelming the fresh flavor of the produce. A chopped ripe, small tomato would be a colorful addition.

2 TABLESPOONS UNSALTED BUTTER

1 LARGE OR 2 SMALL LEEKS *(8 ounces), halved, sliced crosswise into very thin half-moons, and washed well (page 32) (1¼ cups)*

COARSE SALT AND FRESHLY GROUND PEPPER

1 MEDIUM ZUCCHINI OR YELLOW SQUASH, *trimmed and cut into ¼-inch dice (1½ cups)*

2 EARS CORN, *kernels removed (1½ cups)*

2 TABLESPOONS HEAVY CREAM

¼ CUP CHIFFONADE OF BASIL *(page 21), plus whole leaves for garnish if desired*

LIME JUICE, *to taste*

Sauté zucchini and corn Melt butter in a large skillet over medium-high heat until foamy. Add leek and season with salt. Cook, stirring frequently, until leek is translucent, about 2 minutes. Add zucchini and corn and cook until tender and color is bright, about 2 minutes.

Finish dish Stir in cream and basil and season with salt and pepper. Add lime juice, about 1 teaspoon at a time, tasting and adjusting with more as desired.

Serve Serve warm or room temperature, garnished with basil leaves, if desired.

REMOVING CORN KERNELS
To cut kernels from the cob, stand the cob on one end, and slice downward with a sharp knife, keeping the blade against the ear to remove as much corn as possible. Once you've finished one side, turn and repeat until all kernels have been removed.

Varieties of Shell Beans

CRANBERRY BEANS

DRAGON'S TONGUES

PINKEYE PURPLE HULLS

SOYBEANS (EDAMAME)

LIMA BEANS

SAUTÉED KALE AND FRESH SHELL BEANS Serves 4

Fresh shell beans such as cranberry beans and black-eyed peas have a creamy yet dense texture; they are also easier and quicker to prepare than their dried counterparts, since no soaking is required and they cook in a fraction of the time.

For this dish, everything is eventually sautéed in the same pan, although a few preliminary steps are required to make the most of the various components. The beans are simmered in an aromatic liquid until tender and infused with hints of cinnamon and herbs, and the kale is blanched to soften its sturdy leaves. If you want to skip this step, shred the kale finely so it will cook more quickly. Or substitute kale with more tender greens, such as escarole, dandelion, or chard, which can go straight into the sauté pan without being shredded or blanched.

328

For beans

- 6 CUPS WATER
- COARSE SALT
- 1 DRIED BAY LEAF
- 2 PIECES (½ INCH) CINNAMON STICK
- ½ TEASPOON WHOLE BLACK PEPPERCORNS
- 1 SPRIG OREGANO
- ¾ POUNDS CRANBERRY BEANS, *shelled (about 1 cup)*

For kale

- 1 MEDIUM BUNCH KALE *(about 12 ounces)*
- COARSE SALT AND FRESHLY GROUND PEPPER
- ¼ CUP EXTRA-VIRGIN OLIVE OIL, *plus more for drizzling*
- 2 GARLIC CLOVES, *very thinly sliced*
- ¼ TEASPOON RED PEPPER FLAKES
- ½ LEMON, *plus wedges for serving*

fig. 4.19 SIMMERING FRESH
SHELL BEANS

fig. 4.20 SAUTÉING FRESH SHELL BEANS

Cook beans Stir together the water, 2 teaspoons salt, the bay leaf, cinnamon, peppercorns, and oregano in a large saucepan. Bring to a boil over medium-high heat, then add beans, and return to a boil. Reduce to a simmer and cook, partially covered, until beans are tender (they should be soft enough to squeeze with your fingers) but not falling apart, 15 to 20 minutes *fig. 4.19*. Drain.

Meanwhile, blanch kale Remove tough stems from kale and discard. Cut leaves crosswise into 1-inch strips. Wash well and drain. Bring a large pot of water to a boil. Add 1 tablespoon salt and the kale and cook until wilted and color has intensified, about 1 minute. Drain well.

Sauté beans and kale Heat a large skillet over medium-high heat. Add the oil, garlic, and red pepper flakes; cook 20 seconds, stirring constantly. Add the beans and stir well to coat in oil *fig. 4.20*, then add kale and stir to coat. Cook until heated through. Squeeze juice from lemon over kale; stir to combine.

Serve Transfer to a serving platter. Drizzle with olive oil and a serve with lemon wedges.

HERBED ROSTI WITH WILD MUSHROOMS

Serves 4 to 6

Rosti is a favorite Swiss potato dish made with grated potatoes and, depending on the cooking technique (deep-frying, pan-frying or even baking), butter, oil, or a combination. It can be formed into one large cake, as in the recipe below, or shaped into smaller patties. The ideal rosti is crisp and light.

For rosti

- 2 LARGE RUSSET POTATOES *(about 1¼ pounds)*
- ½ SMALL LEEK, *white and pale green parts only, washed and cut into julienne*
- 1 TEASPOON FINELY CHOPPED FRESH THYME LEAVES
  COARSE SALT AND FRESHLY GROUND BLACK PEPPER
- 2 TABLESPOONS UNSALTED BUTTER
- 2 TABLESPOONS OLIVE OIL

Rosti Tips

> The potatoes need to be briefly soaked in cold water to remove some of their starch, which would cause the texture of the rosti to be gummy.

> Squeeze excess water from the potatoes before sautéing; otherwise the rosti will steam rather than turn a golden brown.

> Finishing in the oven deepens the color of the outside while allowing the inside to cook through, ensuring that crisp-fluffy contrast in texture.

Equipment

You will need a 10-inch ovenproof sauté pan; the sloped sides makes it easier to slide the rosti in and out of the pan.

The potatoes can also be grated in a food processor instead of a box grater.

Varieties of Potatoes

WHITE

NEW

PURPLE PERUVIAN

SWEET POTATOES

RUSSETS

YUKON GOLD

RED

FINGERLINGS

For mushrooms

   2 TABLESPOONS UNSALTED BUTTER

   ½ SMALL LEEK, *white and pale green parts only, cut into julienne and washed*

   4 OUNCES FRESH CHANTERELLES, *wiped clean (halved if large)*

   ¼ CUP BASIC CHICKEN STOCK *(page 41)*

For serving

   2 OUNCES FRESH GOAT CHEESE, *softened*

Soak potatoes Heat oven to 400°F. Peel potatoes and grate on the large holes of a box grater. Soak in water to cover for 5 minutes. Lift out with your hands and squeeze out liquid [1], then squeeze out excess liquid in a clean kitchen towel or paper towels [2]. You should have 3 cups potatoes.

Ingredients

Chanterelles are small, trumpet-shaped wild mushrooms with a delicate, nutty taste. They are generally available only during summer and winter and can be found at specialty-food stores and many supermarkets. To clean them, simply wipe with a damp cloth or paper towel; do not rinse or soak, as they will become spongy. Any wild mushrooms, such as shiitake, oyster, or morels, can be used instead, or substitute button or cremini mushrooms.

Rosti, Step by Step

fig. 4.21 SAUTÉING CHANTERELLE
MUSHROOMS WITH LEEKS

Sauté rosti Toss together potato, leek, and thyme, and season with ¾ teaspoon salt and ¼ teaspoon pepper. Melt 1 tablespoon each butter and olive oil in a 10-inch ovenproof pan over medium-high heat, swirling to coat evenly. Add potato mixture, and cook, pressing down lightly with a large spatula [3], until bottom is golden and releases easily from pan, about 4 minutes [4]. Invert rosti onto a plate. Add remaining 1 tablespoon each butter and oil and swirl to coat pan. Carefully slide rosti back into pan uncooked side down and cook until starting to brown underneath, about 3 minutes [5].

Bake rosti Transfer to oven and cook until deep golden brown and cooked through (it should offer no resistance when pierced in the center with the tip of a paring knife), 12 to 15 minutes.

Meanwhile, sauté mushrooms Melt the butter in a medium skillet over medium-high heat. Cook leek until translucent, stirring, about 1 minute. Add chanterelles, season with salt and pepper, and sauté until golden *fig. 4.21*, about 3 minutes. Stir in stock and cook until reduced and slightly thickened and the mushrooms have softened, 2 to 3 minutes.

Serve Slide baked rosti out of pan onto a serving platter. Spoon dollops of goat cheese in center of rosti and spoon mushroom mixture over top. Cut into wedges and serve immediately.

LESSON 4.7

How to Fry

Pan-fried vegetables are partially submerged in oil and flipped halfway through the cooking time to brown each side, while deep-fried vegetables are covered in oil (thus requiring no flipping). The key to creating the crunchy exterior and tender interior that the best fried foods are known for is to keep the cooking oil very hot, generally between 350° and 375°F. Whether pan-frying or deep-frying, at this temperature, the vegetables actually shouldn't absorb any more oil than they would if sautéed; if the oil isn't hot enough, the vegetables will soak up more oil and become soggy. The same oils used for frying meats, poultry, and fish can also be used for vegetables (page 246). As with other cooking methods, cut vegetables into uniform pieces, so that they will cook evenly. If using a coating, choose one that is appropriate for the type of crust you want. Batter, such as tempura, creates a very delicate, airy crust. Battered vegetables are best when served immediately after frying because their coating will become limp or oily if left out too long. Breading, on the other hand, produces a crisper, denser crust that will hold up better after frying. Heat oil slowly on moderate heat; it's easy to lose control of the temperature if heating the oil on the high setting of your stove. Carefully regulate the heat of the frying oil with a deep-fry thermometer (see page 245), and don't let the oil get too hot, lest it start smoking or catch fire (see page 247). Cook vegetables in batches and don't overcrowd the pan—they should always be floating free, not touching. After each batch, allow the heat of the oil to come back up. Have a layer of paper towels set out on a baking sheet close to the stove to drain the fried foods immediately after cooking.

FRENCH FRIES Serves 6

The secret to perfect fries—crisp on the outside and soft within—is to "fry" them twice, first to cook through, then to crisp and color. The first step is called blanching rather than deep-frying, since the temperature of the oil (300°F) is sufficient to soften, but not brown. (If you tried to cook them at a high temperature the whole time, the outsides would burn before the insides were cooked through.) The second step involves true deep-frying: the oil is brought up to 350°F—hot enough to quickly brown the outside without needing to cook the interior further. As with the sautéed rosti (page 329), the potatoes are soaked in water before cooking to remove excess starch, then dried thoroughly.

Whenever deep-frying, remember that the oil should be maintained at the proper temperature, so you will need to adjust the heat as necessary. Unless you have a deep-fryer, use a cast-iron pot; it holds its heat better and distributes heat more evenly than other types. Also, frying can leave oil marks on stainless steel and other surfaces that are difficult to clean. To keep the temperature from dropping too much, add potatoes in batches; this will also ensure that they fry evenly and quickly. If the temperature spikes at any time, cool down the oil by adding some room-temperature oil to the pot.

Be sure to salt the fries immediately after removing from the oil, when they are still piping hot. Any other seasonings (such as the lemon zest and rosemary below) are purely optional. Homemade mayonnaise (page 95) is an indulgent option for dipping. Or drizzle with malt vinegar for a tangy taste.

6 RUSSET POTATOES *(about 3 pounds total)*

2 QUARTS PEANUT OR COLD-PROCESSED SUNFLOWER OR SAFFLOWER OIL

1 TO 2 TABLESPOONS ROSEMARY LEAVES *(optional) or small sprigs*

    JULIENNED ZEST OF 1 LEMON *(page 34, optional)*

    FINE SEA SALT

French Fries, Step by Step

Soak potatoes Peel potatoes and square off sides and ends. Cut lengthwise into ⅓-inch-thick slices [1], then cut into 4-by-⅓-by-⅓-inch sticks [2]. Place in a large bowl and add cold water to cover by 1 inch [3], then let soak in the refrigerator at least 4 hours or up to 24 hours. Drain potatoes and spread on a clean kitchen towel and dry completely, patting off as much water as possible [4].

Blanch potatoes in oil Line baking sheets with a double thickness of paper towels. Heat 2 inches of oil in a heavy stockpot over medium heat to 300°F on a deep-fry thermometer. Working in batches and using a spider, lower potatoes into oil [5] (the temperature will drop significantly, to about 270°F, and slowly climb up again) and stir to separate. Cook just until softened (test one by breaking in half; it should be almost completely cooked through), but not brown, about 3 minutes. Use a spider or slotted spoon to transfer to one of the prepared baking sheets to drain, spreading in a single layer. Allow oil to return to 300°F between each batch. (The potatoes can be blanched and left to drain on the prepared baking sheets for 4 hours in the refrigerator before finishing, replacing the paper towels as necessary.)

Fry Heat oil to 350°F. Again working in batches, add blanched potatoes to oil (the temperature will drop to about 340°F) and stir to separate. Cook until golden brown, 4 to 4½ minutes; if desired, add the rosemary and lemon zest during the last 20 seconds of cooking [6]. Use a spider or slotted spoon to transfer to prepared baking sheets to drain (replace paper towels if you are using the same baking sheets as above). Allow oil to return to 350°F between each batch.

Serve Sprinkle with salt and serve immediately.

TEMPURA VEGETABLES Serves 6 to 8

When prepared properly, Japanese-style deep-fried vegetables are light and crisp and not at all greasy. Baking powder in the batter helps it to puff up in the hot oil, while cornstarch keeps it from being too dense (as it can be when made with all flour). Ice-cold batter is the secret to successful tempura, so be sure to use ice water (drained of ice). You can use any type of vegetable in this recipe, as long as you slice the vegetables thinly and uniformly so they cook evenly. Root vegetables should be sliced a bit thinner since they take longer to cook.

For frying
> PEANUT OR COLD-PRESSED SUNFLOWER OR SAFFLOWER OIL

For batter
> 1½ CUPS ALL-PURPOSE FLOUR
> ¾ CUP CORNSTARCH
> 2 TEASPOONS BAKING POWDER
> 2 LARGE EGGS, *lightly beaten*
> 1½ TO 2 CUPS ICE WATER

For vegetables
> 1 MEDIUM SWEET POTATO, *thinly sliced*
> 1 SMALL JAPANESE EGGPLANT, *thinly sliced*
> 1 MEDIUM YELLOW SQUASH, *thinly sliced*

fig. 4.22 MIXING TEMPURA BATTER

fig. 4.23 FRYING TEMPURA VEGETABLES

TEMPURA DIPPING SAUCE

Makes 2⅔ cups

Mix together 1 cup dashi (page 60), ¾ cup soy sauce, ¼ cup plus 2 teaspoons mirin (Japanese cooking wine), 4½ tablespoons lemon juice, and 1½ teaspoons grated peeled fresh ginger in a bowl to combine.

1 MEDIUM ZUCCHINI, *thinly sliced*
½ HEAD OF BROCCOLI, *stemmed and broken into florets*
COARSE SALT

For serving
TEMPURA DIPPING SAUCE *(recipe at left)*

Heat oil Heat 2 inches of oil in a heavy pot over medium heat to 375°F.

Meanwhile, prepare batter Whisk together flour, cornstarch, and baking powder in a shallow bowl. Whisk together egg and 1½ cup strained ice water until combined, then whisk into flour mixture until incorporated. Add enough additional ice water until mixture is the consistency of a light pancake batter *fig. 4.22* (there will be lumps).

Fry When oil is hot, dip the vegetables one at a time into batter to coat completely, then allow excess to drain into bowl. Working in batches (about 6 pieces at a time) and using a spider, carefully submerge vegetables in oil *fig. 4.23*. Cook, turning once, until light golden, puffed, and cooked through, about 3 minutes for most vegetables (they should be tender when pierced with the tip of a paring knife). Transfer to a baking sheet lined with paper towels to drain and sprinkle with salt.

Serve Transfer to a platter and serve immediately with dipping sauce.

LESSON 4.8
How to Stir-fry

This traditional Chinese cooking technique relies on very high heat to quickly cook vegetables, which are small or cut into bite-size pieces and stirred constantly in a hot wok or skillet. They are usually combined with a classic Chinese flavor base such as the ginger, garlic, and scallion in this recipe, in the same way that French and Italian dishes begin with mirepoix or soffritto. Because of the rapid cooking time, the vegetables tend to stay very crisp and retain their vitamins and bright color. Preparing all ingredients before heating your wok or skillet is essential, as it will ensure you can add each at the appropriate time; wash, cut, and store vegetables in separate bowls.

Stir-frying relies on even hotter heat than sautéing, which is sometimes attainable only on a commercial-grade cooktop. You'll get best results at home if you heat the wok for several minutes before adding oil and if you cook different vegetables separately, allowing the pan to heat between batches. If stir-frying a small quantity or one that doesn't require cooking in batches, add vegetables that will take longest first and those that cook quickest last. Either way, do not overcrowd your pan, or the vegetables will steam rather than sear. For extra browning, press vegetables against the side of the wok for a few seconds with a spatula. Stir-fried dishes are often tossed or served with a sauce, usually made by pouring stock or other flavorings directly to the pan. Sometimes a slurry—a thickening agent made of liquid and cornstarch or flour—is incorporated into the liquid to thicken the sauce. Be sure to bring the slurry to a full boil to activate the thickener, and then to cook for a minute or two to eliminate the starchy taste.

SPICY STIR-FRIED VEGETABLES Serves 6

For slurry

- 1 TABLESPOON CORNSTARCH
- ½ CUP WATER OR BASIC CHICKEN STOCK *(page 41)*

For sauce

- ½ CUP BROAD BEAN PASTE WITH CHILI (DOUBANJIANG)
- 1 CUP SHAO XING RICE WINE
- 3 TABLESPOONS SOY SAUCE
- 2 TABLESPOONS HONEY
- 1 TABLESPOON SUGAR

For stir-fry

- ¼ CUP UNTOASTED SESAME OR PEANUT OIL
- 1 POUND SNOW PEAS, *trimmed (5½ cups)*
- 2 BUNCHES SCALLIONS, *green parts only, sliced into 1- to 2-inch pieces (2¼ cups)*
- 5 GARLIC CLOVES, *minced (2 tablespoons)*
- 1 PIECE (ABOUT 1½ INCHES) FRESH GINGER, *peeled and cut into julienne (page 220) (3 tablespoons)*
- 1 TO 2 JALAPEÑO CHILES, *thinly sliced (seeds removed for less heat if desired)*
- ½ POUND SHIITAKE MUSHROOMS, *stems removed, caps cut into ⅛-inch-thick slices (5 cups)*

INGREDIENTS FOR SPICY
STIR-FRIED VEGETABLES

Ingredients

Broad bean paste, called *doubanjiang*, is a specialty of Szechuan cooking; it is a spicy fermented paste made by combining broad (or fava) beans with soybeans and chiles. It is available at Asian markets. If you can't find it, substitute soybean paste with chile, which is sold at many supermarkets.

Shao xing rice wine is a traditional Chinese cooking wine sold at Asian markets; sake (Japanese rice wine) can be substituted.

Make slurry Add cornstarch to water or stock and stir with a fork until thoroughly incorporated *fig. 4.24*.

Make sauce Whisk together all sauce ingredients in a bowl until smooth and combined.

Stir-fry snow peas Heat wok over high heat for 3 minutes. Add 1 tablespoon oil, then immediately add snow peas [1], pressing down with a spatula to promote searing. Stir briefly and quickly to coat with oil, then let sit 15 seconds without disturbing. Repeat stirring and sitting, pressing against wok, until they are bright green and charred in spots, about two more times. Transfer to a bowl and immediately return wok to high heat, cooking for 1 minute.

Stir-fry scallions Add 1 tablespoon oil, then immediately add scallions [2]. Cook as directed for snow peas, searing until scallions are slightly wilted and charred in spots, then transfer to bowl with the snow peas and immediately return wok to high heat for 1 minute.

fig. 4.24 MAKING SLURRY

Cook aromatics and stir-fry mushrooms Add remaining 2 tablespoons oil, then immediately add garlic, ginger, and chiles [3]. Stir quickly and constantly for 5 to 10 seconds, being careful not to let garlic burn. Add shiitakes and stir to combine [4], then let sit 10 seconds. Repeat stirring and sitting until mushrooms are golden brown, about 1½ minutes.

Finish with sauce and slurry, and serve Pour sauce into wok [5] and stir to combine, then add slurry [6] and stir quickly to incorporate. Allow mixture to come to a boil for 1 to 2 minutes. Return peas and scallions to the wok. Toss to coat in the sauce and cook just to heat through. Serve immediately.

Spicy Stir-Fried Vegetables, Step by Step

LESSON 4.9
How to Braise and Stew

When you want fork-tender vegetables with mellow, multilayered flavors, turn to braising and stewing. With both methods vegetables are simmered in flavorful liquid that is served as a sauce—one of the ways they are distinguished from boiled preparations. Stewed vegetables are cut into smaller pieces and cooked in more liquid than those that are braised. Cabbage, broccoli rabe, onions, and tougher greens, such as collards, are often braised or stewed, but even tender tomatoes, peppers, and eggplant turn out delicious when cooked in this manner— as they are for ratatouille, the classic Provençal dish. Often these recipes start by browning the vegetables in oil, butter, or other fat to add flavor and color. Many vegetable-based braises and stews call for mirepoix and other aromatic ingredients to add flavor. After the vegetables have browned, add a liquid (such as stock or broth) and cook the vegetables until just tender. The liquid can serve as a powerful flavor enhancer and will also end up with many of the vitamins and nutrients from the vegetables. Serving the liquid as a sauce helps ensure that those nutrients aren't lost. Homemade stock is preferable to canned because it has sufficient gelatin to thicken the sauce to a syrupy consistency.

BRAISED SPRING VEGETABLES Serves 4

2 TABLESPOONS OLIVE OIL

12 OUNCES SPRING ONIONS *(or scallions), trimmed to 3 inches of green, halved lengthwise*

1 TO 1½ TEASPOONS COARSE SALT

2 TABLESPOONS UNSALTED BUTTER

1½ TO 2 CUPS BASIC CHICKEN STOCK *(page 41)*

2 OUNCES MORELS, *washed well (halved if large) (1 cup)*

12 OUNCES SMALL POTATOES SUCH AS RED BLISS, FINGERLING, OR YUKON GOLD

1 TABLESPOON CHOPPED FRESH CHERVIL

> ## Braised Spring Vegetables, Step by Step

Brown onions Heat oil in a large straight-sided skillet or stockpot over medium-high heat. Add onions cut sides down and season with salt. Cook until onions are caramelized, about 5 minutes. Turn onions over [1] and add butter.

Add stock and vegetables and braise Pour in 1½ cups stock [2] and bring to a boil, then add mushrooms and potatoes [3] and stir to combine. Cover and reduce to a simmer; cook until vegetables are tender when pierced with the tip of a paring knife, 13 to 15 minutes, adding more stock if pan becomes too dry.

Thicken sauce Remove lid and raise heat to high. Boil liquid until reduced to a syrup, about 3 minutes. Season with more salt, if desired. Stir in chervil.

Serve Transfer to a serving platter and serve immediately.

WASHING MORELS

Morels' many crevices make them more difficult to clean than other mushrooms. Start by brushing grit from the surface of the spongy caps. Then dunk them in a bowl of cold water; drain on a clean paper towel. This method works for any hard-to-clean or exceptionally dirty mushrooms. Wash them and dry thoroughly right before using so that they don't become soggy.

Varieties of Cruciferous Vegetables

BROCCOLI RABE

ROMANESCO

KOHLRABI

BROCCOLI

CAULIFLOWER

RED CABBAGE

SAVOY CABBAGE

BRUSSELS SPROUTS

BOK CHOY

BABY BOK CHOY

GREEN CABBAGE

CHINESE CABBAGES

BRAISED BROCCOLI RABE Serves 4

This is an example of a short braise, where the cooking liquid is not reduced to make a sauce. Many recipes call for broccoli rabe to be blanched and then sautéed to remove some of its bitterness, but if you prefer its natural taste, braising is a better option. It mellows the bitterness without adding an extra step, especially when cooked in chicken stock, which adds a touch of richness.

¼ CUP EXTRA-VIRGIN OLIVE OIL, *plus more for drizzling*

3 MEDIUM GARLIC CLOVES, *crushed and peeled (page 33)*

1 BUNCH (1 ¼ POUNDS) BROCCOLI RABE, *trimmed and cut crosswise into 3-inch pieces*

2 TEASPOONS JULIENNED LEMON ZEST, *plus fresh lemon juice for serving*

   COARSE SALT AND FRESHLY GROUND PEPPER

1 CUP BASIC CHICKEN STOCK *(page 41)*

Sauté garlic Heat oil and garlic in a large straight-sided skillet over medium heat, stirring frequently, until garlic is sizzling and aromatic, but not browned, about 2 minutes.

Braise broccoli rabe Add broccoli rabe, zest, and ¾ teaspoon salt, then use tongs to toss and coat in oil. Add stock and bring to a boil, then reduce heat to a simmer. Cover and cook until broccoli rabe is tender, 7 to 10 minutes.

Serve Transfer contents of pan (including liquid) to a serving bowl. Grind pepper over top and drizzle with olive oil and lemon juice. Serve immediately.

BRAISED RED CABBAGE WITH CARAMELIZED APPLES Serves 6 to 8

The cabbage family takes quite well to braising. Start by caramelizing the apples and onions with some sugar for a pleasant balance of sweet and tart flavors. Not only does the vinegar add a delicious flavor, but the acid helps keep the cabbage a bright purple color.

BRAISED RED CABBAGE
WITH CARAMELIZED APPLES

6 TABLESPOONS UNSALTED BUTTER

½ CUP SUGAR

1¼ TEASPOONS COARSE SALT

2 MEDIUM GRANNY SMITH OR OTHER TART, FIRM APPLES *(1 pound total), peeled, cored, and cut into 1½-inch wedges*

1 LARGE ONION, *peeled and cut into 1½-inch wedges*

1 SMALL (1½ POUNDS) RED CABBAGE, *cored and cut into 1½-inch wedges through the core*

¾ CUP APPLE CIDER VINEGAR

¾ CUP WATER

Caramelize apples Melt butter in a medium stockpot or Dutch oven (at least 11 inches in diameter) over medium-high heat. Add sugar and salt, and stir to dissolve. Add apples and onion, in as close to a single layer as possible. Turn to coat in butter mixture. Let cook, shaking pan occasionally and turning over once, until sugar is beginning to caramelize and coat the apples and onions, about 10 minutes.

Braise Add cabbage, vinegar, and water *fig. 4.25*. Bring to just under a boil. Reduce to a simmer, cover, and cook until cabbage is tender and liquid is reduced to a syrup, 25 to 30 minutes. (If necessary, remove lid in the last five minutes and cook uncovered to reduce liquid to desired consistency; most of the apples will disintegrate.)

Serve Transfer cabbage and apples to a bowl and serve immediately.

fig. 4.25 LAYERING CABBAGE
OVER APPLES

STEWED OKRA AND TOMATOES Serves 6 to 8

For aromatics

- 2 TABLESPOONS EXTRA-VIRGIN OLIVE OIL
- 1 LARGE ONION, *sliced thinly into half-moons lengthwise (about 1½ cups)*
- 4 GARLIC CLOVES, *minced*

For stewing

- 5 MEDIUM BEEFSTEAK TOMATOES *(about 2 pounds), cut into 1-inch chunks (about 5 cups)*
- 1½ TEASPOONS COARSE SALT
- ¼ TEASPOON FRESHLY GROUND BLACK PEPPER, *plus more for garnish*
- PINCH OF CAYENNE PEPPER
- 1 POUND OKRA, *stems removed fig. 4.26, cut into ½-inch-thick rounds*
- 1 TO 2 TEASPOONS FRESH OREGANO LEAVES
- 10 LARGE BASIL LEAVES
- 1 GARLIC CLOVE, *minced (optional)*
- BEST-QUALITY OLIVE OIL, *for drizzling*

STEWED OKRA AND TOMATOES

Sauté aromatics Heat oil in a medium Dutch oven or heavy pot over medium heat. Add onion and sauté for 1 minute [1]. Add garlic and sauté until onion is soft and translucent, about 5 more minutes. Reduce heat if they begin to brown.

Stew vegetables Add tomatoes [2] and cook for 2 minutes until they begin to release some of their liquid. Add salt, pepper, and cayenne. Stir in okra [3] and bring mixture to a simmer. Reduce heat to medium-low, partially cover, and very gently simmer until okra is tender, about 1 hour.

Add herbs and garlic Chop oregano and add to mixture. Tear basil leaves and fold into the stew. Stir in garlic, if using.

Serve Transfer to a serving dish and garnish with a few grindings of pepper and a drizzle of oil.

fig. 4.26 TRIMMING OKRA

Stewed Okra and Tomatoes, Step by Step

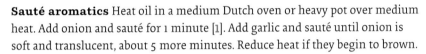

Varieties of Root Vegetables

RUTABAGAS

TURNIPS

CELERY ROOT

BEETS

PARSNIPS

DAIKON RADISHES

RADISHES

CARROTS

GLAZED TURNIPS Serves 4

This recipe relies on the natural gelatin in homemade stock to coat and glaze
the vegetables after most of the liquid has reduced. Brown stock thickens to a nice
glaze and imparts a rich flavor; butter contributes silkiness. Instead of turnips,
you can glaze carrots, rutabagas, potatoes, sweet potatoes, or onions. If you don't
have brown stock (or prefer a vegetarian version), use apple cider instead (the
sugars in the cider should cause it to reduce to a syrupy glaze).

> 2 TABLESPOONS SUNFLOWER OR OTHER NEUTRAL-TASTING OIL
>
> 2 POUNDS MEDIUM PURPLE-TOP TURNIPS, *peeled and cut into 1-inch chunks*
> *(about 8 cups)*
>
> 2 CUPS BASIC BROWN STOCK *(page 50)*
>
> COARSE SALT AND FRESHLY GROUND PEPPER
>
> 2 TABLESPOONS UNSALTED BUTTER

Brown turnips Place a large straight-sided skillet or stockpot with a lid over
medium-high heat; add oil and heat until shimmering. Add turnips and cook,
stirring occasionally, until golden brown [1], about 8 minutes.

Add liquid and braise Add stock [2] and ¼ teaspoon salt and bring to a boil.
Reduce heat to a simmer and cover. Simmer until turnips are just tender when
pierced with the tip of a paring knife, about 10 minutes.

Reduce liquid to a glaze Remove lid and boil until liquid has reduced to a
thick, syrupy glaze, 8 to 10 minutes. Stir occasionally to ensure that turnips are
evenly coated [3]. Season with salt and pepper. Remove from heat. Add butter,
stirring to coat, and heat until melted.

Serve Transfer to a bowl and serve immediately.

Glazed Turnips, Step by Step

How to Grill

Grilled vegetables are so delicious they're worth preparing even if you're not cooking meat or another protein-based main dish on the grill. (For information on setting up a grill, including grill temperature guidelines, see page 162.) To get the char that is so desirable on grilled vegetables, make sure to heat the grill to the temperature recommended in the chart, opposite. If the coals or fire are too hot, the vegetables could burn on the outside while remaining raw on the inside. Softer vegetables such as eggplant, tomatoes, onion, and corn (and any others in the photograph on the opposite page) can be grilled from their raw state, while denser vegetables like potatoes, carrots, and fennel (see photo below) often come out better when parboiled first. Cut large vegetables into uniform slices, but leave slender asparagus stalks and leeks whole so that they do not fall through the grate (and arrange them so they are perpendicular to the lines of the grate). Brush vegetables with olive oil (to keep them from sticking to the grate and to add flavor) or the herb oil below, and season with salt and pepper or a spice mix (see two options below) before cooking. If vegetables begin to blacken before cooking through, move them to a cooler spot on the grill. For kebabs, thread mixed pieces of uniform size onto skewers (soak wooden ones in water first for 30 minutes to prevent scorching). Slide your favorites onto the skewer (add garlic, sprigs of herbs, or lemon wedges for more flavor), and brush all sides with oil.

HERB OIL FOR GRILLED VEGETABLES Makes 1 cup

Whisk together 2 tablespoons coarsely chopped fresh thyme leaves, ¼ cup coarsely chopped fresh basil leaves, 2 tablespoons coarsely chopped fresh flat-leaf parsley, 2 minced garlic cloves, and 1 cup extra-virgin olive oil to combine, then season with coarse salt and fresh ground pepper. Brush on vegetables before cooking, then again halfway through, and immediately after removing them from the grill.

GRILLED PARBOILED VEGETABLES

SPICE MIXES FOR GRILLED VEGETABLES Makes enough for about 2 pounds vegetables

Vegetables such as potatoes and fennel are often parboiled before grilling, for the best texture; you can add additional flavors by tossing them with spice blends between boiling and grilling. Increase the amounts given below if you wish to keep the mixes on hand for convenience. The spice mixes are best stored in an airtight container in a cool, dark spot for up to 6 months.

FOR A SOUTHWESTERN MIX, stir together 1 teaspoon ground cumin, ½ teaspoon paprika, ½ teaspoon chili powder, ½ teaspoon coarse salt, and ¼ teaspoon ground coriander in a small bowl. Toss with 2 pounds of parboiled vegetables such as potatoes before grilling. If desired, sprinkle spiced vegetables with fresh lime juice after they have finished grilling; it's a perfect complement to the southwestern flavors.

For a fennel spice mix, stir together 1 tablespoon plus 1 teaspoon ground fennel seeds, a pinch of cayenne pepper, 1¼ teaspoon dry mustard, 1 teaspoon coarse salt, and ¼ teaspoon ground ginger in a small bowl, and use as directed above.

Perfect Grilled Vegetables

After grilling, brush the vegetables with herb oil (opposite), or drizzle with any of the vinaigrettes on page 356–357. They can also be marinated in vinaigrette or herb oil up to several hours; brush off excess before grilling.

ASPARAGUS
Use spears that are no thicker than ½ inch. If desired, bunch together 6 or 7 trimmed spears; thread a skewer through upper third of spears, gently turning skewer to keep spears from breaking. Repeat at bottom. Or simply place the spears perpendicular to the grates, and take care in turning them. Brush with olive oil or herb oil; season with salt and pepper. Grill over medium-high heat, turning once until marked and just tender, about 9 minutes total. Serve with grilled lemon halves, if desired.

BELL PEPPERS
Grill whole peppers over high heat, turning occasionally until charred all over, 15 to 18 minutes. Remove from grill and place in paper bag or place in a bowl and cover with plastic wrap. Let stand 10 minutes. Rub off skins using paper towels. Halve peppers and discard seeds.

CARROT
Halve lengthwise and cook in salted boiling water until tender, about 8 minutes. Drain. Brush with olive oil or herb oil and season with salt and pepper. Grill over medium heat until heated through and marked, 8 to 10 minutes. Brush with herb oil before serving, if desired.

CELERY ROOT
Peel, halve lengthwise, and cut crosswise into ¾-inch-thick pieces. Cook in salted boiling water until tender, about 8 minutes. Drain. Brush with olive oil or herb oil and season with salt and pepper. Grill over medium heat until heated through and marked, 8 to 10 minutes. Brush with herb oil before serving, if desired.

CORN
Remove husks and silk; discard. Brush cobs with oil. Season with salt. Arrange cobs on grill parallel with the grates. Grill over medium-high heat, turning occasionally until slightly charred and kernels are tender, about 15 minutes total. Serve with regular or compound butter (page 166). In-husk variation: Peel back husks without completely removing. Remove silks. Return husks to original position, and soak corn in water 10 minutes. Grill until charred and cooked through, 15 to 20 minutes. Serve with compound butter.

EGGPLANT
Halve eggplant lengthwise; cut into 1- to 1½-inch wedges (or ½-inch-thick slices lengthwise). Brush cut sides with olive oil or herb oil. Grill slices, one cut side down, over medium-high heat, until just golden and marked in spots, about 3 minutes. Transfer to cooler part of grill (medium heat). Grill, other cut side down, until marked, 5 to 6 minutes. Or grill wedges, skin sides down, until soft, 5 to 7 minutes. Season with salt.

> ## Perfect Grilled Vegetables *continued*

FENNEL BULBS

Trim and cut into ¾-inch wedges or ½-inch-thick slices. Cook in salted boiling water until tender, about 8 minutes. Drain. Brush with olive oil or herb oil and season with salt and pepper. Grill over medium heat until heated through and marked, 8 to 10 minutes. Brush with herb oil before serving, if desired.

LEEKS

Trim leeks. Halve lengthwise, rinse well. Add to a pan of boiling salted water. Reduce heat and simmer until slightly softened, 8 to 10 minutes. Drain and pat dry. Brush with olive oil or herb oil. Grill, cut sides down, over medium-high heat, with grill covered, until marked and softened, about 6 minutes. Flip; grill until soft, about 3 minutes more. Season with salt and pepper.

RED AND YELLOW ONIONS

Cut onions into ½-inch-thick pieces and keep rings intact. Thread a skewer horizontally through several slices. Brush generously with olive oil or herb oil, and season with salt and pepper. Grill onions over low heat with grill covered, until marked and softened, about 15 minutes. Flip; grill until cooked through, 15 to 18 minutes more.

PORTOBELLO MUSHROOMS

Brush with olive oil or herb oil and season with salt and pepper. Grill mushrooms, gill sides up, over medium-low heat, with grill covered, until marked and softened, 10 to 15 minutes. Flip; grill until cooked through (do not char gills), 1 to 2 minutes.

POTATOES

Cover potatoes with cold water. Add salt. Bring to a boil. Reduce to a simmer, and cook until just tender (they should offer slight resistance when pierced with the tip of a knife), 12 to 15 minutes. Drain. Halve or leave whole. Drizzle with olive oil. Season with spice mix (page 348) or salt and pepper. Toss to coat evenly. Thread onto skewers. Grill cut sides down over medium-high heat, turning once, until charred in spots and tender, about 10 minutes total.

RADICCHIO

Halve through stem if small, quarter if large, stem end left intact to hold leaves together. Brush with olive oil or herb oil. Season with salt and pepper. Grill over medium heat until marked and cooked through, 7 to 8 minutes, turning once. Brush with herb oil before serving, if desired.

SCALLIONS

Brush with olive oil and season with salt and pepper. Grill over medium-high heat until charred and tender, about 2 minutes per side.

SWEET POTATOES

Slice lengthwise about ⅓ inch thick. Brush with oil and season with salt and pepper. Grill over medium heat, turning once, 2 to 4 minutes per side.

TOMATOES

Halve tomatoes. Brush with olive oil or herb oil. Season with salt and pepper. Grill tomatoes over medium-high heat until slightly charred and flesh is soft and heated through, 8 to 10 minutes total.

YELLOW SQUASH AND ZUCCHINI

Cut lengthwise into ¼-inch-thick slices. Brush with olive oil; season with salt and pepper. Grill slices over medium-high heat until marked and tender, 6 to 8 minutes total. Or, cook chunks of squash until tender in salted boiling water, about 5 minutes. Brush with olive oil or herb oil and grill over medium heat until marked and heated through, 8 to 10 minutes. Brush with herb oil before serving.

LESSON 4.11
How to Make a Green Salad

Making a great salad is more art than science. There are certain principles worth learning and following, such as the proper way to wash greens and getting the right proportion of oil to vinegar in a dressing. But in terms of hard-and-fast rules, few apply. The best salads layer textures and flavors in interesting combinations: bitter and sweet, crunchy and creamy, crisp and soft. The goal is to create a salad that is well balanced, with no single ingredient dominating the palate or the plate. Once you master the fundamentals of blending flavors, textures, and colors in interesting combinations, you can happily improvise.

Included in this section are the basics of how to prepare greens for a salad mix that is a perfect starter or side for everyday meals. Lessons on vinaigrettes and creamy dressings follow. To make a salad that will delight all of the senses, keep the following suggestions in mind:

■ Use the freshest ingredients available; lettuces, especially, should be eaten as close to picking time as possible. If you have a good source of farm-fresh lettuces, take advantage of it. Because salads involve little, if any, cooking, there's not much of an opportunity to coax out more flavor—after all, no amount of dressing will mask brown lettuce leaves. If a vegetable is not pristine, leave it out.

■ When gathering ingredients, think of a salad as a loose framework. Start with the greens and then layer on any additional vegetables or other components, considering the contrasts you are creating as you go. Choose a mixture of greens for different textures and flavors. For example, romaine adds crunch, spinach imparts sweetness, while peppery arugula or watercress give a salad a pleasant bite.

■ Take the time to arrange the ingredients in a way that is pleasing to the eye. Some salads lend themselves to being plated individually, while others are fine tossed together and served in a salad bowl.

■ To dress, place salad in large bowl, add vinaigrette and season with salt and pepper, and toss with wooden spoons. You can also toss with metal or wooden tongs—just take care not to bruise the greens. The quickest way to ruin a salad is to put too much dressing on, and to leave it for too long. Dress salads lightly and as close to serving time as possible. Test the salad to see if it needs more dressing or salt and pepper after tossing.

■ A salad spinner is the quickest way to dry lettuce leaves and herbs, and can also be used to store cleaned greens for a short time in the refrigerator. The easiest to use— and most durable—spinners on the market are the kind with a pump top. Ones with a string mechanism are less practical, as the pull string tends to break or tangle.

ABOUT DRESSINGS

The word *salad* comes from the Latin *salar*, meaning "to salt," and dates to a time when greens were simply sprinkled with salt. Modern salads are embellished a bit more, usually with a vinaigrette or creamy dressing. Vinaigrettes often include an acidic ingredient (such as lemon juice or vinegar), oil, salt, and pepper. Herbs, spices, citrus zest, crumbled cheeses, and honey are sometimes also added. When making a dressing, always use the finest oils you can find and afford, such as extra-virgin olive oil. Creamy dressings, such as Blue Cheese (page 359), are often made with mayonnaise, yogurt, sour cream, or buttermilk instead of or in combination with oil.

Varieties of Lettuce

RED BOSTON

ICEBERG

BOSTON

FRENCH ICEBERG

BIBB

RED ROMAINE

ROMAINE

SPECKLED ROMAINE

LOLA ROSSA

RED OAK

GREEN LEAF

BUYING SALAD GREENS

More than any other vegetable (besides, perhaps, corn and peas), lettuces are best when they are freshly picked. If you have a vegetable garden, definitely grow your own. A farmers' market is your best bet for buying impeccably fresh salad greens. When shopping, avoid lettuces that are bruised, wilted, or have discoloration on inner leaves or midribs. Also, steer clear of lettuce with brown or tan tips (called "tip burn"), an early sign of rot. Bagged salad mixes are convenient, but the greens will likely have been picked and packaged long before neighboring whole heads of lettuce, so are not a good choice.

WHAT TO LOOK FOR

Romaine: Should have dark green, narrow, stiff leaves, and a loosely folded head.

Butter lettuces, such as Boston or Bibb: Look for light green leaves, with small, round, loosely formed heads.

Crisp heads, such as iceberg: Heads should be tightly formed, with crisp, unblemished leaves.

Leaf lettuces: Choose tender, unblemished leaves; color varies depending on variety.

Endive, chicory, escarole, radicchio, and frisée: These should have crisp, tender leaves that are not discolored.

Mesclun: This loose leaf lettuce mix, which often includes arugula, mizuna, mâche, frisée, sorrel, and radicchio, among others, should have no wilted leaves or those with wet, mushy, or yellow spots. Dig down into the bins for the freshest greens.

Other greens: Dandelion, sorrel, mustard, watercress, arugula, and mâche should have green, tender leaves free from bruising, tears, or any signs of yellowing.

WASHING AND STORING SALAD GREENS

Heads of lettuce grow close to the soil, so they often end up with sand between their leaves. To remove the sand, fill a clean basin or large bowl with cold water. Submerge the lettuce leaves in the water, swishing and agitating to loosen any dirt, which will sink to the bottom of the bowl. Remove the lettuce, drain the sandy water, and refill bowl with clean water. Repeat another time or two, until there is no more residue in the bowl.

If using a salad spinner, put the greens in the spinner in batches. If you try to dry them in one big batch, you may not leave enough room, or to remove water from the leaves, defeating the purpose of the spinner. If you don't have a salad spinner, gently blot the leaves between layers of towel until no water remains.

Washed and dried lettuce can be stored in the refrigerator for three days in a sealed plastic bag (lay leaves on paper towels and loosely roll up before bagging). To prevent the lettuce from turning brown too quickly, don't tear the leaves into smaller pieces until you're ready to serve them.

BASIC GREEN SALAD MIX Makes 9 cups; serves 6

If you like salad with nearly every meal, get in the habit of keeping your own salad mix, washed and dried, in the refrigerator. (You should also have the ingredients and recipe for homemade vinaigrette on hand for quick and effortless salads.) There are no exact proportions for the best salad blend, but a few general guidelines can help you create your own.

Start by recognizing that salads are not just made from lettuces; supplementing them with other greens introduces contrasting flavor and texture components. Fresh herbs add bright notes, and shaved vegetables lend pleasant crunch. Consider all the different lettuces available, some tender (Boston), some crisp (romaine or Bibb), still others in between (red and green leaf).

For contrasting taste (and texture, since some are sturdier than others), include a few greens, some with a peppery bite, such as arugula, watercress, or radish sprouts, and some that are pleasantly bitter, including dandelion, frisée, and chicory. When choosing herbs, steer clear of the sturdy, woody variety (rosemary, thyme, and bay leaf); choose tender, less robust herbs like basil, parsley, chervil, and tarragon, or frilly ones like dill or even fennel fronds. Watch out, too, for any strong-flavored herbs, like cilantro or marjoram, which can upset the balance.

Consider adding fennel, radish (any kind), beets, and carrots to your basic mix. All of these vegetables lend themselves to being shaved paper-thin on a mandoline or grated. Because they will lose some of their crispness over time, wait to add these until just before serving [you can preserve their taste and texture for a few hours by keeping them in a bowl of ice water (acidulated, for fennel); rinse and drain well before using]. If you wish, toss them instead in a little of the dressing that will go into the salad; this will cause them to soften slightly, so dress them sparingly to retain their crunch.

Once you've customized your blend, handle each selected ingredient with care. Except for sturdy lettuces like iceberg and romaine, gently tear lettuces and any large-leaf greens and herbs into bite-size pieces with your fingers instead of cutting (which can easily bruise them). Herbs should be gently blotted dry with paper towels (or a clean kitchen cloth). Once they've all been washed and dried thoroughly, allow them to crisp in the refrigerator before serving.

Plan on 1½ to 2 cups of salad mix per serving, and start with 1 to 2 teaspoons of vinaigrette for every cup of salad. Remember, you can always add more dressing as necessary, but it's impossible to take any away.

Here's but one suggested combination; use the guidelines above to create your own, and any of the dressings on the following pages to finish.

1 HEAD BOSTON LETTUCE *(red, green, or combination)*, *torn into large pieces (3 cups)*

1 HEAD RED LEAF LETTUCE *(or 3 heads lola rossa)*, *torn into bite-size pieces (3 cups)*

1 BUNCH WATERCRESS, UPLAND CRESS, OR ARUGULA, *tough stems trimmed (2 cups)*

1 HEAD BIBB (OR 2 SMALL HEADS BABY BIBB), *torn into bite-size pieces (2 cups)*

Wash and dry Wash the lettuces and watercress well in a large amount of cold water [1]. If they are at all wilted you can add some ice to the water to refresh the greens. Working in small batches, dry the greens thoroughly (but gently) in a salad spinner, pouring out the water from the spinner after each batch.

Crisp and store Roll up lettuces and cress in paper towels [2] and place in a large resealable plastic bag [3]. Place in the crisper drawer of the refrigerator for at least 1 hour so they can become crisp. Salad mix can be kept in the refrigerator for up to 3 days.

Making a Basic Green Salad Mix

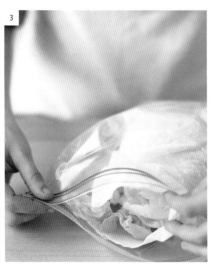

Vinaigrettes

A vinaigrette is a versatile sauce that, in its most basic form, consists of nothing more than an oil, an acid such as vinegar or citrus juice, and salt and pepper. For such a simple preparation, it's vital that you use the very best ingredients, like extra-virgin olive oil and a good-quality wine vinegar. The traditional proportions are three parts oil to one part acid, but these can be varied according to your taste; citrus is less acidic than most vinegars so you can usually get away with a higher percentage of it.

Oil and acid won't combine by simply stirring together; they need to be made into an emulsion, a mixture in which the acid is suspended in the oil. Classically, the method of making a vinaigrette is to pour the acid into a nonreactive bowl, mix in the salt and pepper and other flavorings (some, such as mustard, act as both flavoring and emulsifying agent); next, the oil is added in a very slow, steady stream, whisking constantly until the sauce is emulsified *fig. 4.27*. At this point, the oil and vinegar should be completely blended. In some cases, a jar will approximate the role of the whisk. Combine the acid and flavorings in the jar, add a little oil, then screw on the lid and shake vigorously to combine *fig. 4.28* and continue, adding oil and shaking until the mixture is thickened. The oil and acid will separate over time, so it's best to use the vinaigrette immediately after mixing. You can also make a vinaigrette in a blender. First combine acid and seasonings, then add oil in a slow, steady stream with the blender running *fig. 4.29*. Blended vinaigrette will stay emulsified longer than a whisked or shaken one.

Vinaigrettes, like many simple sauces, are infinitely variable. Common additions include Dijon mustard and shallots, as in the basic vinaigrette here. You can vary the flavor with different oils and acids; experiment with the many specialty nut oils and vinegars available, or try buttermilk or citrus juice in place of or in combination with vinegar (all are acids). You can also create countless unique dressings by adding other ingredients, such as the ones shown opposite *fig. 4.30*: grated or crumbled cheese (such as Parmigiano-Reggiano and Danish Blue); freshly grated citrus zest; roasted garlic and capers (preferably salt-packed); fresh ginger (grated or minced); fresh herbs, such as parsley, tarragon, chervil, and dill; diced red onion (in place of shallot); minced anchovies (or anchovy paste); peeled and diced fruit such as apple or pears; or honey for sweetness.

Before adding the oil, allow flavorings such as garlic, shallots, and onion to macerate for up to 30 minutes (or soak to allow the flavors to infuse). Whisk in any chopped fresh herbs at the end.

fig. 4.27 **WHISKING VINAIGRETTE BY HAND**

fig. 4.28 **SHAKING VINAIGRETTE IN A JAR TO BLEND**

SHALLOT VINAIGRETTE Makes ½ cup

- 3 TABLESPOONS SHERRY VINEGAR
- ½ TEASPOON DIJON MUSTARD
- 1 TEASPOON MINCED SHALLOT
- COARSE SALT AND FRESHLY GROUND PEPPER
- ¼ CUP PLUS 2 TABLESPOONS EXTRA-VIRGIN OLIVE OIL

COMBINE VINEGAR, mustard, shallot, ½ teaspoon salt, and ¼ teaspoon pepper in a bowl and whisk to combine. Whisking constantly, add oil in a slow, steady stream until oil is incorporated and mixture is emulsified. Serve immediately.

RED WINE VINAIGRETTE Makes ½ cup

- 2 TABLESPOONS RED WINE VINEGAR
- 1 GARLIC CLOVE, *smashed*
- 1 TEASPOON COARSE SALT, *or to taste*
- ¼ TEASPOON FRESHLY GROUND PEPPER, *or to taste*
- 3 TABLESPOONS EXTRA-VIRGIN OLIVE OIL
- 3 TABLESPOONS SUNFLOWER OR OTHER NEUTRAL-TASTING OIL

COMBINE VINEGAR, garlic, salt, and pepper in a blender and let macerate 10 minutes, then discard garlic. With blender running, gradually add oils in a slow, steady stream, and continue blending until mixture is emulsified. Season with more salt and pepper, as desired.

fig. 4.29 MIXING VINAIGRETTE IN A BLENDER

LEMON VINAIGRETTE Makes 1 cup

- 2 TEASPOONS DIJON MUSTARD
- 1 TABLESPOON FINELY GRATED LEMON ZEST, *plus ⅓ cup fresh lemon juice (from 3 lemons)*
- ¾ TEASPOON COARSE SALT
- ¼ TEASPOON FRESHLY GROUND PEPPER
- ¾ CUP EXTRA-VIRGIN OLIVE OIL

COMBINE MUSTARD, lemon zest and juice, salt, and pepper in a jar, then add some of the oil. Cover and shake to combine, then continue adding more oil and shaking until all the oil is incorporated and mixture is thickened and uniform in color. Serve immediately.

GINGER-SOY VINAIGRETTE Makes ½ cup

- 1½ TEASPOONS FINELY GRATED FRESH GINGER
- 1 TEASPOON TAMARI SOY SAUCE
- 2 TABLESPOONS RICE WINE VINEGAR
  COARSE SALT AND FRESHLY GROUND PEPPER
- ¼ CUP PLUS 2 TABLESPOONS SUNFLOWER OR SAFFLOWER OIL
  THINLY SLICED SCALLIONS *(optional)*

fig. 4.30 SOME COMMON MIX-INS FOR VINAIGRETTES

WHISK TOGETHER ginger, tamari, vinegar, and salt and pepper to taste in a bowl, then gradually whisk in oil, adding it in a slow, steady stream, and continue whisking until mixture is emulsified. Stir in scallions, if desired.

BLUE CHEESE DRESSING

BUTTERMILK HERB
VINAIGRETTE

CUCUMBER RANCH DRESSING

GREEN GODDESS DRESSING

Creamy Salad Dressings

There is a short list of salad dressings that never go out of fashion, though that doesn't mean that you shouldn't tailor them for modern palates. The four you find here will be familiar in name, if not in taste. For if you've never sampled a homemade version, you are in for a surprise; the fresh flavors are a revelation. The various components are at once discernible and blended in with the others to create a balanced whole. What unifies these four dressings is their creaminess, whether from mayonnaise, sour cream, or yogurt (or a combination), and the addition of buttermilk, which lends acidity as well as a tangy flavor.

Unlike with vinaigrettes, there is no real technique involved beyond balancing the flavors, and only one calls for a food processor (the rest are whisked together in a bowl). The dressings here can be refrigerated in an airtight container for up to three days. You may need to whisk them a few times after storing to smooth their consistency.

All of these dressings pair best with crisp, sturdy lettuces including romaine and iceberg, as well as tender or Boston and leaf lettuce. They can also be served as a dip for crudité (page 303).

GREEN GODDESS DRESSING
This dressing is flavored with the fresh taste of herbs. It would be lovely as a sauce for poached fish and chicken or boiled shrimp.

Pulse 1 small **garlic** clove, pressed in a garlic press or mashed to paste with salt (page 33), ½ teaspoon **coarse salt**, and 2 rinsed and minced **anchovy fillets** (preferably salt-packed) in a food processor to combine. Add ¾ cup **sour cream**, ¼ cup each **buttermilk** and **mayonnaise**, 1 tablespoon **white-wine vinegar**, and a pinch of **cayenne pepper**; pulse a few more times to combine. Add ¼ cup finely chopped **fresh flat-leaf parsley**, 3 tablespoons finely minced **fresh chives**, 1½ teaspoons finely chopped **fresh tarragon**, and 2 tablespoons thinly sliced **scallion**, and process until fully incorporated and mixture is pale green. Makes 1¼ cups.

CUCUMBER RANCH DRESSING
The addition of cucumber to the traditional recipe results in a dressing with a decidedly lighter, fresher flavor.

Stir together 1 medium **cucumber**, peeled, halved lengthwise and seeded, then grated on the large holes of a box grater, 1 tablespoon finely chopped **shallot**, ¾ cup **sour cream**, ¼ cup each **buttermilk** and **mayonnaise**, 3½ tablespoons **fresh lemon juice** (about 1 lemon), 1¼ teaspoons **coarse salt** (or to taste), 3 tablespoons each finely chopped **fresh flat-leaf parsley** and **fresh chives**, and a pinch of **cayenne pepper** in a medium bowl. Season with more salt and cayenne, if desired. Makes 2¼ cups.

BLUE CHEESE DRESSING
Buttermilk and low-fat yogurt replace some of the mayonnaise and the usual sour cream for a lighter, more refreshing dressing. This is a favorite for spooning over chilled wedges of iceberg lettuce, and it also goes well with hearty Belgian endive spears. The dressing can be made with any crumbly blue cheese, ranging from mild Danish blue to the more pungent Roquefort, Stilton, or Gorgonzola.

Whisk together 1 cup **buttermilk**, ¼ cup each **mayonnaise** and **plain low-fat yogurt**, 1 tablespoon **fresh lemon juice**, and ½ teaspoon coarsely chopped **fresh thyme** in a bowl to combine, then stir in 4 ounces crumbled **blue cheese** and season with **coarse salt** and **freshly ground pepper**. Makes 1¾ cups.

BUTTERMILK HERB VINAIGRETTE
The addition of buttermilk to a basic vinaigrette imparts creaminess and reduces the amount of oil needed for thickening. This dressing has a lighter body than the others, perfect for tender lettuces.

Whisk together ¼ cup **buttermilk**, 2 tablespoons **white-wine vinegar**, ½ teaspoon **coarse salt**, and ¼ teaspoon **freshly ground pepper** in a bowl to combine, then slowly whisk in 2 tablespoons **extra-virgin olive oil**. Add ¼ cup chopped **fresh herbs**, such as chives, tarragon, or dill, and ½ teaspoon chopped **fresh herbs** such as thyme, oregano, or marjoram. Makes ½ cup.

5 Pasta

PASTA

WHY BOTHER MAKING FRESH pasta when you can buy it? Well, for several reasons: it is easier than you might think, it is faster than you can imagine, and it is actually quite fun. Tasting fresh pasta is a revelation; it's at once tender and delicate, flavorful and firm to the tooth. The ingredients for the dough are inexpensive, and probably already sitting in your cupboard and refrigerator. But perhaps the most compelling reason to make pasta from scratch

is the tactile pleasure of the process: mixing the simple ingredients, working the dough with your hands, and rolling it into long sheets and strips.

High-quality factory-made pasta has its own virtues: it's delicious, readily available, and makes the perfect vehicle for savory sauces. And though you may think you know everything about store-bought pasta, there are lessons that bear repeating, such as how to cook it to just the right texture and how to pair pasta shapes with sauces. These lessons have less to do with discovering something new than with rethinking a familiar favorite.

On the following pages you'll learn all you need to know about fresh pasta: how to mix the ingredients; how to roll, cut, and shape the dough; and how to cook and store it properly. And once you've made your own pappardelle or tagliatelle, you'll want a sauce to serve it with. The recipes for some classic sauces—fresh tomato, marinara, and Bolognese—are a great place to start. The chapter also includes instructions for making your own filled pastas, such as ravioli and tortellini stuffed with such delectable ingredients as ricotta cheese, butternut squash, and duck confit—consider them a "master class" in pasta making. Gnocchi (light little potato dumplings) and a traditional basil pesto are here, too, along with two well-loved baked pasta dishes: lasagne and macaroni and cheese.

FRESH PASTA

Pasta is essentially a simple paste, or dough, of flour and water. It's a highly adaptable dough—replace the water with egg yolks, for example, and the pasta is instantly more rich. Mix in pureed vegetables, such as spinach, for beautiful color and added flavor. Then roll it out for making all sorts of shapes. Just like a homemade pie or

loaf of bread, part of the charm of making fresh pasta lies in the whimsical irregularity of each piece, especially when you are just learning.

Making the very best pasta depends on using basic, but high-quality, ingredients. Eggs should be fresh, and the flour should preferably have been sitting on the shelf for less than six months. In Italy, fresh pasta is made with soft, white, low-protein flour known as double zero (or "oo"), which is milled from the local wheat of the Po Valley in the northern Emilia-Romagna region (incidentally, an area world-renowned for its pasta). Although it is traditional, using double zero is not imperative (the flour can be difficult to find outside of Italy). All-purpose flour is a perfectly acceptable substitute; like double zero, it's finely milled and low enough in protein that the dough won't produce too much gluten when kneaded. (Too much gluten would cause the dough to become very elastic and hard to roll out.)

MIXING AND ROLLING

Dough can be mixed by hand on a cutting board with a fork (page 366) or in a food processor (page 368), and the dough can then be rolled by hand or machine. Rolling pasta by hand is more challenging than using a machine: the dough must be rolled and stretched rapidly, before it dries out, and rare is the novice who produces a flawless sheet on the first try. But don't be intimidated. Simply rolling the dough with a rolling pin on a lightly floured surface can yield smooth, even sleek, dough. Hand-rolled dough often turns out a little thicker than machine-rolled dough, but it still works, especially in more rustic dishes. A hand-crank pasta machine or pasta-making attachment for a standing mixer is much quicker and easier, and it produces more consistent results than hand rolling. These machines will roll the dough into thinner sheets than can be attained by hand and are useful for creating stuffed pastas.

OTHER EQUIPMENT

A cutting board is a good surface on which to mix dough and a bench scraper is the best tool for scraping up the loose bits of dough as you knead, and to divide dough into uniform pieces for rolling. If you don't have a pasta attachment for your standing mixer, a classic Italian hand-cranked pasta machine is a good (and relatively modest) investment. Use a pastry brush for dusting excess flour off pasta and off your machine or pasta attachment (choose a brush that hasn't previously been used with oil or butter). A pastry cutter or pizza wheel works well for cutting out ravioli and other pasta shapes for filling.

DRIED PASTA

In Italy, fresh pasta is usually not an everyday meal, except perhaps in Emilia-Romagna. Most Italians actually take their daily portion of pasta as *pastasciutta*, or "dried" pasta—factory made of semolina flour from the hard durum wheat grown in the south, which gives the pasta its golden color. In the United States, many people think fresh pasta is superior to the dried variety, but factory-made pastas can be just as good and, in some cases, even better than fresh. Dried semolina pasta holds its shape well when cooked and is more versatile, pairing

amenably with a range of sauces than more delicate-tasting fresh pasta. Some sauces actually call for a specific pasta shape—a creamy Alfredo clings to the flat strands of fettucine, while looser "sauces" like braised broccoli rabe need to be cupped in orecchiette or other short shapes. The general rule of thumb is that, in both texture and flavor, light sauces go with delicate shapes and robust sauces with sturdy ones.

COOKING PASTA

Both fresh and dried pasta should be cooked in an ample amount of well-salted, boiling water. Fill the pot with at least six quarts water per pound of pasta and bring to a rolling boil. Add at least 1 tablespoon of salt for every pound of pasta. Don't add oil to the water, as this will hinder the absorption of sauce later on. As the pasta cooks, it needs a lot of room to move and, in the case of gnocchi and certain filled pastas, to float to the top of the pot.

Monitor the pasta closely while it cooks. It must remain on your proverbial front burner from the moment it hits the water to the moment it hits the sauce. For dried pastas, keeping the noodles moving is key—stir the water frequently, and test the pasta by fishing out pieces and tasting them. You'll know that the pasta is done when it is slightly chewy, or al dente—"firm to the tooth."

Before draining the pasta, reserve a cup or so of the cooking liquid to add to the sauce, if needed. The hot water will help thin a sauce that is too thick, and the starch in the liquid will add a little extra body.

DRYING AND STORING FRESH PASTA

Long, ribbonlike pasta shapes, such as fettuccine and tagliatelle, can be dried, then stored. The noodles must be completely free of moisture, or mold will develop. To dry properly, gather several strands as you cut the pasta and curl them into nests. These circular shapes will be less likely to break when they are stacked in containers. To be sure nests are moisture-free, let them dry on clean, flour-dusted kitchen towels for 24 hours. After drying them, store stacked nests in an airtight container for up to 2 weeks.

Filled pasta should be frozen in a single layer on baking sheets, then transferred to resealable freezer bags; first dust the pieces with semolina flour so that they do not stick to one another. Keep filled pasta up to a month in the freezer; no need to thaw before cooking.

PASTA-SAUCE PARTNERSHIPS

In general, linear shapes, such as spaghetti, fettuccine, and linguine, partner well with smooth tomato or creamy sauces that will coat the strands; the thicker the strand, the more robust the ragù or sauce it can stand up to (think pappardelle with Bolognese).

Short shapes—penne, farfalle, and fusilli—will give chunkier sauces something to hold on to.

Filled pastas call for lighter-bodied sauces with simple flavors, such as browned butter and herbs, that won't compete with or overwhelm the filling.

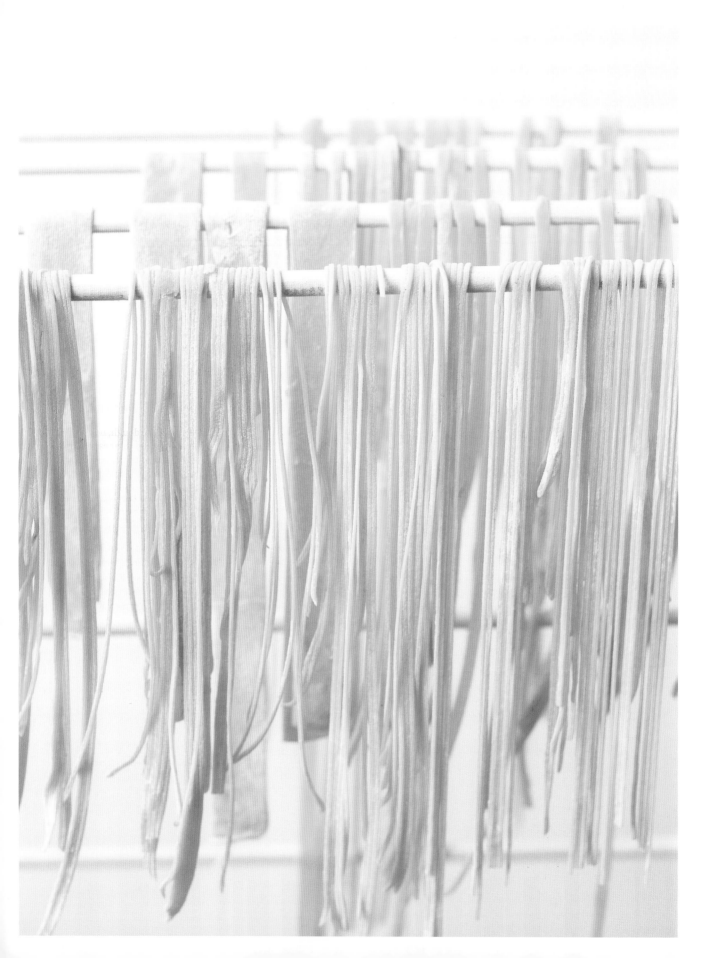

LESSON 5.1
How to Make Fresh Pasta

Pasta purists hold that there is no substitute for making, rolling, and cutting the dough entirely by hand, from start to finish. Anyone who has tasted the incomparable product of the legendary *sfoglinas* of Italy who turn out fresh pasta daily is apt to agree. But unless you have all day to set aside for making the dough, using a pasta roller is better than missing out on the experience entirely. Moreover, it produces sheets of dough that are the perfect thinness for forming pasta that will be just the right texture once cooked.

Pasta dough must be thoroughly worked to release and develop the flour's gluten, which gives the dough the elasticity needed to produce pasta with both bite and tenderness. It must also be given time to rest, to relax the gluten that you've just developed (otherwise it will be on the too-firm side). Never skimp on kneading and resting; these steps will make it much easier to roll out the dough into thin and thinner sheets without rips or tears. The kneading technique is the same as for bread dough: first knead just enough to gather the dough into a cohesive mass, then use the palm of your hand (curling your fingers) to push and pull on the dough, folding it over and then smoothing out the seam. Continue until the dough is smooth and elastic (it should contract when stretched slightly). This can take as long as ten minutes. But be careful not to overwork the dough, or it will become tough.

Rolling pasta is undeniably a challenge, but just remember that perfectly good pasta can come from less-than-perfect sheets. For your first few attempts, it might be worthwhile to mix an extra batch of dough.

FRESH PASTA DOUGH Makes about 12 ounces

Settings on pasta makers vary (some have as many as ten settings, others only six); this recipe was developed using a hand-cranked pasta machine, but you can use any machine as long as you change the settings incrementally.

- 2 CUPS ALL-PURPOSE FLOUR, *plus more for dusting*
- 3 LARGE EGGS, *room temperature*
-   PINCH OF COARSE SALT
-   SEMOLINA FLOUR, *for baking sheet*

Mix dough Mound the all-purpose flour in the center of a clean work surface or in a large wide bowl and form a well in the middle. In a small bowl, lightly beat the eggs and salt with a fork until smooth, then pour into the well [1]. Begin to work the flour into the eggs with the fork [2]. Then use your hands to work the rest of the flour into the mixture, a bit at a time, just to form a sticky dough (don't force all the flour to be incorporated; it's okay if some remains on the work surface).

Knead dough Start working the dough with your hands [3] to form a rounded mass for kneading. Knead dough about 10 minutes, or until smooth and elastic. Scrape any loose bits of dough from the work surface with a bench scraper.

Fresh Pasta Tips

> Before making pasta dough, clear ample counter space for kneading, laying, and cutting the dough.

> You will need room to dry the strands. If you don't have a wooden drying rack (a laundry or dish rack works just fine), get creative. You can lay the strands out on tabletops or drape them over chair backs; cover the chairs with clean dishcloths, and lightly dust the flat surfaces with semolina flour.

> Eggs and flour should be at room temperature to ensure that they combine well.

> When mixing the dough, hold back on adding all of the flour called for in the recipe until you are sure it will be needed, which can vary depending on the freshness of the egg, among other factors.

> Work with just one piece of dough at a time, rolling it out and then immediately cutting it into shapes before starting on the next piece.

> When resting or storing fresh pasta on baking sheets, first sprinkle them lightly and evenly with semolina flour, which is coarser than other types of flour and keeps the dough from sticking more effectively. Coarse-ground cornmeal is a good substitute.

Fresh Pasta, Step by Step

Rest dough Form dough into a ball [4]. Wrap tightly in plastic and let rest 1½ hours at room temperature.

Roll dough with machine Use a bench scraper [5] to cut dough into eight equal pieces (four for filled pasta shapes and lasagne). Working with one piece at a time (keep remaining pieces covered with a clean kitchen towel), flatten dough into an oblong shape somewhat narrower than the pasta machine's thickest setting (number 1). Very lightly dust with all-purpose flour and feed through machine [6]. Fold dough in thirds and rotate 90 degrees [7]. Pass through two more times on the same setting to smooth dough and increase its elasticity. Adjust the setting to the next level (number 2), and pass pasta dough through two times [8], gently supporting it with the palm of your hand as it emerges. Continue to pass through ever-finer settings, once on each setting. End with next-to-thinnest setting for pastas and lasagne; thinnest setting for ravioli [9] (lasagne should be slightly thicker; filled pastas, thinner, almost transparent). If dough bubbles or tears, simply pass through one or two more times to patch the dough (dust lightly with more all-purpose flour if dough is sticking). As each sheet of dough has been rolled to the desired thickness, immediately cut into desired shapes or strands, according to the instructions that follow.

Alternatively, roll pasta by hand Divide dough into pieces, as above. Lightly dust a clean work surface with all-purpose flour. With a rolling pin, vigorously roll out dough to a very thin circle, applying even pressure and working from the center out, without actually rolling over edges (which would cause them to stick to the work surface, and inhibit stretching). Do not bear down too hard or dough will tear. Roll constantly for several minutes, until dough is as thin as possible (it should be almost translucent). If it starts to shrink back as you roll, cover with a clean kitchen towel, and let rest 10 minutes before resuming. To cut strands by hand, working with one sheet at a time, lightly fold dough into thirds, and use a pastry wheel or a sharp knife to cut desired thickness.

FRESH TAGLIATELLE, SPAGHETTI, OR OTHER LONG-STRANDED PASTA
Drape dough over a drying rack until only slightly tacky, 10 to 15 minutes. Run dough sheet through the pasta machine (fitted with the appropriate attachment) to cut into strands, including tagliatelle or spaghetti. (If making pappardelle, cut by hand into 1-inch-thick strands *fig. 5.1*; there is no setting on machines for this shape.) Then immediately drape strands over rack until they are almost dry and do not stick together, about 20 minutes. If not cooking immediately, keep strands flat on a baking sheet lightly dusted with semolina flour (or cornmeal); cover tightly with plastic wrap and refrigerate overnight. To dry and store longer (up to 2 weeks), follow instructions on page 363.

fig. 5.1 FORMING PAPPARDELLE

SPINACH PASTA DOUGH Makes about 12 ounces

This colorful dough should be made in a food processor, which ensures that the vegetable puree is distributed evenly throughout.

6 OUNCES FRESH SPINACH, *washed well and trimmed*
1 LARGE WHOLE EGG PLUS 1 LARGE EGG YOLK
1¼ CUPS PLUS 2 TABLESPOONS ALL-PURPOSE FLOUR, *plus more for dusting*
½ TEASPOON COARSE SALT

Steam spinach Fill a medium saucepan with 2 inches of water and fit with a steamer basket. Bring water to a simmer, then place spinach in basket and cover. Steam until leaves are bright green and softened, about 2 minutes. Let cool slightly, then thoroughly squeeze out liquid in a clean kitchen towel or paper towels. Chop spinach coarsely; you should have about ⅓ cup.

Mix dough Combine spinach with egg and yolk in a food processor [1], and process until well combined. Add 1¼ cups flour and the salt [2] and process until dough just comes together, about 20 seconds [3].

Knead and rest Turn out dough onto a well-floured work surface. Knead until smooth and elastic, about 10 minutes, adding up to 2 tablespoons more flour if dough is too sticky. Form dough into a ball, wrap tightly in plastic, and let rest 1 to 2 hours or refrigerate overnight.

Roll out and cut Follow directions on pages 369–371 for rolling and cutting into desired shapes.

Making Spinach Pasta Dough

LESSON 5.2
How to Make Filled Pasta Shapes

There is little chance of mistaking homemade filled pasta for mass-produced; each piece has its own shape, degree of plumpness, and personality. Once you've mastered the dough-making process, the rest is actually very easy to accomplish. The fillings can be simple or extravagant, depending on your whimsy.

For each of the filled pasta shapes that follow, you will need to follow the directions on page 365 or 368 to make fresh pasta dough, then cut into pieces and roll as directed on page 367. Roll out only one sheet of dough at a time, and then fill and cut that sheet immediately before rolling out the next piece of dough. After the pasta has been rolled through the thinnest setting on a pasta machine, the sheet should be four to five inches wide, 28 to 29 inches long, and almost transparent. The yield will be slightly less for dough that is rolled out by hand.

After filling and shaping the dough, press out any air from inside the shapes and then pinch the edges to seal securely; otherwise, any air trapped inside may cause the pasta shape to burst during cooking. Set the filled pasta shapes on a rimmed baking sheet that has been generously dusted with semolina flour (or cornmeal) while proceeding with the next sheet of dough. If not cooking immediately, cover tightly with plastic wrap and freeze until ready to use, up to 2 months.

TO FORM RAVIOLI

Place one dough sheet on a work surface lightly dusted with all-purpose flour, and cut in half crosswise. Cover half with plastic wrap. Drop teaspoons of filling on the other half in two rows [1], spacing them 1 inch apart and ½ inch from the edges. Moisten dough around filling with a wet pastry brush, then top with remaining half sheet, pressing gently around filling with the side of your hand [2] and gradually working your way to the edge to seal. Use a pastry wheel to first trim edges to make straight, then cut into 1¾-inch squares [3], keeping the

> ### **Forming Ravioli**

fig. 5.2 FORMING AGNOLOTTI WITH SPINACH DOUGH

filling in the center of each one. Sweep away excess flour with a dry pastry brush and set ravioli on a baking sheet generously dusted with semolina flour. Repeat with remaining dough and filling. Makes about 4 dozen ravioli.

AGNOLOTTI ("PRIESTS' CAPS")

Place one dough sheet on a lightly floured surface. Use a 2¾-inch round cookie cutter to punch out as many rounds as possible. Drop 1 teaspoon of filling on one half of each round *fig. 5.2*. Brush the edges lightly with water and fold into half-moon, then pinch edges to seal, eliminating any air inside. Place agnolotti on a rimmed baking sheet generously dusted with semolina flour. Repeat with remaining dough and filling. Makes about 3 dozen.

TORTELLINI

Place one dough sheet on a lightly floured work surface. Use a 2½-inch round cookie cutter to punch out as many rounds as possible. Drop ¼ teaspoon of filling in the center of each round. Brush the edges lightly with water and fold into a half-moon, then pinch edges to seal [1], eliminating any air inside. Wrap the two corners on the folded side around your finger; brush one corner with a little water [2], then pinch to seal [3]. Brush off any excess flour with a dry brush. Place tortellini on a rimmed baking sheet generously dusted with semolina flour. Repeat with remaining dough and filling. Makes about 5 dozen.

Forming Tortellini

TORTELLINI

AGNOLOTTI

TORTELLONI

RAVIOLI

TORTELLONI

For these larger versions of tortellini, cut the dough into squares before folding into triangles (you can also cut into 4-inch rounds). Place one dough sheet on a lightly floured work surface and use a pastry wheel to cut sheet into 4-inch squares. Drop a heaping tablespoon of filling in center of each square, then brush edges lightly with water to moisten. Fold into a triangle and pinch edge to seal, eliminating any air inside. Bring the two corners on the folded side together *fig. 5.3*; brush one corner with a little water, then pinch to seal. Brush off excess flour with a dry brush and set tortelloni on a tray generously dusted with semolina flour. Repeat with remaining dough and filling. Makes about 2½ dozen.

fig. 5.3 FORMING TORTELLONI

RAVIOLI WITH BUTTERNUT SQUASH FILLING Serves 6

For a hint of sweetness and added texture, add a tablespoon of crushed amaretti to the filling, folding it in at the end. Toss these ravioli with melted or browned butter and a chiffonade of sage, and garnish with shaved Parmigiano-Reggiano. Follow the instructions here to make ravioli with other fillings (below); each variation makes enough for 4 dozen ravioli, and can be served with butter and cheese or Marinara Sauce (page 381). Any of these fillings can also be used for the other filled pasta shapes, including agnolotti (page 370); halve the recipes for tortellini (page 370) and make one and a half times the amount for tortelloni (page 371).

1 TABLESPOON EXTRA-VIRGIN OLIVE OIL

COARSE SALT AND FRESHLY GROUND PEPPER

½ SMALL BUTTERNUT SQUASH *(about ½ pound), halved lengthwise and seeds removed*

1 LARGE EGG YOLK

¼ CUP FINELY GRATED PARMIGIANO-REGGIANO CHEESE, *plus shavings for serving*

¼ CUP FRESH WHOLE-MILK RICOTTA CHEESE

   FRESH PASTA DOUGH *(page 365), cut into pieces and rolled as directed*

   ALL-PURPOSE AND SEMOLINA FLOURS, *for forming*

3 TABLESPOONS UNSALTED BUTTER, *room temperature, for serving*

1 TABLESPOON CHIFFONADE OF SAGE *(page 21), for serving*

Roast squash Heat oven to 400°F. Coat a rimmed baking sheet evenly with the oil. Season cut side of squash with salt and pepper; set squash cut side down on baking sheet. Roast until tender and cooked through, 30 to 40 minutes.

Mix filling Scoop flesh from squash. Measure out 1¼ cups (save remaining for another use). Place half the squash in a bowl. Combine the rest in a food processor with the egg yolk and Parmigiano-Reggiano and season with salt and pepper. Pulse until smooth, then add this mixture to the reserved squash along with the ricotta, and gently fold to combine. Cover and refrigerate until well chilled, about 30 minutes.

Fill and shape pasta Follow directions on page 365 to form ravioli. If not cooking the ravioli right away, freeze them on a baking sheet (covered with plastic wrap) until firm, then store in a resealable plastic bag and freeze up to 2 months. Frozen ravioli will take 4 to 5 minutes to cook; no need to thaw first.

Boil ravioli Bring a large pot of water to a boil, then add a generous amount of salt. Working in batches, boil ravioli until they float to the top, 3 to 4 minutes. Remove with a slotted spoon, shaking off excess water.

Serve Toss ravioli gently with butter. Divide among plates and serve immediately, topped with Parmesan shavings and sage.

RICOTTA FILLING

1¼ CUPS FRESH WHOLE-MILK RICOTTA CHEESE

½ CUP FINELY GRATED PARMIGIANO-REGGIANO CHEESE, *plus shavings for serving*

1 LARGE EGG YOLK

   COARSE SALT AND FRESHLY GROUND PEPPER

FOLD TOGETHER the cheeses and egg yolk and season with salt and pepper. Proceed with recipe above. Makes 1½ cups.

SPINACH AND CHEESE FILLING

   COARSE SALT AND FRESHLY GROUND PEPPER

8 OUNCES SPINACH OR OTHER LEAFY GREENS, *such as Swiss chard or dandelion greens, washed well and trimmed*

½ CUP FRESH WHOLE-MILK RICOTTA CHEESE

3 TABLESPOONS FINELY GRATED PECORINO ROMANO CHEESE

3 TABLESPOONS FINELY GRATED PARMIGIANO-REGGIANO CHEESE, *plus shavings for serving*

¾ TEASPOON MINCED FRESH THYME LEAVES

1 LARGE EGG YOLK

   PINCH OF FRESHLY GRATED NUTMEG

Ingredients

Whenever possible, buy fresh ricotta cheese instead of the mass-produced variety; it has an incomparable taste and texture. Look for fresh ricotta at cheese shops, Italian markets, and gourmet grocers.

PREPARE AN ICE-WATER bath. Bring a large pot of water to a boil, then salt generously and cook spinach until tender and bright green, 3 to 5 minutes. Drain well, then let cool and thoroughly squeeze out excess liquid in a clean kitchen towel or paper towels. Finely chop spinach; you should have about ¾ cup. Combine spinach, cheeses, and thyme in a bowl. Stir in egg yolk and nutmeg, and season with salt and pepper. Proceed with ravioli recipe on page 373. Makes 1½ cups.

DUCK CONFIT FILLING

Duck confit is just one example of how leftover meat can be used to make savory fillings. Short ribs, osso bucco, or lamb shanks are other good options. Just make sure to chop the meat finely enough to be wrapped neatly within tender pasta (without tearing the dough). You can alter the flavorings to suit your palate or the type of meat, but the egg yolks are always required for binding. This filling is especially good with the spinach pasta (page 368), as shown for the agnolotti on page 370.

- 1 TABLESPOON OLIVE OIL
- 2 LARGE SHALLOTS, *thinly sliced*
- 1 TEASPOON COARSELY CHOPPED FRESH THYME LEAVES
  COARSE SALT AND FRESHLY GROUND PEPPER
- 2 TABLESPOONS DRY SHERRY
- 2 DUCK CONFIT LEGS *(page 232), meat separated from bones and finely chopped (7 ounces)*
- 2 LARGE EGG YOLKS

HEAT THE OIL in a medium skillet over medium heat. Add shallots and thyme and season with salt and pepper. Reduce heat to medium-low and cook, stirring occasionally, until shallots are golden brown and softened (reduce heat if browning too quickly), 15 minutes. Deglaze the pan with sherry, stirring up browned bits from bottom of pan and cooking until completely evaporated. Fold duck into shallot mixture, then remove from heat and let cool completely. Mix in egg yolks to combine, then cover and refrigerate until ready to use, up to 4 hours. Proceed with ravioli recipe on page 373. Makes 1½ cups.

TORTELLINI EN BRODO Serves 8 to 10

Tortellini are traditionally served in broth; Basic Chicken Stock (page 41) or Basic Brown Stock (page 50) would be equally delicious.

- 4 OUNCES BONELESS PORK SHOULDER, *chilled*
- 2 OUNCES BONELESS SKINLESS CHICKEN BREAST
- 1 OUNCE PROSCIUTTO, *chilled*
- 1 OUNCE MORTADELLA, *chilled*
- 1 TABLESPOON UNSALTED BUTTER
- ¼ CUP FINELY GRATED PARMIGIANO-REGGIANO CHEESE
  PINCH OF FRESHLY GRATED NUTMEG
  COARSE SALT AND FRESHLY GROUND PEPPER
  FRESH PASTA DOUGH *(page 365), rolled as directed on page 370*

ALL-PURPOSE AND SEMOLINA FLOUR, *for forming*

3 QUARTS BASIC CHICKEN STOCK *(page 41) or Basic Brown Stock (page 50)*

Grind meats Grind the pork and chicken through the fine disk of a meat grinder into a bowl. Grind the prosciutto and mortadella into a separate bowl.

Cook filling Melt the butter in a medium skillet over medium-high heat. Add the pork and chicken and cook, breaking up the meat with the back of a wooden spoon, until beginning to brown, about 5 minutes. Add prosciutto and mortadella and cook, stirring occasionally, until pork and chicken are no longer pink, about 5 minutes. Cover and reduce heat to low, then cook 10 minutes longer to allow the flavors to meld. Let cool completely, then stir in Parmigiano-Reggiano and nutmeg and season with salt and pepper.

Fill and shape pasta Follow directions on page 370 to form tortellini.

Equipment

If you don't have a standing mixer with a meat grinder attachment, buy ground pork and chicken, and very finely chop the prosciutto and mortadella by hand.

Reduce stock Bring stock to a boil in a medium saucepan, and cook until reduced by half, about 15 minutes. Divide evenly among serving bowls.

Meanwhile, boil tortellini Bring a large pot of water to a boil, then add a generous amount of salt. Working in batches, boil until tortellini float to the top, 3 to 5 minutes. Remove with a slotted spoon, shaking off excess water.

Serve Transfer tortellini to bowls of hot stock. Garnish with pepper, and serve.

LESSON 5.3
How to Make Gnocchi

Potato gnocchi are one of the small triumphs of the Italian kitchen. These petite dumplings are made primarily from potatoes, with flour added to balance the moisture content and just enough egg to bind the mixture. Properly prepared gnocchi are light in the center, with a surface that is gently resistant and supple.

Making gnocchi is not difficult so long as you remember some simple rules. Start by using russet potatoes, which have the ideal starch content. A ricer will yield the finest texture, but you can also pass the potatoes through a food mill (never use a food processor to puree potatoes—they will turn into a gluey mess). This should be done while the potatoes are still hot, for the most volume. Then make sure the potatoes are as dry as possible and cooled to room temperature so they will not soak up too much flour and become tough. Add just the right amount of flour to the dough; too little and the dumplings will fall apart and dissolve in the water, too much and they'll be dense and rubbery. Under- or overworking the dough can cause similar problems. It will take some practice and patience to perfect your technique and gain a feeling for how much flour the dough needs, but even the trial runs will produce dumplings that are delicious (they can always be topped with grated cheese or coated in a rich cream sauce and then baked to mask any imperfections).

GNOCCHI WITH BASIL PESTO Serves 8 to 10

The hearty flavor of these dumplings lends itself to a range of preparations. Tossing with basil pesto is perhaps the most common, but gnocchi can also be served with brown butter and sage or doused in a hearty ragù, like Bolognese Sauce (page 383).

    2¼ POUNDS RUSSET POTATOES *(about 3 large)*
     1 LARGE EGG, *lightly beaten*
     2 CUPS ALL-PURPOSE FLOUR, *plus more for kneading and dusting*
       COARSE SALT
       BASIL PESTO *(page 379)*
       BASIL LEAVES, *for garnish*

Cook potatoes and pass through a ricer Cover whole (unpeeled) potatoes in a medium pot with 2 inches of water. Bring to a boil, then reduce to a simmer and cook until tender when pierced with the tip of a sharp knife, 35 to 40 minutes. Drain well, then peel: Holding each potato with a thick, dry kitchen towel (they will be too hot to hold directly), remove the skin with a

Gnocchi, Step by Step

GNOCCHI WITH BASIL PESTO

fig. 5.4 PEELING POTATOES

paring knife *fig. 5.4*. Immediately pass the potatoes through a ricer [1]. Spread out on a baking sheet and let cool completely.

Mix dough Turn out potatoes onto a work surface, then pour the egg over the potatoes and sprinkle with 1½ cups of flour and 1 tablespoon salt [2]. Start to work the mixture with your hands [3] and bring it together to form a dough; then gently knead 4 to 5 minutes, adding more flour (up to ½ cup total) as necessary to keep the dough from sticking, until dough is smooth and elastic [4]. (To check, pinch off a piece and roll into a rope; it should not break apart.) Pat dough into a rough rectangle, 2 to 3 inches thick.

Cut and shape Line a rimmed baking sheet with a dry clean kitchen towel (or parchment paper) and sprinkle liberally with flour. Use a bench scraper to divide dough into four to six pieces [5]. Begin gently rolling each piece under the palms of your hands into a rope [6], then continue rolling until it is ½ inch in diameter [7]. Use the bench scraper to cut ropes crosswise into 1-inch pieces [8]. Roll a cut side of each dumpling against the tines of a fork with your thumb [9] (each piece will have ridges on one side and an indentation on the other). Set gnocchi in a single layer on the prepared baking sheet. If not cooking immediately, cover with plastic wrap and refrigerate up to 2 hours.

Cook Bring a large pot of water to a boil, then add a generous amount of salt. Working in small batches, add gnocchi and cook until they float to the top, about 2 minutes. Remove gnocchi with a slotted spoon and gently shake off excess water before placing in a large pasta bowl. (If not serving immediately, plunge gnocchi into an ice-water bath to stop the cooking. Once completely cool, drain thoroughly, toss with a little extra-virgin olive oil, and refrigerate in a covered container for up to 3 hours. Reheat slowly on the stove, with the serving sauce or melted butter. Freezing gnocchi is not recommended.) Toss with pesto while boiling remaining gnocchi.

Serve Once the last batch has been boiled, drained, and tossed with pesto, divide gnocchi among bowls and serve at once, garnished with basil.

BASIL PESTO Makes about 1 cup

Pesto is one of those once-exotic foodstuffs that has become ubiquitous on the American table. It hails from the Italian city of Genoa, in Liguria. Don't limit yourself to pairing it with pasta—it's sensational on sandwiches, pizza, and even as a topping for vegetables such as tomatoes and corn. A mortar and pestle (preferably large) is the best tool to use for crushing the basil, since it produces a sweeter-tasting sauce (a food processor also works, as long as you don't over-mix). It's the traditional equipment, after all, that gives the sauce its name. In this recipe the garlic is blanched first to mellow its flavor; if you prefer the pungent taste of raw garlic, omit this step and use only one or two cloves. For variety, add a little fresh parsley, spinach, or arugula, or substitute pine nuts with walnuts or

> ### Pesto, Step by Step

almonds (chopped after toasting). Store pesto in an airtight container, covered with ¼ inch of olive oil (to preserve color) in the refrigerator.

Toasting pine nuts enhances their flavor. Spread nuts evenly on a baking sheet and toast in a 350°F oven, stirring occasionally, until lightly golden, about 10 minutes. Transfer to a plate to cool.

3 GARLIC CLOVES, *peeled*

2 CUPS LOOSELY PACKED FRESH BASIL LEAVES

3 TABLESPOONS PINE NUTS, *toasted*

½ TEASPOON COARSE SALT

⅓ CUP GRATED PARMIGIANO-REGGIANO CHEESE *(grated on medium holes of a box grater)*

½ CUP BEST-QUALITY EXTRA-VIRGIN OLIVE OIL

Blanch garlic Cover garlic in a small saucepan with water by 1 inch. Bring to a boil over high heat, then immediately drain and let garlic cool to room temperature.

Make pesto With a large mortar and pestle, pound together basil, garlic, pine nuts, and salt [1] until the basil is pulverized and the pine nuts and garlic are pasty, about 10 minutes. Add the cheese and pound to incorporate [2]. Mixing vigorously, pour in the oil in a slow steady stream [3], and mix until combined (it will not be emulsified). Serve immediately or cover with a layer of oil and store in an airtight container in the refrigerator up to 3 days.

LESSON 5.4
How to Make Tomato Sauce

Perhaps more than any other pasta sauce, tomato sauce is versatile and adaptable. In its most basic form, it is just flavorful enough to complement, but not overpower, the taste of the pasta. Tomato sauce can be embellished to take on other flavors, and can be pureed to be perfectly smooth (usually with a food mill) or left chunky. Whether cooked or uncooked, the sauce is an excellent way to use a bumper crop of fresh tomatoes at their peak, but other times of the year it might be better to use good-quality canned tomatoes for cooked sauces. When making the fresh (uncooked) sauce (called *salsa crudo* in Italy) that follows, there's no need to first peel and seed the tomatoes, but cooked sauces usually call for them to be blanched and peeled, as the skins can toughen during cooking; you can strain out the seeds before serving, if you like, though this is a matter of preference.

Fresh tomato sauce is usually reserved for tossing with pasta, while cooked tomato sauce can also be used on pizza or in soups and stews.

FRESH TOMATO SAUCE Makes about 5 cups
(enough for 1 pound of pasta)

With its light taste and texture, this sauce is best paired with slender strands, such as cappellini, spaghetti, or linguine; to serve, toss sauce with freshly boiled and drained pasta, adding a generous handful of fresh basil leaves, torn into pieces. And keep in mind that although the sauce is extremely easy, it does need an hour or two to allow the flavors to meld, so plan accordingly.

- 8 MEDIUM TOMATOES *(about 2 pounds total), coarsely chopped*
- 4 GARLIC CLOVES, *crushed and peeled (page 33)*
- 2 TEASPOONS COARSELY CHOPPED FRESH OREGANO LEAVES *(from 4 sprigs)*
- ½ CUP LOOSELY PACKED FRESH FLAT-LEAF PARSLEY, *coarsely chopped (¼ cup)*
  COARSE SALT AND FRESHLY GROUND PEPPER
- ⅔ CUP BEST-QUALITY EXTRA-VIRGIN OLIVE OIL

Toss together tomatoes, garlic, oregano, and parsley; season with salt and pepper. Pour in olive oil, then toss to combine *fig. 5.5*. Cover and let stand at room temperature for 1 to 2 hours to allow flavors to blend.

fig. 5.5 TOSSING FRESH TOMATO SAUCE
INGREDIENTS

MARINARA SAUCE Makes about 4 cups (enough for 1 to 2 pounds of pasta)

Marinara is the most basic tomato sauce for pasta and pizza, consisting only of tomatoes, olive oil, garlic, and minimal seasonings. With so few ingredients, the quality of the tomatoes and olive oil is critical. The recipe below calls for fresh tomatoes. A combination of very ripe plum and beefsteak is best; plum tomatoes are fleshier with fewer seeds, while beefsteaks have a balanced, delicious flavor. If fresh tomatoes are not in season, by all means substitute canned whole tomatoes, preferably the imported variety from Italy (or other high-quality tomatoes).

It is imperative that the garlic doesn't color at all in the beginning, as this will give the sauce an unpleasant bitterness. That's why the garlic and the oil are heated together briefly over moderate heat. Then the tomatoes are quickly added (after only 30 to 45 seconds), which will help keep the garlic from browning.

This sauce is used in the lasagne on page 386, but it's also perfect over ricotta-filled ravioli (page 369) or tossed with spaghetti and sprinkled with freshly grated Parmigiano-Reggiano or Romano cheese.

- 3 ½ POUNDS FRESH TOMATOES *(or substitute two 28-ounce cans whole, peeled tomatoes)*
- 2 TABLESPOONS BEST-QUALITY EXTRA-VIRGIN OLIVE OIL
- 1 TO 2 LARGE CLOVES GARLIC, *finely chopped*
  PINCH OF RED PEPPER FLAKES *(optional)*
  COARSE SALT AND FRESHLY GROUND BLACK PEPPER

Blanch and peel tomatoes First, slice an X into the bottom of each tomato with a paring knife. Lower tomatoes into a pot of boiling water [1] and blanch for about 10 seconds. Use a slotted spoon or a spider to remove the tomatoes from the pot. Immediately plunge into an ice-water bath [2] until cool enough to handle, about 30 seconds. Then pull off each peel, gripping the skin between your thumb and the flat part of a knife blade, starting at the X [3].

Cook sauce Heat oil, garlic, and red pepper flakes (if using) together in a medium pot over medium heat until fragrant and sizzling, but not brown [4]. Add tomatoes [5] and season with 1½ teaspoons salt and ¼ teaspoon black pepper. Bring to a boil over high heat, then reduce to a rapid simmer and cook until tomatoes are falling apart and juices are reduced slightly, about 15 minutes.

Puree Working in batches, pass through a food mill fitted with the fine disk into a bowl [6] (or puree in a food processor, straining out seeds if desired). If not serving immediately, let cool completely and store in an airtight container in the refrigerator up to 3 days, or the freezer for 3 months.

Marinara Sauce, Step by Step

LESSON 5.5
How to Make Ragù

Ragù—hearty meat sauce—is another staple of Italian cooking, offering a richer, more complex alternative to tomato sauces for tossing with pasta. Think of it as a stew that has been cooked to a thicker consistency, since the process for making the sauce is largely the same: Start by cooking the aromatics (called *soffritto*) until soft and sweet, then brown the meat. Next deglaze the pot with wine to stir up the flavorful bits, and finally add the tomatoes and seasonings and stock (or water) and simmer slowly until the sauce is deeply flavorful.

The most famous example is *ragù alla Bolognese*, made with veal and pork. Duck, rabbit, and veal ragù are also common.

BOLOGNESE SAUCE Makes about 8 cups

Bologna, the capital of the northern region of Emilia-Romagna, is considered by many to be the food capital of Italy. Besides being the birthplace of Parmigiano-Reggiano cheese, balsamic vinegar, and Prosciutto di Parma, Emilia-Romagna differs from the rest of the country in the richness and complexity of its cuisine; Bolognese Sauce, with its delicate aroma and balanced flavors, is no exception. The sauce is hearty but also profoundly elegant, and is especially delicious when tossed with fresh pappardelle (see page 367 for how to roll and cut fresh pasta dough into these flat, long, wide strands). You'll need about 3 cups for 12 ounces of pappardelle. The sauce can also be baked into lasagne (using spinach noodles as the Bolognese do; page 386) or served over gnocchi (page 376).

For the meat sauce to have its characteristic richness and complexity, it must be cooked slowly over low temperature (what many cooks call "slow and low"). You simply cannot rush it, but know that your patience will be rewarded.

For soffritto

- 2 TABLESPOONS UNSALTED BUTTER
- 2 TABLESPOONS EXTRA-VIRGIN OLIVE OIL
- 3 OUNCES PANCETTA, *cut into ¼-inch pieces (⅔ cup)*
- ⅔ CUP MINCED YELLOW ONION *(½ medium)*
- ⅔ CUP MINCED CARROT *(1 medium)*
- ⅔ CUP MINCED CELERY *(1 stalk)*

For sauce

- 1 POUND GROUND VEAL
- 1 POUND GROUND PORK
- 3 TABLESPOONS PLUS 1 TEASPOON TOMATO PASTE
- 1 CUP DRY WHITE WINE
- 1¼ CUPS WHOLE MILK
- 6 TO 7 CUPS BASIC CHICKEN STOCK *(page 41)*
- 1 CAN (28 OUNCES) WHOLE PEELED TOMATOES, *pureed (with juice) in a blender (or through a food mill)*
- 1 DRIED BAY LEAF
- 5 SPRIGS THYME, *tied into a bundle with kitchen twine*
- COARSE SALT AND FRESHLY GROUND PEPPER

Ingredients

A mixture of veal and pork is traditional, but you can substitute one or both meats with ground beef.

Buy the best-quality canned tomatoes you can find; look for those that are imported from Italy.

BOLOGNESE SAUCE WITH
FRESH PAPPARDELLE

Cook soffritto Heat butter and oil in large pot over medium-high heat until butter starts to sizzle, then reduce heat to medium. Add pancetta, and cook until golden and fat has rendered, about 2½ minutes. Add onion, carrot, and celery and cook, stirring often, until just beginning to brown around edges [1], about 10 minutes (adjust heat if mixture is browning too quickly).

Brown meat Add veal and pork and cook over medium heat, stirring frequently and separating meat with the back of a wooden spoon, until no longer pink, 8 to 10 minutes. Once meat is completely browned, pour off any excess fat. Add tomato paste and cook 1 minute, stirring to intensify sweetness [2].

Deglaze pot and add liquids Pour in wine [3] and cook, stirring to scrape up browned bits from bottom of pot, until liquid has evaporated, 6 to 7 minutes. Add 1 cup milk [4] and cook until reduced by half, about 3 minutes (don't worry if it appears slightly curdled, it will smooth out again). Add thyme bundle, then pour in 6 cups stock [5]. Add tomatoes and bay leaf, and season with 1½ teaspoons salt and ¼ teaspoon pepper.

Simmer the sauce Bring to a boil, then reduce heat to a very low simmer and cook, partially covered, 3 to 3½ hours, skimming the fat from the surface with a ladle periodically. If at any time the sauce appears too dry, add up to 1 cup more stock as necessary. The finished sauce should have the consistency of a loose chili [6]. Stir in remaining ¼ cup milk and season with salt and pepper, as desired. If not serving immediately, let cool completely before transferring to airtight containers. Refrigerate up to 3 days or freeze up to 3 months; defrost in the refrigerator before using.

> ## Bolognese Sauce, Step by Step

LESSON 5.6
How to Make Baked Pasta Dishes

Baked pastas are among the ultimate in comfort food, providing substance and nostalgia in every scrumptious, molten bite. While they might remind you of something a grandmother makes, baked pastas actually involve some technique—and a grandmotherly approach to making everything from scratch. This means that you must make the essential sauces, especially béchamel for macaroni and cheese. Béchamel is what transforms dried elbow pasta and relatively ordinary cheese into the familiarly decadent dish (it is also commonly used as a binder for lasagne). Despite its daunting French name, béchamel (another of the "mother sauces") is one of the easiest sauces to master.

One of the best qualities of baked pasta is its ability to turn leftovers into a memorable meal. If you have leftover spaghetti and tomato sauce from one night, simply spread it in a baking dish, sprinkle with grated cheese and some fresh herbs (and fresh bread crumbs), and bake until golden and heated through. Practically any pasta and sauce combination, whether freshly cooked or pulled from the refrigerator, can be handled this way, including gnocchi and filled shapes. Just be sure there's enough sauce to keep the pasta from drying out in the oven; you can always add a bit of flavorful stock to the dish to make up the difference.

LASAGNE Serves 8

In Italy, lasagne is usually made with fresh pasta, either made at home or bought at the local shop (practically every town has one). The quality of the pasta is in fact the key to the dish, since the ratio of noodles to sauce should be fairly equal. The other components should also be of top quality, as they will contribute to the overall dish; buy fresh ricotta and mozzarella if possible—both will lend wonderful flavor and creaminess.

This vegetarian lasagne evokes the Italian flag, with its layers of red (marinara sauce), white (cheese), and green (fresh spinach pasta). If you would like to incorporate some meat, brown a pound of sweet Italian sausage (casings removed), crumbling with a spoon as it cooks, then halve the sausage and sprinkle evenly among the cheese in two layers.

The pasta dough should be made as close to assembling the lasagne as possible, so plan accordingly. There is no need to pre-boil these noodles. Once rolled out to the thinnest setting on your pasta machine, stack the noodles (they should measure 5 inches wide and 26 inches long) on a baking sheet with plenty of semolina in between to keep them from sticking together. The lasagne can be assembled on one day and then baked on the next; cover tightly with plastic wrap and refrigerate until ready to bake.

FRESH SPINACH PASTA DOUGH *(page 368), cut into 4 equal pieces and rolled as directed on page 367*

1 POUND FRESH WHOLE-MILK RICOTTA CHEESE

1 LARGE EGG

1/8 TEASPOON FRESHLY GRATED NUTMEG

COARSE SALT AND FRESHLY GROUND PEPPER

1 POUND FRESH MOZZARELLA CHEESE, *chilled*

MARINARA SAUCE *(page 381)*

5 OUNCES PARMIGIANO-REGGIANO CHEESE, *grated on the medium holes of a box grater (about 1¾ cups)*

Cut pasta Heat oven to 375°F. Trim each rolled pasta sheet to make two 5-by-13-inch rectangles (you should have 8 sheets).

Prepare fillings Stir together ricotta, egg, and nutmeg until well blended; season with ¾ teaspoon salt and ¼ teaspoon pepper. Cut the mozzarella in half, and set half aside. Grate the other half on the large holes of a box grater (you should have about 2 cups; it will be much easier to grate if it's well chilled), then fold into the ricotta mixture.

Make layers Spread 1 cup sauce in the bottom of a 9-by-13-inch baking dish. Make a layer of lasagna sheets in pan, very slightly overlapping them to completely cover the sauce. Use a small offset spatula to spread one-third of the ricotta mixture evenly over the pasta [1], then sprinkle with one-third of the

Parmigiano-Reggiano. Add another layer of pasta, 1 cup of sauce, and another layer of pasta. Spread another one-third of the ricotta mixture over the pasta, then sprinkle with another one-third of the Parmigiano-Reggiano [2]. Add the final layer of pasta, the remaining ricotta mixture and Parmigiano-Reggiano, and the remaining 2 cups of sauce. Tear reserved mozzarella half into shreds with your fingers, placing it evenly over the sauce [3].

Bake and serve Place pan on a parchment-lined rimmed baking sheet, and bake lasagne until cheese is golden brown and sauce is bubbling, 50 to 55 minutes. Let rest for 10 minutes before cutting into squares and serving.

Assembling Lasagne

MACARONI AND CHEESE Serves 8

You might imagine that this dish was a modern creation, but its history dates back to the 1700s, when dried macaroni—one of the few staples that could survive a year aboard ship—was brought from Italy to Britain and to the American colonies. Because there was a lack of other (Italian) ingredients, the imported pasta would often be served with a simple white sauce—milk thickened with flour and butter; sometimes it was baked in a casserole with bread crumbs on top. The earliest recorded recipe was in the *Boston Cooking School Cookbook* in 1896.

This recipe uses a classic variation of béchamel known as sauce Mornay, made by whisking the flour into sautéed onions to form the roux (which is what thickens the sauce; see page 62 for more); then milk is added and the sauce is left to simmer until thick and creamy. Grated cheese is the final touch. Béchamel—and any sauce where flour is used as a thickener—is typically cooked for about 30 minutes to give the starch molecules in the flour enough time to absorb as much liquid as possible (so the flour goes from being granular to smooth, or gelatinized). In this recipe, the sauce is simmered for a much shorter time, since it will continue to cook in the oven after being stirred into the dish. For variety, top some or all of the servings with thin slices of roasted tomato and fresh thyme.

For pasta
> COARSE SALT
> 8 OUNCES DRIED ELBOW MACARONI

For bread crumbs
> 6 SLICES WHITE SANDWICH BREAD, *crusts removed*
> 2 TABLESPOONS UNSALTED BUTTER, *melted*

For sauce and cheese topping
> 3 TABLESPOONS UNSALTED BUTTER, *plus more for baking dishes*
> ¼ CUP FINELY DICED YELLOW ONION
> ¼ CUP ALL-PURPOSE FLOUR
> 3 CUPS WHOLE MILK
> 2 OUNCES ITALIAN FONTINA CHEESE, *grated (½ cup)*
> 3 OUNCES GRUYÈRE CHEESE, *grated (1 cup)*, ⅓ *cup reserved for topping*
> 6 OUNCES EXTRA-SHARP WHITE CHEDDAR CHEESE, *grated (2 cups)*, ⅓ *cup reserved for topping*
> 2 OUNCES PARMIGIANO-REGGIANO CHEESE, *grated (1 cup)*, ½ *cup reserved for topping*
> COARSE SALT AND FRESHLY GROUND BLACK PEPPER
> ⅛ TEASPOON CAYENNE PEPPER
> ⅛ TEASPOON FRESHLY GRATED NUTMEG

For topping (optional)
> SLOW-ROASTED TOMATO SLICES *(page 390)*
> THYME SPRIGS

Heat oven and boil pasta Heat oven to 375°F. Bring a large pot of water to a boil, then add salt generously and cook pasta 2 to 3 minutes less than manufacturer's instructions (the outside should be cooked but the inside under-done). Transfer to a colander, rinse under cold running water, and drain well.

Ingredients

Using a variety of cheeses offers the best balance of flavors. If you want to substitute those suggested below with others, consider their flavors and melting qualities. Combine pungent cheeses, such as sharp Cheddar and Gruyère, with milder ones like fontina or Monterey Jack, then add Parmigiano-Reggiano or pecorino Romano for extra bite.

A good Italian brand of dried elbow macaroni will have the best consistency. Undercook your pasta so that it is the slightest bit crunchy in the center, then rinse it under cold water. This stops the cooking and washes off the extra starch, which, contrary to what you might think, is not useful in thickening the casserole; instead, as it bakes, that extra starch merely expands and lends a mealy texture to the sauce.

MACARONI AND CHEESE

SLOW-ROASTED TOMATO SLICES
Cut 6 small tomatoes into ¼-inch-thick rounds (about 24 total) and arrange in a single layer on rimmed baking sheets. Drizzle with 2 tablespoons extra-virgin olive oil and season with coarse salt and freshly ground pepper. Sprinkle with 1 teaspoon fresh thyme leaves. Roast at 400°F until softened and browned in spots, about 20 minutes. Let cool before storing.

Meanwhile, make bread crumbs Tear bread into large pieces and pulse a few times in a food processor to form very large crumbs. Transfer to a bowl, and add melted butter. Toss to evenly coat.

Prepare baking dishes Butter eight 6-ounce shallow baking dishes or a 1½-quart baking dish.

Make cheese sauce Melt butter in a 4-quart pot over medium heat, then sweat onion until translucent, stirring occasionally, about 5 minutes [1]. Whisk in flour and cook, stirring with a wooden spoon [2], until bubbling but not browning, about 45 seconds. Add milk [3] and whisk to combine [4]. Bring to a simmer, stirring with a wooden spoon (scrape across the bottom and around edge of pot to prevent scorching), until thickened [5], about 4 minutes. Add fontina, ⅔ cup grated Gruyère [6], 1⅔ cups grated Cheddar, and ½ cup Parmigiano-Reggiano, stirring until completely melted and sauce is smooth. Season with salt and pepper, add cayenne and nutmeg, and stir to combine.

Assemble and add cheese topping Add pasta to sauce and stir to thoroughly combine [7]. Pour into prepared baking dishes and sprinkle evenly with the reserved cheeses, followed by the bread crumbs. If using, top with roasted tomato slices and thyme [8].

Bake Place dishes on a parchment-lined baking sheet and bake until bubbling and cheese is golden brown, 25 to 30 minutes. Let cool 5 minutes before serving.

Macaroni and Cheese, Step by Step

6

Dried Beans & Grains

DRIED BEANS AND GRAINS

HUMBLE FOODSTUFFS LIKE DRIED BEANS and grains are such everyday staples, it would be easy to underestimate their culinary prowess. They can be simply prepared and seasoned—say, by simmering in a pot on the stove (or in the oven) with a few aromatics. But witness the transformation of an ordinary dried navy bean as it bakes in the oven for hours in a heady cassoulet, or a cup of plump Arborio rice as it is slowly simmered with stock to

become risotto. Both dishes (along with others in this chapter) borrow many of the techniques explored elsewhere in this book, including building flavor with an aromatic base (such as the rice pilafs on pages 414–415), or layering components in such a way as to improve the whole (in the Indian-Spiced Split Pea Soup on page 401). After you've practiced the techniques introduced in each recipe, try swapping one bean or type of grain for another, or experiment with other seasonings and companion ingredients. To that end you'll find glossaries of beans, grains, and rice, designed to guide you in exploring the wonderful (and broad) world of beans and grains in your own kitchen, as well as at-a-glance charts of cooking times for several varieties of rice and other grains. (You'll notice that there is no chart with cooking times for dried beans. Because the age of a dried bean is the most significant factor in the time it takes to cook, and the age can vary widely, such a chart would not be practical.)

BUYING AND STORING BEANS AND GRAINS

■ Purchase beans and grains from a store with a high turnover. You will know beans are old if they look shriveled. Regardless of type, the beans' freshness has the most direct impact on how your beans will cook and taste. Freshly dried beans (from a current crop, as opposed to those from previous harvests) have more moisture in the center and absorb heat more evenly and efficiently. Older beans require much longer cooking times and will not be as flavorful (and, sadly, no amount of extra cooking will help improve the taste). It's harder to discern the freshness of grains, although some products have helpful use-by dates on them.

■ When you get them home, transfer the beans or grains to widemouth jars (for easier scooping) with airtight lids. Always note the use-by date or date of purchase on the jar. To discourage pantry pests, place a few bay leaves or dried chile peppers in the container.

■ Buy only what you will need within a six-month period and replenish your supply often.

■ When transferring grains to a jar, tape the cooking instructions on the underside of the lid (ratio of water to grains, for example).

LESSON 6.1
How to Cook Dried Beans

Dried beans, which are the seeds of legumes, continue to play an important role in the cuisines of the world: consider Italian pasta e fagioli (pasta and beans), New Orleans–style red beans and rice, Mexican frijoles, and Boston baked beans. In addition to familiar favorites—kidney beans, pinto beans, chickpeas, and lentils—you're likely now to find lesser-known varieties such as flageolet and borlotti beans in supermarkets and specialty stores. Dried beans are always cooked at a simmer, whether on the stove or in the oven. Follow these guidelines when preparing to cook beans:

■ Before cooking, beans should be sorted through. Remove and discard any stones, then rinse beans with cold water.

■ After rinsing, soak dried beans to rehydrate them, which will speed up the cooking process (lentils, split peas, and black beans are the exceptions; they cook just fine without soaking first). Soaking will also soften the skins. It's okay if a few beans float to the top of the water (these floaters should be removed), but if a large number do, the beans are probably old and won't cook well.

Beans can be soaked by two methods:

■ **Long soaking:** Place beans in a large bowl or pot; beans can expand to twice their size, so choose a bowl big enough to accommodate them. Add water to cover generously (about three times as much water as beans), and refrigerate for at least 8 (and up to 24) hours. Drain and rinse before proceeding with your recipe.

■ **Quick soaking:** Place beans in a saucepan, cover with cold water, and bring to a strong boil. Turn off the heat and allow the beans to soak, covered, for 1 hour. Drain and rinse before proceeding with your recipe.

Follow these guidelines when cooking dried beans:

■ Cook beans in cold, fresh water. Don't use the water that the beans were soaked in, as it will contain the oligosaccharides—indigestible sugars that cause flatulence—that have leached from the beans. Water should come about 2 inches above the beans.

■ Many recipes instruct you to season beans with salt only after they have softened (since it is widely believed that adding salt too soon toughens the skins and requires a much longer cooking time), but salting the beans at the beginning actually imparts more flavor with no noticeable difference in either the texture of the bean or the cooking time.

■ To cook, bring to a boil first, then reduce to a gentle simmer. Cook beans until tender; this may take anywhere from 30 minutes to 3 hours, depending on age and type of the beans.

■ If you need to add more cooking liquid at any point, make sure it's very hot water, not cold, which would increase cooking time.

■ Test beans for doneness by pressing one between two fingers. It should mash easily. Also, taste one for texture; the bean should be creamy, not gritty. The degree of doneness—thus texture—you want for a bean will depend on the particular recipe. In salads, for example, beans should be left a little firmer than those for soups.

■ When beans are finished, turn off the heat and let them cool in their own liquid to keep them from drying out. This will also allow flavors from the liquid to further infuse the beans.

■ The flavor of pork pairs very well with beans. Bacon (or pancetta) or prosciutto can take the place of the traditional ham hocks (which are often used to flavor slow-cooked soups such as split pea); in a pinch, you can use smoked turkey. A mirepoix of onions, garlic, celery, and carrots adds rich flavor to the cooking liquid, as do herbs like thyme, rosemary, and bay leaves. Again, the seasonings depend on the type of bean. Sage pairs well with white beans (cannellini), cumin with chickpeas or lentils, and cilantro or Mexican oregano with black beans.

■ If you're short on time, canned beans can be used in almost any dish that calls for dried, but they will not hold up as well in long, slow cooking (such as in cassoulet) or have the same texture as beans cooked from scratch. Sturdier varieties, such as chickpeas, black beans, and black-eyed peas, are a better option from the can than more naturally tender beans, such as lentils. Always drain and rinse canned beans well before using, and adjust the amount of salt in your recipe, as canned beans can be very salty.

CRANBERRY

KIDNEY

FAVA

CANNELLINI

FLAGEOLET

PINTO

BORLOTTI

NAVY

BLACK

GIANT LIMA

GARBANZO

RED LENTILS

BROWN LENTILS

LE PUY LENTILS

GREEN SPLIT PEAS

YELLOW SPLIT PEAS

Varieties of Dried Beans

CRANBERRY

Nutty in flavor, cranberry beans can be used in recipes that call for red or white beans. Related to kidney beans, but beige and slightly mottled, these are alternately called October beans, Roman beans, and borlotti (in Italy).

KIDNEY

This deep reddish-brown bean (part of the red bean family) has a thick skin that helps it keep its shape once cooked; it's often found in hearty chilis and stews. It's also the bean of choice for New Orleans–style red beans and rice.

FAVA

Dense, with a rich, slightly bitter flavor, fava beans are a staple of many Mediterranean cuisines. The fresh variety holds its shape when cooked; dried favas are often integrated into spreads or purees. Fava beans are also called broad or horse beans.

CANNELLINI

Classically used in the Tuscan region of Italy, this white bean is also referred to as a white kidney. It's about the same size as its red cousin, but has a creamier consistency when cooked, and can be used in most recipes that call for white beans.

FLAGEOLET

This small white or pale-green bean's light, fresh taste hints of haricots verts—the long, thin French green bean. Flageolets are technically immature kidney beans. They are traditionally paired with spring lamb. Although flageolets can be used in any white bean recipe, they hold their shape very well, making them particularly good in salads.

PINTO

Subtly flavored, but useful for their close-grained texture, pintos are also part of the red bean family. They retain their shape well when cooked, but their skin is slightly thinner than kidneys, which is why they are often used to make (mashed and) refried beans.

BORLOTTI

The Italian variation of cranberry beans (see above). They are often cooked with pancetta or prosciutto ends to heighten flavor. Borlotti beans are used in Italian soups and pasta dishes.

BLACK

Widely popular in Latin American cuisine, in which they are called *frijoles negros*, these earthy legumes are often enhanced with onions and garlic. Also called turtle beans, they can be integrated into salads, soups, and side dishes, or mashed into dips.

GIANT LIMA

Alternately called butter beans and Ford-hook beans, these large legumes can be used in any white bean recipe. They work well in stews, soups, and side dishes. Don't use dried cooked limas in place of the fresh variety, as the texture and flavor differ greatly. Smaller lima beans, called baby limas or sieva beans, come from a different species than the larger ones.

GARBANZO

A classic of the Middle East and Mediterranean regions, these dense, round beans hold their firm shape very well, making them ideal in stews, soups, and salads. Alternately called chickpeas or ceci beans, they can also be integrated into spreads, such as hummus, mashed and made into falafel, or ground into a flour.

NAVY

Once a staple of the U.S. Navy, these delicately flavored white beans need long cooking time and are superb when baked or stewed. Alternately called Yankee beans, they are often used interchangeably in recipes that call for white beans.

LENTILS

Popular in Middle Eastern, Indian, and Mediterranean cuisines, lentils are one of the few dried beans that don't need to be presoaked before cooking. The larger brown variety (sometimes called green) is the most common. Le Puy lentils—tiny legumes from Auvergne, France—are prized for having a distinctive nutty taste and less starch than other types of lentils, so they cook quickly and remain firm after cooking. They are perfect for salads. Red and yellow lentils turn a golden color once cooked; they don't hold their shape and are commonly used in soups and purees.

SPLIT PEAS

Split peas are the product of steaming whole field peas to remove their skins, then splitting them so that they cook faster. The green variety has a bright flavor, reminiscent of fresh peas, while the yellow type tends to be milder. Both are excellent in soups and stews. Yellow split peas are used in India to make dal.

Dried Beans Recipes

PERFECT BEANS Makes 5 cups

This recipe is for borlotti beans flavored with pancetta and sage, but you can apply the technique to most of the beans on page 397, except for lentils and split peas, neither of which need to be presoaked. (See opposite for a basic lentil recipe, and page 401 for split pea soup.) The cooking time depends on the variety and age of bean, so check the consistency often as they cook. The sage and pancetta used below would also work well for white beans, but omit them if making other types of beans, or substitute with other fresh herbs or meats (such as ham hocks or slab bacon). To serve, finish the beans with extra-virgin olive oil, freshly squeezed lemon juice, coarse salt, and freshly ground pepper. Or simply leave them as is to use in a salad or as part of another recipe.

2 CUPS DRIED BORLOTTI BEANS (¾ pound), picked over and rinsed

8 TO 10 CUPS WATER

2- TO 3-OUNCE PIECE PANCETTA, optional

2 GARLIC CLOVES, crushed and peeled

1 SPRIG OF SAGE

2 TEASPOONS COARSE SALT

Soak Sort through beans, discarding any stones. Place beans in a bowl and add water to cover by 2 inches [1]. Cover with plastic wrap and refrigerate 8 hours or overnight. Drain beans, discarding soaking liquid. (Or quick soak the beans according to the method described on page 395.)

Simmer Place beans in a medium saucepan. Add fresh water to cover by 1 to 2 inches. Add pancetta, garlic, sage, and salt [2]. Bring to a boil, reduce to a simmer, and cook until all the beans are tender, but not split, 1 hour to 1 hour

Perfect Beans, Step by Step

15 minutes (start checking at 45 minutes by pressing beans between your fingers [3]; the beans should mash easily and be tender all the way through). If not using right away, let beans cool in cooking liquid to absorb more of the flavors and keep them from drying out. Store in an airtight container in the refrigerator up to 3 days.

WARM LENTILS WITH MUSHROOMS Serves 4 as a side dish, 2 as a main course

Beans are wonderful for making dishes that are hearty enough to serve as the main part of a meal or, in smaller portions, as an accompaniment to meat, fish, or chicken. Besides protein, they lend chewy texture that holds up well when tossed with vinaigrette. This dressing is made by deglazing the pan that was used to sauté the mushrooms and aromatics with vinegar, then whisking in oil. You may find that you have some left over; if you like, toss it with frisée or other salad greens, then serve the lentils over the greens. The lentils are also delicious with sausages, pan-seared tuna or roasted salmon, and duck confit.

For lentils and aromatics

- 1 CUP LE PUY LENTILS, *picked over and rinsed*
- 1 MEDIUM CARROT, *peeled and cut into small dice (¾ cup)*
- 1 DRIED BAY LEAF
- 3 SPRIGS THYME
- 2 DRIED PORCINI MUSHROOMS
- 2 TEASPOONS COARSE SALT
- 3 CUPS WATER

For mushrooms

- 3 TABLESPOONS EXTRA-VIRGIN OLIVE OIL
- 1 TABLESPOON UNSALTED BUTTER
- 5 OUNCES CREMINI MUSHROOMS *(2 cups), sliced*
  COARSE SALT AND FRESHLY GROUND PEPPER
- 1 MEDIUM SHALLOT, *minced*
- 1 GARLIC CLOVE, *minced*

For vinaigrette

- 2 TABLESPOONS RED-WINE VINEGAR
- 1 TEASPOON DIJON MUSTARD
  COARSE SALT AND FRESHLY GROUND PEPPER
- 3 TABLESPOONS EXTRA-VIRGIN OLIVE OIL
- 2 TABLESPOONS COARSELY CHOPPED FRESH FLAT-LEAF PARSLEY

Ingredients

Regular French green lentils can be used instead of Le Puy lentils, but they may take slightly longer to cook and will not hold up as well.

Cook lentils Combine lentils, carrot, bay leaf, thyme, porcini, salt, and the water in a saucepan *fig. 6.1* and bring to a boil over high heat. Reduce to a simmer and cook, partially covered, until the lentils are tender, about 35 minutes. Drain, discarding herbs, porcini, and liquid, and transfer to a bowl.

Sauté mushrooms Meanwhile, heat a large skillet over high heat until hot, then add 2 tablespoons oil and the butter and swirl until butter is melted. Working in batches if necessary, add cremini mushrooms and season lightly

fig. 6.1 COOKING LENTILS WITH AROMATICS

WARM LENTILS WITH
MUSHROOMS

fig. 6.2 SAUTÉING MUSHROOMS

with salt and pepper; sauté until mushrooms are golden brown and their juices have evaporated, about 5 minutes. Add shallot and garlic *fig. 6.2*; cook, stirring occasionally, until shallot is translucent, about 2 minutes. Add to lentils and stir gently to combine.

Make vinaigrette Deglaze pan: Pour the vinegar into skillet (remove from heat if vinegar spatters) and boil, scraping up any brown bits from the bottom of the pan with a wooden spoon, 10 seconds (do not allow liquid to reduce). Transfer mixture to a small bowl and whisk in mustard, 1 teaspoon salt, and ¼ teaspoon pepper. Whisking constantly, add oil in a slow, steady stream until emulsified.

Toss and serve Stir 3 tablespoons vinaigrette into lentils, then add parsley and toss to combine. Serve warm or at room temperature, drizzled with additional vinaigrette if desired.

INDIAN-SPICED SPLIT PEA SOUP Serves 6

The most well-known pea soups are made with green split peas and flavored with pork, but this lively vegetarian version features split peas and Indian seasonings. Though the end result tastes remarkably different from the classic, the method for making any split pea soup is virtually the same; you start by building a flavor base with sautéed aromatics, then add peas and water and cook until the peas fall apart. For split pea soup with ham, you would add a ham hock to the pot along with the peas, but for this version, spices are fried at the end and stirred into the soup to finish—a technique borrowed from many classic Indian dishes.

For aromatics

- 2 TABLESPOONS SUNFLOWER OR OTHER NEUTRAL-TASTING OIL
- 1 MEDIUM ONION *peeled and minced (1 cup)*
- 3 MEDIUM GARLIC CLOVES, *peeled and minced*
- 1½ -INCH PIECE FRESH GINGER, *peeled and minced (about 2 tablespoons)*
- 6 MEDIUM SCALLIONS, *white and pale-green parts only, trimmed and thinly sliced*
- 1 SMALL DRIED RED CHILE
- 2 TEASPOONS COARSE SALT, *plus more to taste*
- ¼ TEASPOON TURMERIC

For soup

- 1 POUND YELLOW SPLIT PEAS, *picked over and rinsed*
- 8 TO 10 CUPS WATER

For finishing

- 2 TABLESPOONS SUNFLOWER OR OTHER NEUTRAL-TASTING OIL
- ¾ TEASPOON CUMIN SEEDS
- 1 TEASPOON MUSTARD SEEDS
- 2 TABLESPOONS FRESH LIME JUICE *(about 1 to 2 limes), plus wedges for serving (optional)*
- 2 TABLESPOONS COARSELY CHOPPED CILANTRO

Indian-Spiced Split Pea Soup, Step by Step

INDIAN-SPICED SPLIT
PEA SOUP

fig. 6.3 TOASTING SPICES FOR FINISHING
THE SOUP

Cook aromatics Heat the oil in a saucepan over medium-high heat. Add the onion, garlic, ginger, scallions, chile, and salt. Cook, stirring frequently, until onions are translucent and ginger is fragrant, about 3 minutes. Add turmeric [1].

Make soup Add peas and 8 cups water [2]. Bring to a boil, then reduce to a simmer, and cook, partially covered, until peas are falling apart and very tender, 45 minutes to 1 hour 15 minutes. (Check after 30 minutes and add more water if necessary. Remove chile, if desired, and discard.)

Finish and serve Heat the oil in a skillet over medium heat. Add cumin and mustard seeds; cook until mustard seeds start to pop and cumin is fragrant *fig. 6.3*, about 30 seconds. Add spices to the soup, stir to combine [3], and cover pot. Let stand for 10 minutes to allow the flavors to meld. Stir in lime juice and cilantro; season to taste with salt. Serve immediately, with lime wedges, if desired. The soup can be refrigerated in an airtight container up to 3 days. Thin with water before serving, if necessary.

CASSOULET Serves 6 to 8

A specialty of the southwest of France, cassoulet—named for *cassole,* the oval earthenware dish in which it was made—is a rich, slow-cooked bean stew made with white beans, meats (most often pork and sausages), and duck or goose confit. The dish is time consuming—it can take an entire day from start to finish—but is manageable when you break it into three tasks, which can be spaced out over a few days. The first step is to prepare Duck Confit (see page 232). Next the beans (which have to be soaked overnight) are cooked on the stove. Then the confit and beans are layered in a pot, along with pork and sausage, and baked for about three hours.

For bouquet garni

- 4 SPRIGS FLAT-LEAF PARSLEY
- 3 SPRIGS THYME
- 1 SPRIG ROSEMARY
- 1 DRIED BAY LEAF
- 1 CELERY STALK, *halved crosswise*
- 1 LEEK, *dark-green part only, washed well*

For beans

- 1 TABLESPOON OLIVE OIL
- 2 OUNCES FATBACK OR UNCURED PORK BELLY, *cut into small dice*
- ½ POUND PORK SHOULDER, *cut into 1-inch pieces*
- 1 WHOLE CLOVE
- 1 MEDIUM ONION, *unpeeled*
- 1 SMOKED HAM HOCK (¾ *to 1 pound*)
- 1 MEDIUM CARROT, *peeled and halved crosswise*
- 3 WHOLE PEELED TOMATOES (*from a 14.5-ounce can*), *coarsely chopped, with juice*
- 2 CUPS DRIED NAVY BEANS (¾ POUND), *soaked for 12 hours (page 395)*

For cassoulet

- 1 GARLIC CLOVE, *peeled and halved*
- 2 DUCK CONFIT LEGS (*page 232*), *skin removed, separated at the joint*
- ½ POUND FRENCH GARLIC SAUSAGE, *cut into ½-inch-thick half-moons*
- 4 CUPS VERY COARSE FRESH BREAD CRUMBS, *preferably from a rustic loaf*
- 4 TABLESPOONS (½ STICK) UNSALTED BUTTER, *melted*

Make bouquet garni Tie the herbs, celery, and leek into a bundle with kitchen twine, wrapping the string around several times to secure the smaller herbs.

Render fat and brown pork In a large (8-quart) pot, heat olive oil over medium heat. Add fatback or pork belly and cook until fat has rendered and meat is light golden, about 4 minutes. Add the pork shoulder and cook [1], stirring occasionally, until browned, about 5 minutes. Pour off all but ¼ cup fat.

Cook beans Stick the clove in the onion and cut onion in half; add it to the pot along with the bouquet garni, ham hock, carrot, tomatoes and juice, and beans [2]. Cover with water by 2 inches (about 8 cups) [3]. Bring to a boil; reduce heat and cook at a gentle simmer until the beans are tender but not falling apart, about 40 minutes. Remove from heat. Use tongs to remove and discard the onion, carrot, and bouquet garni.

Ingredients

Fatback, which is unsmoked and unsalted, can be substituted with uncured pork belly (not to be confused with salt pork, which also comes from the belly but is very salty). Both can be found at butcher's shops, as can smoked ham hocks, which are also often found at supermarkets.

To save time, you can use store-bought duck confit instead of making your own. It is available through D'Artagnan (www.dartagnan.com) and other specialty food purveyors.

You can use Great Northern or Tarbais beans in place of navy beans, but canned beans are not an acceptable substitution.

Equipment

A large (8-quart) pot is needed to simmer the beans. The traditional pot for cassoulet is an oval earthenware, but any enameled cast-iron Dutch oven or other pot with a tight-fitting lid will do.

INGREDIENTS FOR CASSOULET

CASSOULET

Remove meat from ham hocks Heat oven to 300°F. Remove the ham hocks. When cool enough to handle, cut away and discard the skin. Dice the meat into small pieces and return to the pot.

Layer beans and meat in pot Rub the inside of a large (8-quart) Dutch oven or cast-iron pot with garlic halves. Using a spider or a slotted spoon, transfer half of the bean mixture to the pot [4], spreading in an even layer (reserve the cooking liquid). Arrange the duck and sausage over the beans, then cover with the remaining beans. Pour in cooking liquid [5] until it comes just below the top of the beans (about 3 cups) and reserve the rest of the liquid (there should be 1 to 2 cups remaining).

Bake cassoulet Bake, uncovered, 2 hours; check every half hour or so to make sure the mixture is bubbling (adjust heat if necessary) and that the liquid hasn't fallen more than ½ inch below the surface of the beans (add more reserved cooking liquid or water, if necessary). Remove from oven.

Cassoulet, Step by Step

Top with bread crumbs and finish baking Toss the bread crumbs with the butter. Sprinkle evenly over the mixture in the pot [6] and continue baking 1 to 1½ hours longer, or until the bread crumbs are crisp and golden.

Serve Let cassoulet stand 10 to 20 minutes to allow it to cool and ensure that the beans soak up more of the liquid. Serve individual portions on warmed dishes. Any leftovers can be cooled completely, then refrigerated, covered, for up to 2 days; reheat in a 300°F oven until warmed through.

LESSON 6.2
How to Cook Grains

Whether whole or ground, earthy or subtle, coarse or silky, grains are glorious. They are the basis of cereals, breads, and salads, and act as accompaniments to countless main dishes. In fact, for millennia grains have formed the foundation of most of the world's cuisines. And, as any nutritionist will tell you, whole grains are one of the building blocks of a healthy diet. Technically, grains are the edible seeds of grasses, among them wheat, rice, corn, oats, millet, rye, and barley. But certain seeds of nongrass plants, including amaranth, quinoa, and buckwheat, are also thought of as grains.

In this section, you'll find information and cooking times for some of the most well-known and accessible grains, as well as a few lesser-known examples. Because rice is widely recognized as the most common grain, and there are so many varieties, it appears in a glossary and cooking chart of its own, and you'll find recipes using rice to exemplify a few of the four basic cooking methods: absorption; boiling and draining; pilaf; and risotto. The section ends with a recipe for soft polenta, since it is also made from a grain (cornmeal), and there is definitely a lesson to be learned in getting it right.

For absorption, the most common method, the cooking liquid is completely absorbed by the grains, which can be cooked by this method on the stovetop or in the oven. The liquid is either brought to a boil first, then the grain slowly added and the liquid returned to a boil; or the two are combined at the outset, then brought to a boil. (See the chart on pages 413 for instructions for specific grains cooked by the absorption method.) Next, reduce heat, cover, and simmer for the estimated time, or until the grains are tender and have absorbed all the liquid. (Take care not to overcook; grains should never be soggy or mushy.) The final step—letting them steam off heat for ten minutes—ensures that all liquid is completely absorbed, producing the fluffiest results.

For the boiling method, the grains do not absorb all of the cooking liquid; the excess is drained off and the grains drained in a sieve. Afterward, grains can be returned to the hot pot, covered, and allowed to steam for about ten minutes (as in absorption method) to make them fluffier.

The pilaf method is similar to the absorption method, but the grains are toasted in oil or butter before the cooking liquid (usually stock or broth) is added. Many grains can be cooked into a pilaf, but rice is the most common. Toasting the grains helps to keep them from sticking to one another and to maintain their shape once cooked. (It also adds flavor; see below.) Beyond grains, pilafs often include other ingredients, such as onion, small pastas, or dried fruits. After the initial toasting, pilafs can be finished on the stovetop or in the oven.

Grains prepared by the risotto method are cooked slowly while flavorful stock is added gradually; the grains are stirred very frequently (and at times constantly) until the dish is rich and velvety. Italian risotto (page 416) is made with medium-grain rice, such as Arborio, Carnaroli, or Vialone Nano, which cooks to a firm yet creamy texture, but other types of rice can be used as well. Cheese and seasonings (saffron is added to make risotto Milanese, for example) are very common in risottos, but you will also often find vegetables or seafood; these are usually cooked separately before being stirred into the dish. Although the consistency will be slightly different (but the taste just as delicious), risottos can be prepared from other grains, such as barley or farro.

Depending on the grains you are cooking, you might want to rinse them first in order to remove any dirt or debris. Rinsing can also keep certain grains from becoming gummy once cooked. This is particularly helpful for very starchy Asian rice, such as basmati. Gumminess is less of a concern for rice that comes from the United States or Europe, as it is generally less starchy. Also, American rice that is labeled "enriched" has been coated with vitamins, which will wash away if rinsed.

Many grains, particularly millet, quinoa, and some varieties of rice, are toasted before cooking to impart a nutty flavor. To do so, place the grains in a single layer in a dry skillet and cook over moderate heat, stirring or tossing frequently, until lightly browned and fragrant.

> ## *Grains Recipes*

PERFECT WHITE RICE Serves 4

Cooking rice by the absorption method on the stove is easy, as long as you leave the lid on while cooking to trap as much steam as possible (check only toward the end of the recommended time) and avoid overcooking. Let the rice sit after cooking to absorb the water completely, and fluff rice with a fork just before serving. Although many recipes call for a ratio of 2 cups water to 1 cup rice, using less water (1½ cups) produces lighter, fluffier results.

FOR PERFECT WHITE RICE, bring 1½ cups water to a boil in a medium saucepan. Stir in 1 cup long-grain white rice and ½ teaspoon salt [1] and return to a boil over medium-high heat. Reduce heat to a simmer, cover, and cook until rice is tender and has absorbed all the liquid, 16 to 18 minutes (check only toward end of cooking time). The rice should be studded with craters, or steam holes, when it is ready [2]. Remove from heat and let steam, covered, for 10 minutes. Then fluff with a fork [3] and serve.

> ## Perfect White Rice, Step by Step

SUSHI

BHUTANESE RED

BROWN BASMATI

LONG-GRAIN BROWN

KALIJIRA

JASMINE

BASMATI

LONG-GRAIN WHITE

SHORT-GRAIN BROWN

SPANISH SHORT-GRAIN

ITALIAN SHORT-GRAIN

Varieties of Rice

In many parts of the world—particularly Asia—rice plays such a central role that most meals would be incomplete without it. This grain can carry the flavor of a sauce, tame the fire of spicy food, and lend satisfying substance to lighter dishes.

Most rice is classified as either white or brown; the color is determined by the way the grain is processed. White rice is stripped of its outer husk, as well as its bran and germ (the high-fiber coating and nucleus, respectively); it has a mild taste, which is ideal when you want other flavors to come through. Brown rice, with its bran and germ left intact, has more vitamins and fiber, a stronger flavor, and a chewier texture. It takes longer to cook, and is more perishable, so buy it in smaller quantities and keep it refrigerated.

All rice is classified by grain size. The shorter the grain, the more starchy it will be. Most long-grain rice is fluffy and firm, suited for side dishes, soups, or stuffings. Shorter grains work well with many Asian foods (they hold their shape in sushi, for instance) and have just the right amount of creaminess for puddings.

Of the more than seven thousand varieties of rice grown around the world, here are a few of the more versatile types. Refer to the chart that follows for general cooking guidelines (except for the Italian and Spanish rices, which are best cooked by the risotto method described on page 416).

BASMATI

The aroma and flavor—reminiscent of toasted nuts or popcorn—of this Indian long-grain rice (and its American relative, Texmati) make it delicious on its own. Rinse basmati in a sieve before cooking; the delicate grains will absorb some of the water, keeping them from breaking.

BHUTANESE RED

Also called Himalayan red rice, this ancient short-grained variety is cultivated in the mountainous regions of Central Asia. Earthy red in color, it generally cooks more quickly than brown rice and has a delicate, nutty flavor.

BROWN BASMATI

In India, brown rice has long been thought of as inferior to white, but its nuttiness and healthful properties make it hard to pass up. Brown basmati rice, cooked by the absorption method and fluffed with a fork, is especially good alongside chicken or fish.

ITALIAN SHORT-GRAIN

Starchy Arborio, Carnaroli, and Vialone Nano rice have short, fat grains that readily absorb flavors and take on a creamy texture when cooked properly for risotto.

JASMINE

This long-grain, bright white rice is one of several varieties known as aromatic. As the name implies, jasmine rice produces pleasant aromas when cooked. It resembles basmati, and is commonly served in Thai cuisine as an accompaniment to main dishes.

KALIJIRA

Grown in Bangladesh, this long-grain rice, available in both white and brown varieties, resembles basmati on a smaller scale. Due to its delicate flavor and texture, it is sometimes called the "Prince of Rice" and is traditionally paired with aromatic spices such as cinnamon, cloves, and cardamom.

LONG-GRAIN BROWN

A pleasantly chewy all-purpose brown rice, this type pairs nicely with stews, grilled meats, or hearty vegetable soups.

LONG-GRAIN WHITE

One of the most adaptable rices, and the most popular in America, the grains become dry and fluffy after cooking, so they separate easily.

SHORT-GRAIN BROWN

This somewhat sticky brown rice goes well with Asian food, since it can be picked up easily with chopsticks. To enhance its flavor, briefly toast the grains in a dry pan before cooking.

SPANISH SHORT-GRAIN

Calasparra (pictured) and Bomba have plump grains that readily absorb water (and flavor) and remain firm and separate after cooking. You may be familiar with these rices as key ingredients in Spanish paella.

SUSHI

This short-grain rice has a sticky texture. Like many other Asian varieties of rice, sushi rice is better when rinsed with water before cooking.

QUINOA

MILLET

POLENTA

OAT GROATS

GRITS

DUCKWHEAT

BULGUR

PEARL BARLEY

WILD RICE

WHEAT BERRIES

SPELT

KAMUT

FARRO

Varieties of Grains

BUCKWHEAT

Strong, and yeasty in flavor, buckwheat is most often ground into flour for making pancakes (including Russian blini) and other dishes. The kernels can also be found whole (hulled to remove outer coating) or crushed, and are called groats. When toasted in oil, the groats are called kasha (shown here); popular in Eastern European cooking, they have a sweeter, less bitter taste than untoasted groats. In Japan and Korea, buckwheat noodles, called soba, are a staple starch, appearing in broth-based soups and eaten on their own, with savory sauces for dipping.

BULGUR

Popular in the Middle East, bulgur is made by cooking whole wheat kernels, then drying and grinding them. The result is a quick-cooking grain that is slightly chewy. Bulgur comes in coarse and fine grinds, and is often incorporated into salads, such as tabbouleh.

FARRO

This ancient grain was first cultivated near Damascus and was widely consumed by the ancient Romans. Also known as emmer wheat, farro is a cousin of spelt. Farro is delicious when prepared risotto-style and also as a main component of salads and stuffings.

GRITS

Standard fare in the cuisine of the Southern United States, grits are made of coarsely ground dried corn or hominy, a type of corn treated with an alkali. They can be served as a hot cereal for breakfast or as a side dish, often flavored with butter or cheese. The term *grits* can also refer to any coarsely ground grain, such as oats, buckwheat, or rye.

KAMUT

Named for the ancient Egyptian word for wheat, this grain apparently originated in Egypt more than six thousand years ago. These days kamut is prized for its high-protein qualities and is often used as a substitute for wheat, particularly in pastas and baked goods.

MILLET

Prized in Africa, China, and India for its superior protein content, millet was a staple before wheat and rice became the principal grains. It has a mild flavor, and is served as an accompaniment to main dishes in much the same way as white rice.

OAT GROATS

These are essentially oats in their most basic form—simply hulled whole oats. They are available at health food stores, and can be used in savory dishes such as pilafs, or as a component in multi-grain breakfast cereals.

PEARL BARLEY

Whole, hulled barley is referred to as Scotch or pot barley; barley with the bran layer (and hence some nutrients) peeled off is called pearl barley and is what is most widely available. Barley has a mild, slightly sweet flavor that complements a wide range of dishes, and a hearty texture that adds heft to soups and stews.

POLENTA

A staple in Northern Italy, polenta is made from yellow or white cornmeal ground medium-fine and slowly simmered and stirred until creamy. Served soft, it is similar to porridge, but it can also be cooled in a shallow pan, cut into squares, and baked or fried until firm. Common flavorings include butter, olive oil, and cheese.

QUINOA

Of all grains (though it's technically the fruit of a tree plant), quinoa comes closest to having the most complete protein balance. It has long been a staple of Latin American cuisines, particularly in Peru and Chile, and has traditionally been grown in the Andes mountains. Quinoa comes in a large array of colors, from pink to orange to green to purple, but red and white are the most commonly available. You can use it in place of other grains in salads such as tabbouleh, or as a stuffing for peppers or tomatoes.

SPELT

This native of southern Europe has a subtle flavor, similar to that of hazelnut. Because it contains no gluten and is higher in protein, spelt is a good alternative to wheat flour in baking and other preparations.

WHEAT BERRIES

Tan to reddish-brown in color, this whole, unprocessed wheat kernel is nutrient-rich and high in protein and fiber. Presoaking for several hours, while not necessary, helps soften the outer bran layer and yields plumper grains. The nutty flavor and pleasantly chewy texture works well in pilafs and salads.

WILD RICE

Actually a long-grain marsh grass found in the Great Lakes region of the United States (and traditionally harvested solely by hand, making it more expensive), wild rice is prized for its nutty taste and firm, toothsome texture. Rinse well before cooking.

RICE COOKING CHART

Type of Rice	Rinse	Liquid and Salt Amount (for 1 cup rice)	Cooking Time (Absorption Method)	Standing Time	Yield
BASMATI (REGULAR OR BROWN)	Rinse until water runs clear.	1½ CUPS WATER AND ¼ TEASPOON SALT (1¾ CUPS WATER FOR BROWN)	Bring rice and water to a boil, simmer, covered, 15 minutes (30 minutes for brown).	10 minutes	3 CUPS
JASMINE	Rinse until water runs clear.	1½ CUPS WATER AND ¼ TEASPOON SALT	Bring rice and water to a boil, simmer, covered, 15 minutes.	10 minutes	3 CUPS
KALIJIRA	Rinse until water runs clear.	1½ CUPS WATER AND ¼ TEASPOON SALT	Bring rice and water to a boil, simmer, covered, 25 minutes.	10 minutes	2½ CUPS
LONG-GRAIN WHITE	Do not rinse.	1½ CUPS WATER AND ¼ TEASPOON SALT	Bring water to a boil first, add rice. Return to a boil, then simmer, covered, 16 to 18 minutes.	10 minutes	2½ CUPS
SHORT-GRAIN BROWN	Do not rinse.	2 CUPS WATER AND ¼ TEASPOON SALT	Bring rice and water to a boil, simmer, covered, 40 to 50 minutes.	10 minutes	2½ CUPS
LONG-GRAIN BROWN	Do not rinse.	1¾ CUPS WATER AND ¼ TEASPOON SALT	Bring rice and water to a boil, simmer, covered, 35 to 40 minutes.	10 minutes	2½ CUPS
SUSHI	Rinse until water runs clear, then drain and let dry 20 minutes.	1⅓ CUPS WATER AND ⅓ TEASPOON SALT	Bring rice and water to a boil, simmer, covered, 8 minutes.	10 minutes	2½ CUPS
WILD RICE	Rinse well.	2 CUPS WATER AND ¼ TEASPOON SALT	Bring water to a boil first; add wild rice, return to a boil, then simmer, covered, 45 to 50 minutes.	10 minutes	2½ CUPS

GRAIN COOKING CHART

Type of Grain	Liquid Amount (for 1 cup grain)	Method	Yield
PEARL BARLEY	2 CUPS	Absorption: Rinse thoroughly. Bring water and ½ teaspoon coarse salt to a boil; add grains and return to a boil, then reduce heat, cover, and simmer 35 minutes. Let stand 10 minutes.	3 CUPS
BUCKWHEAT GROATS (OR KASHA)	2 CUPS	Absorption: Bring grains, water, and ¼ teaspoon coarse salt to a boil, then reduce heat, cover, and simmer 12 to 15 minutes.	3 CUPS
BULGUR WHEAT	2 CUPS	Absorption: Bring water and ¼ teaspoon coarse salt to a boil, then pour over grains (do not cook); let stand, covered, 30 to 45 minutes.	2½ CUPS
FARRO	1½ CUPS	Absorption: Bring water, grains, and ¼ teaspoon coarse salt to a boil, then reduce heat, cover, and simmer 20 minutes. Drain excess water; return to pot and let stand 10 minutes.	1¾ CUPS
KAMUT	5 CUPS	Boiling: Rinse thoroughly. Bring grains, water, and ½ teaspoon coarse salt to a boil. Reduce heat and simmer, uncovered, 45 to 60 minutes. Drain.	2 CUPS
MILLET	1½ CUPS	Absorption: Toast in dry pan over medium heat 3 to 4 minutes. Bring water and ¼ teaspoon coarse salt to a boil, then add grains and simmer, covered, 15 minutes. Let stand (covered) 10 minutes more, then fluff with a fork.	2½ CUPS
OAT GROATS	5 CUPS	Boiling: Bring water, grains, and ¼ teaspoon coarse salt to a boil, then reduce heat, cover, and simmer 25 to 35 minutes. Drain off excess liquid.	1¾ CUPS
QUINOA	1½ CUPS	Absorption: Toast grains in dry pan over medium heat 1 to 2 minutes. Add water and ¼ teaspoon coarse salt and bring to a boil, then reduce heat, cover, and simmer 10 to 15 minutes.	2½ CUPS
SPELT	5 CUPS	Boiling: Bring water, grains, and ¼ teaspoon coarse salt to a boil, then reduce heat, cover, and simmer 35 to 45 minutes. Drain off excess liquid.	2 CUPS
WHEAT BERRIES	5 CUPS	Boiling: Bring water, grains, and ¼ teaspoon coarse salt to a boil, then reduce heat, cover, and simmer 30 to 40 minutes. Drain off excess liquid.	2¼ CUPS

BROWN-RICE PILAF WITH
CURRANTS

BASMATI RICE PILAF WITH
POMEGRANATES

RICE PILAF

RICE PILAF Serves 4

Pilafs originated in the Middle East, where they are usually made with rice. The rice is toasted in butter or oil along with aromatic vegetables such as onion, then the mixture is cooked with stock (or water) in the oven. The grain is ready for the liquid to be added when it gives off a nutty, toasted aroma. The desired texture of a pilaf is fluffy, with no grains sticking to each other. Pilafs can contain a variety of other ingredients, such as dried fruit, nuts, and pasta such as orzo. Here is a basic recipe, followed by two variations.

1½ CUPS BASIC CHICKEN STOCK *(page 41), or water*

1 TABLESPOON UNSALTED BUTTER

¼ CUP MINCED ONION

1 SMALL DRIED BAY LEAF

½ TEASPOON COARSE SALT

1 CUP LONG-GRAIN WHITE RICE

Heat oven and stock Heat oven to 350°F. Bring stock to a simmer in a small saucepan.

Meanwhile, sauté aromatics Melt butter in a 2-quart ovenproof saucepan over medium heat. Add onion, bay leaf, and salt [1] and cook until onion is soft and translucent, stirring occasionally, about 3 minutes.

Toast rice Add rice and stir well to coat each grain with butter mixture [2]. Cook until rice is fragrant and starting to turn translucent, stirring frequently, about 3 minutes.

Add stock to rice mixture and bake Add stock [3] and return to a simmer. Transfer to oven, cover, and bake 16 minutes. Remove from oven. Cover and let steam for 10 minutes, then fluff with a fork before serving.

> ## Making Rice Pilaf

BROWN RICE PILAF WITH CURRANTS
Follow recipe above, substituting brown rice for white and increasing stock to 1¾ cups (instead of 1½ cups). Bake 45 minutes, then stir in ¼ cup dried currants before fluffing with a fork. Garnish with toasted sliced almonds and serve.

BASMATI RICE PILAF WITH POMEGRANATES
Follow main recipe above, substituting basmati rice for the white rice. Add a pinch of saffron to the stock and let stand 10 minutes before bringing to a simmer. Proceed with recipe. Garnish with pomegranate seeds and serve.

FARRO RISOTTO WITH
WILD MUSHROOMS

RISOTTO

RISOTTO Serves 4

A well-made risotto is a culinary feat: Small, firm grains of rice float, suspended, in a rich, creamy sauce. When scooped onto a shallow plate or bowl, a good risotto should have a loose consistency, rippling into a tight pool on the plate (it should not be soupy, though). As the Italians say, it should be *all'onda*, or "with waves." Unfortunately, many cooks (home and professional) make risottos that are too thick and dense, more like a porridge. But preparing a successful risotto is actually easier to accomplish than you may imagine. It involves no special tricks, just careful observation (and a lot of stirring). Allow your senses—taste, sight, and smell—to tell you when it's done.

The type of rice is critical to the dish. Italian rices, such as Arborio, Carnaroli, or Vialone Nano, are the best choices for the particular composition of starches risotto requires. During cooking, the soft starch on the outside of the grains readily dissolves to form the intrinsic creaminess, while the inside remains al dente (firm "to the tooth"), giving risotto its characteristic bite. Because its flavor will permeate the dish, the liquid used is equally important, and what you use should depend on what else is being added to the dish. Many recipes call for chicken or vegetable stock, but these can prove too overpowering, especially when the dish will be simply seasoned with a handful each of cheese and herbs, as in the recipe below. So instead, the recipe calls for a simple broth that incorporates some of the ingredients used to flavor the dish, here celery, carrot, onion, garlic, and parsley. Likewise, for a shrimp risotto, you could make a broth by combining the shells with lemons and herbs; or you could sauté or roast the bones from meat, fish, or chicken and then simmer them with water. If you prefer deeper flavor, follow this same principle to enrich existing chicken or vegetable stocks for using in risotto.

Making a risotto is a lot like making a stew: First, you begin by sautéing an aromatic ingredient. Then the rice is stirred in and toasted to give it a nutty flavor (similar to pilafs) and to loosen some of its starch. After a few minutes, as you stir, the grains eventually become slightly more translucent and they begin making a clicking noise, which tells you it's time to add the wine. When the wine is stirred in, the rice releases a bit more starch, turning the liquid slightly milky, a sign of the creaminess to come. Once the wine is absorbed, the stock is added, ladleful by ladleful. Near-constant stirring will ensure that the rice cooks evenly and helps release the soft starch on the outside of the grains. The final step of any great risotto is to "mount" it with butter, which gives the risotto richness, and to add in any final seasonings (in this case, grated cheese, freshly ground pepper, and parsley), just before serving.

In certain regions of northern Italy, the risotto method is used to cook other grains, such as farro, an ancient grain with a nutty taste. It will produce a dish with a slightly chewier and less creamy texture (see the farro variation with wild mushroom on page 419).

For stock

1 CELERY STALK *(preferably from the heart), cut in half crosswise*

1 MEDIUM CARROT, *cut in half crosswise*

½ SMALL ONION, *peeled*

1 GARLIC CLOVE, *smashed and peeled*

1 SPRIG FLAT-LEAF PARSLEY

7 CUPS WATER, OR HALF WATER AND HALF BASIC CHICKEN STOCK *(page 41)*

For aromatic

3 TABLESPOONS EXTRA-VIRGIN OLIVE OIL

½ SMALL ONION, *cut into fine dice (about ⅓ cup)*

For risotto

1 CUP MEDIUM-GRAIN ITALIAN RICE, *such as Arborio, Carnaroli, or Vialone Nano*

⅓ CUP DRY WHITE WINE, *such as Sauvignon Blanc*

For finishing

2 TABLESPOONS UNSALTED BUTTER

½ CUP GRATED PARMIGIANO-REGGIANO CHEESE

COARSE SALT AND FRESHLY GROUND PEPPER

CHOPPED FLAT-LEAF PARSLEY

Perfect Risotto, Step by Step

Make stock Combine stock ingredients in a 4-quart stockpot and bring to a boil over medium-high heat. Reduce heat and simmer 15 minutes. Reduce heat to the lowest setting to keep stock hot but not evaporating.

Meanwhile, cook aromatic and toast rice In another 4-quart pot, heat the olive oil over medium-high heat. Cook onion until translucent [1], stirring, about 2 minutes. Add rice and cook, stirring [2], until just starting to turn translucent (rice will start making a clicking sound), 1 to 2 minutes. Reduce heat if onion begins to brown.

Add wine and stock Pour in wine [3] and cook, stirring, just until absorbed (rice should still be wet and glistening, not dry) [4]. Using a ladle, add ½ cup hot stock to the rice [5]. Stir constantly with a wooden spoon, at a moderate speed, until about three-quarters of the liquid is absorbed (the mixture should be thick enough to hold a trail behind the spoon) [6]. Continue adding stock ½ cup at a time and stirring frequently until rice is almost translucent (the rice should be al dente but not crunchy, and liquid is creamy in consistency) [7]. As rice nears doneness, watch carefully and add smaller amounts of liquid to make sure it doesn't overcook (you may not need to use all the broth). The process should take 20 to 25 minutes total.

Finish and serve Stir in the butter [8] until completely melted (this is called mounting), then stir in cheese [9] and season with salt. Garnish with parsley and pepper and serve immediately.

FARRO RISOTTO WITH WILD MUSHROOMS

Trim ½ pound mixed wild mushrooms (such as oyster, shiitake, and hen of the woods) and halve if large. Heat 2 tablespoons extra-virgin olive oil in a large skillet over high heat. Add half the mushrooms *fig. 6.4* and cook, stirring occasionally, until golden and tender, about 7 minutes. Season with coarse salt and freshly ground pepper and transfer to a bowl. Repeat with 2 more tablespoons oil, remaining mushrooms, and more salt and pepper. Keep warm until ready to serve. Follow the above recipe, using the same proportions of ingredients, but substitute farro for the rice to make risotto (including the stock) and cook for about the same amount of time; the farro should be tender but still firm to the bite (the indentation in the grain will have puffed up). Serve, topped with mushroom mixture.

fig. 6.4 SAUTÉING MUSHROOMS FOR FARRO RISOTTO

PERFECT SOFT POLENTA Serves 6 to 8

Polenta, a staple of northern Italian cooking, is coarsely ground cornmeal that is cooked very slowly simmering on top of the stove (or in the oven). Because of the frequent stirring and the incremental additions of liquid, the cooking method is very similar to that used for risotto. Polenta can be served right away, as in the recipe that follows, or allowed to set and then cut into shapes and fried, grilled, or baked. Water is the most common liquid, but for a richer, more flavorful polenta, replace all or some of the water with chicken stock (page 41) or vegetable stock (page 56), reducing salt accordingly, if necessary. Or substitute half the water with milk (preferably whole) for a creamier consistency.

Polenta Tips

It is not necessary to stir constantly while the polenta cooks, but it is important to stir frequently, taking care to scrape the sides and bottom when you stir.

Adjust the heat as necessary to keep the polenta at a very slow simmer so it is barely bubbling (otherwise it can splatter and you can burn yourself).

Serve soft polenta as soon as it is ready (it should be the consistency of oatmeal); it will thicken as it cools.

This recipe calls for two pots of water for cooking the polenta: one for the initial stage when the cornmeal is whisked into hot water, and the other for additional water that is added gradually while the polenta cooks to reach the desired thickness. Having less water in the first stage helps the cornmeal reach a creamier consistency earlier in the cooking process, so lumps are less likely to form. Once you become familiar with the method and know the thickness you prefer, you won't need to measure the amount in the second pot.

The longer the polenta cooks, the creamier and tastier it becomes (up to a point). The recommended cooking time here is merely the minimum required for the polenta to cook through. If you choose to cook it longer, simply add small amounts of hot liquid as necessary to achieve the desired consistency, making sure that you let the polenta absorb all of the liquid before adding more.

The method described below can be used to cook other types of meal, including semolina (coarsely ground durum wheat often used to make puddings) and grits (coarsely ground corn, also known as hominy grits).

Ingredients

Coarse-ground polenta can be found at gourmet shops and many natural-food stores, either packaged or in bulk. You can substitute stone-ground cornmeal.

Soft polenta can be kept warm for up to an hour; cover pan and set over (not in) a pot of very hot water. Remove any skin that forms on the top before serving.

For polenta

    10 CUPS WATER
     1 HEAPING TABLESPOON COARSE SALT
     2 CUPS COARSE-GROUND POLENTA MEAL

For finishing

     2 TABLESPOONS UNSALTED BUTTER
       FRESHLY GROUND PEPPER
       PARMIGIANO-REGGIANO CHEESE

Heat water Bring 6 cups water and the salt to a boil over high heat in a medium (6-quart) heavy-bottom pot. Bring remaining 4 cups water to a simmer over medium heat in a small saucepan.

Perfect Soft Polenta, Step by Step

PERFECT SOFT POLENTA

Whisk in meal Add polenta to the large pot in handfuls, separating your fingers to let the grain slip through [1], and whisking constantly; cook until cornmeal has absorbed all of the water, about 3 minutes. Lower heat until only one or two large bubbles break the surface at a time (over medium-low or low, adjusting heat as necessary).

Add water and cook polenta Whisk 2 ladles of simmering water into polenta, and cook, stirring frequently with a wooden spoon [2], until water has been absorbed, about 5 minutes. Continue to add 2 ladles of water every 5 minutes, stirring frequently to prevent polenta from scorching and waiting for it to be absorbed before adding more, until polenta is creamy and just pulls away from sides of pot, about 45 minutes. (It may be necessary to adjust heat.)

Finish and serve Stir in butter [3] and season with pepper. Use a damp spoon or ladle to transfer polenta to wide, shallow bowls, and shave cheese over each serving.

7 ▸ Desserts

DESSERTS

WHY DO SO MANY people whip up fantastic dinners, but then choose to run to a bakery or turn to a boxed-mix for dessert? It's a matter of convenience at times, but more pressing seems to be the concern that the alternative—baking something "from scratch"—means risking culinary disaster. While cooking allows for creative improvisation, tasting as you work and substituting ingredients sometimes at will, baking and other

ways to make sweets are all about precision. A double-crust pie, custard, or batch of drop cookies depends on gathering just the right ingredients, measuring them properly, and combining them the right way, in the right order, and at just the right temperature. If making a delicious salad or pot of soup is an art, making great layer cakes and other desserts is more a science.

None of that, however, means that dessert should be intimidating. In fact, some cooks might find the very existence of proper methods and precise recipes to be liberating: more than any other kind of cooking, dessert making can be broken down into component techniques. Master a few of these techniques and you are well on your way to producing dozens of spectacular sweets.

THE BUILDING BLOCKS OF GOOD DESSERTS
Almost every dessert starts with some combination of a fairly short list of ingredients: butter, sugar, flour, and eggs. The remarkable thing about these very simple ingredients is that they can be transformed into such a wide range of enticing foods. The best, and most fun, way to teach the creation of these foods is to start at the beginning and take a step-by-step approach. So this chapter has lessons that focus mainly on those ingredients, and mini lessons that involve other, no less important flavor- and texture-building blocks like milk, cream, and fruit.

For many people, the introduction to baking at home involves chocolate chip cookies (usually with a recipe straight off the back of the chip bag). Though the recipe is pretty straightforward, it's surprising to see how varied a different batch of cookies made from the same recipe can be. And though they all might be tasty, some are certainly closer to the right texture and flavor than others. This has to do with the choice of ingredients (for example,

substituting artificial vanilla flavoring for pure vanilla extract will compromise flavor, to be sure, and using bread flour instead of all-purpose flour will cause the texture to be more tough and not as tender). But all else being equal, there's just one easy-to-overlook technique that makes a huge difference in how your cookies (and cakes, for that matter) turn out: creaming the butter and sugar together. Getting this step right can mean the difference between delicate, tender baked goods and those that are dense and hard.

So the lessons begin with how to cream butter and sugar properly. After a brief primer on how it's done, you get a couple of recipes whose success depends on the well-executed technique—namely, a drop cookie (with multiple variations for add-ins) and a basic layer cake (topped with an uncomplicated buttercream frosting that further illustrates the technique). The lessons move on from there to include other crucial baking components, such as how to cut butter into dry ingredients, a crucial step for producing flaky biscuits and piecrust; how to properly whip eggs, with recipes for meringues and angel food cake (egg whites only) and génoise, or sponge cake (which depends entirely on whole eggs for leavening); how to create a lofty soufflé (again, by learning a thing or two about whipped eggs); how to make rich custards, for flan, crème brulée, or ice cream; and how to make pâte à choux, the delightfully easy—and versatile—dough for cream puffs. You'll also learn simple techniques for cooking fresh fruit and making fruit-juice-based frozen treats like sorbets and granitas that will take your desserts in a new direction.

LESSON 7.1
How to Cream Butter

The purpose of creaming butter with sugar is to create air pockets, or cells, formed when sugar granules are blended with fat. Later, during baking, gases from any chemical leaveners combine with evaporating moisture to inflate the pockets, resulting in a light, nicely textured finished product. For creaming, it's most important to start with butter at room temperature, since air pockets won't form in cold butter. If you forget to take it out of the refrigerator, there are some shortcuts that will speed up the process (see note at right), but use these with care. If the butter gets too warm or soft, it won't hold its structure well enough, and you'll need to chill it again some before you cream it.

You can cream by hand—the old-fashioned way, with a wooden spoon—which takes a fair amount of muscle (and perseverance), or with an electric mixer. There are advantages to doing it by hand at least a few times: You'll get a close-up view of the interaction of the fat with the sugar, as well as a good feeling for when you've achieved the right consistency (without as much of a chance of overbeating). Some recipes will indicate a time frame of at least several minutes for creaming, but most important will be visual cues: the mixture should become paler in color—a creamy shade—and should have increased in volume some and have a fluffy appearance. Don't keep beating once this stage is reached; overdoing it can cause the air cells that have formed to collapse. Other ingredients will then be added to the mix: eggs, like the butter, should be at room temperature (if not, you can place them in a bowl of warm water for about 15 minutes). When you add them, they need to combine thoroughly with the other ingredients, a process that will be inhibited if they are cold (or added all at once); using cold eggs (or cold liquids like milk or buttermilk, for that matter) can cause a batter to separate and look curdled. Once the basic ingredients are fully incorporated, stop mixing to preserve the texture. (Again, there's a risk of overmixing at this point, which is why you'll see the phrase "just until combined" in so many baking recipes.) Any solid ingredients such as chocolate chips, chopped fruit, and nuts should be stirred or folded in at the end.

BASIC DROP COOKIES Makes about 40

Everyone needs one reliable recipe for an old-fashioned drop cookie. This master recipe fills the bill. It's simple (no machines necessary—the butter can be creamed by hand, though you can use a mixer for ease) and infinitely variable (modify the dough with any of the add-ins listed below, or split it into two or three batches so that you can make more than one type of cookie at the same time). And if you want, you can bake a portion of it, then form the remainder into balls (on baking sheets) and place in freezer until frozen. Store the frozen balls of dough in a resealable bag in the freezer until until you're ready to bake; let sit at room temperature for 30 minutes before baking, and bake a few minutes longer than the recommended time. These cookies are somewhat cakey; for a chewier texture, reduce the flour by ½ cup and the baking time by 2 minutes.

THE RIGHT TEMPERATURE FOR BUTTER
What does it mean when a recipe calls for "room temperature" butter? The stick should be soft enough to hold a deep indentation when you press it with your finger, but not so soft that the stick smooshes out of shape. Let butter sit out of the refrigerator, and test its softness by pressing your finger into the top. When the indentation remains but the butter still holds its shape, it's ready. Never microwave or otherwise melt butter to speed things up. Butter that is too warm will separate and won't cream well. To hasten softening, cut the cold butter into slices, or grate it on the large holes of a box grater.

Drop-Cookie Tips

If your cookies turn out dense and hard, you might be using ingredients that are too cold and not creaming them enough. If your cookies spread too much in the oven and are too thin, on the other hand, you might be overdoing the creaming step or using ingredients that are too warm. It's worth the time to chill your dough before baking; this will help to control how much it spreads in the oven as it bakes.

3 CUPS ALL-PURPOSE FLOUR

1½ TEASPOONS COARSE SALT

1¼ TEASPOONS BAKING SODA

1 CUP (2 STICKS) UNSALTED BUTTER, *room temperature*

1 CUP PACKED LIGHT-BROWN SUGAR *(or use dark-brown sugar for deeper flavor and color)*

½ CUP GRANULATED SUGAR

2 LARGE EGGS, *room temperature*

1 TEASPOON PURE VANILLA EXTRACT

2 CUPS DESIRED ADD-INS *(semisweet chocolate chips or chunks; coarsely chopped pecans, walnuts, or peanuts; raisins, dried cranberries, dried sour cherries, or chopped dried fruit such as apricots, dates, or figs)*

Prepare oven and pans Heat oven to 350°F, with one rack in center and one rack in bottom third. Line two large cookie sheets with parchment paper.

Combine dry ingredients In a bowl, whisk together flour, salt, and baking soda [1].

Basic Drop Cookies, Step by Step

BASIC DROP COOKIES
(WITH CHOCOLATE CHIPS AND WALNUTS)

SIFTING CHOPPED NUTS
Before incorporating chopped nuts into doughs or batters, sift out the fine dust in a sieve. This will keep the particles from clouding the color or imparting a grainy texture.

Cream butter and sugars Place butter and both sugars in a mixing bowl. Mash and stir with a wooden spoon [2] until mixture is very light and fluffy (this can take up to 6 minutes, or 2 to 3 minutes if you're using an electric mixer). Add eggs one at a time [3], beating until thoroughly incorporated after each [4]. Stir in vanilla.

Add dry ingredients and mix-ins Add dry ingredients in three additions [5], stirring until completely incorporated after each. Stir in desired add-ins [6]. (Or, if making several types of cookies, first divide dough into equal parts and then stir in appropriate amounts of add-ins: 1 rounded cup for dough split in half, ¾ cup for dough divided into thirds.)

Bake and cool Using a 1½-inch ice-cream scoop, drop dough onto prepared baking sheets, about 2 inches apart *fig. 7.1*. Bake, rotating sheets top to bottom and back to front halfway through, until golden brown at edges and set in center, 13 to 15 minutes. Let cool on sheets 5 minutes, then transfer to a wire rack to cool completely. Cookies can be stored in an airtight container at room temperature up to 1 week, or frozen up to 1 month.

fig. 7.1 SCOOPING COOKIE DOUGH

YELLOW BUTTER CAKE WITH EASY CHOCOLATE BUTTERCREAM Serves 12

A simple butter cake is often referred to as yellow cake, but it's not the butter that produces its distinctive color; most butter cakes also contain whole eggs, so the yolks contribute to the color (as well as the rich flavor). The creaming method is essential to many classic American layer cakes like this one, but here an electric mixer (fitted with the paddle attachment) is used, rather than a wooden spoon. Be sure to cream for the suggested amount of time to create the finest texture and a velvety crumb. Using a combination of flours is equally important; cake flour imparts tenderness and a delicate crumb, all-purpose flour lends structure.

1 CUP PLUS 2 TABLESPOONS (2¼ STICKS) *unsalted butter, room temperature, plus more for pans*

1½ CUPS ALL-PURPOSE FLOUR, *plus more for pans*

3 CUPS CAKE FLOUR *(not self-rising), sifted*

2¼ TEASPOONS BAKING POWDER

¾ TEASPOON BAKING SODA

1½ TEASPOONS COARSE SALT

2¼ CUPS SUGAR

6 LARGE EGGS, *room temperature*

2 CUPS BUTTERMILK, *room temperature*

2 TEASPOONS PURE VANILLA EXTRACT

EASY CHOCOLATE BUTTERCREAM *(page 432)*

Ingredient

When a recipe calls for flour, be sure to follow the order for measuring and sifting. For example, "3 cups sifted flour" means to sift, then measure; "3 cups flour, sifted" calls for measuring before sifting. Cake flour is often sifted, as it is finer and more prone to clumping.

Prepare oven and pans Heat oven to 350°F, with racks in the middle of oven. Brush two 8-inch square or two 9-inch round cake pans with softened butter [1] and line bottoms with parchment paper [2]; butter parchment. Dust pans with all-purpose flour, and tap out excess [3].

Combine dry ingredients Whisk together both flours, baking powder, baking soda, and salt in a medium bowl.

Cream butter and sugar Using an electric mixer fitted with the paddle attachment, beat the butter and sugar [4] on medium-high speed until light and fluffy [5], 4 to 6 minutes, scraping down sides of bowl as needed.

Add remaining ingredients Reduce speed to medium and add eggs one at a time [6], beating to incorporate fully after each and scraping down sides of bowl as needed. Reduce mixer speed to low and gradually add flour mixture [7], alternating with buttermilk [8] and ending with the flour. (Alternating the ingredients helps them incorporate more easily into the batter, while also reducing the risk of losing volume.) Beat in vanilla. The batter should be smooth and very thick.

▷ **Preparing a cake pan**

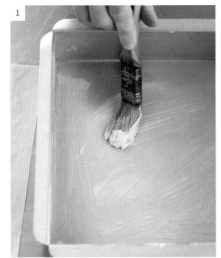

440

Cake tip

There are a few ways to make sure a cake has finished cooking, inside and out. A cake tester inserted in the center should come out clean, with no crumbs or moist batter attached. The top of the cake should be golden (unless it's chocolate) and spring back when lightly touched, and the cake should be beginning to pull away from the sides of the pan.

Bake cakes Divide batter evenly between prepared pans, smoothing tops with an offset spatula [9] (pans should be about half full). Bake, carefully rotating pans halfway through, until cakes spring back when lightly touched, and a cake tester inserted into the centers comes out clean, about 40 minutes.

Cool Transfer pans to wire racks; let cool 20 minutes. Carefully run a paring knife around the outer edge of the cakes to loosen [10]. Holding rack over pan with a dish towel [11] invert cakes onto racks. Carefully lift off pan [12], then remove and discard parchment [13]. Let cool completely. (If not using immediately, wrap layers in plastic and store at room temperature overnight or in refrigerator up to 3 days. Cake layers can also be frozen, tightly wrapped in plastic, up to 2 months.)

Frost cakes Reinvert cakes, top sides up. Place one layer on a cake stand or platter lined with parchment paper. With a long serrated knife, trim top to make level [14]. Using an offset spatula, spread with a ¼-inch-thick layer (about 1¼ cups) of buttercream [15]. Trim top of other layer, then place top side down

Butter Cake, Step by Step

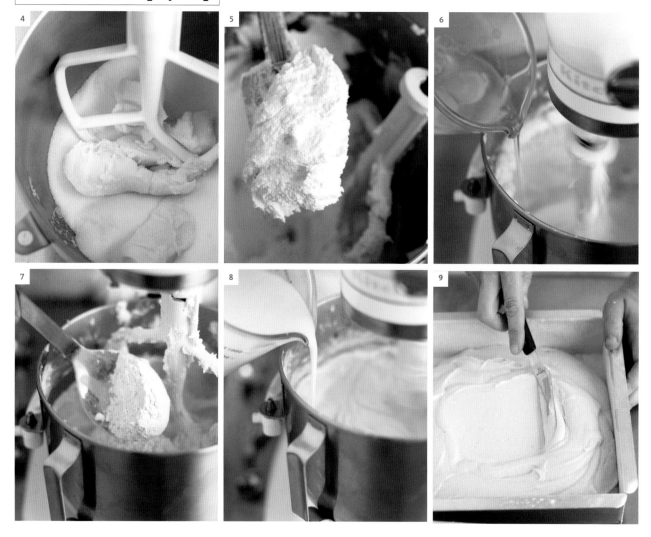

Forming a Layer Cake

on the first, pressing lightly. Smooth layer of frosting flush with sides of cake [16]. Apply a crumb coat: Using an offset spatula, frost the top and sides of cake with a thin layer of buttercream (½ to ¾ cup) [17]. Refrigerate 20 minutes. Then spread cake with a final layer (¼ inch thick) of buttercream [18]. To smooth frosting, run the spatula over entire cake, dipping it in hot water and wiping dry as you go. Cake can be frosted and kept, covered, at room temperature up to 1 day before serving.

YELLOW BUTTER CUPCAKES Makes 42
Follow the recipe above, lining standard muffin tins with paper liners (if you need to bake them in batches, replace liners after each batch has been baked and removed from the tin). Fill each cup halfway with batter, and bake until a tester inserted in centers comes out clean, 15 to 20 minutes. Cool in tin on a wire rack for 10 minutes, then turn out cupcakes onto rack and cool completely. Cupcakes can be stored in an airtight container and refrigerated up to 3 days or frozen up to 1 week before frosting.

EASY CHOCOLATE BUTTERCREAM Makes about 5 cups

When creaming butter for frostings, incorporating air and creating cells is not as important as simply creating a seamless texture. Many traditional buttercream frostings, such as the Swiss Meringue Buttercream on Page 455, incorporate softened butter into a meringue base, but this version is far simpler and quicker. You need only to beat the butter until creamy and then mix in confectioners' sugar and cocoa powder until smooth. This frosting will be grainier than a shiny, glossy meringue-based buttercream, but it is perfectly acceptable for a birthday cake or batch of cupcakes.

1 POUND (4 STICKS) UNSALTED BUTTER, *room temperature*
1 TEASPOON PURE VANILLA EXTRACT
¾ CUP UNSWEETENED DUTCH-PROCESS COCOA POWDER
5¼ CUPS SIFTED CONFECTIONERS' SUGAR

WITH AN ELECTRIC MIXER, cream butter on medium-high speed until pale and fluffy, about 2 minutes. Add vanilla. Reduce speed to medium; add cocoa. Mix until smooth. Add sugar, 1 cup at a time, mixing well after each addition. Mix on high speed until well blended, 10 to 20 seconds more. (If not using immediately, cover with plastic wrap and refrigerate up to 3 days. Before using, bring to room temperature and beat with electric mixer on medium speed until fluffy, 2 or 3 minutes.)

LESSON 7.2
How to Cut Butter into Flour

What distinguishes pie crusts, biscuits, and other so-called short pastries from the cakes and cookies produced by the creaming method is texture. Short pastries are marked by flakes and layers rather than by a smooth and consistent crumb. In order to achieve those flaky layers, you need to cut butter into flour so that the butter remains broken up in solid, cold chunks (hence the name pâte brisée for pie crust, which means "broken pastry" in French). For the recipes that follow, it's imperative that the butter be cold. In fact, everything should be cold. Place the ingredients and tools—the bowl you'll be mixing in, along with a pastry blender, if using—in the freezer before you begin working, especially in the summer or in a warm room. You don't want those chunks of butter to begin to melt until they hit the heat of the oven; there, they will melt and create steam, leading to—you guessed it—pockets of air to be formed in the dough. The result will be a light, flaky finish.

fig. 7.2 **RUBBING IN BUTTER**

For pie crusts especially, a food processor makes easy, quick work of cutting butter into flour. Just take care not to overprocess; you want the mixture to look something like coarse meal, with the largest pieces of butter resembling small peas. If you don't have a food processor or prefer to cut the butter in by hand, rub it in with your fingertips *fig. 7.2*; a pastry blender also does a fine job, just quickly work it through the butter and flour in a chopping motion, until the desired texture is reached. (If you are a novice, you may want to begin by cutting in butter by hand, so you can develop a feel for the proper consistency; it can be easy to overprocess if you haven't used a food processor for this purpose before.) For the sake of preserving those chunks of butter, don't overwork the dough once the liquids are added. Blend just enough to incorporate; the dough should just come together when pressed with two fingers. (It should not come together in a ball, as many recipes suggest; at that point it will be overworked). Pat the dough gently together on your work surface, and form into a neat disk once in plastic. Then leave it alone.

BUTTERMILK SHORTCAKES WITH RHUBARB AND BERRIES Makes 10

A simple buttermilk biscuit serves as the basis for fruit shortcake. As with many easy recipes, your success rate at making biscuits will most likely grow exponentially with each attempt. There's nothing tricky about it; just be sure to work quickly and not to overwork the dough at all, which will cause the biscuits to become heavy and flat. In this recipe, a traditional strawberry shortcake is enhanced by a rhubarb compote to serve along with the macerated berries. You can use one fruit and not the other (by doubling the amount of either topping). Or substitute an equal amount of another fruit for the rhubarb, or macerate any other type of berry. An apricot compote would be lovely with macerated black-berries, for example, or nectarines with raspberries. The whipped cream, however, is not optional; it's a fundamental part of the appeal of fruit shortcake. The biscuits, meanwhile, can be served on their own for breakfast, topped with a pat of butter and your favorite jam. (If you are planning to serve them with savory dishes like eggs and bacon, however, omit the sugar and vanilla bean.)

For shortcakes

    3 CUPS ALL-PURPOSE FLOUR, *plus more for biscuit cutter*

    1 CUP CAKE FLOUR *(not self-rising)*

    ¼ CUP GRANULATED SUGAR

    1 TABLESPOON BAKING POWDER

    1 TEASPOON BAKING SODA

    1 TEASPOON TABLE SALT

    1 CUP (2 STICKS) COLD UNSALTED BUTTER, *cut into small pieces*

    1 VANILLA BEAN, *split lengthwise (see page 469)*

  1½ CUPS COLD BUTTERMILK

    2 TABLESPOONS HEAVY CREAM, *for brushing*

    FINE SANDING SUGAR, *for sprinkling (or use granulated sugar)*

For serving

    WHIPPED CREAM *(page 436)*

    RHUBARB COMPOTE *(page 436)*

    MACERATED STRAWBERRIES *(page 437)*

Prepare baking sheet Line a large cookie sheet with parchment paper.

Cut butter into dry ingredients Whisk together flours, granulated sugar, baking powder, baking soda, and salt. Using a pastry blender [1] or your fingertips, cut the butter into the flour until the largest pieces are the size of small peas [2].

Mix dough Rub the vanilla seeds into the buttermilk with your fingers *fig. 7.3* (this is the best way to disperse the seeds, but alternatively, you can scrape the bean against the side of the measuring cup with a rubber spatula). Add the buttermilk to the flour mixture [3], stirring with a fork until most of the ingredients have come together into a moist dough (it's okay if some flour is left on bottom of bowl).

fig. 7.3 DISPERSING VANILLA SEEDS

Form biscuits Turn out dough onto a clean work surface and gather any loose bits together [4]. Press lightly to fully incorporate all the ingredients while patting into a rough rectangle [5], being careful not to overwork the dough. Fold dough into thirds: Starting with a short end, carefully fold over [6], then fold the other end over the first. [7]. (The folding adds an extra layering of flakiness to the finished biscuits.) Pat out dough until 1¼ inches thick. Using a floured biscuit cutter, cut dough into 2½-inch rounds [8].

Bake Preheat oven to 400°F. Place rounds on prepared cookie sheet, about 1 inch apart [9]. Gather together scraps; pat out again, and cut once. Chill 20 minutes. Brush tops with the cream and sprinkle with sanding sugar. Bake 10 minutes, and rotate sheet. Reduce heat to 375°F, and continue to bake until golden brown and cooked through, about 12 minutes more. Transfer biscuits to a wire rack to cool.

Serve Split biscuits, and layer with whipped cream and rhubarb compote. Serve berries on the side. Or, set out a platter of biscuits and bowls of each topping and let guests build their own shortcakes. Biscuits are best eaten the day they are made.

Shortcakes, Step by Step

BUTTERMILK SHORTCAKES WITH RHUBARB AND BERRIES

fig. 7.4 WHIPPING CREAM OVER
AN ICE BATH

WHIPPED CREAM Makes about 2 cups

The key to perfect whipped cream is to have the cream and bowl very cold, especially when beating by hand.

    1 CUP HEAVY CREAM
    1 TABLESPOON CONFECTIONERS' SUGAR
    ½ TEASPOON PURE VANILLA EXTRACT

IN A DEEP MIXING BOWL set in a large ice-water bath, whisk cream by hand *fig. 7.4* until soft peaks form. Sprinkle with the sugar, add vanilla, and whisk until soft peaks return. Do not overbeat.

RHUBARB COMPOTE Makes about 3½ cups

A compote is a simple fruit sauce that usually serves as one element of a multilayered dessert. It's used to top cakes or scoops of ice cream or as an accompaniment to mildly flavored cookies such as shortbread. Rhubarb requires a higher proportion of sugar than most fruits, since it is naturally sour; here it is also flavored with citrus zests. If you want to use other fruits, such as stone fruits or pears, adjust the amount of sugar depending on their sweetness.

2¼ POUNDS RHUBARB, *ends trimmed and leaves discarded*

  1 CUP PLUS 2 TABLESPOONS SUGAR

  ½ CUP WATER

  3 STRIPS (EACH 2½ BY ½ INCH) ORANGE ZEST

  3 STRIPS (EACH 2½ BY ½ INCH) LEMON ZEST

  ¼ TEASPOON COARSE SALT

Prepare rhubarb Wash rhubarb well and dry thoroughly with paper towels (wipe each stalk to remove any grit). Cut crosswise on the diagonal into 1-inch pieces (you should have about 5 cups).

Make poaching syrup Bring sugar, water, zests, and salt to a boil in a large straight-sided skillet, stirring until sugar is dissolved. Add rhubarb, and stir to coat in sugar syrup. (There won't be enough syrup to cover, but the compote will become more liquidy once the fruit starts to release its juices.) Cover and cook over medium-low heat until rhubarb is just tender, about 5 minutes. (Do not overcook; you want most of the rhubarb pieces to hold their shape.)

Cool Remove from heat and let cool completely, about 1 hour, before using. Compote can be refrigerated in an airtight container up to 1 week.

MACERATED BERRIES Makes about 2½ cups
Macerating is a simple way to turn fresh fruit into a syrupy sauce. Sugar draws out the fruit's juices; lemon juice preserves color and adds flavor.

  1 PINT FRESH STRAWBERRIES, *hulled (large berries halved or quartered lengthwise)*

  2 TABLESPOONS SUGAR

  1 TEASPOON FRESH LEMON JUICE

IN A BOWL, toss berries with sugar and lemon juice to combine. Let stand at room temperature 20 minutes to draw out some of the juices before serving.

PÂTE BRISÉE Makes enough for two 9- or 10-inch single-crust pies or one 9- or 10-inch double-crust pie

There are a handful of dishes that serve as true measures of any good cook: a great omelet, a comforting and well-balanced soup, a perfectly crisp and golden roast chicken, and a tender, flaky pie crust. Perhaps because of the risk of overworking, and turning out something that tears in two or tastes more leaden than light, many home cooks shy away from homemade dough, opting instead for unfold-as-you-go boxed crusts. But making perfect pie dough from scratch should be part of any home cook's basic skills. And the best dough for homemade pies is pâte brisée. Like pasta dough, pâte brisée is a simple paste containing flour and water, but in this case butter is a key component and plays an integral role in creating the flaky texture. Getting the right proportion of butter to flour is crucial, as is using very cold ingredients and a light hand.

2 ¾ CUPS ALL-PURPOSE FLOUR

1 TABLESPOON SUGAR

1 ½ TEASPOONS COARSE SALT

1 CUP PLUS 2 TABLESPOONS (2 ¼ STICKS) COLD UNSALTED BUTTER, *cut into ¾-inch pieces*

7 TABLESPOONS ICE WATER, *plus more if needed*

Combine dry ingredients Pulse flour, sugar, and salt in a food processor to combine (or whisk together by hand in a bowl).

Cut in butter Add butter [1], and pulse until coarse crumbs form, about 10 seconds (or quickly cut in with a pastry blender or your fingertips). The mixture should have pieces ranging from coarse crumbs to the size of small peas [2].

Add water Add the water (start with 7 tablespoons and add up to 2 tablespoons more water only if necessary, 1 tablespoon at a time) and pulse until dough just

Pâte Brisée, Step by Step

holds together when pinched [3] (do not process longer than 30 seconds). The mixture should retain a crumbly texture at this point; it should not be sticky. (If mixing by hand, drizzle water over flour mixture, and mix with a fork until dough just holds together.)

Shape and chill dough Turn out dough onto a clean work surface. Knead once or twice to incorporate loose bits. Divide in half. Pat each half into a thick disk [4], then place on a piece of plastic wrap and gather wrap to flatten disk [5]. Wrap tightly in plastic and refrigerate at least 1 hour (or overnight). Dough can be frozen up to 1 month; thaw in refrigerator overnight before using.

How to Roll Out Pâte Brisée

Rolling out dough is not difficult, but it can take a bit of practice to get it right. Here are a few pointers to keep in mind before you begin.

First, cool temperature is extremely important in keeping the butter from melting (remember: no butter pieces, no flakes). Don't try to roll out dough in a hot room; the dough will soften too quickly and become difficult to work with. Make sure the dough is well chilled (but after chilling, let it sit out for 10 minutes or so before you start rolling, or it may crack); you can soften the edges a bit by pressing between fingertips. A cool work surface is best. Professional pastry counters, as an example, are often made of marble or stainless steel because of their ability to remain cool.

Roll out the dough on a lightly floured surface or a piece of parchment paper. (The latter will allow you to shift the dough and turn it more easily than if you roll directly on the work surface). If the dough gets too soft to work with, transfer it to the refrigerator until it firms up, about 10 minutes.)
1 Start rolling, working from the center of the dough out to the edges. To preserve the shape, turn dough ⅛ turn every time you roll. Avoid rolling directly over the edges, which can cause them to stick. Lift edges with a bench scraper to loosen and allow dough to continue thinning. As you go, run your fingers around the edges of the dough to feel if the thickness is even (and if not, to find where you need to roll more). 2 Use a pastry brush to remove excess flour from the dough (too much flour will toughen it). 3 If the dough loses its circular shape, place the end of the rolling pin near the crooked edge and roll, working that area by pressing with one hand while holding the pin loosely with the other.

Ingredients

This recipe uses plums, but you can substitute an equal weight of other stone fruits. Halved figs, whole berries, or sliced ripe pears also make great fillings. If using figs, which tend to be less juicy than plums, reduce the cornstarch to $1^{1}/_{2}$ teaspoons.

An acidic ingredient is essential for brightening the flavor of the fruit; lemon juice is used with the plums, but lime juice would be nice with apricots.

Cornstarch is the preferred thickener for pies made with stone fruit and berries, as the juices will be less cloudy, but you can use all-purpose flour in its place, particularly if you are baking pears or apples (whose juices are naturally cloudy). Bear in mind that you will need to substitute twice the amount of flour for the cornstarch.

To make the egg wash, you can use either a whole egg or just a yolk. A crust brushed with a whole-egg wash will be shinier; the yolk produces a browner finish. Heavy cream enhances the color.

FRUIT GALETTE Serves 6 to 8

Making this rustic, free-form pie couldn't be more elementary. You still have to know how to prepare the dough and roll it out, but after that it's quite forgiving. The foldover crust requires less fuss than does a pastry shell baked in a pan. Just arrange the sweetened fruit in the center of the dough, then fold the border up and over the filling and bake. Make sure to taste the fruit before you begin, adding more sugar if it tastes very tart.

For crust

　½ RECIPE PÂTE BRISÉE *(page 437), chilled*

　　ALL-PURPOSE FLOUR, *for dusting*

For filling

　1¾ POUNDS RIPE BUT FIRM PLUMS, *pitted and cut into ½-inch wedges (about 3 cups)*

　2 TEASPOONS FRESH LEMON JUICE

⅓ CUP SUGAR *(if plums are very tart, use a little more)*

1 TABLESPOON CORNSTARCH *(or 2 tablespoons all-purpose flour)*

½ TEASPOON COARSE SALT

For finishing

1 LARGE WHOLE EGG *or egg yolk*

1 TABLESPOON HEAVY CREAM

SANDING SUGAR, *for sprinkling (or use granulated sugar)*

Prepare oven and baking sheet Heat oven to 375°F. Line a large rimmed baking sheet with parchment paper or a nonstick baking mat (such as Silpat).

Roll out dough and chill Let dough sit out at room temperature until slightly malleable, about 10 minutes. Roll out on a lightly floured surface into a 14-inch round (it doesn't have to be a perfect circle; the shape can be rough). Transfer to prepared baking sheet by rolling it around the rolling pin, then unrolling onto sheet [1]; refrigerate 15 minutes.

Make filling Mix together fruit, lemon juice, sugar, cornstarch, and salt in a bowl. Remove pastry from refrigerator and arrange fruit over center, leaving a 1½-inch border all around. Fold border over filling, allowing the dough to fall naturally into creases [2].

Finish crust and bake Whisk together egg (or yolk) and cream, and brush over edges of galette. Sprinkle crust generously with sanding sugar [3]. Bake until filling is bubbling in the center and crust is dark golden brown, about 1¼ hours. (It's very important that the juices are bubbling; if they are not, the cornstarch will not be activated and will not thicken the juices.) If a lot of juices have leaked out, run an offset spatula under tart to release it from the sheet. Transfer sheet to a wire rack; cool 15 minutes. Transfer galette to rack, and let cool completely before serving. Galette is best eaten the same day it is baked.

Equipment

Make sure to use a rimmed baking sheet for a galette; a rimless sheet will allow the juices to run over the sides and burn on the oven floor. Line the sheet with parchment paper for easier cleanup.

Forming a Galette

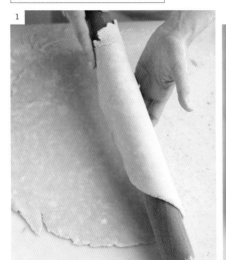

Pie Tips

> Butter is a natural thickener; if your recipe doesn't already call for it, dot a few pats atop the filling after pouring it into the crust.

> Always cut vents in the top crust of the pie to let steam escape during baking, and keep the crust from getting soggy.

> Chill pie thoroughly before baking to ensure crust holds its shape.

> It's important to bake at the precise temperature called for, until the bottom crust is golden brown, and the juices bubble up (this is a sign that the thickening agent has been activated, assuring the filling will set properly).

> Tent pie with foil if crust is browning too quickly.

> Let fruit pies cool completely before cutting and serving, to give the filling plenty of time to set.

DOUBLE-CRUST APPLE PIE Serves 8

When you think of fruit pie, a double-crust beauty with juices bubbling up and out of the top probably comes to mind. And though you will often hear that baking requires precision to turn out right, once you get in the habit of baking fruit pies, you will begin to see an opportunity for some flexibility with the fillings. With a little practice, you can learn to adapt the basic formula depending on what fruit is in season, and to adjust the amount of sugar or thickener (such as flour or cornstarch) based on the juiciness of the fruit. You might even begin to experiment with combinations of fruits, or flavorings such as zests and spices, to suit your own tastes. Apricots and cherries taste great together, as do peaches and blueberries. If you want to combine fresh and dried fruits, try pears with dried sour cherries; up the ante with a pinch of Chinese five-spice powder. In order to get to that improvisational stage, however, you have to start with something very basic, and what's better than starting with the American standard—apple?

For filling

3 POUNDS ASSORTED BAKING APPLES *(such as Granny Smith, Rome, Cortland, Mutsu, Golden Russet, or Empire), peeled, cored, and cut into ½-inch-thick slices*

½ TO ¾ CUP GRANULATED SUGAR

¼ CUP ALL-PURPOSE FLOUR *or 2 tablespoons cornstarch*

1 TABLESPOON FRESH LEMON JUICE

¾ TEASPOON GROUND CINNAMON

¼ TEASPOON GROUND GINGER

½ TEASPOON COARSE SALT

2 TABLESPOONS UNSALTED BUTTER, *cut into pieces*

For crust

ALL-PURPOSE FLOUR, *for dusting*

PÂTE BRISÉE *(page 437), chilled*

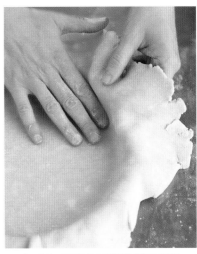

fig. 7.5 FITTING DOUGH INTO PAN

Double-Crust Pie, Step by Step

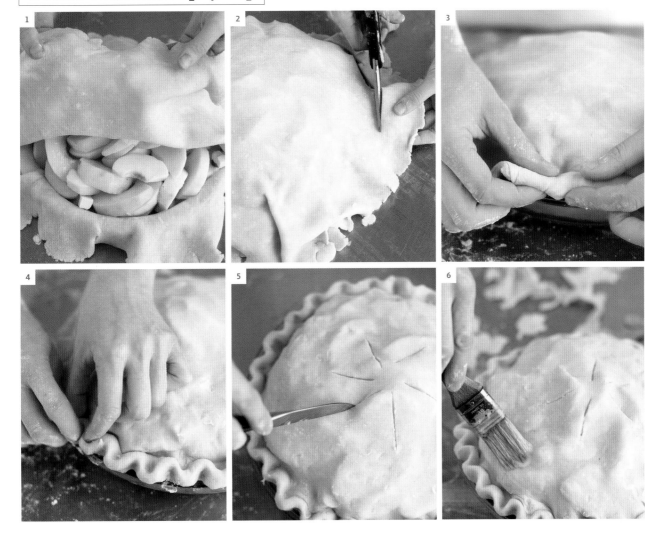

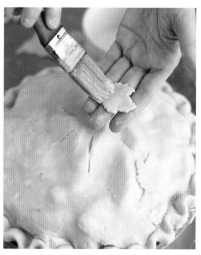

fig. 7.6 EMBELLISHING CRUST

For finishing

1 LARGE EGG YOLK

1 TABLESPOON HEAVY CREAM

FINE SANDING SUGAR, *for sprinkling*

Prepare filling Stir together apples, granulated sugar, flour, lemon juice, cinnamon, ginger, and salt in a large bowl to combine.

Assemble pie On a lightly floured surface, roll out one disk of dough until ⅛ inch thick (and at least 13 inches in diameter). Roll dough around rolling pin and unroll it over a 9-inch glass pie plate, pressing gently to fit into pan *fig 7.5*. Fill with apple mixture. Dot with butter. Roll out remaining disk of dough in the same manner. Drape over filling [1]. Use kitchen shears to trim overhang of both crusts to 1 inch [2]. Press edges to seal. Fold overhang under [3], and crimp edges: With thumb and index finger of one hand, gently press dough against index finger of other hand. Continue around pie [4]. Make several 3-inch slits in top crust [5]. Refrigerate pie 20 minutes. Meanwhile, heat oven to 400°F.

Finish crust and bake Whisk egg yolk and cream in a bowl; brush over top crust [6]. (If desired, use cutters to cut chilled scraps into leaves or other

FRUIT PIES				
	Rhubarb	**Sour Cherry**	**Peach**	**Blueberry**
FRUIT	2¼ POUNDS, TRIMMED AND CUT CROSSWISE INTO ½-INCH PIECES (8 CUPS)	2 POUNDS FRESH, PITTED (6 CUPS), OR 1¾ POUNDS FROZEN AND PARTIALLY THAWED	2¾ POUNDS, CUT INTO ½-INCH WEDGES (8 CUPS)	3 PINTS
LEMON JUICE	1 TABLESPOON	NONE	1 TABLESPOON	1 TABLESPOON
SUGAR	1½ CUPS	1 CUP	½ TO ¾ CUP	½ CUP
THICKENER	¼ CUP PLUS 1 TABLESPOON CORNSTARCH	3 TABLESPOONS CORNSTARCH	¼ CUP CORNSTARCH	3 TABLESPOONS
SEASONING	¼ TEASPOON SALT 1½ TEASPOONS FINELY GRATED LEMON ZEST	¼ TEASPOON SALT ⅛ TEASPOON CINNAMON	¼ TEASPOON SALT ¼ TEASPOON GROUND GINGER	¼ TEASPOON SALT ¼ TEASPOON CINNAMON
BUTTER	2 TABLESPOONS	2 TABLESPOONS	2 TABLESPOONS	2 TABLESPOONS
BAKE	400°F FOR 10 MINUTES; REDUCE TO 375°F; BAKE 50 TO 80 MINUTES MORE.	400°F FOR 10 MINUTES; REDUCE TO 375°F; BAKE 50 TO 80 MINUTES MORE.	400°F FOR 10 MINUTES; REDUCE TO 375°F; BAKE 50 TO 80 MINUTES MORE.	425°F FOR 20 MINUTES; REDUCE TO 375°F; BAKE 40 TO 75 MINUTES MORE.

shapes; adhere to top crust with egg wash *fig. 7.6*. This is a good way to hide imperfections.) Sprinkle with sanding sugar. Place in oven, lining rack below with foil (to catch juices). Bake 10 minutes; reduce heat to 375°F. Continue baking until bottom and top crusts are golden and juices are bubbling in center, 70 to 85 minutes. Tent pie with foil if browning too quickly.

Cool Transfer pan to a wire rack; let cool completely, at least 4 hours (or up to overnight). If keeping pie overnight, tent loosely with foil and store at room temperature; do not refrigerate, which makes crust soggy.

PÂTE SUCRÉE Makes enough for two 4 by 14-inch tarts or two
9- or 10-inch round tarts

Pâte sucrée is another type of pastry dough. The method for making it is the same as for pâte brisée; you just have to add a bit more sugar and a couple of egg yolks. The presence of sugar results in a sturdier crust—ideal for the more structured crusts used for tarts. The flour and butter are processed slightly longer than for pâte brisée, as there should be no pieces of butter remaining. Both sugar and egg soften the dough a bit, making it a little harder to roll out perfectly than pâte brisée; it's easier to patch, however, because any tears can simply be pressed together. Pâte sucrée is often used for blind-baked tart shells (meaning the crust is baked before the filling is added; see note on page 448). Because it is tender (due to the eggs), it will hold its shape better than a flaky crust would. A baked pâte sucrée shell is delightfully crisp, providing a nice contrast to soft, unbaked fillings, such as the panna cotta in the recipe that follows.

2½ CUPS ALL-PURPOSE FLOUR

3 TABLESPOONS SUGAR

¾ TEASPOON TABLE SALT

1 CUP (2 STICKS) COLD UNSALTED BUTTER, *cut into small pieces*

2 LARGE EGG YOLKS, *lightly beaten*

¼ CUP ICE WATER, *plus more if needed*

Combine dry ingredients Pulse flour, sugar, and salt in a food processor to combine (or whisk together by hand in a bowl).

Cut in butter Add butter. Process until mixture resembles coarse meal, 10 to 15 seconds; the butter pieces should be ⅛ inch or smaller, with no pea-size pieces remaining. (Or quickly cut in with a pastry blender or your fingertips.)

Mix in egg yolks Add yolks; pulse to combine (or stir with a fork by hand).

Add water With machine running, add ice water in a slow, steady stream through feed tube until dough just holds together. Do not process longer than 20 seconds; check by stopping machine and pressing some between fingers. Do not wait until dough comes together in machine. (If mixing by hand, slowly add water and stir with a fork until mixture just comes together.)

Form, wrap, and chill Divide in half, and shape into rectangles or disks, depending on shape of tart pan. Wrap in plastic, and refrigerate for at least 1 hour (or up to overnight). Pâte sucrée can be frozen up to 1 month; defrost overnight in refrigerator before using.

Varieties of Berries and Cherries

BLACK RASPBERRIES

SOUR CHERRIES

STRAWBERRIES

SWEET CHERRIES

RED RASPBERRIES

WHITE CURRANTS

GOOSEBERRIES

BLUEBERRIES

RED CURRANTS

PANNA COTTA TART Serves 8

Made with a sturdy pâte sucrée shell, this dessert is a variation on the well-known fruit-topped tarts of traditional French pastry. The most recognizable of those depends on a generous amount of creamy filling such as pastry cream (*crème pâtissière,* page 476) or lemon curd (page 477), topped with a selection of ripe sliced fruits or whole berries. This one uses panna cotta—"cooked cream," thickened with gelatin—instead, which is less rich than butter-thickened fillings. It is also a little less formal than the pâtissèrie tarts, as the fruit is macerated and casually served on the side rather than painstakingly arranged. In fact, the cherries in the photo are intended only as a suggestion; top the tart with any type of macerated fruit you prefer. It's equally delicious unadorned. The crust should be cool before you make panna cotta since the filling needs to set in the shell. The cherries can be macerated up to one hour ahead and refrigerated; however, not more than that because the fruit loses flavor and texture if refrigerated too long, and also will begin to oxidize and brown on the edges.

fig. 7.7 **MAKING PANNA COTTA**

For crust

ALL-PURPOSE FLOUR, *for dusting*

½ RECIPE PÂTE SUCRÉE *(page 445)*

For panna cotta

1 TEASPOON UNFLAVORED POWDERED GELATIN

3 TABLESPOONS COLD WATER

¾ CUP WHOLE-MILK PLAIN YOGURT *or buttermilk*

⅓ CUP HEAVY CREAM

3 TABLESPOONS SUGAR

¼ TEASPOON COARSE SALT

1 VANILLA BEAN, *split lengthwise (see page 469)*

For topping

1½ POUNDS CHERRIES *(a mixture of sweet, white, and sour, if available), pitted and halved*

3 TABLESPOONS SUGAR

1 TABLESPOON FRESH LIME JUICE, *or to taste*

PINCH OF COARSE SALT

Roll out and chill dough On a lightly floured surface, roll out dough into a ⅛-inch-thick rectangle (about 7 by 17 inches). Transfer to a 4 by 14-inch fluted rectangular tart pan with a removable bottom, gently fitting dough into bottom and up sides. Trim dough flush with pan by rolling across top with a rolling pin. Prick bottom of dough all over with a fork (this is called docking, which keeps the dough from puffing during baking). Refrigerate until cold, about 1 hour.

Blind bake Heat oven to 375°F. Line chilled tart dough with parchment paper and fill to top with pie weights or dried beans. Bake until just starting to color around the edges, 20 to 25 minutes. Carefully remove parchment and weights. Return to oven, and bake until center is golden and dry, 12 to 15 minutes more (cover edges with foil if darkening too quickly). Transfer to a wire rack to cool completely. Carefully remove tart shell from pan and place on a baking sheet.

Make panna cotta filling Sprinkle gelatin over the cold water in a small bowl. Let stand until softened (and all water absorbed), about 5 minutes. (This makes it easier for the gelatin to dissolve in the hot cream.) Place yogurt in a medium bowl and whisk to soften and remove any lumps *fig 7.7*. Combine cream, sugar, salt, and vanilla seeds and pod in a small saucepan. Bring to just under a boil, then reduce heat to low. Remove vanilla pod and discard. Whisk softened gelatin into cream mixture, whisking over low heat until completely dissolved. Pour through a fine sieve (to remove any undissolved gelatin) into yogurt, then whisk to combine. Pour panna cotta into cooled tart shell and refrigerate until firm, at least 2 hours (or up to overnight, covered).

Macerate fruit About 30 minutes before you are ready to serve tart, combine cherries, sugar, lime juice, and salt. Stir well, then let stand at room temperature until some of the juices are drawn out of the cherries and the sugar is completely dissolved, about 30 minutes.

Serve Place the fruit mixture in a bowl and serve alongside sliced tart, or spoon it down the center.

BLIND BAKING

Many recipes call for tart shells or pie crusts to be blind baked before they are filled. This step ensures the crust will hold its shape and not become soggy, especially important with unbaked fillings such as the panna cotta here. To do this, fit rolled-out dough into pan, prick all over with a fork, line with parchment paper, and weigh with dried beans (or pie weights). Chill thoroughly before baking, either partially or completely—partially for custards and other fillings that will be baked in the crust, completely for unbaked fillings.

LESSON 7.3
How to Make Meringue

Eggs are a versatile ingredient for a baker, and whipped egg whites, in particular, can do spectacular things, such as adding height to a cake or baking up on their own into a fragile meringue. When making meringue, handle those egg whites with care. Room-temperature whites whip up better than cold ones. Cold eggs, however, are easier to separate, so you might want to separate your eggs right out of the refrigerator (see page 95), then let the whites warm up before you continue with your recipe.

When whipping, start slowly: whip the whites on low to medium speed, and add sugar—gradually—only once soft peaks begin to form. The point is to allow the sugar to dissolve before adding more, to prevent meringue from collapsing. Then increase speed and beat meringue until it is stiff and glossy, but don't overbeat: this can cause curdling (a cottage-cheese–type effect), and create a meringue that won't hold its structure. And remember that one speck of fat, even the tiniest bit of egg yolk, can prevent whites from whipping, so always separate each egg individually, in a separate bowl, and take care to clean and dry your mixing bowl and beaters very well. Last but not least, you need cool, dry conditions to make a baked meringue such as Pavlova (page 452), so avoid attempting one when the weather is hot and humid.

Although an electric mixer is perfectly acceptable, many chefs prefer to beat egg whites by hand, in a copper bowl. A chemical reaction between the copper and the egg whites produces a fluffy, stable foam; beating by hand also reduces the risk of overbeating. Just before using copper, clean it with salt and lemon juice or vinegar, then rinse with cold water and dry thoroughly. If you choose to beat egg whites by hand, a balloon whisk will incorporate more air than narrower whisks, making it easier to beat whites to stiff peaks. A small amount of cream of tartar is added to meringue (especially when not made in a copper bowl) as a stabilizer, lowering the pH of the egg white to counter the effects of overbeating.

ANGEL FOOD CAKE Serves 10 to 12

Delightfully airy and light, this spongy dessert is a good example of the adaptability of a French-meringue base. The cake gets its lift from stiffly beaten egg whites rather than chemical leaveners, such as baking soda or baking powder. (Incidentally, there are no butter or egg yolks either, making the cake fat-free.) Whisking up the perfect meringue is crucial: Overbeating can deflate the whites, and underbeating won't allow enough air to be incorporated. Similarly, don't skimp on sifting; you will need to sift the flour and a portion of the sugar together no fewer than five times in order to achieve a featherlight texture. Mix on medium-high speed (never high) to strengthen the cake's structure. When it comes time to fold in the flour, cut the spatula down through the center of the egg whites, make a sweeping motion up the side of the bowl, then turn spatula over (as if you were making the letter "J"). Repeat until just combined, rotating bowl as you go. Before serving, dust the cake lightly with confectioners' sugar and scatter fresh berries around it; dollop freshly whipped cream alongside each slice.

TYPES OF MERINGUE

There are several types of meringues; each calls for a slightly different technique when it comes to combining the egg whites and sugar, and is suitable for slightly different usages.

French Meringue To make this type, sugar is added to beating egg whites as soon as they reach the soft peak stage. French meringue is usually used to fold into cakes or soufflés or baked into a pavlova or simple meringue cookies.

Italian Meringue For this version, sugar is cooked to 238°F and poured down the side of the bowl while the whites are whisked. This is the most stable and solid of the meringues and is usually used for buttercream and meringue frostings.

Swiss Meringue Egg whites and sugar are heated over a bowl of simmering water until hot to the touch and sugar is dissolved, then beaten to stiff glossy peaks. This step adds volume and stability. Swiss meringue is second in stability after Italian meringue, and is used for buttercream frostings and cookies.

fig. 7.8 SIFTING FLOUR AND SUGAR

Equipment

If using a standing mixer, you will need to gently transfer meringue to a large, wide bowl before folding in the flour.

Angel food cake pans have removable bottoms and legs for easy removal and cooling. A 10-inch tube pan can be used in its place.

A comb cutter is the traditional tool for slicing angel food cake; it keeps the cake from flattening. If you don't have one, use a serrated knife and slice with a sawing motion.

For cake

1 ¼ CUPS SIFTED CAKE FLOUR *(not self-rising)*

1 ½ CUPS GRANULATED SUGAR

12 LARGE EGG WHITES, *room temperature*

½ TEASPOON SALT

1 TEASPOON CREAM OF TARTAR

1 TEASPOON PURE VANILLA EXTRACT

For serving

FRESH RASPBERRIES

CONFECTIONERS' SUGAR

2 RECIPES WHIPPED CREAM *(page 436)*

Heat oven and sift flour Heat oven to 325°F, with rack in lower third of oven. Use a fine sieve to sift together flour and ¾ cup granulated sugar over a sheet of parchment paper or a bowl *fig. 7.8*. Repeat sifting four times.

> ## Angel Food Cake, Step by Step

ANGEL FOOD CAKE

Make meringue Beat egg whites in a large, wide bowl with an electric mixer on low speed until foamy [1]; add salt, cream of tartar, and vanilla. Beat on medium speed until soft peaks form, about 3 minutes. With mixer running, add remaining ¾ cup sugar a little at a time [2], beating no more than 1 minute after each. Raise speed to medium-high and beat until stiff glossy peaks form [3] (when beater is lifted, only the tip of the peak should fall over slightly).

Fold flour into meringue Sift flour mixture over meringue in six parts [4], gently folding in each addition with a flexible spatula [5]. Be careful not to overmix or the egg whites will deflate.

Bake and cool Scrape batter into a 10-inch angel-food pan (or tube pan). Run a knife through the batter to release any large air bubbles [6], and smooth with an offset spatula. Bake until cake is golden brown and springy to the touch, 30 to 45 minutes. Invert pan onto its legs (if using an angel-food pan) or a wire rack, and let cool about 1½ hours. Carefully run a paring knife around side of cake to loosen, then turn out onto the rack.

Serve Place the cake on a serving platter and surround with berries; dust with confectioners' sugar. Slice cake with a comb cutter or serrated knife; serve slices with berries and whipped cream. Cake will keep up to 2 days at room temperature in an airtight container or wrapped well in plastic.

SAVING EGG YOLKS

One way to put yolks to good use is to make lemon curd (page 477) to serve with angel food cake. For a savory alternative, use extra egg yolks to prepare mayonnaise (page 95) or hollandaise sauce (page 96).

If you're not planning to use raw egg yolks right away, refrigerate them up to three days in an airtight container, or freeze up to four months. When refrigerating yolks, press a piece of plastic wrap directly onto the surface to prevent a skin from forming. To prevent them from becoming gelatinous when frozen, add ⅛ teaspoon salt or 1½ teaspoons sugar (add salt to yolks intended for savory dishes and sugar to yolks for baked desserts) to each ¼ cup of yolks (about four). Beat the yolks lightly before mixing in the salt and sugar, and freeze the mixture in an airtight container. Be sure to label the container with the date and number of yolks. When using them in a recipe, use 1 tablespoon of thawed yolk for each large yolk needed.

PAVLOVA Serves 6

To make this Australian dessert—named for Russian ballerina Anna Pavlova, who toured Australia in the 1920s—whipped cream and fresh fruit are layered atop a crisp French-meringue shell. Properly baked, the meringue stays completely white and develops a crunchy outer shell and a soft, marshmallow-like interior. Pavlova is traditionally topped with passionfruit, strawberries, or kiwi fruit, but this recipe features poached apricots and fresh black raspberries. Feel free to top a pavlova with other fresh, macerated, poached, or even roasted fruits.

For meringue shell

4 LARGE EGG WHITES, *room temperature*
PINCH OF SALT
2 TEASPOONS CHAMPAGNE VINEGAR
1 TEASPOON CORNSTARCH
1 CUP PLUS 2 TABLESPOONS SUPERFINE SUGAR
1 TEASPOON PURE VANILLA EXTRACT

Pavlova Tip

Do not try to make pavlova on a hot or humid day. The meringue will brown long before it sets and also will not dry but remain tacky.

For whipped cream

¾ CUP HEAVY CREAM

2 TO 3 TABLESPOONS GRANULATED SUGAR

For topping

1 CUP POACHED APRICOTS *(about 7 apricots; page 490)*

½ CUP FRESH BLACK RASPBERRIES

Prepare oven and pan Heat oven to 200°F, with a rack in lower third. Use an 8-inch bowl as a guide to trace a circle with a pencil onto a piece of parchment. Place the parchment, marking side down, on a baking sheet.

Make meringue In the bowl of an electric mixer fitted with the whisk attachment, beat egg whites on low speed until foamy. Add salt, vinegar, and cornstarch, and beat on medium speed until soft peaks form, about 3 minutes. Add superfine sugar in four additions, beating on medium-high speed until meringue is stiff and glossy, about 5 minutes. Beat in vanilla.

Bake Use a flexible spatula to spread the meringue to fill the marked circle on the parchment *fig. 7.9*, then use the back of a spoon to thin out the center while slightly building up the sides (they should be about 1½ inches high). Bake until the meringue is glossy and hard to the touch, about 1 hour 40 minutes; reduce temperature if the meringue begins to take on color. When meringue has finished cooking, turn off oven and let it cool in oven for at least 2 hours (or up to overnight). The pavlova should lift easily off the parchment *fig. 7.10*.

Assemble pavlova Whip cream and sugar until soft peaks form. Spoon whipped cream into center of pavlova shell, then spread evenly but loosely with the back of the spoon. Top with fruit (or serve fruit on the side).

Serve Cut into slices and serve. Pavlova is best eaten immediately after it is assembled, although you can bake the shell and keep it in an airtight container at room temperature up to 2 days.

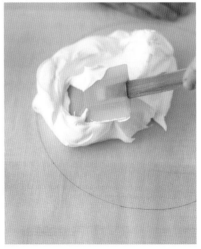

fig. 7.9 SPREADING MERINGUE

fig. 7.10 LIFTING SHELL

ONE-BOWL CHOCOLATE CUPCAKES WITH SWISS MERINGUE BUTTERCREAM Makes 24

Just like a great drop-cookie recipe, every home cook needs a fuss-free cake that can be mixed in a flash and is adaptable enough for layer cakes and cupcakes. One-Bowl Chocolate Cupcakes are so effortless, they don't even warrant their own technique lesson; you simply combine dry ingredients and whisk in a few liquid ones. There is no need for an electric mixer, and best of all, you have to use only one bowl in the process.

1 ¼ CUPS UNSWEETENED DUTCH-PROCESS COCOA POWDER, *plus more for pans*

2 ½ CUPS ALL-PURPOSE FLOUR

2 ½ CUPS SUGAR

2 ½ TEASPOONS BAKING SODA

1 ¼ TEASPOONS BAKING POWDER

1 ¼ TEASPOONS TABLE SALT

ONE-BOWL CHOCOLATE CUPCAKES
WITH SWISS MERINGUE BUTTERCREAM

2 LARGE WHOLE EGGS PLUS 1 LARGE EGG YOLK

1¼ CUPS WARM WATER

1¼ CUPS BUTTERMILK

½ CUP PLUS 2 TABLESPOONS (1¼ STICKS) UNSALTED BUTTER, *melted and cooled*

1¼ TEASPOONS PURE VANILLA EXTRACT

SWISS MERINGUE BUTTERCREAM *(recipe follows)*

Prepare oven and tins Heat oven to 350°F. Line two standard muffin tins with paper cupcake liners.

Combine ingredients In a large bowl, whisk together cocoa, flour, sugar, baking soda, baking powder, and salt. Whisk in eggs, yolk, water, buttermilk, butter, and vanilla until smooth and combined, about 3 minutes.

Bake Divide batter evenly among lined cups, filling each about halfway. Bake cupcakes, rotating tins halfway through, until a cake tester inserted into the centers comes out clean, about 20 minutes.

Cool and frost Transfer to a wire rack; cool 10 minutes, then turn out cupcakes onto rack. Let cool completely before frosting. Unfrosted cupcakes can be stored in an airtight container, up to 3 days at room temperature or frozen up to 1 month.

CHOCOLATE LAYER CAKE

Coat two 8-by-2-inch round cake pans with nonstick cooking spray. Line bottoms with parchment paper rounds; spray parchment. Follow instructions for cupcakes above, dividing batter evenly between prepared pans. Bake, rotating pans halfway through, until a cake tester inserted in the centers comes out clean, about 45 minutes. Transfer pans to a wire rack to cool 10 minutes. Invert cakes onto the rack; peel off parchment. Reinvert cakes, and cool completely, top sides up, before frosting.

SWISS MERINGUE BUTTERCREAM Makes about 6 cups

Of the three types of meringue, Swiss meringue is perhaps the easiest for the home cook to master. This recipe is by no means as simple as the Easy Chocolate Buttercream on page 432, but it is a good next step on the way to more involved icings such as Italian meringue.

You begin by combining egg whites and sugar in a mixing bowl and then whisking them over a pan of simmering water. Because the heat is more gentle, you won't have to use a candy thermometer. Once the sugar has melted, and the egg whites are warm, the bowl is transferred to an electric-mixer stand and the mixture whipped to stiff peaks. When the mixture is completely cool, softened butter is beaten in piece by piece, to create a silky smooth icing. It is ultrarich and delicious, and can be used on cakes that run the gamut from homespun to oh-so-fancy.

1½ CUPS SUGAR

6 LARGE EGG WHITES

PINCH OF SALT

¼ TEASPOON CREAM OF TARTAR

1 POUND (4 STICKS) UNSALTED BUTTER, *cut into tablespoons, room temperature*

1 TEASPOON PURE VANILLA EXTRACT

Heat sugar and eggs Bring a saucepan filled with about 2 inches of water to a simmer. Meanwhile, combine sugar, egg whites, and salt in a large heatproof mixing bowl. Set bowl over (not in) simmering water, and whisk until whites are warm to the touch and sugar is dissolved, 2 to 3 minutes [1]. (Heating the eggs relaxes their proteins, enabling the eggs to whip up higher and more quickly; the sugar also melts, for a silky smooth consistency.) Test by rubbing between your fingers; the mixture should feel smooth.

Whip meringue Attach bowl to a standing electric mixer fitted with the whisk attachment, and beat on low speed until foamy. Add cream of tartar, and beat on medium-high speed until stiff, glossy peaks form and mixture is cooled completely, about 10 minutes.

Mix in butter Reduce speed to medium-low; add butter 2 tablespoons at a time [2], beating to incorporate fully after each addition. Don't worry if the buttercream appears curdled at this point; it will become perfectly smooth again with continued beating. After all the butter has been incorporated, beat in vanilla.

Finish Switch to the paddle attachment. Beat on the lowest speed [3] to reduce air bubbles, 3 to 5 minutes. Let stand, covered with plastic wrap, at room temperature. (If not using the same day, transfer to airtight containers and store in the refrigerator up to 3 days or the freezer up to 1 month. Before using, bring to room temperature; beat with the paddle attachment on the lowest speed until smooth and pliable, about 10 minutes.)

CHOCOLATE SWISS MERINGUE BUTTERCREAM
Follow recipe above, adding 5½ ounces melted and completely cooled semisweet chocolate along with the vanilla.

Swiss Meringue Buttercream, Step by Step

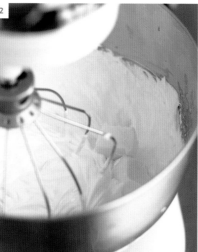

WHITE CAKE WITH LEMON CURD AND ITALIAN MERINGUE Serves 12

White cakes, as opposed to butter cakes like the one on page 428, are made with egg whites only, and they offer another good lesson in how French meringue can help give loft, or leavening, to a cake. (The heat of the oven causes the beaten whites to expand; in this case, they are helped by a chemical leavener, namely baking powder.) It's important to beat the whites until they are stiff but not dry, and to make sure that you fold them into the batter very gently, in parts, so that they retain their volume. First, you fold in just a third of the beaten whites to "lighten" the creamed batter (so it is easier to incorporate the rest without overmixing), then you very gently fold in the rest *fig. 7.11* and quickly transfer the batter to the prepared pans, lest it lose any volume. True to its name, the cake remains pure white inside after baking, save for the brown flecks of flavor-enhancing vanilla seeds.

For cake layers

1 CUP (2 STICKS) UNSALTED BUTTER, *room temperature, plus more for pans*

3 CUPS SIFTED CAKE FLOUR *(not self-rising), plus more for pans*

2 TEASPOONS BAKING POWDER

1 TEASPOON SALT

1¾ CUPS SUGAR

1 VANILLA BEAN, *split lengthwise (page 469)*

fig. 7.11 **FOLDING BEATEN WHITES INTO BATTER**

fig. 7.12 MEASURING CAKE FOR SPLITTING

fig. 7.13 SLICING LAYER IN HALF

fig. 7.14 FILLING A LAYER

1 CUP MILK, *room temperature*

8 LARGE EGG WHITES *(reserve yolks for the lemon-curd filling)*

¼ TEASPOON CREAM OF TARTAR

For filling

1½ CUPS LEMON CURD *(page 477)*

For frosting

ITALIAN MERINGUE *(recipe follows)*

Prepare oven and pans Heat oven to 350°F, with racks in middle. Butter two 8-inch round cake pans, and line bottoms with parchment paper rounds. Butter paper and dust both pans with flour, tapping out excess.

Combine dry ingredients In a mixing bowl, whisk together flour, baking powder, and salt.

Cream butter and sugar In the bowl of an electric mixer fitted with the paddle attachment, beat butter and 1¼ cups sugar until light and fluffy, about 4 minutes, scraping down the sides of the bowl as necessary. Scrape the vanilla seeds into the bowl with a paring knife, reserving pod for another use.

Make batter With mixer on low speed, add dry ingredients in 3 batches, alternating with milk and starting and ending with dry ingredients; scrape down sides of bowl once or twice to ensure proper combining.

Make meringue and fold into batter In the clean bowl of an electric mixer fitted with the whisk attachment, beat egg whites on low speed until foamy. Add cream of tartar, and beat on medium speed until soft peaks form. Gradually add remaining ½ cup sugar, beating on medium-high speed until stiff, glossy peaks form. (Do not overmix the whites; if they appear curdled or broken, the cake will not rise.) Whisk one-third of the whites into the batter to lighten, then carefully fold in the rest of the whites.

Bake and cool Divide the batter between prepared cake pans (about 4 cups batter each). Bake until a cake tester inserted in the centers comes out clean and cakes are just beginning to pull away from sides of pans, 30 to 40 minutes. (Do not overbake.) Transfer pans to wire racks and cool for 10 minutes. Run an offset spatula around the edge of each cake, then invert cakes onto racks. Remove parchment; cool cakes completely. Refrigerate 1 hour or up to overnight, wrapped well in plastic (or freeze up to 1 month).

Fill Reinvert cakes and trim tops with a serrated knife to make level. Using a ruler as a guide, insert toothpicks halfway up side of cake, all around *fig. 7.12*. Slice each cake in half horizontally using toothpicks as your guides *fig. 7.13*. Place one cake layer on a piece of parchment or a cardboard cake round. Top with ½ cup curd, spreading evenly *fig. 7.14*. Top with another cake layer; repeat with remaining curd and cake layers, ending with cake. Let set in refrigerator 2 hours.

Frost Just before serving, frost the top and sides of the cake evenly with Italian meringue.

ITALIAN MERINGUE Makes 4½ cups

Making Italian meringue is a bit tricky, as it involves bringing the sugar syrup up to the right temperature and then immediately pouring it into beaten egg whites in a slow, steady stream. The hot syrup helps make the meringue stable; the higher ratio of sugar to eggs also contributes to its stability (making it ideal for wedding or other display cakes). Lemon juice or vanilla is added here to complement the flavors of the cake, but they are not essential ingredients for Italian meringue.

Equipment

A reliable candy thermometer is crucial.

You will also need a pastry brush for washing down the sides of the saucepan as the sugar syrup cooks, to prevent crystals from forming.

- 1 CUP PLUS 3 TABLESPOONS SUGAR
- ⅓ CUP WATER
- 4 LARGE EGG WHITES
- PINCH OF CREAM OF TARTAR
- PINCH OF SALT
- 1 TABLESPOON FRESH LEMON JUICE *or 1 teaspoon vanilla extract (optional)*

Cook sugar syrup Bring sugar and the water to a boil in a small saucepan, swirling pan to dissolve sugar, and washing down sides of pan with a wet pastry brush to prevent crystals from forming. (Do not stir.) Boil until syrup registers 238°F on a candy thermometer [1].

Meanwhile, whip egg whites Beat egg whites in the bowl of an electric mixer fitted with the whisk attachment on low speed until foamy. Add cream of tartar and salt. Raise speed to medium; mix until soft peaks form. (If the egg whites reach soft peaks before the syrup reaches 238°F, reduce the mixer speed to low. Do not stop mixing, as the meringue will start to separate if not continually mixed. Continuing to mix on high speed, however, could cause the egg whites to be overbeaten.)

Combine syrup and whites With mixer running, slowly pour hot sugar syrup down the side of the mixing bowl, without touching whisk attachment [2]. Mix on medium-high speed until stiff, glossy peaks form and mixture has partially cooled, 5 to 7 minutes. Beat in lemon juice or vanilla. Use immediately.

> **Making Italian Meringue**

How to Make Soufflé

This elegant and notoriously temperamental dish is another preparation that depends on eggs: the whipped whites provide lift to a soft, thick, yolk-rich batter as it bakes. Very shortly after the soufflé comes out of the oven, it loses that lift and the soufflé falls—so a dramatic presentation at the table requires moving quickly. In fact, the most important words in any soufflé recipe might be the last two: serve immediately.

In order to get to that stage, you must start with a good base. For a sweet soufflé, that might be a thick pastry cream. Then you add egg whites, which should be beaten to medium-stiff peaks; if you go too far the whites won't be able to hold their structure and the whole creation will be a flop. The whites should be carefully folded into the base, and the mixture transferred to prepared ramekins or soufflé dishes. That's an important step, too: preparing the dishes properly means buttering them well on every inside surface, then coating them with granulated sugar. This will create texture for the soufflé to "grab onto" as it rises, and help ensure an even result. You can hold your prepared soufflé base for a bit, if you need to, but once you fold in those whites you should bake it right away for the loftiest result.

INDIVIDUAL CHOCOLATE SOUFFLÉS Makes 5

Chocolate soufflé, with its chewy exterior and warm, puddinglike center, might be considered the more refined cousin of molten chocolate cake. With or without a sauce of Crème Anglaise (basically the ice-cream base on page 468 before it's frozen), a soufflé is a showstopper. And although it has earned a reputation for difficulty, following a few key techniques will reward you with a masterpiece every time. Before whipping the egg whites, be sure your bowl and whisk are thoroughly clean and dry; just a drop of grease, yolk, or water will prevent the whites from expanding properly. Avoid overbeating the egg whites; you've taken them too far if they lose their glossiness and become clumpy. Above all else, don't open the oven door until the end of the baking time, since any fluctuation in temperature, as well as an accidentally slammed oven door, can cause a soufflé to fall.

This recipe will produce the best results when baked in five 10-ounce ramekins; you can divide the batter among six dishes, but the soufflés won't reach the same height as those shown here (though they will be just as delicious).

For dishes

> 2 TABLESPOONS UNSALTED BUTTER, *melted*
> SUGAR, *for dusting*

For chocolate base

> 5 OUNCES BEST-QUALITY BITTERSWEET CHOCOLATE (*such as Valrhona 71% cocoa*), *coarsely chopped*
> 2 OUNCES BEST-QUALITY SEMISWEET CHOCOLATE (*such as Valrhona 55% cocoa*), *coarsely chopped*

For batter

> 1½ CUPS WHOLE MILK
> ¼ CUP PLUS 2 TABLESPOONS SUGAR
> 6 LARGE EGG YOLKS

Equipment

A soufflé dish has straight sides that enable the soufflé to climb.

You will need parchment paper and kitchen twine to form a collar that supports the soufflé as it rises. (If you don't have twine, secure the collar with tape.) The collars help the soufflés to rise straight up; you can eliminate this step if you want, but the tops will be uneven.

¼ CUP PLUS 2 TABLESPOONS ALL-PURPOSE FLOUR

1 TEASPOON PURE VANILLA EXTRACT

PINCH OF SALT

For egg whites

8 LARGE EGG WHITES, *room temperature*

⅛ TEASPOON CREAM OF TARTAR *(optional; if not using a copper bowl)*

2 TABLESPOONS SUGAR

Prepare oven and dishes Heat oven to 400°F, with rack in lower third. Do not open oven door until ready to bake. Place five 10-ounce ramekins on a rimmed baking sheet. Brush the inside of the ramekins with melted butter [1]. Dust with sugar and tap out excess [2]. Wrap a strip of parchment paper around each ramekin so that parchment extends 2 inches above the rim [3], and secure with kitchen twine (or tape). Chill in freezer at least 15 minutes.

Melt chocolates Bring about 2 inches of water to a simmer in a medium saucepan. Melt chocolates in a large heatproof bowl set over the simmering water [4] (the bowl should not touch the water, since the slightest drop of condensation can cause the chocolate to seize, or harden). Stir chocolates until smooth.

Make batter Scald the milk (heat it until it's just about to simmer) in a saucepan over medium heat; remove from heat. Combine sugar and yolks [5] in the bowl of an electric mixer fitted with the whisk attachment; beat on high speed until pale [6], about 4 minutes. On low speed, beat in flour. Beat in half the hot milk, ladling it in a little at a time (this is called tempering and prevents the yolks from scrambling). Whisk this mixture into remaining hot milk in pan [7]. Bring to a simmer and cook, whisking, until thickened [8], about 2 minutes. Pour into melted chocolate, stirring to combine, then stir in vanilla and salt. Let cool 10 minutes.

▷ **Preparing Soufflé Dishes**

Chocolate Soufflé, Step by Step

INDIVIDUAL
CHOCOLATE SOUFFLÉS

Whip egg whites In a copper bowl (or use an electric mixer fitted with the whisk attachment), beat egg whites with a handheld whisk until foamy [9]. Add cream of tartar (if using). Continue beating (on medium if using electric mixer) until soft peaks form. Gradually add the sugar [10], beating (on medium-high with mixer) until medium-stiff peaks form [11]. (Do not overbeat or the soufflé will not rise as high; if the eggs are overbeaten, start again.)

Combine custard and whipped whites Whisk one-third of egg whites into the chocolate mixture to lighten until mostly combined [12]. Gently but thoroughly fold in remaining whites.

Bake and serve Carefully spoon mixture into the prepared dishes, dividing evenly. Bake 10 minutes. Reduce heat to 375°F (do not open oven door); bake until set (the outside should look firm), about 13 minutes longer. Remove parchment collars, and serve immediately.

How to Make Génoise

Génoise, a sponge cake, has been popular in European—particularly French—pastry making for more than a century. It serves as the base for petits fours and other shaped cakes, and is a traditional building block for rolled cakes (also called roulades) such as jelly roll and Swiss roll. The finished desserts may look involved, but a basic génoise requires surprisingly few ingredients and is exceptionally sturdy and amenable. After meringue and soufflé, the génoise method is the ideal next step in any dessert-making course, as it illustrates the leavening power of whole eggs, rather than just whites.

Unlike many cakes, which rely on chemical leaveners such as baking powder to attain height in the oven, génoise relies solely on eggs, beaten with sugar until thick and voluminous. Heating the eggs and sugar in a bowl over a pan of simmering water relaxes the egg proteins, enabling the eggs to whip up higher and more quickly. (This process also melts the sugar, resulting in a fine-crumbed cake.) Heat the mixture, whisking, until the eggs are warm to the touch and you can't feel any grains of sugar when you rub the mixture between your fingers. When it comes time to whip the eggs, remember that the more air you incorporate at this stage, the lighter the génoise will be. Beat the eggs on high speed until they are pale white, doubled in volume, and hold a thick ribbon.

Vulnerable to deflation, the batter—and the beaten eggs upon which it's built—can be challenging to work with. To maintain volume, handle these components with care. Add the flour by lightly sifting it over the beaten egg mixture, and folding it gently but thoroughly with a large flexible spatula. Melt and cool the butter completely (warm butter will cause the mixture to collapse), before carefully pouring it down the side of the mixing bowl and into the batter. When you transfer the batter to the baking sheet, the mixture should be thick, not runny, in order to produce the most ethereal result.

JELLY ROLL Serves 8 to 10

For this nostalgic dessert, a génoise cake is baked and spread with raspberry jam and a thick layer of whipped cream before being rolled into a log. If you've never made a rolled cake before, you are in for a surprise: the génoise sheet cake will readily roll up without the slightest resistance (and any slight rips or tears will be concealed with a generous dusting of confectioners' sugar). It's so simple to prepare and so utterly delicious to eat, it's a wonder it ever went out of style. Make it once or twice and you might be inspired to bring it back into fashion.

For cake

- VEGETABLE-OIL COOKING SPRAY
- ⅔ CUP SIFTED CAKE FLOUR (not self-rising), plus more for pan
- PINCH OF SALT
- 3 LARGE WHOLE EGGS PLUS 2 LARGE EGG YOLKS
- ½ CUP GRANULATED SUGAR
- 4 TABLESPOONS (½ STICK) UNSALTED BUTTER, melted and cooled completely
- CONFECTIONERS' SUGAR, for dusting

CHOCOLATE-RUM SWISS ROLL

JELLY ROLL

For filling

1 ¼ CUPS BEST-QUALITY FRUIT JAM, *such as raspberry, strawberry, or blackberry*

1 CUP HEAVY CREAM

For finishing

CONFECTIONERS' SUGAR

Prepare oven and baking sheet Heat oven to 450°F, with rack in bottom half. Coat a 12½- by 17½-inch rimmed baking sheet with cooking spray. Line with parchment paper; coat with cooking spray. Dust with flour, and tap out excess.

Combine dry ingredients Whisk together flour and salt in a bowl.

Combine eggs and sugar Bring about 2 inches of water to a simmer in a medium saucepan. In the heatproof bowl of an electric mixer set over (not in) simmering water, whisk eggs, yolks, and granulated sugar until sugar has dissolved and mixture is warm to the touch [1]. Attach bowl to mixer fitted with

Ingredients

For the most tender crumb, use cake flour; it's a very fine flour made entirely from soft wheat (all-purpose flour, by contrast, is made from a blend of hard and soft wheats).

Jelly Roll, Step by Step

whisk attachment; beat on medium-high speed for 2 minutes. Raise speed to high; beat until mixture is pale and thick [**2**], about 4 minutes more.

Add dry ingredients Sift flour mixture over egg mixture [**3**]; using a large rubber spatula, carefully fold [**4**]. When almost incorporated, pour melted butter down side of bowl [**5**]; gently fold to combine.

Bake Using an offset spatula, spread batter evenly into prepared sheet [**6**]. Bake cake until golden brown and springy to the touch, 6 to 7 minutes. Meanwhile, dust a clean kitchen towel with confectioners' sugar. Run a knife around sides of cake. Invert onto prepared towel, and remove parchment.

Roll into a log and cool While the sheet cake is still warm, gently roll, starting from one short side, into a log, incorporating the kitchen towel [**7**]. Let the cake cool completely, rolled. (This will give the cake a "shape memory," so it will be easier to roll again with filling.)

Fill cake and reroll Unroll cake. Spread with jam, leaving a ½-inch border on all sides. In a mixing bowl with a whisk or electric mixer, whip cream until soft peaks form; spread evenly over jam with an offset spatula [**8**]. Roll cake to enclose filling (without towel), starting at a short end [**9**]. Wrap the towel around rolled cake, securing the clips *fig. 7.15* (or clothes pins) to help retain the shape.

Chill and serve Refrigerate cake 30 minutes (or up to 3 hours). Dust with confectioners' sugar, cut into slices with a serrated knife, and serve.

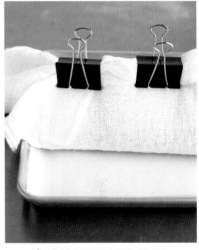

fig. 7.15 **SETTING THE SHAPE**

CHOCOLATE-RUM SWISS ROLL *Serves 8 to 10*

Basically a chocolate génoise rolled around rum-flavored whipped cream, this is another supremely simple dessert that always manages to please. It's a not-too-rich ending for any celebratory meal.

For cake

> VEGETABLE-OIL COOKING SPRAY
> ¼ CUP SIFTED UNSWEETENED DUTCH-PROCESS COCOA POWDER, *plus more for pan*
> ⅓ CUP PLUS 2 TABLESPOONS SIFTED CAKE FLOUR *(not self-rising)*
> PINCH OF SALT
> 3 LARGE WHOLE EGGS PLUS 2 LARGE EGG YOLKS
> ½ CUP SUGAR
> 4 TABLESPOONS (½ STICK) UNSALTED BUTTER, *melted and cooled completely*

For filling

> ¼ CUP WATER
> ¼ CUP PLUS 1 TABLESPOON SUGAR
> 2 TABLESPOONS LIGHT RUM
> 1¼ CUPS HEAVY CREAM

For finishing

> UNSWEETENED DUTCH-PROCESS COCOA POWDER

Mix batter and make cake Follow the directions for Jelly Roll (page 464), dusting pan with cocoa powder instead of flour. For batter, whisk cocoa powder with other dry ingredients before folding into beaten egg-sugar mixture. While cake is baking, dust kitchen towel with cocoa powder. Once baked, roll up cake (incorporating towel) and let cool completely.

Meanwhile, make rum syrup In a small saucepan, combine the water and ¼ cup sugar. Bring to a boil; reduce heat, and simmer until sugar has dissolved, about 3 minutes. Remove from heat; add rum, then let cool completely.

Fill cake and reroll Unroll cake. Brush entire surface generously with cooled rum syrup. Whip cream and remaining tablespoon sugar until soft peaks form; spread over cake, leaving a ½-inch border all around. Roll cake to enclose filling (without towel), starting at a short end. Wrap with towel and secure with clips.

Chill and serve Refrigerate 30 minutes (or up to 3 hours). Serve, dusted with cocoa powder.

LESSON 7.6
How to Make Custard

Mastering the art of making custard opens up the home cook's repertoire to many sophisticated preparations. The velvety texture is a result of the gelling effect of the egg, which, when blended with cream or milk and gently heated, becomes neither solid nor liquid but somewhere in between. The key is to combine the ingredients carefully. Most custards use either whole eggs or just egg yolks, combined with sugar, milk, cream, and flavorings such as vanilla or citrus. Typically, the eggs are beaten, and the milk or cream heated; then comes the delicate part: you need to temper the eggs so they don't curdle.

Fortunately, tempering isn't hard to do. Simply add a ladleful of hot milk or cream to the eggs, and stir well to incorporate. Repeat this a couple of times. This will slowly warm the eggs so they don't cook and form curds. Once the egg mixture is warmed, you can add it to the rest of the hot milk and cook gently, stirring until thick. As an added precaution, in case there are a few small bits of cooked egg in the mix, strain the custard through a sieve before baking it or using it as a base for a sauce or for ice cream. Your custard will be smooth as silk.

VANILLA ICE CREAM Makes about 1½ quarts

Custard serves as an incomparable ice-cream base. Also called French ice cream, frozen custard usually consists of a combination of egg yolks, milk, and cream. What makes it different from other ice cream, such as Philadelphia-style (which contains no egg), is the base, which is a variation of crème anglaise, a cold sauce that often accompanies soufflés, cakes, poached fruit, and meringues. (To make the sauce, simply follow the recipe below, substituting 3 cups whole milk for the skim milk and cream and omitting corn syrup; do not freeze after straining and chilling.)

Unlike many store-bought versions, ice cream made from scratch has a deeply luxurious texture. It's voluminous and soft, able to envelop whatever delectable flavors you plan to blend into it. And as long as you have an ice-cream machine, there's not much to the preparation. It's just a matter of cooking the custard,

Equipment

Ice cream machines with internal condensers are excellent, though they can be expensive. Less costly models should work just fine. If your machine relies on a prefrozen canister, remember to place it in the freezer at least one day ahead (or store it there, if you have the space). For the same reason, it's worth buying an extra canister and freezing both. This way, you can make more than one batch at a time.

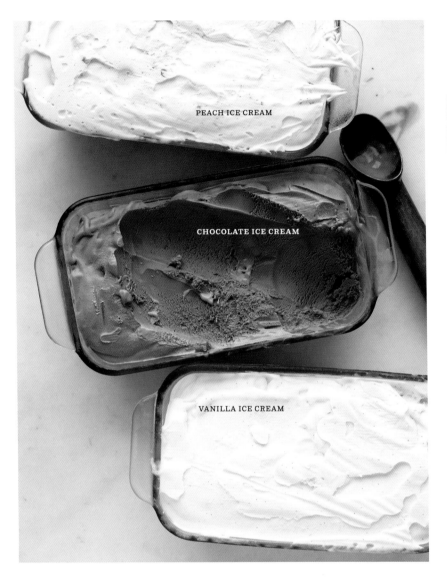

PEACH ICE CREAM

CHOCOLATE ICE CREAM

VANILLA ICE CREAM

USING VANILLA BEANS

Vanilla beans have a deeper, more complex flavor than extract. To expose the tiny seeds, split the pod: Lay it flat on a cutting board, and hold one end while slicing bean open lengthwise with a paring knife. When a recipe calls for the seeds to be scraped, run the tip of the knife along each cut side. And since the pod itself is flavorful, don't toss it out after scraping the seeds. Place a whole pod in a jar of sugar, sealing the lid. Leave it for at least one week, shaking daily to be sure the flavor is absorbed evenly. Use vanilla sugar in baking and to sweeten drinks; it should keep for several months.

chilling it, and then letting the machine handle the bulk of the work. Ice cream has the best texture when it has just finished churning; it's somewhere between soft-serve and regular ice cream. If making ice cream ahead of time, make sure to take it out of the freezer 15 to 30 minutes before serving (depending on the room temperature) to soften slightly.

- 1½ CUPS HEAVY CREAM
- 1½ CUPS SKIM MILK
- ¼ TEASPOON TABLE SALT
- ¾ CUP SUGAR
- 1 VANILLA BEAN, *split lengthwise*
- 6 LARGE EGG YOLKS
- 3 TABLESPOONS LIGHT CORN SYRUP

Ingredients

- Skim milk might seem like an unusual addition, but, when it is combined with heavy cream in the custard base, the resulting texture of the ice cream is light and airy.

- A small amount of corn syrup added to the custard base helps maintain the creamy texture and prevents crystals from forming, particularly when you are adding fruit.

Infuse milk and cream Combine cream, milk, salt, and half the sugar (¼ cup plus 2 tablespoons) in a medium saucepan over medium-high heat. Scrape vanilla seeds with the tip of a small paring knife into pan; add pod. Heat the mixture over medium heat until hot (do not let boil), about 2 minutes. Remove from heat; cover and let stand 30 minutes.

Temper yolks Prepare an ice-water bath. Whisk together yolks and remaining sugar in a medium bowl [1]. Add a ladle of the cream mixture in a slow stream, whisking to combine [2] (this is called tempering and prevents the eggs from curdling). Add another ladle of cream mixture and whisk to combine. Pour this mixture into remaining cream mixture in pan [3]. Cook over medium heat, stirring constantly, until custard is thick enough to coat the back of a spoon (it should hold a line drawn by your finger) [4] and registers 170°F on an instant-read thermometer, 5 to 7 minutes.

> **Ice Cream, Step by Step**

Strain and chill Strain mixture through a fine sieve (to remove vanilla pod and any cooked pieces of egg) into a bowl set in the ice-water bath [5]. Stir in corn syrup. Let stand until cold, stirring occasionally.

Freeze and serve Pour mixture into ice-cream maker. Freeze according to manufacturer's instructions. The ice cream is ready when it will hold its shape when the machine is stopped but it still sags slightly [6]. Serve immediately, or transfer to a chilled container, cover tightly, and freeze up to 3 days.

CHOCOLATE ICE CREAM

Stir 6 ounces melted bittersweet chocolate into warm cream mixture just before tempering yolks, and proceed with recipe.

PEACH ICE CREAM

Reduce sugar to ½ cup and add ½ cup high-quality store-bought jam (or the homemade version that follows), when the ice cream is almost done churning. Just before putting it in the freezer, fold in another ½ cup jam.

PEACH JAM Makes 2 cups

Peaches are used in this very basic recipe for fruit jam, but you could substitute an equal amount of apricots or plums in their place. Add it to ice cream, or use it to fill a jelly roll cake such as the one on page 464. The jam is quickly made and can be kept refrigerated in an airtight container up to 2 weeks. If you prefer, strain the jam in a fine sieve before storing.

1½ POUNDS FRESH PEACHES, *pitted and cut into 1-inch chunks*

1½ CUPS SUGAR

1 TEASPOON FRESH LEMON JUICE

PINCH OF COARSE SALT

PLACE A FEW small plates in the freezer (to test for consistency later). Stir together peaches, sugar, lemon juice, and salt in a large, heavy-bottom pot. Bring to a boil, stirring to dissolve sugar and mashing fruit lightly with a potato masher. Skim foam from surface. Cook, stirring more frequently as jam thickens, until it is the consistency of very loose jelly, 5 to 6 minutes. Remove pot from heat. Drop a spoonful of jam onto one of the chilled plates. Return to freezer for 1 to 2 minutes, then gently nudge edge of jam with a finger. Jam is ready when it holds its shape. If jam is too thin and spreads out, return to the stovetop and boil, stirring frequently and testing every minute, until it reaches the proper consistency.

Equipment

For this recipe, the custards are baked in traditional brûlée dishes, which are shallow (1 inch high) and wide, to allow more surface area for caramelizing the sugar; any individual-size baking dish can be used instead.

You will need a roasting pan to set the ramekins in to create a bain-marie.

A small kitchen propane torch works best to "brûlée" the tops of each custard; you can use your broiler, but it's far more difficult to control the heat and to cook the sugar crust evenly (and to achieve the same degree of caramelization).

CRÈME BRÛLÉE Serves 8

The allure of crème brûlée, French for "burnt cream," lies in its apparent contradiction: a topping of sugar, singed to golden brown, crackles over a cool, creamy-smooth custard. To achieve that silky consistency in baked custards, it's critical that the oven temperature be regulated (to be both even and gentle). This is why the custard molds are set in a bain-marie, or hot-water bath, made by pouring water around molds into a roasting pan, which insulates the custard from hot spots in the oven. Another precautionary measure is to eliminate any excess bubbles in the custard after it is poured into the ramekins (just before baking). These bubbles will rise as the custard bakes, causing holes to form in the top. To get rid of them, pass the flame of a kitchen torch briefly over the liquid in the ramekins. Don't worry if some remain, since the tops will be caramelized, hiding any imperfections.

For custard

- 4 CUPS HEAVY CREAM
- ¾ CUP SUGAR
- 1 VANILLA BEAN, *split lengthwise (see page 469)*
- 7 LARGE EGG YOLKS
- ¼ TEASPOON COARSE SALT

For topping

- ¾ CUP SUGAR

Prepare oven and baking dishes Heat oven to 300°F. Bring a kettle or pot of water to a boil. Place eight 5-ounce baking dishes in a large roasting pan.

Gently heat cream In a medium saucepan, combine cream and half of the sugar (¼ cup plus 2 tablespoons). Scrape vanilla seeds into pan, then add pod. Heat over medium just until mixture starts to bubble around the edge of the pan, 7 to 8 minutes (do not let boil).

Meanwhile, whisk egg yolks In a large mixing bowl, whisk the egg yolks with the remaining sugar (¼ cup plus 2 tablespoons), and the salt.

Temper eggs Use a ladle to pour a small amount of the hot cream mixture into the egg mixture, then whisk to combine. (This is called tempering and prevents the eggs from curdling.) Add two more ladles of cream mixture, one at a time, whisking to combine after each addition. Gradually whisk in remaining cream mixture. Strain through a fine sieve into a large liquid measuring cup (to remove the vanilla pod and any cooked bits of egg).

Bake Divide custard evenly among baking dishes. Place pan in oven. Add enough boiling water to come halfway up the sides of the dishes. Bake until custards are just set (they should tremble slightly in center when shaken), 30 to 40 minutes.

Chill Remove pan from oven. Use tongs to carefully remove dishes from hot-water bath and place on a wire rack for 30 minutes. Then cover with plastic wrap and chill for at least 2 hours (or up to 3 days) before serving. The custards will finish setting in the refrigerator. If you like, transfer the custards to the freezer 15 minutes before serving to ensure they stay cold after being brûléed (this is especially important if using the broiler).

FLAN

CRÈME BRÛLÉE

Caramelize tops and serve Sprinkle about 1½ tablespoons granulated sugar over each custard. Working with one at a time, pass the flame of the torch in a circular motion 1 to 2 inches above the surface of each custard *fig. 7.16* until the sugar bubbles, turns amber, and forms a smooth surface. Serve immediately.

fig. 7.16 CARAMELIZING THE SUGAR ON TOP

FLAN Makes 8

Flan, also known as crème caramel, is very similar to Crème Brûlee (opposite), in that a custard (here made with whole eggs and milk, rather than yolks and cream) is combined with a layer of caramel. But with flan, the caramel is poured into the dish before the custard is added; once the custard has baked and chilled, it is inverted before serving, so the caramel—which first hardens and then turns to liquid again in the warm oven—on the bottom becomes a sauce on top.

There are two critical steps in making the caramel: First is to prevent the sugar from crystallizing. The second is to stop the caramel from cooking any more as soon as it has reached the desired color. Combining the sugar with water at the outset makes it much less likely to crystallize, so long as the sugar is dissolved (adding lemon juice can also help). Also, avoid stirring the mixture, as crystals can form on the spoon; swirl the pan to dissolve the sugar instead. Finally, keep a pastry brush and small bowl of water within easy reach for washing away any crystals that form on the sides of the pan, and set up an ice bath, to help stop the cooking when the time comes.

For caramel

¾ CUP SUGAR

¼ CUP WATER

JUICE OF HALF A LEMON *(optional)*

For custard

3 CUPS WHOLE MILK

¾ CUP SUGAR

4 LARGE WHOLE EGGS PLUS 3 LARGE EGG YOLKS

¼ TEASPOON COARSE SALT

1 TEASPOON PURE VANILLA EXTRACT

Prepare oven and ramekins Heat oven to 325°F. Place a small bowl of cold water and a pastry brush near the stovetop, and prepare an ice-water bath. Place eight 4-ounce ramekins in a large roasting pan. Bring a large kettle or pot of water to a boil.

Make caramel In a saucepan over medium-high heat, stir together sugar, water, and lemon juice (if using), stirring to combine [1]. Do not stir again. Cook, washing down sides of pan with a pastry brush dipped in water to prevent crystals from forming [2], until caramel is amber [3], about 8 minutes, swirling pan to color evenly. Remove from heat, and immerse bottom of pan in ice-water bath [4] for 3 seconds to stop cooking. Dry bottom of pan. Working quickly, pour about 1 tablespoon caramel into each ramekin [5], swirling each to coat bottoms evenly.

Make custard In a small saucepan, heat milk with half the sugar (¼ cup plus 2 tablespoons) over medium heat just until mixture starts to steam and bubble around the edges, 5 to 6 minutes (do not let it boil).

Meanwhile, whisk egg yolks In a large mixing bowl, whisk together the eggs, yolks, remaining sugar (¼ cup plus 2 tablespoons), and salt.

Temper eggs Add a ladle of hot milk mixture to the egg mixture and whisk to combine. (This is called tempering and it prevents the eggs from curdling.) Add two more ladles of milk mixture, one at a time, whisking to combine after each addition. Gradually whisk in remaining milk mixture.

Strain Strain through a fine sieve into a large liquid measuring cup or a bowl (to remove any cooked bits of egg). Stir in vanilla.

Bake Divide custard evenly among ramekins [6]. Place pan in oven. Add enough boiling water to pan to come halfway up the sides of ramekins [7]. Bake until

Equipment

You will need a pastry brush for washing down the sides of the pan as well as eight 4-ounce ramekins, and a large roasting pan that can hold all the ramekins for the bain-marie (water bath).

Flan, Step by Step

custards are just set (they should tremble slightly in center when shaken), 35 to 42 minutes.

Chill and serve Remove pan from oven. Use tongs to carefully remove ramekins from hot-water bath and place on a wire rack for 30 minutes. Then cover with plastic wrap and chill for at least 8 hours (or up to 3 days). To unmold, run a sharp knife around inside of ramekins [8], and place a rimmed serving plate upside down over the top of each. Invert, and gently lift ramekin to remove [9]. Serve immediately.

Variation To make a large flan, prepare caramel as directed above and pour into an 8-inch round cake pan. Top with custard, then set pan in a hot-water bath and bake, chill, and serve as directed above.

EXTRA CREDIT
Pastry Cream and Lemon Curd

Because it is cooked on the stove, unlike flan and other baked custards, pastry cream (crème pâtissiére)—along with crème anglaise (see note on page 468)—is called a stirred custard. Though not technically a custard, fruit curd is similar in that it is also "set" with eggs; the difference is that curd doesn't include milk or cream. The cooking method is comparable (minus the need for tempering) and results in an equally creamy texture. These two classic "custards" also play comparable roles in dessert-making, especially as fillings for cakes, tarts, and other pastries, so it makes sense to combine them into one extra credit lesson.

PASTRY CREAM Makes about 1¾ cups

Unlike crème anglaise, which is pourable, pastry cream is intended to hold its shape, requiring the addition of starch for structure (cornstarch is preferred over flour for producing a silkier texture). For this reason, pastry cream must be brought to a full boil to activate the starch and ensure proper thickening. Contrary to its name, pastry cream contains no cream, only milk; butter is added at the end for richness. Pastry cream is used to fill tarts, cream pies (such as Boston or banana), pâte à choux (cream puffs, éclairs, and profiteroles), and puff-pastry confections, notably napoleons and mille-feuille.

2 CUPS WHOLE MILK

½ CUP SUGAR

½ VANILLA BEAN, *split lengthwise and seeds scraped (see page 469)*

    PINCH OF SALT

3 LARGE EGG YOLKS

3 TABLESPOONS PLUS 1½ TEASPOONS CORNSTARCH

2 TABLESPOONS UNSALTED BUTTER, *cut into small pieces*

Simmer milk and flavorings Bring milk, ¼ cup sugar, vanilla seeds, and salt to a simmer in a saucepan over medium heat, whisking to disperse seeds.

Temper eggs Whisk egg yolks and remaining ¼ cup sugar in a medium bowl. Whisk in cornstarch, 1 tablespoon at a time. Ladle ½ cup hot-milk mixture into yolk mixture, whisking [1]. Add remaining milk mixture, ½ cup at a time. Pour mixture into pan [2], and heat over medium-high, whisking constantly, until mixture comes to a full boil and is thick enough to hold its shape when lifted with a spoon [3], about 2 minutes. Stir in butter and vanilla.

Chill Remove from heat and pour mixture into a bowl; place plastic wrap directly on surface to prevent a skin from forming. Refrigerate until cold, at least 2 hours (or up to 2 days).

> ### Pastry Cream, Step by Step

LEMON CURD Makes about 1¾ cups

A high proportion of lemon juice gives curd its intense flavor. Since it is an acidic ingredient, it also prevents the yolks from curdling, eliminating the extra step of tempering. Lemon curd makes a delicious filling for a cake like the one on page 457 but it's equally welcome spread into a tart shell or on slices of pound cake or Buttermilk Shortcakes (page 433). Gelatin is added primarily to make a sturdier cake filling; leave it out if you are making the curd to serve on its own. Other citrus curds can be made using the formula below; replace ½ cup of the lemon juice with other fresh citrus juice and use an equal measure of zest.

- 2 TABLESPOONS COLD WATER *(optional; only if using gelatin)*
- ½ TEASPOON UNFLAVORED POWDERED GELATIN *(optional)*
- 4 LARGE WHOLE EGGS PLUS 6 LARGE EGG YOLKS
- 1 CUP SUGAR
- FINELY GRATED ZEST OF 2 LEMONS (ABOUT 5 TEASPOONS) PLUS ¾ CUP FRESH LEMON JUICE *(from 5 or 6 large lemons)*
- 6 TABLESPOONS (¾ STICK) UNSALTED BUTTER, *cut into small pieces and well chilled*

Dissolve gelatin (if using) Pour water into a small bowl, then sprinkle with gelatin; let stand until gelatin has softened and all water is absorbed, about 5 minutes.

Ingredients

Lemons should feel heavy for their size, with thin smooth skins. Those with thick, bumpy skins are usually less juicy. Before juicing a lemon, roll it on a countertop to soften the membranes slightly before cutting and juicing; this helps it to release more juice.

Lemon Curd, Step by Step

fig. 7.17 STRAINING CURD

Cook curd In a small, heavy-bottom saucepan, whisk together eggs and yolks. Add sugar and lemon zest and juice. Cook over medium-low heat, whisking constantly [1], until thick enough to coat the back of a wooden spoon (it should hold a line drawn by your finger) [2], 8 to 10 minutes.

Thicken curd Remove pan from heat and add the gelatin mixture (if using), stirring until dissolved. Stir for a few minutes to cool slightly. Stir in butter a few pieces at a time [3], stirring until smooth after each addition.

Strain and chill Strain through a fine sieve into a bowl (to remove any undissolved bits of gelatin and egg), pressing with a flexible spatula to remove as much curd as possible *fig. 7.16*. Press a piece of plastic wrap directly onto the surface to prevent a skin from forming, and refrigerate until set, at least 2 hours (or up to overnight). Whisk until smooth before using.

LESSON 7.7
How to Make Pâte à Choux

Cream puffs usually look as if they came from a pastry shop, but the pastry dough itself, pâte à choux, is so simple to prepare, you should master it at home with your first batch. Also known as cream-puff pastry, the French pâte à choux loosely translates to "cabbage dough." As the pastries bake in the oven and puff up in little rows, their resemblance to a cabbage patch is undeniable. Unlike pâte brisée, pâte à choux requires no rolling and no guesswork about the proportions of cold butter or ice water. Mix the dough on the stovetop, pipe it onto a baking sheet, and it's ready for the oven. (The lined baking sheets can be marked with flour-dipped cookie cutters first to help guide you in piping dough into uniform shapes. Space the circles two inches apart. *fig. 7.18*) Pâte à choux is also the foundation for éclairs, savory hors d'oeuvres called gougères, and the towering

pyramid of pastry known as croquembouche, and is ideal for cream-filled pastries because, as it bakes, the dough puffs up and forms a pocket inside. The moisture of the eggs in the dough turns to steam and is trapped within, causing a slight hollow inside a shell that is golden brown and crisp on the outside.

CREAM PUFFS Makes about 3 dozen

For pâte à choux

 1 CUP WATER, *plus more as needed*

 ½ CUP (1 STICK) UNSALTED BUTTER

 1 TEASPOON GRANULATED SUGAR

 ½ TEASPOON TABLE SALT

 1 CUP ALL-PURPOSE FLOUR

 4 TO 5 LARGE EGGS

fig. 7.18 MARKING BAKING SHEETS
FOR PIPING

For puffs

- 1 LARGE EGG
- 1 TABLESPOON WATER
- SUNFLOWER OR OTHER NEUTRAL-TASTING OIL, *for plastic wrap*
- ⅓ CUP HEAVY CREAM
- 1 RECIPE PASTRY CREAM *(page 476)*

For finishing

- CONFECTIONERS' SUGAR *(optional)*
- BERRY GLAZE *(optional; recipe follows)* OR CHOCOLATE GLAZE *(optional; recipe follows)*

Prepare oven and baking sheets Heat oven to 400°F, with a rack in the center. Line two baking sheets with nonstick baking mats.

Make pâte à choux Combine the water, butter, sugar, and salt in a medium saucepan over medium-high heat. Bring to a boil, and immediately remove from

Cream Puffs, Step by Step

heat. Using a wooden spoon, stir in the flour [1]. When flour is combined, return to heat. Dry the mixture by stirring constantly over heat until it pulls away from the sides and a film forms on the bottom of the pan [2], about 4 minutes. Transfer mixture to the bowl of an electric mixer fitted with the paddle attachment, and mix on low speed, about 2 minutes, until slightly cooled. Add 4 eggs, one at a time, on medium speed [3], letting each one incorporate completely before adding the next. Test the batter by touching it with a flexible spatula or your finger, then lifting; it should form a string [4]. If a string does not form, lightly beat the last egg and add it, a teaspoon at a time, until the batter is smooth and shiny. If you have added all the egg and the batter still doesn't form a string, add water, 1 teaspoon at a time, until it does.

Pipe Fill a pastry bag fitted with a plain round ¾-inch tip (such as Ateco #806) with pâte à choux, and pipe 1½-inch rounds (¾ inch high) onto baking sheets [5]. Beat together egg and the water; use your finger to rub egg wash over entire surface, being careful not to let it drip onto the baking sheet (it will inhibit rising), and flatten tips [6].

Bake Cover one sheet with lightly oiled plastic wrap, and place in refrigerator. Bake the other sheet 15 minutes; reduce oven heat to 350°F. Bake about 20 minutes more, or until puffs are golden brown. Transfer to a wire rack to let cool completely. Return oven heat to 400°F, and repeat process for remaining batch.

Fill and finish Whip heavy cream to medium peaks in a small bowl. Stir pastry cream to soften. Add whipped cream to pastry cream in two batches, folding to combine after each. Fill a pastry bag fitted with a coupler and plain round tip (such as Ateco #806). Insert tip into the underside of each cream puff, and fill *fig. 7.19*. Cool completely before dusting with confectioners' sugar or dipping tops in glaze, as desired.

fig. 7.19 FILLING CREAM PUFFS
WITH PASTRY CREAM

BERRY GLAZE Makes about ¾ cup

- 1½ CUPS SIFTED CONFECTIONERS' SUGAR
- 2 TABLESPOONS STRAINED RASPBERRY OR OTHER RED PRESERVES
  PINCH OF SALT
- 1 TABLESPOON WATER, *plus more if needed*
- 1 TEASPOON FRESH LEMON JUICE

STIR TOGETHER ingredients in a medium bowl until smooth. Add more water, ½ teaspoon at a time, stirring to achieve desired consistency. Glaze can be stored in an airtight container at room temperature up to 3 days.

CHOCOLATE GLAZE Makes about ¾ cup

- ¼ CUP WATER
- ¼ CUP LIGHT CORN SYRUP
- ½ CUP SUGAR
- 4½ OUNCES SEMISWEET CHOCOLATE, *finely chopped*

COMBINE WATER, corn syrup, and sugar in a small bowl. Stir over medium-high heat until sugar is dissolved. Bring mixture to a boil, washing sides of pan with a wet pastry brush to prevent crystals from forming. Once at a boil, remove from heat; add chocolate. Let stand 2 minutes; stir gently until smooth.

LESSON 7.8
How to Make Sorbets and Granitas

Making sorbets and granitas is no-heat (or almost no-heat) cooking at its best. Sorbet is a nothing more than a combination of fruit puree or juice with water and simple syrup, which is chilled and then frozen in an ice-cream maker. In this section, you'll find a handy chart of sorbet recipes using a variety of fruits.

A granita, by contrast, is really just fruit juice and sugar syrup, with an optional dash of flavoring, combined and frozen. No ice-cream maker is required: just freeze the mixture in a pan, then scrape with a fork into icy crystals for serving — the ultimate in easy, sweet refreshment.

With both of these frozen treats, the key is to experiment with different fruits and flavorings, discovering how they combine and complement one another. Learn the basics and you can serve a different frozen dessert for any occasion.

WATERMELON SORBET Makes about 1 quart

Because no two batches of fruit have the same sweetness, it's important to adjust the mix before freezing. This will affect more than flavor because sugar lowers the freezing point of water; so the sweeter your mix, the slushier your sorbet. Too little sugar and the sorbet will be icy hard. Some chefs use a saccharometer (which gauges a liquid's density by how much of the instrument floats above the surface), but a large uncooked egg stands in quite well (see step 4, opposite).

Watermelon is one of the simplest flavors to make, since it requires no added water. Follow the amounts in the chart on page 485 to make the suggested flavor variations. When using only juice, you can skip the first step. Citrus fruit can be squeezed by hand. For the kiwi and pineapple sorbets, you will need to add fresh lime or lemon juice along with water in the first step. All liquids should be strained into a deep bowl or plastic container as directed. If desired, add up to 3 tablespoons of other flavorings such as liqueur before adding the simple syrup.

> 3 CUPS CUBED WATERMELON (*about one-eighth of a whole melon*)
> 1 CUP SIMPLE SYRUP *(page 485), plus more if needed*

Make puree and strain Place fruit (and water, when using) in a food processor [1], and process until very smooth [2]. Pass through a fine sieve into a deep bowl or a large glass measuring cup, pressing on solids with a flexible spatula to extract as much liquid as possible [3]. Don't press too hard, or some of the seeds (if there are any) may be forced through the strainer into the liquid. Discard any solids that remain in the strainer.

Sweeten puree and chill Transfer strained puree (or, for citrus sorbets, strained juice) to a deep bowl or plastic storage container. Add simple syrup (start with 1 cup syrup, then add more as needed) and stir until it is well combined. (To determine whether you need more syrup, gently drop a just-cleaned and dried egg into puree and push to submerge completely; when the sugar content is right, a piece of egg about the size of a quarter should be exposed [4]. If the egg doesn't float to the top, add more syrup; if too much egg is exposed, add more fruit puree.) Cover bowl or container, and refrigerate until completely chilled before freezing, at least 1 hour (or overnight).

Freeze Pour mixture into an ice-cream maker and freeze according to manufacturer's instructions [5]. Transfer sorbet to a large airtight container; freeze at least 2 hours (or overnight) before serving.

> ## Watermelon Sorbet, Step by Step

LEMON SORBET

GRAPEFRUIT GRANITA

WATERMELON SORBET

FRUIT SORBET RECIPES

Fruit	Make the Flavor Base (each yields 2 cups)	Add Simple Syrup
BERRIES	Puree together; then strain.	
BLACKBERRY	4 CUPS BLACKBERRIES *(1 ⅛ pounds)* + ¼ CUP WATER	2 CUPS
STRAWBERRY	5 CUPS CHOPPED STRAWBERRIES *(1 ⅓ pounds)* + ¼ CUP PLUS 2 TABLESPOONS WATER	1 ¼ CUPS
RASPBERRY	6 CUPS RASPBERRIES *(1 ⅔ pounds)* + ½ CUP PLUS 4 TABLESPOONS WATER	1 ¾ CUPS
BLUEBERRY	5 CUPS BLUEBERRIES *(1 ⅔ pounds)* + ¼ CUP PLUS 2 TABLESPOONS WATER	1 ¼ CUPS
CITRUS	Squeeze juice from the following, then strain.	
LEMON	8 LEMONS	1 ½ CUPS
ORANGE	5 ORANGES	1 ¼ CUPS
LIME	8 LIMES	1 ½ CUPS
GRAPEFRUIT	2 ½ GRAPEFRUIT	1 ¼ CUPS
TROPICAL	Puree together; then strain.	
MANGO	6 CUPS CHOPPED *(3 mangoes)* + ¼ TO ½ CUP WATER *(depending on juiciness)*	1 ¼ CUPS
KIWI	4 CUPS CHOPPED *(16 kiwi)* + ½ CUP WATER + 1 TABLESPOON FRESH LIME JUICE	1 ¼ CUPS
PINEAPPLE	3 CUPS CHOPPED *(⅔ pineapple)* + ¼ CUP WATER + 1 TABLESPOON FRESH LIME JUICE	1 ¼ CUPS

SIMPLE SYRUP Makes 1 quart

Simple syrup has countless uses—here it is combined with fruit to make frozen desserts, but it can also be used to poach fruits (see page 489) and to sweeten iced tea, lemonade, and cocktails.

    3 CUPS SUGAR
    3 CUPS WATER

In a large saucepan, bring the sugar and the water to a boil over medium-high heat. Cook, stirring occasionally, until sugar has completely dissolved, about 10 minutes. Let cool. Use immediately, or transfer to an airtight container, and refrigerate up to 2 months.

Variation To infuse Simple Syrup with tender herbs such as basil, mint, or tarragon sprigs, ladle syrup over ½ bunch of herbs and let steep at least 30 minutes (and up to 2 hours, depending on desired strength). For other flavorings, such as sliced fresh ginger, cinnamon sticks, strips of citrus peel, and vanilla bean, it helps to bring the syrup to a simmer with the aromatics first, before steeping. Strain syrup, discarding aromatics, before using.

fig. 7.20 FLAVORING SIMPLE SYRUPS

fig. 7.21 SCRAPING GRANITA

GRAPEFRUIT GRANITA Makes about 3 cups

Fresh citrus juice is ideal for making granita; it is easy to extract and it freezes particularly well. For variety, use an equal amount of any type of citrus juice in place of grapefruit. Campari lends a pleasant bitterness and dash of color to grapefruit granita; add 3 tablespoons to the proportions below. To make apple granita, puree four peeled and cored apples in a food processor with ½ cup water and the juice of one lemon (to preserve the color); strain, and you should have 2 cups juice. For watermelon granita, puree about 3 cups cubed melon in a processor; strain.

> 2 CUPS STRAINED FRESH GRAPEFRUIT JUICE
> 1 CUP SIMPLE SYRUP (page 485)

COMBINE ALL INGREDIENTS in a deep-sided metal baking pan. Freeze, uncovered, until mixture is nearly set, at least 4 hours, whisking mixture every hour. Remove mixture from freezer and scrape surface with the tines of a fork *fig. 7.21* until it is the texture of shaved ice. (Mixture can be frozen overnight without whisking; remove from freezer in the morning, and let sit at room temperature about 10 minutes to allow it to slightly soften before scraping with a fork as instructed.)

EXTRA CREDIT
Cooking Fruit

There's nothing fresher and easier to offer at the end of a meal than a bowl of perfectly ripe, in-season fruit. Most culinary experts agree, in fact, that fruit is at its very best and most nutritious when you leave it alone and simply eat it raw. That doesn't mean, however, that the flavors and textures of fresh fruit can't be enhanced by a variety of cooking methods. Almost any fruit can be cooked, and it's a nice option if the fruit you have on hand is less than perfect. A little heat and sugar can transform a slightly too tart, slightly underripe (or overripe) fruit into a tantalizing dessert. It's also just the solution when you've made a trip to an orchard or farm stand and have bushels of fruit on hand—much more than you can consume by simple snacking. To cook fruit on its own, there are three primary techniques to know: roasting, poaching, and caramelizing. After familiarizing yourself with these basic techniques, consider the recipes that follow as jumping-off points, and have fun from there.

ROASTING FRUIT

Roasting is an extremely easy way to cook fruit. It is done in the oven, at a high heat, and has the effect of drawing out the fruit's sweetness and transforming its texture. A small amount of sugar tossed with the fruit helps it maintain its shape while it cooks, and encourages the caramelizing process. A couple of table-spoons of butter contribute flavor and moisture. Finally, sprinkle the fruit with a bit of fresh lemon juice at the end, for brightness. All kinds of fruit can be roasted, but this technique is particularly successful with stone fruit (apricots, peaches, plums, and nectarines) and pineapple. You can alter the flavor of roasted fruit with aromatics. Hearty fresh herbs such as rosemary are welcome additions, especially with pineapple, but take care to use only a couple of sprigs—anything more will be overpowering.

ROASTED PINEAPPLE Serves 4 to 6

1 MEDIUM PINEAPPLE *(about 1½ pounds)*

⅓ CUP SUGAR

¼ TEASPOON COARSE SALT

2 TABLESPOONS UNSALTED BUTTER, *cut into pieces*

1 SPRIG ROSEMARY *(optional)*

Prepare oven and fruit Heat oven to 450°F. Cut top and bottom ends off pineapple, then stand it on end and cut off skin (following the curve of the fruit). Remove "eyes" with the tip of the knife. Cut pineapple in half lengthwise; cut lengthwise into 1-inch-wide spears. Cut out core and discard.

Roast Stir together sugar and salt and sprinkle evenly over both sides of pineapple pieces. Arrange pineapple in a single layer on a rimmed baking sheet. Dot evenly with butter; add rosemary. Roast, turning over twice during cooking and brushing with pan juices, until fruit is soft and browned in spots, about 45 minutes. Serve fruit warm or at room temperature.

Varieties of Stone Fruits

PEACHES

DONUT PEACHES

NECTARINES

BLACK PLUMS

APRICOTS

RED PLUMS

ITALIAN PLUMS

DINOSAUR PLUMS

POACHED APRICOT HALVES

POACHING FRUIT

To poach fruit means to cook it in liquid, often a simple syrup, at a low simmer to achieve a soft, tender result. Since fruits break down quickly when exposed to heat, and the addition of liquid expedites this process, it's important not to boil the fruit unless complete disintegration is what you're after. You could poach fruit in plain water, but simple syrup adds more than flavor; sugar helps to support the structure of the fruit as it cooks, so it breaks down more slowly, softening but not completely losing its shape. This is a nice choice if you want to serve the warm fruit with ice cream or a slice of cake. Good fruits for poaching include stone fruits such as peaches, nectarines, plums, apricots, and cherries; the method also works well for figs, pineapples, quince, and pears (remove the core from the bottom first). You can also poach assorted dried fruits to soften them and infuse them with flavor.

The technique is simple: Make a simple syrup by bringing equal parts water and granulated sugar to a boil, reduce to a simmer, add fruit, cover with parchment (to keep moisture in), and simmer until tender. Once you've mastered the basics, you're ready to begin experimenting with the poaching liquids and flavorings. Swap some or all of the water with red or white wine, Champagne, or Port (this is particularly delicious with figs). And try adding different herbs and spices or other aromatics to the poaching liquid to suit the fruit (and your tastes). Favorite flavorings include vanilla beans, cardamom pods, black peppercorns, whole cloves, bay leaves, dried chamomile flowers, sliced fresh ginger, cinnamon sticks, star anise, and citrus peels.

fig. 7.22 POACHING FRUIT

fig. 7.23 COVERING WITH PARCHMENT

POACHED APRICOTS Makes 12

When poaching delicate fruit, such as apricots and peaches, use a large shallow pan so the fruit can be in a single layer, rather than piled on top of each other. Also, keep the fruit submerged in poaching liquid with a round of parchment paper to prevent it from turning brown. After you serve the fruit, mix the poaching liquid with seltzer water to make a refreshing apricot fizz.

3 CUPS WATER

3 CUPS SUGAR

3 STRIPS (EACH ABOUT ½ BY 2 INCHES) FRESH LEMON PEEL

6 SLICES (¼ INCH THICK) PEELED FRESH GINGER

1 CINNAMON STICK

1 TABLESPOON FRESH LEMON JUICE

12 SMALL RIPE APRICOTS, *halved and pitted*

Make poaching syrup Cut a piece of parchment paper to fit inside a large straight-sided skillet. In the same skillet, stir to combine the water, sugar, lemon peel, ginger, and cinnamon stick. Bring mixture to a boil over high heat, and cook until sugar dissolves. Reduce heat to low. Simmer (uncovered) until liquid has thickened slightly, about 10 minutes. Stir in lemon juice.

Poach fruit Add apricots to pan *fig. 7.22*. Place parchment round on top of fruit *fig. 7.23*. Return to a simmer and cook until apricots soften slightly (this will depend on the ripeness of the fruit).

Cool Remove from heat and let cool completely (the fruit will continue to soften a bit as it cools). Use immediately, or transfer fruit and poaching liquid to a storage container. Make sure fruit is completely submerged in liquid. Refrigerate until ready to use, up to 4 days.

CARAMELIZING FRUIT

Caramelizing fruit is as quick and as simple as can be. This technique is great for figs, but it works equally well with peaches, plums, pears, apples, and bananas. Cut the fruit (halve and pit stone fruits, slice apples and pears and other larger fruit), dip it in sugar, and place fruit sugar side down in a pan over medium-high heat. The caramelizing is complete in just a few minutes, in most cases. Then, after turning the fruit over, all you need do is deglaze the pan (using wine or liqueur or a flavorful vinegar) to produce a rich, glossy sauce. Port wine (or balsamic vinegar) is an ideal deglazing liquid for figs, rum for pineapple and banana, brandy for apricots and peaches, and poire William (a pear liqueur) for pears. If you like, swirl a tablespoon or two of butter into the pan to create a richer and more unctuous sauce. Serve the fruit over ice cream or yogurt or alongside slices of pound or sponge cake. Naturally, the fruit is also delicious on its own.

7.24 DIPPING IN SUGAR

fig. 7.25 CARAMELIZING IN PAN

CARAMELIZED FIGS Makes about 12

¼ TO ½ CUP SUGAR

¼ TEASPOON COARSE SALT

1 PINT FIGS *(about 12 ounces or a dozen figs), halved lengthwise*

¼ CUP RUBY OR TAWNY PORT WINE, MARSALA WINE, OR BALSAMIC VINEGAR

2 TABLESPOONS UNSALTED BUTTER, *room temperature*

1 TEASPOON FRESH LEMON JUICE

Caramelize fruit Stir together sugar and salt in a shallow bowl. Press cut side of each fig half into sugar mixture to coat *fig. 7.24*. Heat a large skillet over high heat. Add figs, cut sides down, and cook until sugar and juices caramelize, 3 to 4 minutes, turning over fruit as it browns and shifting position of pan over burner, if necessary, to evenly cook fruit *fig. 7.25*.

Deglaze pan and make sauce Remove skillet from heat and add port. Return to heat and cook to reduce syrup, about 30 seconds, carefully scraping up caramelized bits on bottom of pan. Remove from heat and add butter. Add lemon juice; swirl to combine. Serve figs warm or at room temperature.

Acknowledgments

I HAVE HAD MANY HELPERS in the creation of this book and in my mission to teach the fundamental techniques of home cooking.

I would like to thank everyone who worked so hard to help me accomplish that goal, especially food editor Sarah Carey, who spent a year tirelessly leading the team in creating excellent recipes and styling the most beautiful and instructive photographs. Sarah was joined in her efforts to organize and produce the contents and all accompanying text by executive editor Ellen Morrissey. The book represents the hard work and talent of art director William van Roden, who translated the material into such an enticing, easy-to-follow, and practical design. Amy Conway, editor-in-chief of special projects at MSLO, provided invaluable support along the way. Evelyn Battaglia lent her considerable food knowledge to recipe writing and editing. Christine Cyr contributed research and editing talents to the text that opens the chapters, all of which is designed to help demystify cooking techniques and teach readers how to choose and work with the best ingredients. Yasemin Emory assisted in developing and implementing the beautiful design. Photographer Marcus Nilsson, a delight to work with, created the gorgeous images that accompany the lessons and recipes; Ditte Isager photographed the portraits on the cover and chapter openers. The work of talented prop stylist Tanya Graff lent such a clean, distinctive look to the photographs. Heather Meldrom and Lesley Stockton created wonderful recipes under the direction of Sarah Carey and Lucinda Scala Quinn, executive editorial director of food and entertaining. The recipes were carefully tested by Christina Garcia, Lisa Leonard Lee, and Charlotte March; kitchen assistance was provided by Aida Ibarra, Gertrude Porter, Ruby Sanchez, and Simon Andrews. Sarah Rutledge did an excellent job of keeping everything on track and in order. Evan Lobel, of Lobel's Butcher Shop in New York City, was kind enough to give us expert advice about meat, as well as to recommend the best cooking methods for particular cuts. Chef Pierre Schaedelin provided recipes, ideas, and inspiration.

Others at MSLO were instrumental as well, including Jennifer Aaronson, Matthew Axe, Andrea Bakacs, Dora Cardinale, Denise Clappi, Lawrence Diamond, James Dunlinson, Aimee Epstein, Stephanie Fletcher, Heloise Goodman, Susan Lyne, Wenda Harris Millard, Matthew Papa, Ayesha Patel, Eric A. Pike, George Planding, Laura Regensdorf, Gael Towey, and Laura Wallis. And I am grateful, as always, to our fine publishing partners at Clarkson Potter, including Jenny Frost, Lauren Shakely, Doris Cooper, Rica Allannic, Amy Boorstein, Mark McCauslin, Marysarah Quinn, Jane Treuhaft, Derek Gullino, and Lindsay Miller.

Index

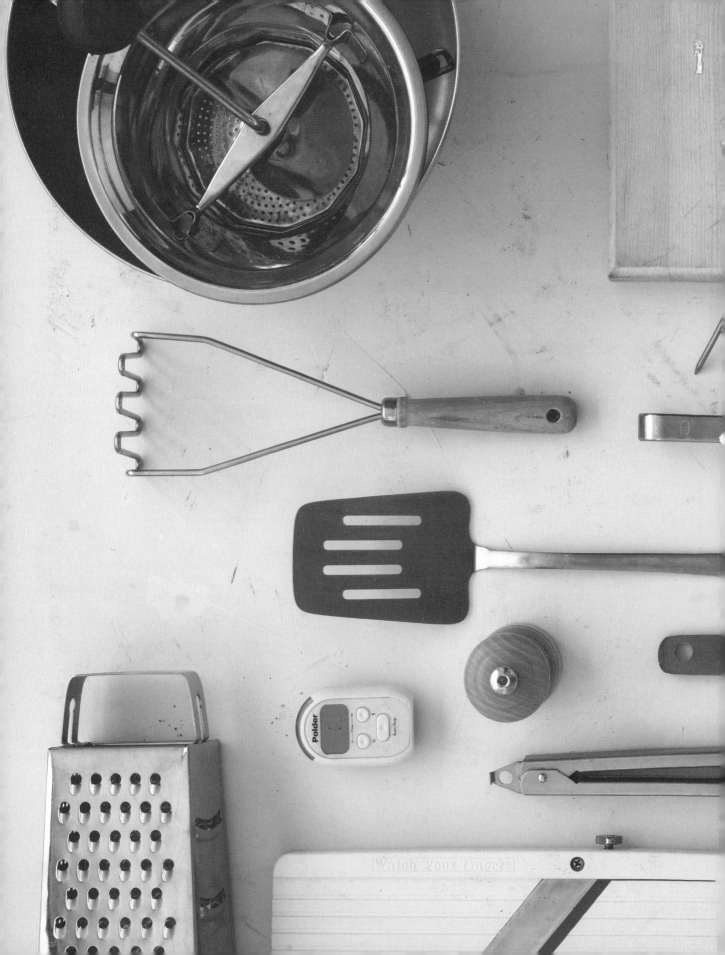